Advances in Economics and Econometrics

Eleventh World Congress, Volume I

This is the first of two volumes containing papers and commentaries presented at the Eleventh World Congress of the Econometric Society, held in Montréal, Canada in August 2015. These papers provide state-of-the-art guides to the most important recent research in economics today. They include surveys and interpretations of key developments in economics and econometrics, and discussion of future directions for a wide variety of topics, covering both theory and application. The first volume includes theoretical and applied papers addressing topics such as dynamic mechanism design, agency problems, and networks.

Bo Honoré is Class of 1913 Professor of Political Economy and Professor of Economics at Princeton University. He is Director of the Gregory C. Chow Econometric Research Program at Princeton University, and was formerly a member of the Board of Trustees of the Danish National Research Foundation. Honoré is a Fellow of the Econometric Society and conducts research in econometrics.

Ariel Pakes is the Thomas Professor of Economics at Harvard University. His research has been in industrial organization, the economics of technological change, and in econometric theory. He is a Fellow of the Econometric Society, and received the Frisch Medal of the Econometric Society in 1986. He has been elected to the National Academy of Sciences and the American Academy of Arts and Sciences, was the distinguished Fellow of the Industrial Organization Society in 2007, and was the winner of the Jean Jaques Laffont Prize in 2017.

Monika Piazzesi is the Joan Kenney Professor of Economics at Stanford University, and she is also the Program Director of the NBER Asset Pricing Group. She conducts research in finance and macroeconomics. Piazzesi is a Fellow of the Academy of Arts and Sciences, the Econometric Society, and the Society of Financial Econometrics.

Larry Samuelson is the A. Douglas Melamed Professor of Economics at Yale University and is Director of the Cowles Foundation at Yale University. His research is in economic theory, with an emphasis on game theory. He has served as a co-editor of *Econometrica* and the *American Economic Review*.

Econometric Society Monographs

Editors:

Jeffrey Ely, Northwestern University
Donald W.K. Andrews, Yale University

The Econometric Society is an international society for the advancement of economic theory in relation to statistics and mathematics. The Econometric Society Monograph series is designed to promote the publication of original research contributions of high quality in mathematical economics and theoretical and applied econometrics.

Other titles in the series:

G. S. Maddala, *Limited dependent and qualitative variables in econometrics*, 9780521241434, 9780521338257

Gerard Debreu, *Mathematical economics: Twenty papers of Gerard Debreu*, 9780521237369, 9780521335614

Jean-Michel Grandmont, *Money and value: A reconsideration of classical and neoclassical monetary economics*, 9780521251419, 9780521313643

Franklin M. Fisher, *Disequilibrium foundations of equilibrium economics*, 9780521378567

Andreu Mas-Colell, *The theory of general equilibrium: A differentiable approach*, 9780521265140, 9780521388702

Truman F. Bewley, Editor, *Advances in econometrics – Fifth World Congress (Volume I)*, 9780521467261

Truman F. Bewley, Editor, *Advances in econometrics – Fifth World Congress (Volume II)*, 9780521467254

Hervé Moulin, *Axioms of cooperative decision making*, 9780521360555, 9780521424585

L. G. Godfrey, *Misspecification tests in econometrics: The Lagrange multiplier principle and other approaches*, 9780521424592

Tony Lancaster, *The econometric analysis of transition data*, 9780521437899

Alvin E. Roth and Marilda A. Oliviera Sotomayor, Editors, *Two-sided matching: A study in game-theoretic modeling and analysis*, 9780521437882

Wolfgang Hardle, *Applied nonparametric regression*, 9780521429504

Jean-Jacques Laffont, Editor, *Advances in economic theory – Sixth World Congress (Volume I)*, 9780521484596

Jean-Jacques Laffont, Editor, *Advances in economic theory – Sixth World Congress (Volume II)*, 9780521484602

Halbert White, *Estimation, inference and specification*, 9780521252805, 9780521574464

Christopher Sims, Editor, *Advances in econometrics – Sixth World Congress (Volume I)*, 9780521444590, 9780521566100

Christopher Sims, Editor, *Advances in econometrics – Sixth World Congress (Volume II)*, 9780521444606, 9780521566094

Roger Guesnerie, *A contribution to the pure theory of taxation*, 9780521629560

David M. Kreps and Kenneth F. Wallis, Editors, *Advances in economics and econometrics – Seventh World Congress (Volume I)*, 9780521589833

David M. Kreps and Kenneth F. Wallis, Editors, *Advances in economics and econometrics – Seventh World Congress (Volume II)*, 9780521589826

David M. Kreps and Kenneth F. Wallis, Editors, *Advances in economics and econometrics – Seventh World Congress (Volume III)*, 9780521580137, 9780521589819

(Continued after the index)

Advances in Economics and Econometrics

Eleventh World Congress
Volume I

Edited by

Bo Honoré
Princeton University

Ariel Pakes
Harvard University

Monika Piazzesi
Stanford University

Larry Samuelson
Yale University

CAMBRIDGE
UNIVERSITY PRESS

CAMBRIDGE
UNIVERSITY PRESS

University Printing House, Cambridge CB2 8BS, United Kingdom

One Liberty Plaza, 20th Floor, New York, NY 10006, USA

477 Williamstown Road, Port Melbourne, VIC 3207, Australia

314-321, 3rd Floor, Plot 3, Splendor Forum, Jasola District Centre, New Delhi - 110025, India

79 Anson Road, #06-04/06, Singapore 079906

Cambridge University Press is part of the University of Cambridge.

It furthers the University's mission by disseminating knowledge in the pursuit of education, learning and research at the highest international levels of excellence.

www.cambridge.org
Information on this title: www.cambridge.org/9781316510520
DOI: 10.1017/9781108227162

First published 2017

A catalogue record for this publication is available from the British Library

ISBN 978-1-108-22724-7 Set of 2 hardback volumes
ISBN 978-1-316-51052-0 Volume 1 Hardback
ISBN 978-1-108-41498-2 Volume 2 Hardback
ISBN 978-1-108-22725-4 Set of 2 paperback volumes
ISBN 978-1-108-40000-8 Volume 1 Paperback
ISBN 978-1-108-40002-2 Volume 2 Paperback

Contents

Contributors

Sanjeev Goyal
University of Cambridge

Igal Hendel
Northwestern University

Johannes Hörner
Yale University

Fuhito Kojima
Stanford University

Rachel E. Kranton
Duke University

Parag A. Pathak
Massachusetts Institute of Technology

Áureo de Paula
University College London and São Paulo School of Economics

Alessandro Pavan
Northwestern University and CEPR

Bernard Salanié
Columbia University

Andrzej Skrzypacz
Stanford University

Editors' Note

These volumes constitute the invited proceedings of the Eleventh World Congress of the Econometric Society, held in Montréal, August 17–21, 2015. It was our great pleasure to invite the papers, and we thank the authors and discussants for their contributions.

CHAPTER 1

Dynamic Mechanism Design: Robustness and Endogenous Types

Alessandro Pavan

This article was prepared for an invited session at the 2015 World Congress of the Econometric Society. Through a unifying framework, I survey recent developments in the dynamic mechanism design literature and then introduce two new areas that I expect will draw attention in the years to come: robustness and endogenous types.

1 INTRODUCTION

Long-term contracting plays an important role in a variety of economic problems including trade, employment, regulation, taxation, and finance. Most long-term relationships take place in a *"changing world,"* that is, in an environment that evolves (stochastically) over time. Think, for example, of (a) the provision of private and public goods to agents whose valuations evolve over time, as the result of shocks to their preferences or learning and experimentation, (b) the design of multi-period procurement auctions when firms' costs evolve as the result of past investments, (c) the design of optimal tax codes when workers' productivity evolves over time as the result of changes in technology or because of learning-by-doing, (d) the matching of agents whose values and attractiveness is learned gradually over time through private interactions.

Changes to the environment (either due to exogenous shocks, or to the gradual resolution of uncertainty about constant, but unknown, payoffs) are often anticipated at the time of initial contracting, albeit rarely jointly observed by the parties. By implication, optimal long-term contracts must be flexible to

I thank the organizers of the 2015 World Congress of the Econometric Society, and in particular Larry Samuelson, for the invitation, and my discussant Juuso Välimäki for useful comments and suggestions. I also thank my co-authors on related projects, Daniel Fershtman, Daniel Garrett, Miltos Makris, Ilya Segal, and Juuso Toikka, without whom this work would have not been possible. Finally, I thank Laura Doval, Jonas Mishara-Blomberger, and Bela Szabadi for excellent research assistance.

accommodate such changes, while at the same time provide the parties with incentives to share the information they receive over time.

Understanding the properties of optimal long-term contracts is important both for positive and for normative analysis. It permits one to address questions such as: How does the provision of quantity/quality evolve over time under profit-maximizing contracts? How do the dynamics of the allocations under profit maximization compare to their counterparts under welfare maximization? In particular, when do distortions due to profit maximization decrease over time and vanish in the long run? In what environments does the private observability of the "shocks" (i.e., the changes to the environment subsequent to the signing of the initial contract) play no role? When is the nature of the shocks (i.e., whether they are transitory or permanent) relevant for the dynamics of the decisions under optimal contracts?

The last fifteen years have witnessed significant interest in these questions. Important contributions have been made in extending mechanism design tools to economies in which information evolves over time and a stream of decisions is to be made.[1]

In this article, I first provide a brief overview of the recent dynamic mechanism design literature. I then introduce a simple yet flexible framework that I use in the subsequent sections to review some of the recent contributions. Finally, I discuss two new areas that I expect will attract attention in the near future: robustness and endogenous types.

1.1   Brief Review of the Dynamic Mechanism Design Literature

This section builds on a recent overview that I prepared with Dirk Bergemann for the Journal of Economic Theory Symposium Issue on Dynamic Contracts and Mechanism Design (Bergemann and Pavan, 2015).

An important part of the dynamic mechanism design literature studies how to implement efficient allocations in dynamic settings with evolving private information. The pioneering contributions in this area are Bergemann and Välimäki (2010) and Athey and Segal (2013). The first paper constructs a dynamic pivot transfer scheme under which, in each period, all agents receive their expected marginal flow contribution to social welfare. The scheme guarantees that, in each period, all agents are willing to remain in the mechanism and report truthfully their incremental information, regardless of their beliefs

---

[1] Mechanism design has been used in static settings to examine a variety of problems including: auctions (Myerson, 1981; Riley and Samuelson, 1981; Cremer and McLean, 1988; Maskin and Riley, 1989); nonlinear pricing (Mussa and Rosen, 1978; Wilson, 1993); bargaining (Myerson and Satterthwaite, 1983; Ausubel and Deneckere, 1989, 1993); regulation (Baron and Myerson, 1982; Laffont and Tirole, 1986); taxation (Mirrlees, 1971); political economy (Dasgupta et al., 1979; Acemoglu et al., 2011); public goods provision (Vickrey, 1961; Clarke, 1971; Groves, 1973; Green and Laffont, 1979); organization design (Cremer, 1995), and voting (Gibbard, 1973, 1977; Satterthwaite, 1975). The reader is referred to Börgers (2015) for an excellent overview of the static mechanism design literature.

about other agents' past and current types (but provided they expect others to report truthfully).[2] The scheme can be thought of as the dynamic analog of the various Vickrey–Clarke–Groves (VCG) schemes proposed in static environments. The paper by Athey and Segal (2013), instead, proposes a transfer scheme under which each agent's "incentives payment," at each period, coincides with the variation in the net present value of the expected externality the agent imposes on other agents, with the variation triggered by the agent's own incremental information. The proposed scheme can thus be thought of as the dynamic analog of the type of schemes proposed by d'Aspremont and Gérard-Varet (AGV) for static settings. Relative to the dynamic pivot mechanism of Bergemann and Välimäki (2010), the Athey and Segal (2013) mechanism has the advantage of guaranteeing budget balance in each period. Contrary to Bergemann and Välimäki (2010), however, it need not guarantee that agents have the incentives to stay in the mechanism in each period.[3]

A second body of work investigates properties of profit-maximizing mechanisms in settings with evolving private information. Earlier contributions include Baron and Besanko (1984), Besanko (1985), and Riordan and Sappington (1987). For more recent contributions, see, among others, Courty and Li (2000), Battaglini (2005), Eső and Szentes (2007), Board (2007), and Kakade et al. (2013).

Pavan, Segal, and Toikka (2014) summarize the above contributions and extend them to a general dynamic contracting setting with a continuum of types, multiple agents, and arbitrary time horizon. The model allows for serial correlation of the agents' information and for the dependence of this information on past allocations. The approach to the design of optimal mechanisms in Pavan, Segal, and Toikka (2014) can be thought of as the dynamic analog of the approach pioneered by Myerson (1981) for static settings, and subsequently extended by Guesnerie and Laffont (1984), Maskin and Riley (1984), and Laffont and Tirole (1986), among others. This approach consists in first identifying necessary conditions for incentive compatibility that can be summarized in an envelope formula for the derivative of each agent's equilibrium payoff with respect to the agent's type. This formula in turn permits one to express transfers as a function of the allocation rule and thereby to express the principal's objective as virtual surplus (i.e., total surplus, net of handicaps that control for the cost to the principal of leaving the agents information rents). The second step then consists in maximizing virtual surplus across all possible allocation rules, including those that need not be incentive compatible. The final step consists in verifying that the allocation rule that solves the relaxed program, along with the transfer rule required by the necessary

---

[2] The formal solution concept capturing the above properties is periodic ex-post equilibrium.

[3] See also Liu (2014) for an extension of the Bergemann and Välimäki (2010) mechanism to a setting with interdependent valuations.

envelope conditions, constitute a fully incentive-compatible and individually-rational mechanism. This last step typically involves "reverse-engineering," i.e., identifying appropriate primitive conditions guaranteeing that the allocation rule that solves the relaxed program satisfies an appropriate monotonicity condition.

The approach in Pavan, Segal, and Toikka (2014) – reviewed in Section 4, below – adapts the above steps to a dynamic environment. The cornerstone is a dynamic envelope theorem that yields a formula for the evolution of each agent's equilibrium payoff and that must be satisfied in any incentive-compatible mechanism. This formula combines the usual direct effect of a change in the agent's current type on the agent's utility (as in static mechanism design problems) with novel effects stemming from the effect that a change in the current type has on the distribution of the agent's future types. These novel effects, which are specific to dynamic problems, are summarized by *impulse response functions* that describe how a change in the current type propagates throughout the entire type process. A second contribution of Pavan, Segal, and Toikka (2014) is to show that, in Markov environments, the aforementioned dynamic envelope formula, combined with an appropriate *integral monotonicity condition* on the allocation rule, provides a complete characterization of incentive compatibility. The integral monotonicity condition is the dynamic analog of the monotonicity conditions identified in static problems with unidimensional private information but multidimensional decisions (see, among others, Rochet, 1987; Carbajal and Ely, 2013; and Berger et al., 2010). This condition requires that the allocations be monotone in the reported types "on average," where the average is both across time and states, and is weighted by the impulse responses of future types to current ones.

As in static settings, the Myersonian (first-order) approach yields an implementable allocation rule only under fairly stringent conditions. An important question for the dynamic mechanism design literature is thus the extent to which the predictions identified under such an approach extend to environments where global incentive-compatibility constraints bind. This topic is addressed in two recent papers, Garrett and Pavan (2015) and, Garrett, Pavan, and Toikka (2016).[4] These papers do not fully solve for the optimal mechanisms. Instead, they use variational arguments to identify certain properties of the optimal contracts. More precisely, they use perturbations of the allocation policies that preserve incentive compatibility to identify robust properties of the dynamics of the allocations under optimal contracts. I review this alternative variational approach in Section 5, below.[5]

---

[4] See also Battaglini and Lamba (2015).

[5] The notion of robustness considered in these papers is with respect to the details of the type process. Robustness with respect to the agents' higher-order beliefs is the topic of a by now rich literature well summarized in the monograph by Bergemann and Morris (2012). The type of problems examined in this literature are typically static. For some recent developments to

Another body of the literature studies the design of efficient and profit-maximizing mechanisms in dynamic settings where the agents' private information is static, but where agents or objects arrive stochastically over time. A recent monograph by Gershkov and Moldovanu (2014) summarizes the developments of this literature (see also Bergemann and Said, 2011; Board and Skrzypacz, 2016; Gershkov et al., 2014; and Said, 2011, 2012). Most of the papers in this literature assume that the agents' information is stationary. Instead, Garrett (2016a, 2016b), Hinnosaar (2016), and Ely et al. (2016) combine dynamics originating from stochastic arrivals with dynamics generated by evolving private information. A recent new addition to this literature is Akan et al. (2015); the paper studies a sequential screening environment à la Courty and Li (2000), but in which different agents learn their valuations at different times, with the timing of learning correlated with the agents' initial valuations.[6]

Dynamic mechanism design has also been applied to study optimal insurance, taxation, and redistribution in the so-called "New Dynamic Public Finance" literature. For earlier contributions, see Green (1987), Atkenson and Lucas (1992), and Fernandes and Phelan (2000). For more recent contributions, see Kocherlakota (2005), Albanesi and Sleet (2006), Farhi and Werning (2013), Kapicka (2013a), Stantcheva (2014) and Golosov et al. (2016).

In all the papers above, the evolution of the agents' private information is exogenous. In contrast, the evolution of the agents' information is endogenous in the experimentation model of Bergemann and Välimäki (2010), in the procurement model of Krähmer and Strausz (2011), in the sponsored-search model of Kakade et al. (2013), in the bandit-auction model of Pavan, Segal, and Toikka (2014), in the matching model of Fershtman and Pavan (2016), and in the taxation model of Makris and Pavan (2016). This last paper is reviewed in Section 6, below; it considers a dynamic taxation problem in which the agents' productivity evolves endogenously as the result of learning-by-doing.

Related is also the literature on dynamic managerial compensation. Most of this literature studies optimal compensation schemes in a pure moral hazard setting (see, for example, Prendergast, 2002 for an earlier overview; Sannikov, 2013 for a more recent overview of the continuous-time contracting literature; and the references in Board, 2011 for the subset of this literature focusing on relational contracting). The part of this literature that is most related to the dynamic mechanism design literature is the one that assumes that the manager observes shocks to the cash flows prior to committing his

dynamic environments, see Aghion et al. (2012), Mueller (2015), and Penta (2015). Another strand of the literature studies screening and moral hazard problems in settings in which the principal lacks information about the type distribution, the set of available effort choices, or the technology used by nature to perturb the agent's action. See, for example, Segal (2003), Frankel (2012), Chassang (2013), Garrett (2014), Carroll (2015), and the references therein.

[6] See also Krähmer and Strausz (2016) for a discussion of how the analysis of sequential screening in Courty and Li (2000) can be reconducted to a static screening problem with stochastic allocations.

effort (as in the taxation and in the regulation literature); see, for example, Edmans and Gabaix (2011), Edmans et al. (2012), Garrett and Pavan (2012), and Carroll and Meng (2016). This timing is also the one considered in the variational-approach paper by Garrett and Pavan (2015) reviewed in Section 5, below.

Most of the analysis in the dynamic mechanism design literature is in discrete time. One of the earlier papers in continuous time is Williams (2011). For a discussion of the developments of the continuous-time dynamic adverse selection literature and its connection to discrete time, see the recent paper by Bergemann and Strack (2015a) and the references therein.[7]

The dynamic mechanism design literature typically assumes that the designer can commit to her mechanism, with the dynamics of the allocations originating either in evolving private information or in the stochastic arrival and departure of goods and agents over time. A related literature on dynamic contracting under limited commitment investigates the dynamics of allocations in models in which the agents' private information is static but where the principal is unable to commit to future decisions. For earlier contributions to this literature, see, for example, Laffont and Tirole (1988), and Hart and Tirole (1988). For more recent contributions, see Skreta (2006, 2015), Battaglini (2007), Galperti (2015), Maestri (2016), Gerardi and Maestri (2016), Liu et al. (2015), Strulovici (2016), and the references therein. A particular form of limited commitment is considered in Deb and Said (2015). In that paper, the seller can commit to the dynamic contract she offers to each agent, but cannot commit to the contracts she offers to agents arriving in future periods. Partial commitment is also the focus of a recent paper in continuous time by Miao and Zhang (2015), in which both the principal and the agent can walk away from the relationship at any point in time after observing the evolution of the agent's income process.

Another assumption typically maintained in the dynamic mechanism design literature is that transfers can be used to incentivize the agents to report their private information (and/or to exert effort). A few papers investigate dynamic incentives in settings with or without evolving private information, in which transfers are not feasible. An early contribution to this literature is Hylland and Zeckhauser (1979). More recent contributions include Abdulkadiroğlu and Loertscher (2007), Miralles (2012), Kováč et al. (2014), Johnson (2015), Li et al. (2015), Frankel (2016), Johnson (2015), and Guo and Hörner (2016).

Related is also the literature on information design. For a survey of earlier contributions see Bergemann and Välimäki (2006). For more recent developments, including dynamic extensions, see Gershkov and Szentes (2009), Rayo and Segal (2010), Kamenica and Gentzkow (2011), Gentzkow and Kamenica (2015), Bergemann and Morris (2016), Ely et al. (2016), Doval and Ely (2016), Ely, Garrett, and Hinnosaar (2016), and the references

---

[7] See also Prat and Jovanovic (2014), Strulovici and Szydlowski (2015), and Williams (2015) for recent contributions.

therein. Hörner and Skrzypacz (2016) offer a useful survey of these recent developments. The canonical persuasion model assumes that the designer (the sender) can choose the information structure for the receiver at no cost. In contrast, Calzolari and Pavan (2006a, 2006b), consider models in which a principal first screens the private information of one, or multiple agents, and then passes a garbled version of this information to other agents, or other principals. The design of optimal disclosure rules in screening environments is also the focus of Bergemann and Pesendorfer (2007), Eső and Szentes (2007), Bergemann and Wambach (2015), and Nikandrova and Pancs (2015); all these papers study the design of optimal information structures in auctions.

Finally, dynamic mechanism design is related to the literature on information acquisition in mechanism design (see Bergemann and Välimäki (2002, 2006) and the references therein for earlier contributions, and Gershkov and Szentes (2009), and Krähmer and Strausz (2011) for some recent developments).

2   SIMPLE DYNAMIC SCREENING MODEL

In this section, I introduce a simple dynamic screening model that I use in the next four sections to illustrate some of the key ideas in the dynamic mechanism design literature.

The principal is a seller, the agent is a buyer. Their relationship lasts for $T \in \mathbb{N} \cup \{\infty\}$ periods, where T can be either finite or infinite. Time is discrete and indexed by $t = 1, 2, \ldots, T$. Both the buyer and the seller have time-additively-separable preferences given, respectively, by

$$U^P = \sum_t \delta^{t-1}(p_t - C(q_t)) \quad \text{and} \quad U^A = \sum_t \delta^{t-1}(\theta_t q_t - p_t)$$

where $q_t \in \mathcal{Q} \subset \mathbb{R}$ denotes the quantity exchanged in period t, $\theta_t \in \Theta_t$ denotes the buyer's period-t marginal value for the seller's product, p_t denotes the *total* payment from the buyer to the seller in period t, $\delta \geq 0$ denotes the common discount factor, and $C(q_t)$ denotes the cost to the seller of providing quantity q_t.[8] The function $C(\cdot)$ is strictly increasing, convex, and differentiable.

Let $F \equiv (F_t)$ denote the collection of kernels describing the evolution of the buyer's private information, with F_1 denoting the initial distribution over Θ_1 and, for all $t \geq 2$, $F_t(\cdot \mid \theta_{t-1})$ denoting the cdf of θ_t given θ_{t-1}. Note that the above specification assumes the process is Markov and exogenous.

The sequence of events is the following.

- At $t = 0$, i.e., prior to entering any negotiations with the principal, the buyer privately learns θ_1.

---

[8] The results for a static relationship can be read from the formulas below for the dynamic environment by setting $\delta = 0$.

- At $t = 1$, the seller offers a mechanism $\varphi = (\mathcal{M}, \phi)$. The latter consists of a collection of mappings

$$\phi_t : \mathcal{M}_1 \times \cdots \times \mathcal{M}_t \to \mathcal{Q} \times \mathbb{R}$$

specifying a quantity–price pair for each possible history of messages $m^t \equiv (m_1, \ldots, m_t) \in \mathcal{M}_1 \times \cdots \times \mathcal{M}_t$, with $\mathcal{M} \equiv (\mathcal{M})_{t=1}^T$ and $\phi \equiv (\phi_t)_{t=1}^T$. A mechanism is thus equivalent to a menu of long-term contracts. If the buyer refuses to participate in φ, the game ends and both players obtain a payoff equal to zero. If the buyer chooses to participate in φ, he sends a message $m_1 \in \mathcal{M}_1$, receives quantity $q_1(m_1)$, pays a transfer $p_1(m_1)$, and the game moves to period 2.
- At the beginning of each period $t \geq 2$, the buyer privately learns θ_t. He then sends a new message $m_t \in \mathcal{M}_t$, receives the quantity $q_t(m^t)$, pays $p_t(m^t)$ to the principal, and the game moves to period $t + 1$.
- $\cdots$
- At $t = T + 1$ the game is over (in case T is finite).

Remark The game described above assumes that the principal (here the seller) perfectly commits to the mechanism φ. It also assumes that at any period $t \geq 2$ the buyer is constrained to stay in the relationship if he signed on in period 1. When the agent has "deep pockets," there are, however, simple ways to distribute the payments over time so that it is in the interest of the buyer to remain in the relationship at all periods, irrespective of what he did in the past.[9] ‖

The principal's problem consists in designing a mechanism that disciplines the provision of quantity and the payments over time. Because the principal can commit, the Revelation Principle[10] applies and one can without loss of optimality restrict attention to direct mechanisms in which $\mathcal{M}_t = \Theta_t$ all t and such that the agent finds it optimal to report truthfully at all periods. For simplicity, hereafter, I drop the message spaces and identify such a mechanism directly with the policies $\chi = \langle \mathbf{q}, \mathbf{p} \rangle$ that it induces, where, for any $t \geq 1$, $q_t : \Theta^t \to \mathcal{Q}$ is the period-t output policy and $p_t : \Theta^t \to \mathbb{R}$ the payment policy, with $\Theta^t = \Theta_1 \times \cdots \times \Theta_t$.[11] The principal designs χ so as to maximize

$$\mathbb{E}\left[\sum_t \delta^{t-1}(p_t(\theta^t) - C(q_t(\theta^t)))\right]$$

[9] See also Krähmer and Strausz (2015a) for a discussion of interim vs ex-post participation constraints in sequential secreening models.

[10] See, among others, Gibbard (1977), Green and Laffont (1979), Myerson (1979, 1986).

[11] A similar notation will be used hereafter to denote sequences of sets. For example, $\mathcal{A}^t = \mathcal{A}_1 \times \cdots \times \mathcal{A}_t$ with generic element $a^t = (a_1, \ldots, a_t)$.

subject to

$$\mathbb{E}\left[\sum_t \delta^{t-1}(\theta_t q_t(\theta^t) - p_t(\theta^t)) \mid \theta_1\right] \geq 0 \text{ for all } \theta_1 \in \Theta \qquad \text{(IR-1)}$$

$$\mathbb{E}\left[\sum_{s \geq t} \delta^{s-t}(\theta_s q_s(\theta^s) - p_s(\theta^s)) \mid \theta^t\right]$$

$$\geq \mathbb{E}\left[\sum_{s \geq t} \delta^{s-t}(\theta_s q_s^{\sigma}(\theta^s) - p_s^{\sigma}(\theta^s)) \mid \theta^t\right] \text{ for all } t, \ \theta^t \in \Theta^t, \text{ and } \sigma,$$

$$\text{(IC-t)}$$

where σ denotes an arbitrary continuation strategy for the game that starts in period t after the agent has reported truthfully at all previous periods. For any $s \geq t$, any $\theta^s \in \Theta^s$, $q_s^{\sigma} : \Theta^s \to Q$ and $p_s^{\sigma} : \Theta^s \to \mathbb{R}$ are the state-contingent policies induced by the continuation strategy σ under the mechanism $\chi = \langle \mathbf{q}, \mathbf{p} \rangle$. Hereafter, unless otherwise specified, the expectation operator $\mathbb{E}[\cdot]$ is with respect to the entire type sequence $(\theta_s)_{s=1}^T$ under the kernels F.

Note that the above constraints require that the buyer finds it optimal to participate in period 1 and report truthfully "on path," i.e., conditional on having reported truthfully in previous periods. Because the environment is Markov, holding fixed the agent's reports at each period $s < t$, the agent's incentives in period $t \geq 2$ are invariant in the agent's true type θ_s, $s < t$. Hence, the above (IC-t) constraints guarantee that the agent finds it optimal to report truthfully at all histories, not just "on-path."

3 TWO-PERIOD DISCRETE EXAMPLE

To illustrate the trade-offs that determine the dynamics of allocations under optimal mechanisms in the simplest possible way, consider the following environment in which $T = 2$, $\Theta_1 \equiv \{\bar{\theta}, \underline{\theta}\}$, $\underline{\theta} > 0$, $\Delta\theta \equiv \bar{\theta} - \underline{\theta} > 0$, and $\Theta_2 \equiv \{\underline{\theta} - \Delta\theta, \underline{\theta}, \bar{\theta}, \bar{\theta} + \Delta\theta\}$. That is, the buyer has either a high or a low valuation in period 1. In period 2, he then experiences a shock that either raises his valuation by $\Delta\theta$, leaves his valuation unchanged, or reduces his valuation by $\Delta\theta$. To simplify, also assume that the principal's production cost is quadratic, with $C(q) = q^2/2$, all q.

The probability that the buyer is a high type in period 1 (equivalently, the proportion of high types in the cross-section of the population) is $\Pr(\theta_1 = \bar{\theta}) = v$. Conditional on θ_1, the transition probabilities are as follows: $\Pr(\bar{\theta}+\Delta\theta|\bar{\theta}) = \bar{x}$, $\Pr(\bar{\theta}|\bar{\theta}) = \bar{\alpha}$, $\Pr(\underline{\theta}|\bar{\theta}) = 1 - \bar{x} - \bar{\alpha}$, $\Pr(\bar{\theta}|\underline{\theta}) = \underline{x}$, $\Pr(\underline{\theta}|\underline{\theta}) = \underline{\alpha}$, and $\Pr(\underline{\theta}-\Delta\theta|\underline{\theta}) = 1-\underline{x}-\underline{\alpha}$. Figure 1 illustrates the situation under consideration.

As usual, the game is solved backwards. Let $U_2^A(\theta_2; \hat{\theta}_1, \hat{\theta}_2) \equiv \theta_2 q_2(\hat{\theta}_1, \hat{\theta}_2) - p_2(\hat{\theta}_1, \hat{\theta}_2)$ denote the agent's period-2 flow payoff when the true period-2 type is θ_2 and the agents reported $(\hat{\theta}_1, \hat{\theta}_2)$ in the two periods. Note

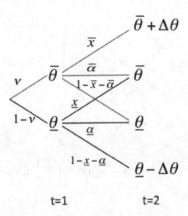

t=1   t=2

Figure 1 Evolution of Agent's Type.

that the flow period-2 payoff $U_2^A(\theta_2; \hat{\theta}_1, \hat{\theta}_2)$ does not depend on the agent's true period-1 type, θ_1.

Next, let $V_2^A(\theta_1, \theta_2) \equiv U_2^A(\theta_2; \theta_1, \theta_2)$ denote the agent's period-2 flow payoff under truthful reporting (because it is irrelevant whether or not the period-1 report coincides with the true period-1 type, I am replacing $\hat{\theta}_1$ with θ_1 to facilitate the notation).

Incentive compatibility in period 2 then requires that, for all $\theta_1 \in \Theta_1$, all $\theta_2, \hat{\theta}_2 \in \Theta_2$,

$$V_2^A(\theta_1, \theta_2) \geq U_2^A(\theta_2; \theta_1, \hat{\theta}_2).$$

Because the flow payoffs $\theta_t q_t - p_t$ satisfy the increasing differences property, it is well known, from static mechanism design, that incentive compatibility in period 2 requires that, for all $\theta_1 \in \Theta_1$, the output schedules $q_2(\theta_1, \cdot)$ be nondecreasing in θ_2 and the payments $p_2(\theta_1, \cdot)$ satisfy the following conditions:

$$\Delta\theta q_2\left(\theta_1, \bar{\theta}\right) \leq V_2^A(\theta_1, \bar{\theta} + \Delta\theta) - V_2^A(\theta_1, \bar{\theta}) \leq \Delta\theta q_2\left(\theta_1, \bar{\theta} + \Delta\theta\right)$$
(1)

$$\Delta\theta q_2\left(\theta_1, \underline{\theta}\right) \leq V_2^A(\theta_1, \bar{\theta}) - V_2^A(\theta_1, \underline{\theta}) \leq \Delta\theta q_2\left(\theta_1, \bar{\theta}\right)$$
(2)

$$\Delta\theta q_2\left(\theta_1, \underline{\theta} - \Delta\theta\right) \leq V_2^A(\theta_1, \underline{\theta}) - V_2^A(\theta_1, \underline{\theta} - \Delta\theta) \leq \Delta\theta q_2\left(\theta_1, \underline{\theta}\right),$$
(3)

both for $\theta_1 = \bar{\theta}$ and for $\theta_1 = \underline{\theta}$. Along with the monotonicity of the output schedules $q_2(\theta_1, \cdot)$, the above constraints are not only necessary but also sufficient for period-2 incentive compatibility.

Next, let

$$U_1^A(\theta_1; \hat{\theta}_1) \equiv \theta_1 q_1(\hat{\theta}_1) - p_1(\hat{\theta}_1) + \delta\mathbb{E}\left[V_2^A(\hat{\theta}_1, \theta_2) \mid \theta_1\right]$$

denote the payoff that a buyer with initial type θ_1 expects from reporting $\hat{\theta}_1$ in period 1 and, then, reporting truthfully at $t = 2$. Observe that the same period-2 incentive-compatibility constraints (1)–(3) that guarantee that it is optimal for the buyer to report truthfully in period 2 after having reported truthfully in period 1 also guarantee that it is optimal for him to report truthfully after having lied in period 1. Also, note that the expectation in the above definition of $U_1^A(\theta_1; \hat{\theta}_1)$ is over θ_2 given the true period-1 type θ_1. Finally, let $V_1^A(\theta_1) = U_1^A(\theta_1; \theta_1)$ denote the payoff that the buyer expects over the entire relationship under a truthful strategy in both periods, given his period-1 type θ_1. The following is then a necessary condition for incentive-compatibility at $t = 1$:

$$
\begin{aligned}
V_1^A(\bar{\theta}) \geq{} & V_1^A(\underline{\theta}) + \Delta\theta q_1(\underline{\theta}) + \delta\{\bar{x} V_2^A(\underline{\theta}, \bar{\theta} + \Delta\theta) \\
& + (\bar{\alpha} - \underline{x}) V_2^A(\underline{\theta}, \bar{\theta}) + (1 - \bar{\alpha} - \bar{x} - \underline{\alpha}) V_2^A(\underline{\theta}, \underline{\theta}) \\
& - (1 - \underline{\alpha} - \underline{x}) V_2^A(\underline{\theta}, \underline{\theta} - \Delta\theta)\}.
\end{aligned}
\tag{4}
$$

Importantly, note that the right-hand side of (4) is written so as to highlight the extra payoff (or, equivalently, the informational rent) that a period-1 high type enjoys relative to a period-1 low type. The term $\Delta\theta q_1(\underline{\theta})$ is the familiar term from static mechanism design capturing the extra utility that the high type derives from the period-1 quantity $q_1(\underline{\theta})$ supplied to the period-1 low type. The term in curly brackets is the novel effect specific to the dynamic setting. It captures the discounted expectation of the second-period continuation payoff $V_2^A(\underline{\theta}_1, \theta_2)$ that follows the reporting of a low type in period 1, but where the discounting combines the time factor, δ, with terms that capture the differences in the transition probabilities between the period-1 high and low types.

Now observe that the period-1 IC constraint (4) can be conveniently rewritten as

$$
\begin{aligned}
V_1^A(\bar{\theta}) \geq{} & V_1^A(\underline{\theta}) + \Delta\theta q_1(\underline{\theta}) + \delta\left\{ \bar{x}\left[V_2^A(\underline{\theta}, \bar{\theta} + \Delta\theta) - V_2^A(\underline{\theta}, \bar{\theta}) \right]\right. \\
& + (\bar{x} + \bar{\alpha} - \underline{x})\left[V_2^A(\underline{\theta}, \bar{\theta}) - V_2^A(\underline{\theta}, \underline{\theta}) \right] \\
& \left. + (1 - \underline{\alpha} - \underline{x})\left[V_2^A(\underline{\theta}, \underline{\theta}) - V_2^A(\underline{\theta}, \underline{\theta} - \Delta\theta) \right]\right\}.
\end{aligned}
\tag{5}
$$

It is then evident from (5) that it is not the level of the continuation payoffs $V_2^A(\underline{\theta}, \theta_2)$ that determines the expected surplus that the high type can guarantee for himself over and above the one of the low type, but the "rate" by which such continuation payoffs change with the period-2 type θ_2. Also, note that the terms in the round brackets in (5) are the differences in the *survival rates* across the two period-1 types. That is,

$$
\bar{x} = \Pr(\theta_2 \geq \bar{\theta} + \Delta\theta | \bar{\theta}) - \Pr(\theta_2 \geq \bar{\theta} + \Delta\theta | \underline{\theta})
$$
$$
\bar{x} + \bar{\alpha} - \underline{x} = \Pr(\theta_2 \geq \bar{\theta} | \bar{\theta}) - \Pr(\theta_2 \geq \bar{\theta} | \underline{\theta})
$$
$$
1 - \underline{\alpha} - \underline{x} = \Pr(\theta_2 \geq \underline{\theta} | \bar{\theta}) - \Pr(\theta_2 \geq \underline{\theta} | \underline{\theta}).
$$

To reduce the informational rent of the period-1 high type, the principal can then either distort downwards the period-1 output provided to the period-1 low type, $q_1(\underline{\theta})$, or the various differences in the period-2 continuation payoffs across adjacent period-2 types, following a report $\underline{\theta}$ of a low type in period 1. Incentive compatibility in period 2, however, imposes lower bounds on such differentials, as one can see from (1)–(3). Consider then a *relaxed program* in which the following constraints are neglected: (a) the period-1 participation constraint of the high type; (b) the period-1 incentive-compatibility constraint of the low type; (c) all period-2 incentive compatibility constraints in the contract for the period-1 high type (that is, (1)–(3) for $\theta_1 = \bar{\theta}$); (d) all period-2 upward adjacent incentive-compatibility constraints in the contract for the period-1 low type (i.e., the right-hand inequalities in the constraints (1)–(3) for $\theta_1 = \underline{\theta}$). Formally, the relaxed program can be stated as follows:

$$
\mathcal{P}_r : \begin{cases}
\max_{\chi = \langle \mathbf{q}, \mathbf{p} \rangle} \mathbb{E}\left\{ \theta_1 q_1(\theta_1) - C(q_1(\theta_1)) + \delta \left[\theta_2 q_2(\theta_1, \theta_2) - C(q_2(\theta_1, \theta_2)) \right] \right. \\
\qquad\qquad \left. - V_1^A(\theta_1) \right\} \\
\text{subject to } V_1^A(\underline{\theta}) \geq 0, \text{ (5) and} \\
V_2^A(\underline{\theta}, \bar{\theta} + \Delta\theta) - V_2^A(\underline{\theta}, \bar{\theta}) \geq \Delta\theta q_2\left(\underline{\theta}, \bar{\theta}\right) \\
V_2^A(\underline{\theta}, \bar{\theta}) - V_2^A(\underline{\theta}, \underline{\theta}) \geq \Delta\theta q_2\left(\underline{\theta}, \underline{\theta}\right) \\
V_2^A(\underline{\theta}, \underline{\theta}) - V_2^A(\underline{\theta}, \underline{\theta} - \Delta\theta) \geq \Delta\theta q_2\left(\underline{\theta}, \underline{\theta} - \Delta\theta\right).
\end{cases}
$$

Now suppose the process is *stochastically monotone* (in the sense that the distribution of θ_2 given $\theta_1 = \bar{\theta}$ first-order-stochastic dominates the distribution of θ_2 given $\theta_1 = \underline{\theta}$), which is the case if and only if $\bar{x} + \bar{\alpha} - \underline{x} \geq 0$. The following result is then true:

Proposition 1 *Suppose the process is* stochastically monotone. *Then any solution to the relaxed program is such that all constraints in $\mathcal{P}_r$ bind, and is characterized by the following output schedules:*[12]

$$q_1(\bar{\theta}) = q_1^{FB}(\bar{\theta});$$

$$q_2(\bar{\theta}, \theta_2) = q_2^{FB}(\bar{\theta}, \theta_2), \ \forall \theta_2 \in \Theta_2;$$

$$q_1(\underline{\theta}) = \max\{q_1^{FB}(\underline{\theta}) - \tfrac{\nu}{1-\nu}\Delta\theta; 0\};$$

$$q_2(\underline{\theta}, \bar{\theta}) = \max\{q_2^{FB}(\underline{\theta}, \bar{\theta}) - \left(\tfrac{\nu}{1-\nu}\right)\left(\tfrac{\bar{x}}{\underline{x}}\right)\Delta\theta; 0\};$$

$$q_2(\underline{\theta}, \underline{\theta}) = \max\{q_2^{FB}(\underline{\theta}, \underline{\theta}) - \left(\tfrac{\nu}{1-\nu}\right)\left(\tfrac{\bar{x}+\bar{\alpha}-\underline{x}}{\alpha}\right)\Delta\theta; 0\};$$

$$q_2(\underline{\theta}, \underline{\theta} - \Delta\theta) = \max\{q_2^{FB}(\underline{\theta}, \underline{\theta} - \Delta\theta) - \left(\tfrac{\nu}{1-\nu}\right)\Delta\theta; 0\},$$

where $q_1^{FB}(\theta_1) = \theta_1$, and $q_2^{FB}(\theta_1, \theta_2) = \theta_2$ are the first-best output schedules (i.e., the schedules that would be implemented under complete information). The solution to the relaxed program $\mathcal{P}_r$ coincides with the solution to the full program if and only if the schedule $q_2(\underline{\theta}, \cdot)$ is nondecreasing in θ_2.

---

[12] Not surprisingly, the output schedules that solve the relaxed and the full programs are not uniquely defined at $(\bar{\theta}, \underline{\theta} - \Delta\theta)$ and $(\underline{\theta}, \bar{\theta} + \Delta\theta)$, for these histories have zero measure.

Hence, the solution to the relaxed program entails no distortions in either period in the output provided to the period-1 high type and downward distortions in either period in the output provided to the period-1 low type. Importantly, the distortions in the output provided to the period-1 low type need not decrease over time or be monotone in the period-2 type.

Corollary 1 *The output schedule $q_2(\underline{\theta}, \cdot)$ that solves the relaxed program is nondecreasing in θ_2 (and hence part of an optimal contract) if and only if*

$$-\frac{v}{1-v} \leq 1 - \left(\frac{v}{1-v}\right)\left(\frac{\bar{x}+\bar{\alpha}-x}{\alpha}\right) \leq 2 - \left(\frac{v}{1-v}\right)\left(\frac{\bar{x}}{\underline{x}}\right).$$

Distortions are weakly higher in period 2 than in period 1 if and only if

$$1 \leq \frac{\bar{x}+\bar{\alpha}-x}{\underline{\alpha}} \leq \frac{\bar{x}}{\underline{x}}.$$

Because the above two sets of conditions are not mutually exclusive, distortions under optimal contracts need not be monotone in type or in time.

The example also illustrates the importance of not restricting attention to oversimplified processes. Suppose, for example, that one were to assume that the agent's marginal value for the principal's product takes only two values, $\underline{\theta}$ or $\bar{\theta}$, in each period. In the context of our example, this amounts to imposing that $\bar{x} = 0 = 1 - \underline{\alpha} - \underline{x}$. In this case, $q_2(\underline{\theta}, \bar{\theta}) = q_2^{FB}(\underline{\theta}, \bar{\theta})$ whereas

$$q_1(\underline{\theta}) = \max\{q_1^{FB}(\underline{\theta}) - \tfrac{v}{1-v}\Delta\theta; 0\}; \tag{6}$$

$$q_2(\underline{\theta}, \underline{\theta}) = \max\{q_2^{FB}(\underline{\theta}, \underline{\theta}) - \left(\tfrac{v}{1-v}\right)\left(\tfrac{\bar{\alpha}+\underline{\alpha}-1}{\alpha}\right)\Delta\theta; 0\};$$

$$q_2(\underline{\theta}, \bar{\theta}) = q_2^{FB}(\underline{\theta}, \bar{\theta}).$$

In this case, as soon as the agent's type turns high, he receives first-best output. Furthermore, distortions in the output provided to the period-1 low type decrease monotonically over time. As shown in Battaglini (2005), these properties extend to arbitrary horizons, as long as the process takes only two values, and remains stochastically monotone.

A central question for the dynamic mechanism design literature is then what properties of the process governing the evolution of the agents' private information are responsible for the dynamics of the distortions under optimal contracts. A conjecture in the earlier literature is that distortions should decline over time when the correlation between the initial type, θ_1, and the subsequent ones, θ_t, declines over time. To see the problem with this conjecture, consider the same example above in which the type process takes only two values in each period. However, assume now that $\bar{\theta}$ is an absorbing state so that $\bar{\alpha} = 1$. It is easy to see from the formulas in (6) that, while in this case distortions decrease in expectation over time, they remain constant as long as the agent's type remains low. Furthermore, even the property that distortions decline in expectation should not be taken for granted. Suppose, for example that the agent's type follows a random walk. In the example above, this amounts to assuming that $\theta_2 = \theta_1 + \varepsilon$ with $\varepsilon \in \{-\Delta\theta, 0, +\Delta\theta\}$ and with the distribution over ε independent of θ_1 so that $\bar{x} = \underline{x}$ and $\bar{\alpha} = \underline{\alpha}$. Then use the formulas in Proposition 1 to verify that the distortions in the contract of the period-1 low type remain constant over time. As I discuss further in the next section, this property extends to arbitrary horizons and to general random walk processes. Hence, despite the fact that, when the process is a random walk, the correlation between the agent's period-1 type and his period-t type declines with t, distortions remain constant over time.

Another observation that the example offers is that the volatility of the shocks, or their persistence, need not matter for the dynamics of distortions. To see this, suppose that $\bar{\alpha} = \underline{\alpha} = 1$, in which case the agent's type is constant over time. Clearly, this is a special case of the random walk case discussed above, where the volatility of the period-2 shocks is zero. Then, again, distortions are constant over time. In fact, as shown first in Baron and Besanko (1984), when types are constant over time and payoffs are time-additively-separable, as assumed here, the optimal allocations can be implemented by offering the same static contract in each period.

Another polar case of interest is when types are independent over time. In the context of this simple example, this amounts to assuming that $\bar{x} = 1 - \underline{\alpha} - \underline{x} = 0$ and that $\bar{\alpha} = \underline{x}$. In this case there are no distortions in the second period allocation, irrespective of the first-period type.

It should be clear from the discussion above that, as in static problems, distortions in optimal contracts are driven by the familiar trade-off between efficiency and rent-extraction, *evaluated from period 1's perspective*. That is, from the perspective of the period at which the participation constraints bind. It should also be clear that neither the correlation between the initial type and his future types, nor the agent's ability to forecast his future types (as captured, for example, by the inverse of the volatility of the forecast error) is what determines the way the principal solves the above trade-off intertemporally. The question is then what specific properties of the process governing the evolution of the agents' private information are responsible for the dynamics of distortions under optimal contracts? I will provide a formal answer to this question in the next section, after developing an approach that permits one to extend the analysis to a broader class of processes (and of contracting problems). Before doing so, it is, however, instructive to rewrite (5) as follows:

$$\frac{V_1^A(\bar{\theta}) - V_1^A(\underline{\theta})}{\Delta\theta} = q_1(\underline{\theta}) + \delta\mathbb{E}\left[I_2(\underline{\theta}, \theta_2) \cdot q_2\left(\underline{\theta}, \theta_2\right) \mid \theta_1 = \underline{\theta}\right], \quad (7)$$

where

$$I_2(\underline{\theta}, \theta_2) = \frac{\Pr(\tilde{\theta}_2 > \theta_2 | \bar{\theta}) - \Pr(\tilde{\theta}_2 > \theta_2 | \underline{\theta})}{\Pr(\tilde{\theta}_2 = \theta_2 | \underline{\theta})}. \quad (8)$$

The function $I_2(\underline{\theta}, \theta_2)$ in (8) captures the different probability the two period-1 types assign to having a period-2 type above θ_2, normalized by the probability that the period-1 low type assigns to having a period-2 type equal to θ_2. As it will become clear below, these functions are the discrete-type analogs of what Pavan, Segal, and Toikka (2014) refer to as *"impulse response functions."*

As in static mechanism design, the surplus the principal must grant to the period-1 high type to induce him to report truthfully originates from the surplus that this type can guarantee himself by mimicking the period-1 low type. Contrary to static mechanism design, though, such surplus combines the difference in the period-1 utility of consuming the quantity $q_1(\underline{\theta})$ sold to the low type with the difference in the continuation payoffs. The latter are in turn determined by the quantities supplied in the second period to the period-1 low type (which are responsible for the period-2 informational rents) scaled by the different probabilities the two period-1 types assign to being able to enjoy such rents, as captured by the impulse response functions.

4 MYERSONIAN APPROACH

The example in the previous section illustrates some of the key ideas in the design of optimal dynamic mechanisms. It also shows the importance of not over-simplifying the model when it comes to the predictions the theory delivers for the dynamics of the distortions under optimal contracts. In particular, the example shows the importance of accommodating for more than two types. As in other contexts, working with a large but finite number of types is more tedious than working with a continuum of types. The literature has thus investigated ways of extending the analysis of mechanism design with a continuum of types to dynamic settings. The approach is similar to the one pioneered by Myerson (1981), but adapted to account for the gradual resolution of uncertainty and for the possibility of a stream of decisions. I revisit some of the key results of this approach in this section.

There are a few difficulties in extending the Myersonian approach to dynamic settings. The first is in identifying primitive properties (on payoffs and type processes) under which it is a necessary condition for incentive compatibility that each agent's equilibrium payoff satisfies, at each period, an *envelope formula* analogous to the familiar one

$$V^A(\theta) = V^A(\underline{\theta}) + \int_{\underline{\theta}}^{\theta} q(s)ds \tag{9}$$

for static environments.

A second difficulty is in identifying appropriate *dynamic monotonicity conditions* on the allocation rule that, when paired with the envelope formulas for the equilibrium payoffs, guarantee that the agents have the incentives to report truthfully at all histories.

The difficulty in identifying primitive conditions implying that the envelope representation of the equilibrium payoffs is a necessary condition for incentive compatibility comes from the fact that (a) the policies in the mechanism cannot be assumed to be "smooth," for this may affect the characterization of the optimal mechanisms, and (b) one cannot use directly the conditions justifying the envelope theorem in static models (e.g., Milgrom and Segal, 2002), for the latter require each agent's payoff to be smooth in the agent's type *across all possible strategies* and, in dynamic settings, such a property cannot be guaranteed, at least not for arbitrary mechanisms.

Importantly, these difficulties are conceptual, not technical. In particular, the difficulty in guaranteeing that each agent's payoff is smooth in the initial type, across all possible continuation strategies, is akin to the difficulty in establishing revenue equivalence in multiagent static settings with correlated information. Similarly, the difficulty in identifying appropriate dynamic monotonicity conditions is akin to the difficulty in identifying minimally sufficient conditions in static screening problems with multidimensional types and allocations.

In this section, I describe the approach in Pavan, Segal, and Toikka (2014) to address such difficulties. The exposition here is informal. I refer the reader to the original paper for details.

4.1   Incentive Compatibility, Envelopes, and Payoff Equivalence

In order to identify primitive conditions (on payoffs and type processes) implying that the equilibrium payoffs must satisfy an envelope representation akin to the one in static models, across all possible mechanisms, Pavan, Segal, and Toikka (2014) use a state representation of the evolution of the agents' private information similar to the one in Eső and Szentes (2007) – see also Eső and Szentes (2015).[13] That is, let $\theta_t = Z_t(\theta_1, \varepsilon)$ where ε is a vector of random variables, independent of θ_1, drawn from some distribution G over $\mathcal{E} \equiv \prod_{t=1}^{T} \mathcal{E}_t$, with each $\mathcal{E}_t \subset \mathbb{R}$. Any stochastic process can be described this way. For example, given the kernels $F \equiv (F_t)$, for any $t \geq 2$, one can let $F_t^{-1}(\varepsilon_t|\theta_{t-1}) \equiv \inf\{\theta_t : F_t(\theta_t|\theta_{t-1}) \geq \varepsilon_t\}$ with each ε_t drawn from a Uniform distribution over $(0, 1)$, independently of θ_1 and of any ε_s, $s \neq t$. The random variable $F_t^{-1}(\varepsilon_t|\theta_{t-1})$ is then distributed according to the cdf $F_t(\cdot|\theta_{t-1})$. One can then let $Z_t(\theta_1, \varepsilon) = F_t^{-1}(\varepsilon_t|Z_{t-1}(\theta_1, \varepsilon))$, with $Z^{t-1}(\theta_1, \varepsilon) \equiv (Z_\tau(\theta_1, \varepsilon))_{\tau=1}^{t-1}$, constructed inductively starting from $Z_1(\theta_1) \equiv \theta_1$.[14] The above representation is referred to as the *canonical representation* of F in Pavan, Segal, and Toikka (2014). While the canonical representation is a valid representation for all processes, it is sometimes convenient to work with alternative state representations. For example, suppose that θ_t evolves according to an AR(1) process, so that $\theta_t = \gamma\theta_{t-1} + \varepsilon_t$. Then a natural state representation is

$$\theta_t = Z_t(\theta_1, \varepsilon) = \gamma^{t-1}\theta_1 + \gamma^{t-2}\varepsilon_2 + \cdots + \gamma\varepsilon_{t-1} + \varepsilon_t.$$

[13] These papers use the state representation as a tool to study optimal disclosure policies as opposed to a tool to identify primitive conditions validating the envelope theorem.

[14] This construction is standard; see the second proof of Kolmogorov's extension theorem in Billingsley (1995, p.490).

A similar state representation can be used to describe the agent's private information at any period t as a function of his period-s type history $\theta^s \equiv (\theta_1, \ldots, \theta_s)$, $s < t$, and subsequent shocks. Thus, for any $s \geq 1$, any $t > s$, let $Z_{(s),t}(\theta^s, \varepsilon)$ denote the representation of θ_t as a function of θ^s and independent shocks ε that, along with θ^s, are responsible for θ_t. Hereafter, the index s is dropped from the subscripts when $s = 1$ to ease the exposition (that is, for any t, any (θ_1, ε), $Z_t(\theta_1, \varepsilon) \equiv Z_{(1),t}(\theta_1, \varepsilon)$).

Next, let $\|\cdot\|$ denote the discounted L-1 norm on $\mathbb{R}^\infty$ defined by $\|y\| \equiv \sum_{t=0}^{\infty} \delta^t |y_t|$.

Definition 1 *The process is* regular *if, for any $s \geq 1$, there exist a function $C_{(s)} : \mathcal{E} \to \mathbb{R}^\infty$ satisfying $\mathbb{E}[\|C_{(s)}(\varepsilon)\|] \leq B$ for some constant B independent of s, such that for all $t \geq s$, $\theta^s \in \Theta^s$, and $\varepsilon \in \mathcal{E}$, $Z_{(s),t}(\theta^s, \varepsilon)$ is a differentiable function of θ_s with $\left|\partial Z_{(s),t}(\theta^s, \varepsilon)/\partial \theta_s\right| \leq C_{(s),t-s}(\varepsilon)$.*[15]

In words, a process is regular if it admits a state representation where the $Z_{(s),t}$ functions are differentiable with bounded derivatives (but where the bounds are allowed to vary with the state).

Given the above notation, the *impulse response* of θ_t to θ_s is then defined as follows:[16]

$$I_{(s),t}(\theta^t) \equiv \mathbb{E}\left[\frac{\partial Z_{(s),t}(\theta^s, \varepsilon)}{\partial \theta_s} \mid Z_{(s),t}(\theta^s, \varepsilon) = \theta^t\right],$$

where the expectation is over the shocks ε given θ^s. Again, when $s = 1$, to simplify the notation, drop the index (s) from the subscripts so that by $I_t(\theta^t) \equiv I_{(1),t}(\theta^t)$ all $t > 1$ all θ^t. Finally, for all $s \geq 1$, all θ^s, $I_{(s),s}(\theta^s) \equiv 1$. For example, when θ_t follows an AR(1) process, the impulse response of θ_t to θ_1 is simply $I_t(\theta_1, \varepsilon) = \gamma^{t-1}$. More generally, the impulse response functions are themselves stochastic processes capturing how variations in types at any given period propagate through the entire process. For example, when

$$\theta_t = Z_t(\theta_1, \varepsilon) = \theta_1 \times \varepsilon_2 \times \cdots \times \varepsilon_t$$

the period-1 impulse response functions are given by $I_t(\theta_1, \varepsilon) = \varepsilon_2 \times \cdots \times \varepsilon_t$. When the process is Markov and the kernels $F_t(\theta_t | \theta_{t-1})$ are continuously differentiable in (θ_t, θ_{t-1}), the canonical representation introduced above yields

---

[15] For any ε, the term $C_{(s),t-s}(\varepsilon)$ is the $(t-s)$-compoment of the sequence $C_s(\varepsilon)$.

[16] Special cases of the impulse response functions (and of the ICFOC conditions below) have been identified by Baron and Besanko (1984), Besanko (1985), Courty and Li (2000), and Eső and Szentes (2007), among others. In particular, Baron and Besanko (1984) refer to these functions as to "the informativeness measure." For reasons discussed in detail in Pavan, Segal, and Toikka (2014), we favor the expression "impulse response functions" to highlight that the information that early types contain about future ones is not the precise property of the type process responsible for the dynamics of distortions under optimal contracts – recall the discussion in the previous section.

the following expression for the impulse responses:

$$I_{(s),t}(\theta^t) = \prod_{\tau=s+1}^{t} \left(-\frac{\partial F_\tau(\theta_\tau|\theta_{\tau-1})/\partial\theta_{\tau-1}}{f_\tau(\theta_\tau|\theta_{\tau-1})} \right).$$

Note that, when $s = 1$ and $t = 2$, the impulse response function of θ_2 to θ_1 is then given by

$$I_2(\theta_1, \theta_2) = -\frac{\partial F_2(\theta_2|\theta_1)/\partial\theta_1}{f_2(\theta_2|\theta_1)} = \frac{\partial[1 - F_2(\theta_2|\theta_1)]/\partial\theta_1}{f_2(\theta_2|\theta_1)},$$

which is the continuous-type analog of the discrete formula in (8). For the analogs of such formulas in continuous time, see Bergemann and Strack (2015a).

The advantage of the state representation when it comes to identifying primitive conditions under which the dynamic analog of the envelope representation of the equilibrium payoffs is a necessary condition for incentive compatibility is that it permits one to focus on a subset of possible continuation strategies for the agent that are indexed by state variables, the shocks, that are orthogonal to the initial private information. To see this, let $T = 2$ and assume the agent observes the shocks ε in addition to his types (Notice that (θ_1, θ_2) remains a sufficient statistic for $(\theta_1, \theta_2, \varepsilon)$ when it comes to the agent's payoff). Because there are only two periods, then, without loss of generality, ε can be assumed to be unidimensional. Given any mechanism $\chi = \langle \mathbf{q}, \mathbf{p} \rangle$, then construct an auxiliary mechanism $\tilde{\chi} = \langle \tilde{\mathbf{q}}, \tilde{\mathbf{p}} \rangle$ in which the agent is asked to report θ_1 in period 1 and the shock ε in period 2. The mechanism $\tilde{\chi} = \langle \tilde{\mathbf{q}}, \tilde{\mathbf{p}} \rangle$ is obtained from $\chi = \langle \mathbf{q}, \mathbf{p} \rangle$ by letting $(\tilde{q}_1(\cdot), \tilde{p}_1(\cdot)) = (q_1(\cdot), p_1(\cdot))$ and then letting $\tilde{q}_2(\theta_1, \varepsilon) = q_2(\theta_1, Z_2(\theta_1, \varepsilon))$ and $\tilde{p}_2(\theta_1, \varepsilon) = p_2(\theta_1, Z_2(\theta_1, \varepsilon))$, where $Z_2(\theta_1, \varepsilon)$ is the function describing the state representation of the process introduced above. Then let

$$U^A(\theta_1; \hat{\theta}_1, \sigma) \equiv \theta_1 \tilde{q}_1(\hat{\theta}_1) - \tilde{p}_1(\hat{\theta}_1) + \delta \mathbb{E}\left[Z_2(\theta_1, \varepsilon)\tilde{q}_2(\hat{\theta}_1, \sigma(\varepsilon)) - \tilde{p}_2(\hat{\theta}_1, \sigma(\varepsilon))|\theta_1 \right]$$

denote the payoff that the initial type θ_1 expects from reporting the message $\hat{\theta}_1$ in period 1 and then following the reporting strategy $\sigma(\varepsilon)$ in period 2, where $\sigma(\varepsilon)$ is the report the agent makes in period 2 when the period-2 shock is ε, and where the expectation is over the shocks ε, given θ_1. Once the agent's behavior is indexed this way, fixing $(\hat{\theta}_1, \sigma)$, a variation in θ_1 no longer triggers a variation in the agent's reports. This is convenient, for it bypasses the problem alluded to above of guaranteeing that the agent's payoff be differentiable in the true type θ_1 for all possible reporting strategies.[17]

---

[17] Notice that if, instead, one were to index the agent's reporting plan by $(\hat{\theta}_1, \sigma)$ with the period-2 report $\sigma(\theta_2)$ now depending on θ_2, as opposed to the orthogonalized innovation ε, then a variation in θ_1, by triggering a variation in the period-2 report, would possibly lead to non-differentiability of $U^A(\theta_1; \hat{\theta}_1, \sigma)$ in θ_1.

The construction above, in turn, can be used to validate the envelope theorem. Provided $U^A(\theta_1; \hat{\theta}_1, \sigma)$ is differentiable and equi-Lipschitz continuous in θ_1, the value function $\sup_{(\hat{\theta}_1, \sigma)} U^A(\theta_1; \hat{\theta}_1, \sigma)$ is then Lipschitz continuous in θ_1 (this follows from the same arguments as in Milgrom and Segal (2002)'s atemporal analysis).[18] Now, if the mechanism $\chi = \langle \mathbf{q}, \mathbf{p} \rangle$ is incentive compatible in the primitive environment, then reporting $\hat{\theta}_1 = \theta_1$ in period 1 and then reporting the shocks ε truthfully in period 2 (that is, following the strategy $\sigma^{truth}(\varepsilon) = \varepsilon$) must be optimal for the agent in the auxiliary mechanism $\tilde{\chi} = \langle \tilde{\mathbf{q}}, \tilde{\mathbf{p}} \rangle$. The envelope theorem then implies that a necessary condition for incentive compatibility of $\chi = \langle \mathbf{q}, \mathbf{p} \rangle$ is that, under $\chi = \langle \mathbf{q}, \mathbf{p} \rangle$, $V_1^A(\theta_1)$ is Lipschitz continuous with derivative equal to

$$
\begin{aligned}
\frac{dV_1^A(\theta_1)}{d\theta_1} &= q_1(\theta_1) + \delta\mathbb{E}\left[\frac{\partial Z_2(\theta_1, \varepsilon)}{\partial \theta_1} \tilde{q}_2(\theta_1, \varepsilon) \right] \\
&= \mathbb{E}\left[\sum_{s=1}^{s=2} \delta^{s-1} I_s(\theta^s) q_s(\theta^s) \mid \theta_1 \right],
\end{aligned}
\tag{10}
$$

where the last equality uses the definition of the impulse response functions along with the relation between the policies $\chi = \langle \mathbf{q}, \mathbf{p} \rangle$ and the policies $\tilde{\chi} = \langle \tilde{\mathbf{q}}, \tilde{\mathbf{p}} \rangle$. Note that the above envelope formula is the continuous-type analog of Condition (7) in the discrete case. As mentioned above, this formula is a necessary condition for incentive compatibility; it must hold in order for the agent to prefer reporting truthfully in both periods than lying in period 1 and then reporting the orthogonalized shocks truthfully. To obtain a complete characterization of incentive compatibility, one first extends the above envelope formula to arbitrary horizons and then combines it with appropriate monotonicity conditions on the allocation rule $\mathbf{q}$ guaranteeing that one-stage deviations from truthful reporting are suboptimal. When applied to a Markov environment (such as the one under consideration here), this approach yields a complete characterization of incentive compatibility, as shown in Theorem 1, below (for a general treatment in richer environments with an arbitrary number of agents and decision-controlled processes, see Pavan, Segal, and Toikka, 2014).[19]

---

[18] The differentiability and equi-Lipschitz continuity of U^A in θ_1 in turn can be guaranteed by assuming differentiability and equi-Lipschitz continuity of the Z_2 functions with appropriate bounds on the expected NPV of the quantity schedules. See Pavan et al. (2014) for details.

[19] Here, I assume that the principal is restricted to offering contracts such that, for any $t \geq 1$, any θ^t, $\mathbb{E}\left[\sum_{s \geq t} \delta^{s-t} I_{(s),t}(\theta^s) q_s(\theta^s) \mid \theta^t \right] \leq K$ for some $K \in \mathbb{R}_{++}$ arbitrarily large. This restriction, which is stronger than needed, is used to validate the representation of the equilibrium payoffs in the theorem below. Note that the restriction is vacuous if one assumes bounded impulse responses (in the sense of condition F-BIR in Pavan, Segal, and Toikka, 2014) and bounded output.

For all t, all $\theta^t \in \Theta^t$, all $\hat{\theta}_t \in \Theta_t$, let

$$D_t(\theta^t; \hat{\theta}_t) \equiv \mathbb{E}\left[\sum_{s \geq t} \delta^{s-t} I_{(t),s}(\theta^s) q_s(\theta^s_{-t}, \hat{\theta}_t) \mid \theta^t\right]. \tag{11}$$

Theorem 1 (Pavan, Segal, and Toikka, 2014) *Suppose the process F is regular. The mechanism $\chi = \langle q, p \rangle$ is incentive compatible if and only if, (a) for all $t \geq 1$, all θ^{t-1}, $V_t^A(\theta^t)$ is equi-Lipschitz continuous in θ_t with*

$$\frac{\partial V_t^A(\theta^t)}{\partial \theta_t} = \mathbb{E}\left[\sum_{s \geq t} \delta^{s-t} I_{(t),s}(\theta^s) q_s(\theta^s) \mid \theta^t\right] \quad a.e. \ \theta_t \in \Theta_t, \quad \text{(ICFOC)}$$

and (b), for all $t \geq 1$, all θ^{t-1}, all $\theta_t, \hat{\theta}_t \in \Theta_t$,

$$\int_{\hat{\theta}_t}^{\theta_t} [D_t((\theta^{t-1}, x); x) - D_t((\theta^{t-1}, x); \hat{\theta}_t)] dx \geq 0. \tag{Int-M}$$

Note that the result in Theorem 1 is not specific to quasilinear settings. Conditions (ICFOC) and (Int-M) characterize the entire set of implementable allocations also in settings in which payments are either absent, or agents' payoffs are not linear in the payments (see also the discussion in Section 6, below). Also observe that, in quasilinear settings, there always exist payments p that guarantee that the (ICFOC) conditions are satisfied at all histories (see Pavan, Segal, and Toikka, 2014 for the construction of such payments, and Corollary 2, below, for a discussion of the extent to which such payments are unique). In such quasilinear environments, (ICFOC) imposes restrictions on the payments p, while the integral monotonicity conditions (Int-M) impose restrictions on the output schedule q.

Sketch of the proof. The formal arguments supporting the claim that (ICFOC) is a necessary condition for incentive compatibility are in Pavan, Segal, and Toikka (2014). For a heuristic intuition, see the discussion for the case $T = 2$ preceding the theorem. Here I focus on the necessity of the integral monotonicity conditions (Int-M) and on the fact that (ICFOC) and (Int-M), jointly, imply incentive compatibility. For this purpose, fix t and θ^{t-1} and drop θ^{t-1} to ease the exposition. Let $U_t(\hat{\theta}_t; \theta_t)$ denote the agent's continuation payoff when his period-t type is θ_t, he reports $\hat{\theta}_t$ in period t, and then reports truthfully at all subsequent periods. Observe that $U_t(\theta_t; \theta_t) = V_t^A(\theta_t)$. Incentive compatibility then requires that, for all $\hat{\theta}_t \in \Theta_t$,

$$\hat{\theta}_t \in \arg\max_{\theta_t} \left\{ U_t(\hat{\theta}_t; \theta_t) - V_t^A(\theta_t) \right\}.$$

Next, note that (ICFOC) implies that, for $\hat{\theta}_t$ fixed, the function $g_t(\cdot; \hat{\theta}_t) : \Theta_t \to \mathbb{R}$ given by $g_t(\theta_t; \hat{\theta}_t) \equiv U_t(\hat{\theta}_t; \theta_t) - V_t^A(\theta_t)$ is Lipschitz continuous with derivative equal to

$$g_t'(\theta_t; \hat{\theta}_t) = \partial U_t(\hat{\theta}_t; \theta_t)/\partial \theta_t - dV_t^A(\theta_t)/d\theta_t$$

for almost all θ_t. If the mechanism $\chi = \langle \mathbf{q}, \mathbf{p} \rangle$ is incentive compatible, then reporting truthfully from period $t + 1$ onwards must be optimal for the agent after reporting truthfully in period t. Because the environment is Markov (that is, payoffs separate over time and the process governing the evolution of the agent's type is Markov), then reporting truthfully from period $t + 1$ onward must also be optimal after any deviation in period t. Consider then a fictitious environment in which the agent's period-t report is exogenously fixed at $\hat{\theta}_t$. Incentive compatibility of the mechanism $\chi = \langle \mathbf{q}, \mathbf{p} \rangle$ in the primitive environment implies incentive compatibility of the same mechanism in the fictitious environment. The same arguments that establish the necessity of condition (ICFOC) in the primitive environment then also imply that, in the fictitious environment, $U_t(\hat{\theta}_t; \theta_t)$ must be equi-Lipschitz continuous in θ_t with $\partial U_t(\hat{\theta}_t; \theta_t)/\partial \theta_t = D_t((\theta^{t-1}, \theta_t); \hat{\theta}_t)$ for almost all θ_t. Because $dV_t^A(\theta_t)/d\theta_t = D_t((\theta^{t-1}, \theta_t); \theta_t)$, one then has that

$$g_t(\hat{\theta}_t; \hat{\theta}_t) - g_t(\theta_t; \hat{\theta}_t) = \int_{\theta_t}^{\hat{\theta}_t} \frac{\partial g_t(x; \hat{\theta}_t)}{\partial \theta_t} dx = \int_{\theta_t}^{\hat{\theta}_t} \Big[D_t((\theta^{t-1}, x); \hat{\theta}_t)$$
$$- D_t((\theta^{t-1}, x); x) \Big] dx. \qquad (12)$$

Hence, $\hat{\theta}_t \in \arg\max_{\theta_t} \left\{ g_t(\theta_t; \hat{\theta}_t) \right\}$ only if (Int-M) holds. This establishes that (ICFOC) and (Int-M) are jointly necessary. To see that they are also jointly sufficient, observe that, when these conditions are satisfied, no single one-stage deviation from truthful reporting is optimal (to see this, note that (ICFOC) and (Int-M) imply that $U_t(\hat{\theta}_t; \theta_t) \leq V_t^A(\theta_t)$ all $\theta_t, \hat{\theta}_t \in \Theta_t$ all t, all θ^{t-1}). Along with the facts that (a) payoffs are continuous at infinity, and (b) the environment is Markov, the above result then implies that all other deviations are also suboptimal.[20] QED

In a Markov environment, the combination of integral monotonicity (Int-M) with the envelope representation of the equilibrium payoffs (ICFOC) thus fully characterizes incentive compatibility. That the environment is Markov implies that the agent's incentives in any period depend only on his current true type and his past reports, but not on his past true types. In turn this implies that, when a single departure from truthful reporting is suboptimal, then truthful reporting (at all histories) dominates any other strategy. Importantly, note that every environment can be "Markovized" by expanding the state space (e.g., by letting the state be equal to $\omega_t = \theta^t$ all t). In this case, Myerson's (1986) revelation principle takes the form of Doepke and Townsend's (2004) revelation principle – without loss of generality, one can restrict attention to mechanisms in which the agent reports $\omega_t = \theta^t$ at each period. When the agent is asked to report $\omega_t = \theta^t$ in all periods, it is always without loss of generality to consider

---

[20] Recall that the Markov assumption implies that, when no single deviation from truthful reporting is profitable at any truthful history (i.e., conditional on having reported truthfully in the past) then single deviations from truthful reporting are also suboptimal at all other non-truthful histories.

mechanisms in which the agent reports truthfully at all periods, irrespective of his past behavior. This property, however, does not necessarily make the characterization of incentive compatibility easier. The advantage is that it allows one to focus on "strongly truthful" strategies (that is, strategies prescribing truthful reporting at all histories); The disadvantage is that one needs to deal with incentive compatibility on a multidimensional state space. In certain environments, the dimensionality of the state space is irrelevant, so "Markovizing" the state space is the way to go (this is the case, for example, when implementing efficiency using VCG/AGV-type of mechanisms, or when maximizing profits in environments in which virtual surplus takes the form of an additive or multiplicative transformation of the true surplus, as in Kakade et al., 2013 or in Fershtman and Pavan, 2016). Working with this alternative state representation is also useful in environments in which the agent possesses private information not only about the realizations of a process but also about the process itself (which amounts to assuming that the agent's private information is multidimensional, with a component that is fully persistent – see, e.g., Boleslavsky and Said, 2013).

Static versions of the integral-monotonicity conditions appeared in the literature on implementability (see Rochet, 1987 or Carbajal and Ely, 2013 and the references therein). This condition generalizes the more familiar monotonicity conditions typically encountered in static settings with supermodular payoffs, unidimensional types, and unidimensional decisions by which an allocation rule is implementable if and only if it is monotone. As the above integral monotonicity condition reveals, what is required by incentive compatibility in more general settings is that the derivative of the agent's payoff with respect to his true type be sufficiently monotone in the reported type. In particular, note that (Int-M) holds in the dynamic environment under examination if the NPV of expected future output, *discounted by impulse responses*

$$
\mathbb{E}\left[\sum_{s \geq t} \delta^{s-t} I_{(t),s}(\theta^t) q_s(\theta^s_{-t}, \hat{\theta}_t) \mid \theta^t \right],
$$

is *nondecreasing* in the current report $\hat{\theta}_t$. Even if payoffs are supermodular, as in the environment under consideration here, output need not be monotone in each of the reported types (a property referred to in the literature as *strong monotonicity*). It suffices that it is sufficiently monotone, on average, where the average is both over states and time.

The sufficiency results in the literature are typically based on stronger notions of monotonicity (see, for example, Battaglini, 2005, or Eső and Szentes, 2007) with the exception of the mean-preserving-spread case of Courty and Li (2000). However, there are interesting environments where the optimal allocation rule fails to be strongly monotone (that is, where the nonmonetary allocation in certain periods fails to be increasing in either the current or past reports), and/or where the kernels naturally depend on past decisions, or fail first-order stochastic dominance. For instance, the optimal allocation rule in Pavan, Segal, and Toikka (2014)'s bandit auction, as well as the optimal matching rule in Fershtman and Pavan (2016) fail to be strongly monotone and yet they satisfy integral monotonicity.

The above result has two important implications, which are summarized in the next two corollaries.

Corollary 2 (payments equivalence)   *Let $\chi = \langle q, p \rangle$ and $\bar{\chi} = \langle q, \bar{p} \rangle$ be any two mechanisms implementing the same non-monetary decisions q. There exists a constant K such that for F-almost every θ^T*

$$\sum_{t=1}^{T} \delta^t p_t(\theta^t) = \sum_{t=1}^{T} \delta^t \bar{p}_t(\theta^t) + K.$$

Corollary 3 (irrelevance result)   *Let $\tilde{\chi} = \langle \tilde{q}, \tilde{p} \rangle$ be an incentive-compatible mechanism for the environment in which the agent is asked to report the orthogonal shocks ε starting from $t = 2$. Suppose now the principal can observe the shocks ε. In any mechanism $\tilde{\chi}' = \langle \tilde{q}, \tilde{p}' \rangle$ implementing the same non-monetary decisions $\tilde{q}$, there exists a constant K such that, for any $\theta_1 \in \Theta_1$,*

$$\mathbb{E}\left[\sum_{t=1}^{T} \delta^t \tilde{p}_t(\theta_1, \varepsilon) \right] = \mathbb{E}\left[\sum_{t=1}^{T} \delta^t \tilde{p}'_t(\theta_1, \varepsilon) \right] + K.$$

The first result is a strong version of revenue-equivalence that says that any two mechanisms implementing the same non-monetary decisions yield the same revenues, not just in expectation, but in each state of the world. The result is obtained by using inductively the necessary envelope conditions in (ICFOC) at all histories. In other words, in each state of the world, the NPV of the payments is pinned down by the quantity schedule q and the payoff of the lowest period-1 type, $V_t^A(\underline{\theta}_1)$. This stronger version of payment-equivalence is particularly relevant for settings in which the utility the agent derives from the payments is not linear, as in most managerial compensation and taxation models (see, e.g., Farhi and Werning, 2013, Garrett and Pavan, 2015, and Makris and Pavan, 2016). For a discussion of how the above result extends to settings with multiple agents, see Pavan, Segal, and Toikka (2014).

The second result says that the observability of the shocks is irrelevant for the principal's payoff. The two results are obviously related in the sense that they both follow from the necessary conditions for incentive compatibility summarized by the envelope representation in (ICFOC). For a discussion of how the irrelevance result in the above corollary extends to certain environments combining adverse selection with moral hazard, see Eső and Szentes (2015). For a discussion of how this result may fail when the agents' initial type is drawn from a discrete distribution, see Pavan (2007) and Krähmer and Strausz (2015b).

4.2   Full and Relaxed Programs and the First-Order Approach

The results discussed above can be used to arrive at properties of optimal dynamic mechanisms. In particular, the complete characterization of the set of incentive compatible rules $\chi = \langle \mathbf{q}, \mathbf{p} \rangle$ in the previous theorem implies that the principal's *full program* can be stated as follows:

$$
\mathcal{P}: \begin{cases}
\max_{\chi = \langle \mathbf{q}, \mathbf{p} \rangle} \mathbb{E}\left[\sum_t \delta^{t-1}(p_t(\theta^t) - C(q_t(\theta^t)))\right] \\
\text{subject to} \\
V_1^A(\theta_1) \geq 0 \text{ all } \theta_1, \\
\text{ICFOC-}(t):\, V_t^A(\theta^{t-1}, \theta_t) \text{ abs. cont. in } \theta_t \text{ with } \frac{\partial V_t^A(\theta^t)}{\partial \theta_t} = D_t(\theta^t; \theta_t) \text{ a.e. } \theta_t, \\
\quad \text{all } t, \text{ all } \theta^{t-1}, \\
\text{Int-M: } \int_{\hat{\theta}_t}^{\theta_t} [D_t((\theta^{t-1}, x); x) - D_t((\theta^{t-1}, x); \hat{\theta}_t)]dx \geq 0 \text{ all } t, \text{ all } (\theta^t, \hat{\theta}_t),
\end{cases}
$$

with the functions $D_t(\theta^t; \hat{\theta}_t)$ as defined in (11). Solving the above problem can still be tedious. The approach followed in most applied papers consists in solving a relaxation of the above program, in which all the envelope conditions ICFOC-(t), for $t > 1$, all the integral-monotonicity conditions, and all the participation constraints but the one for the lowest period-1 type are dropped. Dropping all these constraints leads to the following *relaxed program:*

$$
\mathcal{P}^r: \begin{cases}
\max_{\chi = \langle \mathbf{q}, \mathbf{p} \rangle} \mathbb{E}\left[\sum_t \delta^{t-1}(p_t(\theta^t) - C(q_t(\theta^t)))\right] \\
\text{subject to} \\
V_1^A(\underline{\theta}) \geq 0, \\
\text{ICFOC-}(1):\, V_1^A(\theta_1) \text{ abs. cont. with } \frac{dV_1^A(\theta_1)}{d\theta_1} = D_1(\theta_1; \theta_1) \text{ a.e.}
\end{cases}
$$

Once the solution to the relaxed program is at hand, by "reverse engineering," one then identifies primitive conditions (on the process F and, in more general settings, on the utility functions) guaranteeing that the remaining constraints are also satisfied. This approach is often referred to as "first-order approach."

Using ICFOC-(1), and integrating by parts, one can rewrite the principal's objective as "*Dynamic Virtual Surplus*"

$$
\mathbb{E}\left[\sum_t \delta^{t-1}\left(\left(\theta_t - \frac{1 - F_1(\theta_1)}{f_1(\theta_1)}I_t(\theta^t)\right)q_t(\theta^t) - C(q_t(\theta^t))\right)\right] - V_1^A(\underline{\theta}). \quad \text{(DVS)}
$$

Hence, in any incentive-compatible mechanism, irrespective of whether or not the mechanism solves the relaxed program, the principal's payoff takes the form of Dynamic Virtual Surplus. The latter combines the sum of the principal and the agent's gross payoffs with handicap terms that account for the cost to the principal of leaving information rents to the agents. In a dynamic setting, such handicaps combine the familiar term from static mechanism design, $[1 - F_1(\theta_1)]/f_1(\theta_1)$, with the impulse response functions $I_t(\theta^t)$ that link the period-t type to the period-1 type. While the period-1 inverse hazard rate $[1 - F_1(\theta_1)]/f_1(\theta_1)$ controls for the importance the principal assigns to rent-extraction relative to efficiency, the impulse responses $I_t(\theta^t)$ control for the effect of distorting period-t output on the agent's expected rent, as perceived at the moment of contracting, i.e., in period 1.

In the context of the simple screening problem under examination here, the Dynamic Virtual Surplus function can be maximized history by history. Assume, for example, that C is quadratic and that $Q = \mathbb{R}_+$, as in the discrete example in the previous section. The allocation rule that maximizes (DVS) is such that, for any t, any θ^t

$$q_t(\theta^t) = \max \left\{ \theta_t - \frac{1 - F_1(\theta_1)}{f_1(\theta_1)} I_t(\theta^t); 0 \right\}. \tag{13}$$

These optimality conditions are the continuous-type analogs of the conditions in the discrete-type example in the previous section. In particular, they imply (a) "no-distortion at the top" (that is, $q_t(\theta^t) = q_t^{FB}(\theta^t)$ if $\theta_1 = \bar{\theta}$, all t, all θ_{-1}^t) and (b), in case impulse responses are positive (which is always the case when the process satisfies first-order stochastic dominance), downward distortions for all histories for which $\theta_1 < \bar{\theta}$ and $I_t(\theta^t) \neq 0$. As in the example in the previous section, the dynamics of distortions are then driven by the dynamics of the impulse responses of future types to the initial ones. The smaller the impulse responses, the smaller the distortions. Furthermore, if impulse responses decline, on average, over time, so do the distortions.

The formula in (13) provides useful information about how the principal distorts the provision of output over time. However, the formula is valid only insofar as the solution to the relaxed program satisfies all the remaining constraints of the full program. It is easy to see that, when output is non-negative and the process satisfies first-order stochastic dominance, the solution to the relaxed program satisfies the remaining participation constraints for all period-1 types above the lowest one. In fact, ICFOC-(1) implies that

$$V_1^A(\theta_1) = V_1^A(\underline{\theta}) + \int_{\underline{\theta}}^{\theta_1} \mathbb{E}\left[\sum_{t \geq 1} \delta^{t-1} I_t(\theta^t) q_t(\theta^t) \mid x \right] dx \geq V_1^A(\underline{\theta})$$

for all $\theta_1 > \underline{\theta}$. Also, note that the remaining ICFOC-(t) constraints for $t > 1$ neglected in the relaxed program can always be satisfied by letting the payments be equal to

$$p_t\left(\theta^t\right) = \theta_t q_t(\theta^t) - \int_{\underline{\theta}}^{\theta_t} \mathbb{E}\left[\sum_{s \geq t} \delta^{s-t} I_{(t),s}(\theta^s) q_s(\theta^s) \mid (\theta^{t-1}, x) \right] dx$$

$$+ \delta \mathbb{E}\left[\int_{\underline{\theta}}^{\theta_{t+1}} \mathbb{E}\left[\sum_{s \geq t+1} \delta^{s-t-1} I_{(t+1),s}(\theta^s) q_s(\theta^s) \mid (\theta^t, x) \right] dx \mid \theta^t \right].$$

Finally, note that the remaining (Int-M) constraints are satisfied if the quantity schedule $\mathbf{q}$ that solves the above relaxed program is sufficiently monotone, in the sense that

$$\mathbb{E}\left[\sum_{s \geq t} \delta^{s-t} I_{(t),s}(\theta^s) q_s(\theta^t_{-s}, \hat{\theta}_t) \mid \theta^t\right]$$

is nonincreasing in $\hat{\theta}_t$ all t all θ^t. Using (13), one can easily verify that, when the cost is quadratic and output is nonnegative, these conditions are trivially satisfied if, for example, the agent's type follows an AR(1) process (in which case, $I_t(\theta^t) = \gamma^{t-1}$) and the period-1 distribution F_1 is log-concave. Interestingly, note that, in this case, the volatility of the shocks ε_t is irrelevant for the dynamics of the distortions. I refer the reader to Pavan, Segal, and Toikka (2014) for other examples where the solution to the relaxed program solves the full program and for a more detailed discussion of how the dynamics of the impulse responses drive the dynamics of the distortions when the output schedules in the optimal contracts are the ones that solve the relaxed program.

5 ROBUST PREDICTIONS: VARIATIONAL APPROACH

As mentioned in the Introduction, the predictions about the dynamics of distortions under optimal contracts identified in the literature are confined to environments in which the output schedules coincide with those that solve the relaxed program (equivalently, to settings in which the "first order approach" is valid). In this section, I illustrate an alternative approach, which does not permit one to fully characterize the optimal schedules, but offers a way of identifying certain predictions for the dynamics of the average distortions that do not rely on technical assumptions on the stochastic process governing the evolution of the agents' private information or the cost function made to validate the first-order approach. The first paper to follow such an approach is Garrett and Pavan (2015), in the context of managerial compensation. That paper is discussed in Section 6, below. The exposition in this section follows from Garrett, Pavan, and Toikka (2016), where the environment is similar to the one under consideration here.

For simplicity, assume $\Theta_t = \Theta = [\underline{\theta}, \bar{\theta}]$, for all t, and then denote by $\mathcal{B}(\Theta)$ the Borel sigma-algebra over Θ. For any $A \in \mathcal{B}(\Theta)$, any $t \geq 1$, then let $P^t(A; \theta)$ denote the probability that $\theta_t \in A$ given that $\theta_1 = \theta$.

Definition 2 *The type process F is* ergodic *if there exists a unique (invariant) probability measure π on $\mathcal{B}(\Theta)$ whose support has a nonempty interior such that for all $\theta \in \Theta$,*

$$\sup_{A \in \mathcal{B}(\Theta)} \left| P^t(A; \theta) - \pi(A) \right| \to 0 \text{ as } t \to \infty. \tag{14}$$

Definition 3 *The type process F is* stochastically monotone *if, for all $t \geq 2$, $\theta' > \theta \Rightarrow F_t(\cdot \mid \theta') \succsim_{FOSD} F_t(\cdot \mid \theta)$.*

Definition 4   *The type process F is* stationary *if $F_1 = \pi$ and $F_t = F_s$, all* $t, s > 1$.

The above properties are "economic properties" as opposed to technical conditions meant to validate certain first-order conditions. For example, ergodicity captures the idea that the probability the agent assigns to his type reaching a certain level in the distant future is invariant in his current type. Likewise, the property that F is stochastically monotone captures the idea that an agent who, in the present period, assigns a higher marginal value to the principal's product than another agent, expects to derive a higher value also in the next period. Finally, stationarity captures the idea that, at the time of contracting, the process has already evolved for long enough to have converged to the invariant distribution. The nature of these conditions is very different from, say, the log-concavity of the period-1 distribution F_1, or the monotonicity of the impulse response functions $I_t(\theta^t)$ in the realized types, which are technical conditions assumed in applications to validate the first-order approach (via reverse engineering), but which do not have a strong economic appeal.

The aim here is to identify predictions about the dynamics of distortions under optimal contracts that do not hinge on the validity of the first-order approach. In general, solving the full program is hard, if not impossible. The idea in Garrett, Pavan, and Toikka (2016) is that various properties of optimal contracts can be identified without fully solving for the optimal contracts. To see this, suppose that $\chi = \langle \mathbf{q}, \mathbf{p} \rangle$ is an optimal mechanism. Then use the results in the previous section to observe that any perturbation $\mathbf{q}'$ of the output schedule $\mathbf{q}$ that preserves (Int-M) along with any adjustment $\mathbf{p}'$ of the payment schedule $\mathbf{p}$ that preserves (ICFOC) and the period-1 participation constraints yield a mechanism $\chi' = \langle \mathbf{q}', \mathbf{p}' \rangle$ that is individually rational and incentive compatible. For the original mechanism $\chi = \langle \mathbf{q}, \mathbf{p} \rangle$ to be optimal, it must be that any such perturbation is unprofitable. One can then use such perturbations to identify properties of the optimal mechanisms.[21]

To illustrate, assume the period-1 participation constraints bind only at the bottom, i.e., only for $\theta_1 = \underline{\theta}$ (note that this is always the case when the process is stochastically monotone and output is nonnegative). For a moment, assume also interior solutions. A simple perturbation that preserves (Int-M) is to add a constant $a \in \mathbb{R}$ to the entire period-t output schedule $q_t(\theta^t)$. Then, use the fact that, under any incentive-compatible mechanism, the principal's payoff must coincide with Dynamic Virtual Surplus (DVS), to verify that a necessary condition for the optimality of the output schedule $\mathbf{q}$ is that the derivative of Dynamic Virtual Surplus (DVS) with respect to a evaluated at $a = 0$ must vanish. In the context of the economy under consideration here, the above requirement is fulfilled if and only if

$$\mathbb{E}\left[\theta_t - \frac{1 - F_1(\theta_1)}{f_1(\theta_1)} I_t(\theta^t) \right] = \mathbb{E}\left[C'(q_t(\theta^t)) \right]. \tag{15}$$

---

[21] The existence of optimal mechanisms is proved in Garrett, Pavan, and Toikka (2016).

The left-hand side in (15) is the *average* marginal benefit of expanding the period-t output uniformly across the period-t histories. The benefit is in virtual terms to account for the effect of higher output on the surplus the principal must leave to the agent at the time of contracting (recall that the impulse responses $I_t = I_{(1),t}$ are the ones with respect to the period-1 types). The right-hand side is the *average* marginal cost. Optimality requires that the average period-t distortion be equal to the average period-t handicap, where the former is given by

$$\mathbb{E}[\text{period-}t \text{ distortion}] \equiv \mathbb{E}[\theta_t - C'(q_t(\theta^t))]$$

whereas the latter is given by

$$\mathbb{E}[\text{period-}t \text{ handicap}] \equiv \mathbb{E}\left[\frac{1-F_1(\theta_1)}{f_1(\theta_1)} I_t(\theta^t)\right].$$

The optimality condition in (15) is thus the analog of the optimality condition (13) describing the solution to the relaxed program, but with the condition required to hold only *in expectation* as opposed to pathwise.

To derive predictions about the dynamics of the average distortions, one then investigates the dynamics of the average handicap.

Theorem 2 (Garrett, Pavan, and Toikka, 2016) *Assume the process F is regular and ergodic. Then*

$$\mathbb{E}\left[\frac{1 - F_1(\theta_1)}{f_1(\theta_1)} I_t(\theta^t)\right] \to 0 \text{ as } t \to \infty.$$

Moreover, if F is stochastically monotone, convergence is from above. If, in addition, F is stationary, then convergence is monotone in time.

Hence, the dynamics of the average handicaps are entirely driven by three economic properties of the type process: ergodicity, stationarity, and stochastic monotonicity. When output is interior and participation constraints bind only at the bottom, the above result thus implies that, when the process is ergodic, average distortions vanish in the long run. If, in addition, the process is stochastically monotone, average distortions vanish from above, meaning that the average distortion is positive (equivalently, output is distorted downward relative to the first best). Finally, if, in addition, the initial distribution coincides with the invariant distribution, then convergence is monotone in time, meaning that the average period-t distortion is larger than the average period-s distortion, for any $s > t$. The above predictions can be generalized as follows.

Definition 5 *Given the output process* $\mathbf{q}$, *period-t output is strictly interior if there exists $\varepsilon_t > 0$ such that*

$$\min \mathcal{Q} + \varepsilon_t \leq q_t(\theta^t) \leq \max \mathcal{Q} - \varepsilon_t \quad \text{for all } \theta^t.$$

The output schedule $\mathbf{q}$ *is strictly interior if the above condition holds for all t. It is eventually strictly interior if the condition holds for all sufficiently large t.*

Definition 6   *Given the output process* **q**, *the period-t distortions are* downwards *if* $\theta_t \geq C'(q_t)$ *almost surely. Distortions are* eventually downward *if the above condition holds for all sufficiently large t.*

Theorem 3 (Garrett, Pavan, and Toikka, 2016)   *Suppose F is regular and ergodic. (a) If* **q** *is eventually strictly interior, then* $\lim_{t\to\infty} \mathbb{E}[\theta_t - C'(q_t)] = 0$. *(b) If distortions are eventually downward, then* $q_t \overset{P}{\to} q_t^{FB}$.

Hence, if output is eventually strictly interior (which is necessarily the case when $\mathcal{Q} = \mathbb{R}$, that is, when the principal can either buy or sell output to the agent, as in certain trading models), then distortions eventually vanish in expectation. When, instead, $\mathcal{Q} = \mathbb{R}_+$, that is, when the principal can sell to, but not buy from the agent, then

$$\limsup_{t\to\infty} \mathbb{E}[\theta_t - C'(q_t)] \leq 0.$$

In this case, long-run average distortions are either zero or upward. Together, the above results imply that, if convergence to the first best fails, it must be because, eventually, within the same period, certain types over-consume, while others are completely excluded, and this pattern must occur infinitely often.

Part (b) in Theorem 3 in turn implies that, when distortions are eventually downward, as is always the case when F is strongly monotone and the optimal schedules solve the relaxed program, then convergence to the first-best is not just in expectation but in probability.

Importantly, note that the variational approach briefly described in this section (and which is still in its infancy) is different from the one in the earlier literature, and which is extensively used in the new dynamic public finance literature. The earlier approach perturbs the agent's compensation over multiple periods, holding fixed the agent's expected payoff at any history (thus trivially preserving incentive compatibility). Such an approach yields an inverse Euler equation that links average compensation over consecutive periods (see, e.g., Rogerson, 1985). It does not permit one, however, to identify predictions about the dynamics of the non-monetary allocations (e.g., output or effort). The new approach, instead, perturbs the agent's continuation payoff across different type histories. As such, the new approach builds on Theorem 1, above, to identify perturbations of the non-monetary allocations that preserve incentive compatibility.

6   BEYOND THE QUASI-LINEAR CASE

The results reviewed above are for environments in which the utility the players derive from the numeraire is linear. In such environments, the way the principal distributes the payments over time is irrelevant. For certain applications, this is clearly not a desirable assumption. For example, both in the managerial compensation literature as well as in the optimal taxation literature it is customary to assume that the agent's utility over the payments he receives from the principal, or over his consumption, is nonlinear. In this section, I show how the above results must be adapted to accommodate for non-quasi-linear payoffs. In the context of the environment examined thus far, such an extension could be accommodated by letting the agent's payoff be equal to $U^A \equiv \sum_{t=1}^{T} \delta^{t-1} \left[\theta_t q_t - v^A(p_t) \right]$ for some concave function $v^A(\cdot)$. It is easy to see that this enrichment does not affect the characterization of incentive compatibility, which continues to be determined by Conditions (ICFOC) and (Int-M) in Theorem 1. The point where the analysis departs from the discussion above is in the characterization of the optimal policies. When one of the two players' payoff is non-quasi-linear (that is, in the absence of transferable utility), the optimal policies cannot be obtained via simple point-wise maximization of the Dynamic Virtual Surplus function. Furthermore, the first-best allocations cannot be described in terms of the usual equalization of marginal cost of production to marginal value, for one must take into account the non-transferability of the principal's cost to the agent (or, equivalently, of the agent's utility from consuming the good to the principal).

In this section, I show how the Myersonian and the variational approaches discussed in the previous sections must be adapted to accommodate for these complications. To facilitate the connection to the pertinent literature, I consider a slightly different environment that is meant to capture, in reduced form, the non-quasi-linear applications typically considered in the literature. To this purpose, suppose that the principal's and the agent's payoffs are now given by

$$ U^P \equiv \sum_{t=1}^{T} \delta^{t-1} \left[y_t - c_t \right] \text{ and } U^A \equiv \sum_{t=1}^{T} \delta^{t-1} \left[v(c_t) - \psi(y_t, \theta_t) \right]. $$

In the case of managerial compensation, one can interpret y_t as the cash flows the manager generates for the firm, c_t as the agent's period-t consumption, and $\psi(y_t, \theta_t)$ as the disutility the agent derives from generating cash flows y_t when his period-t productivity is θ_t. In a procurement/regulation model, y_t can be interpreted as the gross surplus the regulated firm generates to society, c_t as the period-t compensation paid by the regulator to the firm, and $\psi(y_t, \theta_t)$ as the cost incurred by the firm when its period-t efficiency parameter is θ_t. In the case of nonlinear income taxation, one can interpret y_t as the income produced by the worker in period t, c_t as the period-t consumption (i.e., the net-of-tax disposable income), $y_t - c_t$ as the tax collected by the government, and θ_t as the worker's effective wage (or productivity). In the first two applications, the principal's problem consists in maximizing the ex-ante expectation of U^P subject to the usual incentive compatibility and participation constraints. In the case of optimal taxation, the planner's dual problem consists in maximizing tax revenues subject to the usual IC constraints and the constraint that

$$ \int q(V^A(\theta_1)) d F_1(\theta_1) \geq \kappa, $$

for some $\kappa \geq 0$, where the function $q(\cdot)$ captures the nonlinear Pareto weights that the planner assigns to different period-1 types (see also the discussion in the next section).

Here, I focus on the case of managerial compensation. As in Garrett and Pavan (2015), assume that

$$\psi(y_t, \theta_t) = \frac{1}{2}(y_t - \theta_t)^2 \text{ and } \theta_t = \gamma \theta_{t-1} + \varepsilon_t$$

with ε_t drawn from an absolutely continuous distribution G_t with mean zero, independently across t. The difference $e_t = y_t - \theta_t$ should be interpreted as the agent's period-t effort. For simplicity, assume $T = 2$. Both $(\theta_1, \theta_2) \in \Theta_1 \times \Theta_2$ and $(e_1, e_2) \in \mathbb{R}^2$ are the manager's private information. Instead, the cash flows $y \equiv (y_1, y_2)$ are verifiable, and hence can be used as a basis for the manager's compensation. The function $v : \mathbb{R} \to \mathbb{R}$ is strictly increasing, weakly concave, surjective, Lipschitz continuous, and differentiable. The case where v is linear corresponds to the case where the manager is risk-neutral, while the case where v is strictly concave corresponds to the case where he is strictly risk-averse. Let $w \equiv v^{-1}$ and $\psi_y(y_t, \theta_t) \equiv \partial \psi(y_t, \theta_t)/\partial y_t$.

That productivity follows an autoregressive process (in which case the impulse responses of period-2 types, θ_2, to period-1 types, θ_1, are constant and equal to γ) simplifies the exposition, but is not essential for the results. The perturbations considered in Garrett and Pavan (2015) preserve incentive compatibility under more general processes in which impulse responses are neither constant nor monotone. I will refer to $\gamma = 1$ as to the case of "full persistence" (meaning that, holding effort fixed, the effect of any shock to period-1 productivity on the firm's average cash flows is constant over time). To ease the comparison to the results in the previous section, I describe a mechanism $\chi = \langle \mathbf{y}, \mathbf{c} \rangle$ in terms of its cash flows and compensation policy. I refer the reader to Garrett and Pavan (2015) for a discussion of how one can alternatively describe a mechanism in terms of recommended effort policy and a payment scheme (with the latter defined also for off-path cash flow observations).

The result below parallels the one in Theorem 1, above, for the case of transferable utility by providing a complete characterization of incentive compatibility. Let $\theta \equiv (\theta_1, \theta_2)$ and for any $(\theta; \mathbf{y})$, let

$$W(\theta; \mathbf{y}) \equiv \psi(y_1(\theta_1), \theta_1) + \psi(y_2(\theta), \theta)$$

$$+ \int_{\underline{\theta}_1}^{\theta_1} \left\{ \psi_y(y_1(s), s) + \gamma \mathbb{E}\left[\psi_y(y_2(s, \theta_2), \theta_2) \mid s \right] \right\} ds \qquad (16)$$

$$+ \int_{\underline{\theta}_2}^{\theta_2} \psi_y(y_2(\theta_1, s), s) ds - \mathbb{E}\left[\int_{\underline{\theta}_2}^{\theta_2} \psi_y(y_2(\theta_1, s), s) ds \mid \theta_1 \right].$$

Theorem 4 (Garrett and Pavan, 2015) *The mechanism $\chi = \langle \mathbf{y}, \mathbf{c} \rangle$ satisfies all incentive-compatibility and participation constraints if and only if the following conditions jointly hold: (A) for all $\theta \in \Theta$,*

$$v\left(c_1\left(\theta_1\right)\right) + v\left(c_2\left(\theta\right)\right) = W\left(\theta; \mathbf{y}\right) + K \tag{17}$$

where $K \geq 0$ is such that

$$\mathbb{E}\left[W\left(\theta; \mathbf{y}\right) - \psi(y_1(\theta), \theta_1) + \psi(y_2(\theta), \theta) \mid \theta_1\right] + K \geq 0 \quad \forall \theta_1 \in \Theta_1; \tag{18}$$

and (B)(i) for all $\theta_1, \hat{\theta}_1 \in \Theta_1$,

$$\int_{\hat{\theta}_1}^{\theta_1} \left\{\psi_y\left(y_1(\hat{\theta}_1), s\right) + \gamma \mathbb{E}\left[\psi_y\left(y_2(\hat{\theta}_1, \theta_2), \theta_2\right) \mid s\right]\right\} ds$$

$$\leq \int_{\hat{\theta}_1}^{\theta_1} \left\{\psi_y\left(y_1(s), s\right) + \gamma \mathbb{E}\left[\psi_y(y_2(s, \theta_2), \theta_2) \mid s\right]\right\} ds, \tag{19}$$

and B(ii) $y_1(\theta_1) + \gamma \mathbb{E}\left[y_2(\theta_1, \theta_2) \mid \theta_1\right]$ is nondecreasing in θ_1 and, for all $\theta_1 \in \Theta_1$, $y_2(\theta_1, \theta_2)$ is nondecreasing in θ_2.

Condition (A) is the strong form of payoff-equivalence alluded to in Corollary 1, above: in each state θ, the utility the agent derives from the compensation he receives from the principal is uniquely pinned down by the policy $\mathbf{y}$, up to a scalar $K \geq 0$ chosen to guarantee participation. Such compensation must provide the agent a payoff, net of the disutility of effort,

$$v\left(c_1\left(\theta_1\right)\right) + v\left(c_2\left(\theta\right)\right) - \psi(y_1(\theta_1), \theta_1) - \psi\left(y_2(\theta), \theta_2\right)$$

equal to his period-1 expected payoff

$$V^A(\theta_1) = V^A(\underline{\theta}_1) + \int_{\underline{\theta}_1}^{\theta_1} \left\{\psi_y\left(y_1(s), s\right) + \gamma \mathbb{E}\left[\psi_y(y_2(s, \theta_2), \theta_2) \mid s\right]\right\} ds \tag{20}$$

augmented by a term

$$\int_{\underline{\theta}_2}^{\theta_2} \psi_y(y_2(\theta_1, s), s) ds - \mathbb{E}\left[\int_{\underline{\theta}_2}^{\theta_2} \psi_y(y_2(\theta_1, s), s) ds \mid \theta_1\right],$$

that guarantees that the manager has the incentives to report truthfully not only in period 1 but also in period 2. Note that the expectation of this last term vanishes when computed based on period-1's private information, θ_1. Part (A) thus imposes a restriction on the compensation scheme and is the analog of condition (ICFOC) in Theorem 1, above, applied jointly to $t = 1$ and $t = 2$. Note that the surplus that type θ_1 expects over and above the one expected by the lowest period-1 type $\underline{\theta}_1$ is increasing in the effort that the firm asks of managers with initial productivities $\theta_1' \in (\underline{\theta}_1, \theta_1)$ in each of the two periods. This surplus is necessary to dissuade type θ_1 from mimicking the behavior of these lower types. Also note that the scalar K in (17) corresponds to the expected payoff $V^A(\underline{\theta}_1)$ of the lowest period-1 type. Using (20), it is easy to see that, when the effort requested is nonnegative, then, if $\underline{\theta}_1$ finds it optimal to accept the contract, so does any manager whose initial productivity is higher. This property, however, need not hold in case the firm requests a negative effort from a positive-measure set of types.

Next consider condition (B). This condition is the analog of the integral monotonicity Condition (Int-M), above, applied to the environment under examination. It imposes restrictions on the cash flow policy that are independent of the manager's felicity function, v. In particular, Condition (B)(ii) combines the familiar monotonicity constraint for the second-period cash flows from static mechanism design (e.g., Laffont and Tirole, 1986) with a novel monotonicity constraint that requires the NPV of the expected cash flows, weighted by the impulse responses (which here are equal to one in the first period and γ in the second period) to be nondecreasing in period-1 productivity.

Garrett (2015) show how the above results can be used to derive implications for the dynamics of distortions under optimal contracts. Because the environment features non-transferable utility, distortions are captured by *wedges*, as in the public finance literature.

Definition 7 (wedges) *For each $t = 1, 2$ and each $\theta = (\theta_1, \theta_2)$, the (local expost) distortions in the provision of incentives under an (incentive-compatible) mechanism $\chi = \langle \mathbf{y}, \mathbf{c} \rangle$ are given by the wedge*

$$D_t(\theta) \equiv 1 - \frac{\psi_y\left(y_t(\theta), \theta_t\right)}{v'\left(c_t(\theta)\right)} \tag{21}$$

between the marginal effect of higher effort on the firm's cash flows and its marginal effect on the compensation necessary to preserve the manager's utility constant.

As discussed above, the approach typically followed in the literature to identify optimal policies is the following. First, consider a *relaxed program* that replaces all incentive-compatibility constraints with Condition (17) and all individual-rationality constraints with the constraint that $K = V^A(\underline{\theta}_1) \geq 0$. Second, choose policies (y_1, y_2, c_1) along with a scalar K so as to maximize the firm's profits subject to the aforementioned constraints. However, recall that Condition (17) alone is necessary but not sufficient for incentive compatibility. Furthermore, when the solution to the relaxed program yields policies prescribing a negative effort over a positive-measure set of types, satisfaction of the participation constraint for the period-1 lowest type $\underline{\theta}_1$ does not guarantee satisfaction of all other participation constraints. Therefore, one must typically identify auxiliary assumptions on the primitives of the problem guaranteeing that the policies that solve the relaxed program are implementable.

The approach in Garrett and Pavan (2015) consists, instead, in using variational techniques analogous to those used in the previous section to arrive at properties of the optimal contracts, without fully solving for the optimal contracts. First, one uses the result in the previous theorem to express the principal's profits as

$$\mathbb{E}[U^P] = \mathbb{E}\left[y_1(\theta) + y_2(\theta) - c_1(\theta_1) - v^{-1}\left(W(\theta; \mathbf{y}) + K - v(c_1(\theta_1))\right)\right].$$
(22)

One then proceeds by identifying "admissible perturbations" to implementable policies such that the perturbed policies remain implementable (i.e., continue to satisfy the conditions for incentive compatibility, as in the previous theorem). Finally, one uses such perturbations as test functions to identify properties of optimal policies.[22]

Through the above variational approach, Garrett and Pavan (2015) establish a series of results relating the dynamics of the expected wedges to (a) the agent's risk aversion, and (b) the persistence of the productivity process.

Theorem 5 (Garrett and Pavan, 2015) *Suppose the densities of the type process F are bounded.[23] Fix the level of persistence $\gamma < 1$ of the manager's productivity, and assume that the manager's preferences over consumption in each period are represented by the function $v_\rho(\cdot)$, with lower values of ρ indexing lower degrees of risk aversion.[24] Then there exists $\bar{\rho} > 0$ such that, for any $\rho \in [0, \bar{\rho}]$, under any optimal contract $|\mathbb{E}[D_2(\theta)]| < |\mathbb{E}[D_1(\theta_1)]|$, with $sign(\mathbb{E}[D_2(\theta)]) = sign(\mathbb{E}[D_1(\theta_1)])$.*

The result says that, for small degrees of risk aversion, average distortions decline over time, when the agent's type is less than fully persistent. While the result in the proposition focuses on the dynamics of distortions, the same properties apply to expected effort. Precisely, expected effort increases over time. Importantly, note that the result is established without imposing restrictions on the utility function v and the period-1 distribution F_1 necessary to validate the first-order approach.

The intuition for why, for low degrees of risk aversion, distortions decline, on average, over time is best illustrated in the case of positive effort (for the case where effort takes on negative values, see Garrett and Pavan, 2015). Asking the manager to exert higher effort requires increasing the surplus that the firm must leave to the manager to induce him to reveal his productivity (this surplus is over and above the minimal compensation required to compensate

---

[22] For certain results, the perturbations in Garrett and Pavan (2015) consist in adding nonnegative constant functions $\alpha(\theta_1) = a > 0$ and $\beta(\theta) = b > 0$, all θ, to the original cash flow policies $y_1(\theta_1)$ and $y_2(\theta)$ and then adjusting the compensation policy c so that the payments continue to satisfy the conditions in the previous theorem. For other results, instead, they consider perturbations that preserve not only incentive compatibility but also the agent's expected payoff conditional on his period-1 type θ_1. This is obtained by considering joint perturbations of y_1 and y_2 of opposite sign.

[23] Formally, there exist $a, b \in \mathbb{R}_{++}$ such that, for almost all $\theta_1 \in \Theta_1$, $\theta_2 \in \Theta_2(\theta_1)$, $a < f_1(\theta_1)$, $f_2(\theta_2|\theta_1) < b$, where $\Theta_2(\theta_1) = Supp[F_2(\cdot|\theta_1)]$.

[24] Formally, let $(v_\rho)_{\rho \geq 0}$ be a collection of functions $v_\rho : \mathbb{R} \to \mathbb{R}$ with the following properties: (i) for each $\rho > 0$, v_ρ is surjective, continuously differentiable, increasing, and strictly concave, with $v_\rho(0) = 0$ and $v'_\rho(0) = 1$; (ii) v_0 is the identity function; (iii) v'_ρ converges to one, uniformly over c as $\rho \to 0$.

the manager for his disutility of effort). In this case, the firm distorts downward the effort asked of those managers whose initial productivity is low to reduce the rents it must leave to those managers whose initial productivity is high. When productivity is not fully persistent, these distortions are more effective in reducing managerial rents when introduced in earlier periods than in later ones. Distortions are therefore smaller at later dates. The correction is most pronounced when productivity is least persistent. Indeed, as one approaches the case where productivity is independent over time (i.e., when γ is close to zero), the expected effort the firm asks of each manager in the second period is close to the first-best level (here $e^{FB} = 1$).

The levels of risk aversion for which the result in the previous proposition holds (i.e., how large one can take $\bar{\rho}$) depends on the persistence γ of the initial productivity θ_1. For a fixed level of risk aversion, if γ is close to 1, i.e., if the agent's productivity is highly persistent, then dynamics opposite to those in the previous theorem obtain: distortions increase, on average, over time, as illustrated in the next theorem.

Theorem 6 (Garrett and Pavan, 2015) *Assume the agent is strictly risk-averse.*

(a) Suppose productivity is fully persistent (i.e., $\gamma = 1$). Then distortions weakly increase over time, i.e., for almost all θ_1,

$$\mathbb{E}\left[D_2(\theta) \mid \theta_1\right] \geq D_1(\theta_1). \tag{23}$$

(b) Suppose densities and cash flows are uniformly bounded[25] and that, for $\gamma = 1$, the inequality in (23) is strict. There exists $\bar{\gamma} < 1$ such that, for all $\gamma \in \left[\bar{\gamma}, 1\right]$, (23) holds as a strict inequality.

Again, to ease the discussion, suppose that the effort asked by the firm in each period is strictly positive and that distortions are nonnegative (the result in the proposition also applies to the case where the effort asked of certain types as well as the distortions are negative). When the manager is risk-averse, incentivizing high effort in period 2 is more costly for the firm than incentivizing the same effort in period one. This is because high effort requires a high sensitivity of pay to performance. When done in period 2, such a sensitivity exposes the manager to volatile compensation as a result of the manager's own private uncertainty about his period-2 productivity. Since the manager dislikes this volatility, he must be provided additional compensation by the firm. To save on managerial compensation, the firm then distorts, on average, period-2 incentives more than in period 1. Note that, when the agent's type is fully persistent (i.e., $\gamma = 1$), distortions increase over time, for any strictly concave v. The result extends to persistence levels that are sufficiently high.

---

[25] Formally, suppose there exists $b \in \mathbb{R}_{++}$ such that, for all $\theta_1 \in \Theta_1$, $\theta_2 \in \Theta_2(\theta_1)$, $f_2(\theta_2|\theta_1) < b$. In addition, suppose there exists $M \in \mathbb{R}_{++}$ and $\gamma' < 1$ such that, for all $\gamma \in [\gamma', 1]$, the optimal cash flow policy $y_t(\theta)$ is uniformly bounded (in absolute value) by M.

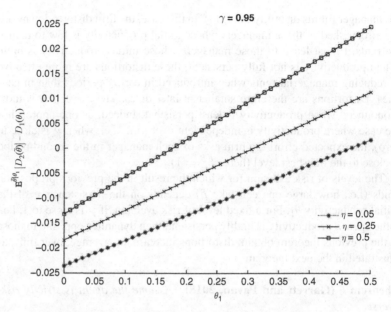

Figure 2 Differential between period-2 and period-1 distortions: $\gamma = 0.95$, $\eta = 0.05$, $\eta = 0.25$ and $\eta = 0.5$.

The above two results are illustrated in the two figures for the special case in which the optimal policies coincide with those that solve the relaxed program and the agent's utility function is isoelastic (i.e., $v(c) = (c^{1-\eta} - 1)/(1 - \eta)$). Figure 2 fixes the level of persistence to $\gamma = .95$ and shows how the difference $\mathbb{E}^{\tilde{\theta}|\theta_1}\left[D_2(\tilde{\theta})\right] - D_1(\theta_1)$ between the period-2 distortions and the period-1 distortions is affected by the degree of managerial risk aversion, η. As indicated in the two theorems above, higher degrees of risk aversion imply a higher differential between period-2 distortions and period-1 distortions. In particular, when $\eta = .05$ (that is, when the manager is close to being risk-neutral) the expected period-2 distortions are smaller than the period-1 distortions, for all but the period-1 very highest types. For higher degrees of risk aversion, instead, expected period-2 distortions are smaller than period-1 distortions over a smaller set of period-1 types θ_1.

Figure 3, instead, fixes the coefficient of relative risk aversion to $\eta = 1/2$ and depicts the difference $\mathbb{E}^{\tilde{\theta}|\theta_1}\left[D_2(\tilde{\theta})\right] - D_1(\theta_1)$ between period-2 distortions and period-1 distortions for three different levels of persistence, $\gamma = .9$, $\gamma = .95$, and $\gamma = 1$. When productivity is perfectly persistent ($\gamma = 1$), the difference is strictly positive for all θ_1. When, instead, $\gamma = .95$, or $\gamma = .9$, the difference continues to be positive, but only for sufficiently high values of θ_1. That, for low values of θ_1, the difference is negative reflects the fact that, for these types, period-1 effort is small. The firm can then afford to ask of these types a higher period-2 effort without having to pay them significant additional compensation.

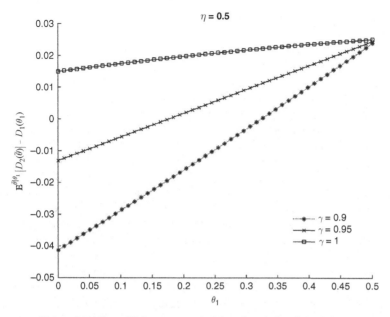

Figure 3 Differential between period-2 and period-1 distortions: $\eta = 1/2$, $\gamma = 0.9$, $\gamma = 0.95$ and $\gamma = 1$.

7 ENDOGENOUS TYPES

Most of the dynamic mechanism design literature assumes that the process governing the evolution of the agents' private information is exogenous. For many problems of interest this is a reasonable assumption. However, there are important applications in which accommodating for an endogenous process is essential. Consider, for example, the sale of experience goods. The buyers' valuations evolve over time as the result of the buyers' experimentation. The dynamics of the allocation of the good then determine the evolution of the buyers' valuations. Similar problems emerge in the presence of habit formation, addiction, and learning-by-doing.

The general model of Pavan, Segal, and Toikka (2014) is flexible enough to accommodate for endogenous (that is, decision-controlled) processes. That paper also offers an application to the design of dynamic auctions for the sale of experience goods. The authors show that the profit-maximizing mechanism takes the form of a sequence of bandit auctions where in each period the seller allocates the good (in limited capacity) to the bidders whose virtual Gittins index is the highest. The virtual index is the same as in the multi-arm bandit literature, but adjusted by a handicap that controls for the cost of informational rents. Interestingly, the optimal allocation rule is not strongly monotone, as a higher report at present, by inducing the agent to consume, may trigger a reduction in consumption in future periods in case the result of the experimentation is negative. Despite such complications, the paper shows that the allocations sustained under the virtual index policy are sufficiently monotone in expectation, thus permitting the construction of payments that implement the desired allocations. The application thus illustrates the broader point that, in dynamic problems, it is important not to impose ad-hoc strong monotonicity requirements on the allocation rule as a way of facilitating incentive compatibility. Many dynamic problems naturally call for allocation rules that are not strongly monotone, and yet implementable.

Two other recent papers on dynamic experimentation with private information are Kakade et al. (2013) and Fershtman and Pavan (2016). The former paper considers a dynamic allocation problem similar to the one in the bandit auction application in Pavan, Segal, and Toikka (2014). The approach, however, is slightly different. The authors confine attention to a family of problems in which payoffs are sufficiently separable (either additively, or multiplicatively) in the agents' initial types. Such separability, in turn, permits the authors to propose an implementation of the virtual index rule based on payments that are similar to those in the dynamic pivot mechanism of Bergemann and Välimäki (2010). The "trick" in the proposed mechanism is to have the agents re-report in each period their initial type. Such re-reporting "Markovizes" the environment by guaranteeing that, when the payments are the virtual VCG payments, and the allocation rule is virtually efficient both on- and off-path, each agent finds it optimal to stay in the mechanism and report truthfully at any history, as long as he/she expects all other agents to do the same. This is because, under the virtual VCG mechanism, when payoffs are sufficiently separable in the first component, each agent's continuation payoff at any history is proportional to the agent's contribution to the aggregate virtual surplus in the continuation game. Arguments similar to those in the literature on the implementation of efficient rules (see, e.g., Vickrey, 1961; Clarke, 1971; and Groves, 1973 for static settings, and Bergemann and Välimäki, 2010 and Athey and Segal, 2013 for dynamic settings) then imply that it is in each agent's own interest to induce a virtually efficient allocation in each continuation game, which can be accomplished by (a) correcting possible period-1 lies and then (b) reporting the current and future innovations truthfully.

An approach similar to the one in Kakade et al. (2013) is also used in Fershtman and Pavan (2016) in the design of dynamic matching auctions. That paper considers the problem of a platform (a matchmaker) controlling the interactions between two sides of a market. Each side is populated by agents whose value for interacting with agents from the opposite side is their own private information and evolves over time, either as the result of shocks that affect the attractiveness of individual interactions, or as the result of gradual resolution of uncertainty about fixed but unknown payoffs.[26]

---

[26] The paper also considers the possibility that valuations vary (stochastically) over time because of preferences for variety, by which the attractiveness of each individual match decreases with the number of past interactions.

The paper accommodates for preferences that combine elements of vertical differentiation (certain agents value interacting with all other agents more than others) with elements of horizontal differentiation (the relative attractiveness of any pair of agents from the opposite side may vary across individuals and can change over time).[27] It also accommodates for constraints on the number of possible matches that can be maintained in each period. The analysis identifies the properties of welfare- and profit-maximizing mechanisms and shows how the optimal matching dynamics can be sustained via "matching auctions." In such auctions, agents from each side first select a membership status in each period (a higher status grants preferential treatment in the auctions). They then bid for each possible partner from the opposite side. Each bilateral match is then assigned a "score" that combines the involved agents' reciprocal bids for one another, the agents' membership status, and the number of past interactions between the two agents. The matches with the highest nonnegative score are then implemented, up to capacity. The payments are designed so as to make each agent's continuation payoff proportional to the agent's contribution to the continuation weighted surplus. Depending on the designer's objective, the latter may coincide with total welfare, with the platform's profits, or, more generally, with a combination of the two. The payments are similar, in spirit, to those in the Generalized Second Price (GSP) auction used in sponsored search, but adjusted to take into account (a) the cost of leaving the agents information rents, and (b) the value of generating information that can be used in later periods. Importantly, in equilibrium, all agents find it optimal to remain in the mechanism after all histories and bid truthfully their myopic values for all partners, despite their own private value for experimentation.

The paper also compares matching dynamics under profit maximization with their counterparts under welfare maximization. When all agents derive a nonnegative value from interacting with any other agent, profit maximization involves fewer and shorter interactions than welfare maximization. In particular, when the capacity constraint is not binding, under profit maximization, each pair of agents is matched for an inefficiently short period of time. When, instead, the capacity constraint is binding, certain matches last longer under profit maximization than under welfare maximization. In each period, however, the aggregate number of interactions, is higher under welfare maximization than under profit maximization. Importantly, the paper shows that the above conclusions need not extend to markets in which certain agents dislike certain interactions. In this case, in each period, profit maximization may involve an inefficiently large volume of matches. The above conclusions have implications for government intervention in matching markets, an area that is attracting significant attention both from policy makers and market designers.

---

[27] Static matching design with vertically and/or horizontally differentiated preferences is examined in Gomes and Pavan (2016a, 2016b).

7.1   Taxation Under Learning-by-Doing

Allowing for endogenous types (that is, for decision-controlled processes governing the evolution of the agents' private information) not only opens the door to novel applications, it may also change some of the results established by confining attention to exogenous processes. This possibility is illustrated in a recent paper by Makris and Pavan (2016). They consider a dynamic model of income taxation over the life cycle, where the agents' productivity evolves endogenously over time as the result of learning-by-doing.[28]

Learning-by-doing (hereafter LBD) refers to a situation where, by working harder in the present period, a worker increases (stochastically) his future average productivity (or wages). One can think of LBD as investment in human capital that occurs "on the job," that is, through the production process (as opposed to, say, through training that occurs outside the working process).[29]

Makris and Pavan (2016) study the effects of LBD on the dynamic provision of incentives under optimal tax codes. They consider a fairly general Markovian setting with endogenous types, non-quasilinear payoffs, and (imperfect) type persistence, that embeds most models in dynamic public finance and certain models in the dynamic managerial compensation literature (e.g., the two-period model in Garrett and Pavan, 2015, discussed in the previous section[30]). In particular, the paper focuses on the effects of LBD on the dynamics of wedges (that is, distortions relative to the first-best benchmark, introduced to limit information rents). LBD affects the cost of incentives (equivalently, the expectation of future information rents) through two channels. The first one is by changing, for given future information rents, the distribution of future types. The second one is through its effect, for given distribution of future types, on future information rents via its effect on the impulse response functions. These effects are absent under an exogenous type process. They are also absent in models where the agents' productivity is endogenous, possibly because of past investment in human capital, but where the agents' private information is exogenous (e.g., Kapicka and Neira, 2014; Best and Kleven, 2013; and Stantcheva, 2016). Importantly, these effects may overturn some of the conclusions established in the literature assuming an exogenous type process. For example, the paper shows that LBD may result in wedges (equivalently,

---

[28] Related models of dynamic taxation with and without human capital accumulation include Krause (2009), Best and Kleven (2013), Farhi and Werning (2013), Kapicka (2013a, 2013b), Golosov, Troshkin, and Tsyvinski (2015), Kapicka and Neira (2014), Stantcheva (2016), and Heathcote et al. (2014).

[29] A vast literature in labor economics documents the effect of labor experience on wages. See, for instance, Willis (1986), Topel (1991), Jacobson et al. (1993), Altuğ and Miller (1998), and Dustmann and Meghir (2005).

[30] For a related model of dynamic managerial compensation where the principal may fire the agent and replace him with a new hire and where each new relationship is affected by shocks to managerial productivity that are privately observed by the managers, see Garrett and Pavan (2012).

marginal tax rates) that are decreasing over the life cycle, in the same environment in which the opposite dynamics obtain under an exogenous process (see, e.g., Farhi and Werning, 2013 and Garrett and Pavan, 2015).

Furthermore, LBD can contribute to higher wedges (equivalently, higher marginal taxes) at all productivity levels. Finally, LBD can contribute to a higher progressivity of the wedges, that is, to an increase in wedges that is more pronounced at the top of the current-period type distribution than at the bottom. Interestingly, in the presence of LBD, marginal taxes may be increasing in earnings in the same environments in which optimal tax codes have been shown to be regressive abstracting from LBD effects. I illustrate these possibilities below in a simplified version of the model considered in Makris and Pavan (2016).

7.1.1   The Environment

The economy is the same as in the simple two-period model of Section 6, above, except for the fact that the agents' period-2 productivity is drawn from a distribution $F_2(\theta_1, y_1)$ that depends on period-1 output y_1. The dependence of F_2 on y_1 is what captures LBD effects. These effects in turn may originate either in past "effort/labor supply," or directly in past "output." While the notation in this section is for an economy in which $T = 2$, some of the key formulas and results will be described for arbitrary time horizons.

Denote by $F_2(\theta_2|\theta_1, y_1)$ the cdf of the kernel $F_2(\theta_1, y_1)$. For any $\theta_2 \in \Theta_2$, $F_2(\theta_2|\theta_1, y_1)$ is assumed to be nonincreasing in (θ_1, y_1). Next, let $\lambda[\chi]$ denote the endogenous ex-ante probability distribution over Θ under the rule $\chi = \langle \mathbf{y}, \mathbf{c} \rangle$ (as in the previous section, the rule χ comprises output and consumption policies that specify the evolution of the relevant allocations, as a function of the history of the agent's productivity). Finally, let $\lambda[\chi]|\theta_1, y_1$ denote the distribution over Θ, starting from (θ_1, y_1), and $\lambda[\chi]|\theta_1 = \lambda[\chi]|\theta_1, y_1(\theta_1)$, where $y_1(\theta_1)$ is the output generated in period one by an agent of productivity θ_1.

To make some of the formulas below easier to read, I will denote by $\mathbb{E}^{\lambda[\chi]|\theta^t}[\cdot]$ the expectation over Θ, under the endogenous process $\lambda[\chi]$, starting from $\theta^t, y^t(\theta^t)$.

The principal designs the rule χ so as to maximize the ex-ante expected value of her payoff subject to the rule being incentive compatible and satisfying the constraint

$$\int q(V^A(\theta_1))dF_1(\theta_1) \geq \kappa. \tag{24}$$

As in the previous section, the function $q(\cdot)$, which is assumed to be increasing and (weakly) concave, captures the nonlinear Pareto weights the principal assigns to the agent's expected lifetime utility. This formulation captures, in reduced form, various problems considered in the literature. For example, in a taxation economy, the principal is a government maximizing tax revenues under the constraint that the agent's lifetime utility be above a minimal level (equivalently, in the dual of this problem, the government maximizes the agents' lifetime utility subject to a budget constraint). In this problem, the function q captures the planner's inequality aversion (see, for instance, Farhi and Werning, 2013, and Best and Kleven, 2013).

In this section, I consider the simplest possible version of this problem where the agents are risk-neutral (using the notation from the previous section, this amounts to assuming that $v^A(c_t) = c_t$, for all c_t) and the principal has a Rawlsian's objective (which amounts to replacing the constraint in (24) with the simpler constraint that $V^A(\theta_1) \geq \kappa$). I also assume that the disutility of effort takes the familiar isoelastic form

$$\psi(y_t, \theta_t) = \frac{1}{1+\phi} \left(\frac{y_t}{\theta_t}\right)^{1+\phi}, \tag{25}$$

which implies that both the elasticity of the disutility of effort and the elasticity of the marginal disutility of effort with respect to the agent's productivity are constant and equal to

$$\epsilon_\theta^\psi(y_t, \theta_t) \equiv -\frac{\theta_t \psi_\theta(y_t, \theta_t)}{\psi(y_t, \theta_t)} = 1 + \phi = \epsilon_\theta^{\psi_y}(y_t, \theta_t) \equiv -\frac{\theta_t \psi_{y\theta}(y_t, \theta_t)}{\psi_y(y_t, \theta_t)},$$

with ϕ parametrizing the inverse Frisch elasticity.[31] Because these restrictions are not important for the qualitative results, in the discussion below I will specialize the notation to the above functional form only when presenting some numerical results. For a more general treatment of the problem in which (a) the agents live, and work, for arbitrarily long horizons, (b) agents are risk-averse, (c) the planner has smoother aversion to inequality (captured by arbitrary q functions), (d) the agents' productivity evolves according to a general type process, I refer the reader to Makris and Pavan (2016). In addition to generalizing the insights discussed below, the paper also shows how the dynamics of allocation under optimal tax codes can be derived through a recursive approach that explicitly accounts for the endogeneity of the agents' private information.

7.1.2   The First-Best Benchmark

In order to appreciate how LBD affects the level, progressivity, and dynamics of the wedges, consider first the allocations that solve the principal's problem, in the absence of information frictions, when the process governing the evolution of the agents' productivity is endogenous. Let

$$LD^{FB;\chi}(\theta_1) \equiv \delta \frac{\partial}{\partial y_1} \int \{y_2(\theta) - \psi(y_2(\theta), \theta_2)\} dF(\theta_2|\theta_1, y_1(\theta_1)) \tag{26}$$

denote the effect of a marginal change in period-1 output on the expected sum of the principal's and the agent's continuation payoffs, under the policy χ, evaluated at history $(\theta_1, y_1(\theta_1))$.

---

[31] As in the previous section, the notation $\psi_\theta(y_t, \theta_t)$ and $\psi_y(y_t, \theta_t)$ stands for the partial derivative of the ψ function with respect to θ_t and y_t, respectively, whereas $\psi_{y\theta}(y_t, \theta_t)$ stands for the cross derivative.

Proposition 2 (Makris and Pavan, 2016) *The first-best rule* $\chi^* = \langle \mathbf{y}^*, \mathbf{c}^* \rangle$
satisfies the following optimality conditions (at all interior points with $\lambda[\chi^*]$-
probability one)[32]

$$1 + LD^{FB;\chi^*}(\theta_1) = \psi_y(y_1^*(\theta), \theta_1) \text{ and } 1 = \psi_y(y_2^*(\theta), \theta_2). \quad (27)$$

The principal thus equalizes the marginal benefit of asking the agent for
higher output (taking into account, in period one, the effect from LBD) with
its marginal cost. When the agent is risk-neutral, the latter is simply the cost
of increasing the agent's compensation by an amount equal to the agent's
marginal disutility of effort. As to the marginal benefit, observe that the sum of
the principal's and of the agent's continuation payoffs is increasing in θ_2 (recall
that $\psi_y(y_2, \theta_2)$ is decreasing in θ_2). Because LBD shifts the distribution in a
first-order-stochastic-dominance way, $LD^{FB;\chi^*}(\theta_1) \geq 0$. Hence, LBD naturally induces the principal to ask for a higher output in period 1 compared to
the level she would ask in the absence of LBD.

As shown in Makris and Pavan (2016), under risk aversion, the above optimality conditions must be paired with other optimality conditions that require
the equalization of the marginal utility of consumption between any two consecutive histories. Furthermore, with more general objectives (that is, with less
extreme preferences for redistribution than in the Rawlsian case assumed here),
optimality also requires equalizing across period-1 types the "weights" the
principal assigns to the agent's period-1 marginal utility of consumption.

7.1.3 Dynamics of Wedges (or Marginal Distortions) under
Second-Best Policies

In contrast to the previous section, here I follow the First-Order Approach
(FOA) by considering a *relaxed program* in which the incentive compatibility constraints are replaced by the envelope conditions requiring that, for all
t, all θ^{t-1}, the agents' equilibrium continuation payoff under χ be Lipschitz
continuous in θ_t, with derivative equal, for almost all $\theta_t \in \Theta_t$, to

$$\frac{\partial V_t^A(\theta^t)}{\partial \theta_t} = -\mathbb{E}^{\lambda[\chi]|\theta^t} \left[\sum_{\tau=t}^T \delta^{\tau-t} I_{(t),\tau}(\theta^\tau, y^{\tau-1}(\theta^{\tau-1})) \psi_\theta(y_\tau(\theta^\tau), \theta_\tau) \right].$$
$$(28)$$

The discussion of the various channels through which LBD affects the dynamics of distortions below should therefore be understood as being conditional
on the First-Order Approach being valid. Note that the assumption that each
$F_t(\theta_t|\theta_{t-1}, y_{t-1})$ is nonincreasing in θ_{t-1} implies that the impulse responses
are nonnegative, and hence that each agent's expected lifetime utility is nondecreasing in θ_t. In particular, that $V_1^A(\theta_1)$ is nondecreasing in θ_1 implies that

---

[32] Here I focus on the optimality conditions for the output schedule. The optimality conditions for
consumption are discussed in Makris and Pavan (2016).

the taxation problem with a risk-neutral agent and a planner with a Rawlsian objective under examination here is formally equivalent to a managerial-compensation problem with interim individual-rationality constraints (where ensuring the participation constraint of the period-1 lowest types implies that all other types' participation constraints are also satisfied, as discussed above).

As in the previous section, to limit the agents' information rents, the principal distorts production downwards. In the presence of LBD, the distortions in labor supply are captured by labor wedges, defined as follows:

Definition 8 (wedges with LBD)   *The period-t "wedge" or "marginal distortion" (equivalently, the "effective marginal income tax rate" in the taxation problem) under the rule χ is given by* [33]

$$W_1(\theta) \equiv 1 - \frac{\psi_y(y_1(\theta), \theta_1)}{1 + LD^{FB;\chi}(\theta_1)} \ \text{and} \ W_2(\theta) = 1 - \psi_y(y_2(\theta), \theta_2).$$

The definition parallels the one in the previous section, adjusted for the presence of LBD. Recall that efficiency requires that the marginal disutility of extra period-t output be equalized to the social marginal benefit, where, in period one, the latter takes into account both the extra output collected by the principal, 1, and the effect of higher period-1 output on the principal's and the agent's joint future surplus, as captured by the term $LD^{FB;\chi}(\theta_1)$ introduced above. The wedge is the discrepancy between the ratio of marginal cost and marginal benefit of higher period-t output under the first-best allocation, 1, and the corresponding ratio at the proposed allocation. Importantly, in the case of an endogenous process, such discrepancy is computed holding fixed the rule χ that determines future allocations, so as to highlight the part of the inefficiency that pertains to the period under consideration. As is standard in the public finance literature, hereafter I will focus on the dynamics of the following monotone transformation of the wedges

$$\hat{W}_t(\theta) \equiv \frac{W_t(\theta)}{1 - W_t(\theta)}$$

and refer to $\hat{W}_t(\theta)$ as to the *relative period-t wedge*. In a taxation problem, the wedge is directly related to the period-t marginal tax rate; that is, the sensitivity of current taxes to current income, holding fixed past incomes and all future tax schedules (with the latter allowed to depend on the entire history of reported earnings). One can easily verify that the relative period-t wedge $\hat{W}_t(\theta)$ satisfies

$$1 + LD_t^{FB;\chi}(\theta) = \left[1 + \hat{W}_t(\theta)\right] \psi_y(y_t(\theta), \theta_t). \tag{29}$$

---

[33] Obviously, y_1 and W_1 naturally depend on $\theta = (\theta_1, \theta_2)$ only through θ_1. The reasons why these functions, in the formulas below, are allowed to depend on the entire type history θ is just to economize on notation by introducing homogeneity in the arguments across different periods.

One can thus also think of the relative wedge as the rate by which the principal inflates the agent's marginal disutility of labor to account for the effects that higher output has on informational rents.

Finally, let

$$h_2(\theta, y) \equiv \frac{1 - F_1(\theta_1)}{f_1(\theta_1)} I_2(\theta, y_1) \epsilon_\theta^{\psi}(y_2, \theta_2) \frac{\psi(y_2, \theta_2)}{\theta_2}.$$

This function is the analog in the taxation environment under consideration here of the "handicap" function $I_2(\theta)\psi_y(y_2, \theta_2)\left[1 - F_1(\theta_1)\right]/f_1(\theta_1)$ in the managerial-compensation model in the previous section. It measures the welfare losses of asking the agent to produce higher output at history $\theta = (\theta_1, \theta_2)$.

The second-best allocation rule χ satisfies the following optimality conditions (at all interior points with $\lambda[\chi]$-probability one):

$$1 = \psi_y(y_2(\theta), \theta_2)\left[1 + \frac{1 - F_1(\theta_1)}{f_1(\theta_1)} I_2(\theta, y_1(\theta_1)) \frac{\epsilon_\theta^{\psi_y}(y_2(\theta), \theta_2)}{\theta_2}\right] \quad (30)$$

$$1 + LD^{FB;\chi}(\theta_1) = \psi_y(y_1(\theta), \theta_1)$$

$$\times \left[1 + \frac{1 - F_1(\theta_1)}{f_1(\theta_1)} \frac{\epsilon_\theta^{\psi_y}(y_1(\theta), \theta_1)}{\theta_1} + \delta \frac{\partial}{\partial y_1} \mathbb{E}^{\lambda[\chi]|\theta_1, y_1(\theta)}[h_2(\theta, y(\theta))]\right]$$

$$(31)$$

The first optimality condition is essentially the same as in Mirrlees (1971), but adjusted for the impulse responses. At each period-2 history $\theta = (\theta_1, \theta_2)$, the optimal choice of $y_2(\theta)$ is obtained by equalizing the marginal benefit of asking the agent for higher output, the left-hand side in (30), with the marginal cost. The latter combines the cost of reimbursing the agent for the higher disutility of effort, $\psi_y(y_2(\theta), \theta_2)$, with the marginal cost of increasing the rents left to all period-1 types whose productivity is above θ_1. The latter cost is given by

$$\frac{\partial}{\partial y_2} h_2(\theta, y(\theta)) = \frac{1 - F_1(\theta_1)}{f_1(\theta_1)} I_2(\theta, y_1(\theta_1)) \frac{\epsilon_\theta^{\psi_y}(y_2(\theta), \theta_2)}{\theta_2} \psi_y(y_2(\theta), \theta_2).$$

The optimality condition in (31), instead, combines the above static effects with the dynamic effects that a higher y_1 has on the principal's payoff, net of the agents' informational rents. As discussed above, holding fixed the period-2 policies, as specified in $\chi = \langle \mathbf{y}, \mathbf{c}\rangle$, the term $LD^{FB;\chi}(\theta_1)$ captures the effect on total surplus of shifting the agent's period-2 productivity towards higher levels. The interesting novel effects here are those captured by the term

$$\frac{\partial}{\partial y_1} \mathbb{E}^{\lambda[\chi]|\theta_1, y_1(\theta)}[h_2(\theta, y(\theta))] = \frac{1 - F_1(\theta_1)}{f_1(\theta_1)} \frac{\partial}{\partial y_1} \mathbb{E}^{\lambda[\chi]|\theta_1, y_1(\theta)}$$

$$\times \left[I_2(\theta, y_1(\theta_1)) \frac{\epsilon_\theta^{\psi_y}(y_2(\theta), \theta_2)}{\theta_2} \psi_y(y_2(\theta), \theta_2)\right].$$

Recall that the term $h_2(\theta, y(\theta))$ captures the welfare losses coming from the information rents the principal must leave to the agents to induce them to report truthfully in period 2. Asking the agents to work harder in period one has two effects on such expected losses. The first one comes from the change in the distribution of θ_2, holding the handicap function $h_2(\theta, y(\theta))$ constant. The second comes from the direct effect that a higher period-1 output has on the period-2 handicap $h_2(\theta, y(\theta))$ via the endogenous impulse response of θ_2 to θ_1, holding the period-2 type distribution constant.

In most cases of interest, the period-2 handicap (equivalently, the period-2 information rent) $h_2(\theta, y(\theta))$ is increasing in θ_2. In this case, the first effect contributes to higher expected welfare losses. The sign of the second effect in turn depends on whether the impulse response of θ_2 to θ_1 is increasing or decreasing in y_1. When period-1 type and period-1 output are complements in the determination of the period-2 type, impulse responses are increasing in y_1, in which case the second effect also contributes to a positive effect of LBD on expected future welfare losses. The opposite is true when period-1 type and period-1 output are substitutes in the determination of the period-2 type. In this case, this second effect operates against the first one in alleviating the positive effects of LBD on expected future rents.

The above results can be used to interpret the dynamics of wedges under optimal contracts. To this purpose, let

$$\hat{W}_t^{RN}(\theta^t) \equiv \frac{1 - F_1(\theta_1)}{f_1(\theta_1)} I_t(\theta^t, y^{t-1}(\theta^{t-1})) \frac{\epsilon_\theta^{\psi_y}(y_t(\theta^t), \theta_t)}{\theta_t}$$

and

$$\Omega(\theta_1) \equiv \frac{\delta \frac{\partial}{\partial y_1} \mathbb{E}^{\lambda[\chi]|\theta_1, y_1(\theta)}[h_2(\theta, y(\theta))]}{\psi_y(y_1(\theta_1), \theta_1)}.$$

From (29), (30) and (31), one can see that

$$\hat{W}_1(\theta_1) = \hat{W}_1^{RN}(\theta_1) + \Omega_1(\theta_1) \text{ and } \hat{W}_2(\theta) = \hat{W}_2^{RN}(\theta).$$

The functions $\hat{W}_t^{RN}(\theta^t)$ represent the relative wedges that the principal would select at each type history θ^t if the process governing the evolution of the agents' productivity determined by the rule χ were exogenous (when the agents are risk-neutral and the principal's objective is Rawlsian, as assumed here). Because there are no LBD effects in the last period (here $t = 2$), naturally, $\hat{W}_2(\theta) = \hat{W}_2^{RN}(\theta)$. The function $\Omega_1(\theta_1)$, instead, captures the effects of LBD on the period-1 wedge. As explained above, it summarizes all the effects of changing the period-1 output on the expected informational rents the principal must leave to the agents in period 2 to induce them to report θ_2 truthfully.

Makris and Pavan (2016) show that the above decomposition holds more generally; that is, it extends to environments in which the agents are risk-averse, the principal's inequality aversion is less than Rawlsian, and there are arbitrarily many periods. In particular, continue to denote by $\hat{W}_t^{RN}(\theta^t)$ and $\Omega_t(\theta^t)$, respectively, the relative wedge in the absence of LBD and the effect of LBD on the period-t wedge in the case the agents are risk-neutral and the principal's objective is Rawlsian. Then let $RA_t(\theta^t)$ be a correction that applies when the agents are risk-averse and/or the principal's inequality aversion is less than Rawlsian.

Theorem 7 (Makris and Pavan, 2016) *At any period $t \geq 1$, with $\lambda[\chi]$-probability one, the relative wedges are given by*

$$\hat{W}_t(\theta^t) = RA_t(\theta^t)\left[\hat{W}_t^{RN}(\theta^t) + \Omega_t(\theta^t)\right].$$

Theorem 7 is established using a recursive solution to the principal's problem that controls for the endogeneity of the type process. The value of the theorem is in highlighting the different forces that contribute to the determination of the dynamics of the wedges. The theorem also unifies the various special cases examined in the literature.

To see how the endogeneity of the type process shapes the dynamics of the wedges in the simplest possible way, consider the following specification often assumed in the taxation and in the labor economics literature. The period-2 productivity is given by

$$\theta_2 = z_2(\theta_1, y_1, \varepsilon_2) = \theta_1 y_1^\zeta \varepsilon_2, \tag{32}$$

where $\zeta \geq 0$ parametrizes the intensity of LBD (the case of no LBD corresponds to $\zeta = 0$) and where ε_2 is a shock drawn from a distribution G. The specification in (32) implies that the impulse responses of θ_2 to θ_1 are invariant in y_1 and are given by $I_1(\theta) = 1$ and $I_2(\theta) = \theta_2/\theta_1$, all $\theta = (\theta_1, \theta_2)$. This specification has the advantage of isolating the effects of LBD coming from the shift in the distribution of period-2 productivity (the other channel by which LBD affects the expectation of the period-2 rents via its direct effect on the impulse response functions is mute under the above specification). A second advantage of this specification is that it implies that the period-2 wedges are invariant in ζ, which facilitates the comparison to the case without LBD. In particular, one can use the results above to verify that, when the disutility of effort takes the isoelastic form in (25) and LBD takes the multiplicative form in (32),

$$\hat{W}_1^{RN}(\theta_1) = \hat{W}_2^{RN}(\theta) = (1+\phi)\frac{1 - F_1(\theta_1)}{f_1(\theta_1)\theta_1}$$

and

$$\Omega_1(\theta_1) = \delta\left(\frac{\theta_1}{y_1(\theta_1)}\right)^\phi \frac{1 - F_1(\theta_1)}{f_1(\theta_1)} \frac{\partial}{\partial y_1}\mathbb{E}^{\lambda[\chi]|\theta_1, y_1(\theta_1)}\left[\left(\frac{y_2(\theta)}{\theta_2}\right)^{1+\phi}\right]. \tag{33}$$

Hence, when $[1 - F_1(\theta_1)]/\theta_1 f_1(\theta_1)$ is nonincreasing in θ_1, as typically assumed in the taxation literature, $\hat{W}_1^{RN}(\theta_1)$ and $\hat{W}_2^{RN}(\theta)$ are nonincreasing in θ_1 and independent of θ_2. That is, in the absence of LBD, marginal taxes are constant over time and decreasing in earnings. Instead, with LBD, wedges are given by

$$\hat{W}_1(\theta^t) = \hat{W}_1^{RN}(\theta_1) + \Omega_1(\theta_1) \text{ and } \hat{W}_2(\theta) = \hat{W}_2^{RN}(\theta).$$

As shown in Makris and Pavan (2016), in this economy, as well as in most cases considered in the literature, the period-2 handicap is increasing in θ_2 (equivalently, $y_2(\theta)/\theta_2$ is increasing in θ_2). As a result, $\Omega_1(\theta_1) > 0$. The following is then true:

Proposition 3 (Makris and Pavan, 2016) *Consider the two-period economy described above. (i) For all θ_1, the period-1 wedge in the presence of LBD is strictly higher than the corresponding period-1 wedge in the absence of LBD; (ii) Under LBD, in each state of the world, period-1 wedges are strictly higher than period-2 wedges; (iii) There exits a function $\Gamma : \Theta_1 \rightarrow \mathbb{R}$ such that the progressivity of the period-1 wedge at productivity level θ_1 is higher under LBD than in its absence if and only if $\Gamma(\theta_1) \geq 0$.*

As an illustration, suppose θ_1 is drawn from a Pareto distribution (in which case, $\theta_1 f_1(\theta_1)/[1 - F_1(\theta_1)] = \lambda$ for all θ_1), as assumed in the earlier taxation literature. In the absence of LBD, the wedges are constant over time and across types and are given by $\hat{W}_1(\theta_1) = \hat{W}_2(\theta) = (1 + \phi)/\lambda$, for all $\theta = (\theta_1, \theta_2)$. Instead, in the presence of LBD, $\hat{W}_1(\theta_1) > \hat{W}_2(\theta) = (1 + \phi)/\lambda$ with $\hat{W}_1(\theta_1)$ strictly increasing in θ_1. Furthermore, one can verify that, whenever the period-1 wedge in the absence of LBD, $\hat{W}_1^{RN}(\theta_1)$, is nonincreasing in θ_1, as is the case here, the solution to the relaxed program also solves the full program, implying that the properties above are truly features of optimal tax codes. This situation is illustrated in Figure 4. The figure depicts the period-1 wedge $\hat{W}_1(\theta_1)$ for four different levels of LBD, $\zeta = 0, 0.2, 0.4, 0.6$. As the figure illustrates, stronger LBD effects (here captured by higher levels of the parameter ζ) call for higher and more progressive wedges.[34]

The intuition is the one anticipated above. LBD affects the cost of future incentives (equivalently, expected future information rents) through two channels. The first one is by changing the distribution of future types, for given future handicaps (recall that the latter measure future welfare losses due to asymmetric information). The second channel is through its direct effect on future handicaps for given distribution of future types. As mentioned above,

---

[34] The parameter *eta* $= 0$ in the Figure's caption indicates that the results are for the case of risk-neutral agents. Also note that the figure assumes $\phi = 2$, i.e., a Frisch elasticity of 0.5, as in Farhi and Werning (2013), Kapicka (2013a), and Stantcheva (2016). Finally, the parameter *rho* $= 1$ in the figure's caption indicates that the skill-persistence parameter has been set equal to one, as in the rest of this section (i.e., $\theta_2 = \theta_1^\rho y_1^z \varepsilon$, with $\rho = 1$).

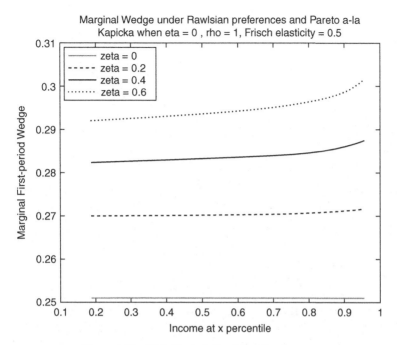

Figure 4 The Risk-Neutral, Rawlsian, Pareto case.

this second channel is absent under the specification in (32). More generally, this second channel adds to the first one in amplifying the effects of LBD on expected future rents when impulse responses of future types to current ones are increasing in output.

To reduce the effects of LBD on expected future rents, the principal induces the agents to work less in the early periods of their career, which explains why LBD contributes to higher wedges. Because the effects of LBD on expected future rents are most pronounced in the early periods, LBD also contributes to wedge dynamics whereby wedges decline over time.

Finally, to see why LBD may contribute to the progressivity of the wedges, note that the benefit of distorting downwards labor supply in the present period so as to economize on future information rents is stronger for higher types, given that these are the types that expect, on average, larger rents in future periods. This is indeed the case, for all θ_1, when θ_1 is drawn from a Pareto distribution. More generally, Makris and Pavan (2016) show that this is true, in the simple economy under consideration here, at any open interval of period-1 types at which $\theta_1 f_1(\theta_1)/[1 - F_1(\theta_1)]$ is almost constant, as in the upper tail of the Pareto Lognormal distribution typically assumed to calibrate the model to US earnings data.

The next four figures illustrate that the properties discussed above hold more generally. In particular, Figure 5 illustrates the effects of LBD on the period-1 wedge $\hat{W}_1$ when θ_1 and the second-period shock ε_2 are drawn

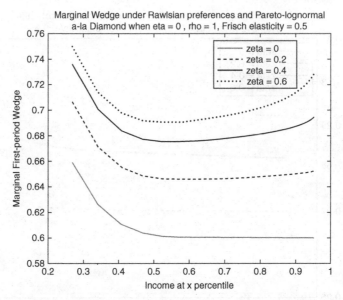

Figure 5 The Risk-Neutral-Rawlsian-Paretolognormal case.

from a Pareto Lognormal distribution with the same parameters as in Diamond (1998). As the figure shows, stronger LBD effects (here parametrized by a higher level of ζ) are responsible for higher period-1 wedges and for more progressivity at all income percentiles, and in particular at high percentiles (the lowest blue curve corresponds to the economy without LBD of Diamond, 1998).

Similar results obtain when the agents are risk-averse and/or the planner's aversion to inequality is less extreme than in the Rawlsian case. Figure 6 depicts the wedges in the case the agents' utility over consumption is CRRA for four different levels of the coefficient of relative risk aversion, namely for $\eta = 0$, 0.2, 0.5, and 0.8 (recall that $\eta = 0$ corresponds to the case of risk-neutral agents). The distribution of θ_1 and ε_2 is Pareto-lognormal and the principal's objective is Rawlsian, as in Figure 5 (higher curves correspond to higher degrees of risk aversion, whereas higher levels of the zeta parameter correspond to stronger LBD effects).

As the figure illustrates, risk aversion contributes to an amplification of the period-1 wedge and to more progressivity. The reason is that, when the agent is risk-averse, the cost of compensating him for his marginal disutility of effort is higher as it now takes $\psi_y(\theta_t, y_t)/v'(c_t)$ units of consumption. Hence, risk aversion, by itself, contributes to higher wedges. What the figure illustrates is that the increase in the cost of compensation also amplifies the effects of LBD on the level and progressivity of the wedges. This is because, by increasing the cost of future information rents, risk aversion also increases the benefits of shifting the distribution of future types towards levels that command lower informational rents, and, as in the risk-neutral case, this effect is most

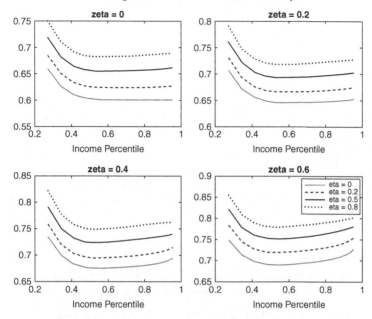

Figure 6 The CRRA Rawlsian Pareto Lognormal case.

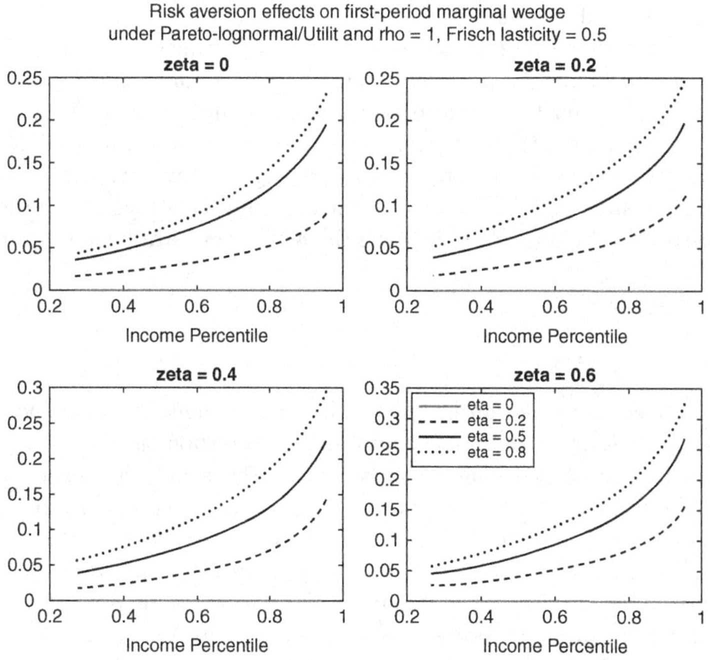

Figure 7 The CRRA Utilitarian Pareto Lognormal case.

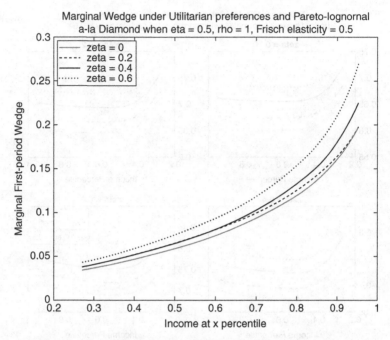

Figure 8 Effects of LBD in CRRA Utilitarian Pareto Lognormal case.

pronounced at the top of the period-1 type distribution where the expectation of future rents is the highest.

Similar results obtain for less extreme forms of inequality aversion on the planner's side. Figure 7 reports the results for the case of a planner with util-itarian objective function – the parameters are as in Figure 6. Once again, risk aversion contributes to an amplification of the effects discussed above, at all levels of LBD. Furthermore, fixing the degree of relative risk aversion to $\eta = 0.5$, stronger LBD effects contribute to higher wedges and to more progressivity, as highlighted in Figure 8 (higher curves correspond to stronger LBD effects).

8   CONCLUSIONS

Dynamic mechanism design has proved useful to conduct positive and nor-mative analysis in environments in which information arrives over time and a sequence of decisions is to be made. The approach pioneered by Myerson (1981) for static design problems can be extended to dynamic envi-ronments. An important tool of this approach is an envelope representation of the agents' equilibrium payoffs summarizing necessary local incentive com-patibility conditions. The key difference with respect to static problems is the presence in the envelope formula of "impulse response functions" capturing the marginal effects of current types on future ones. In quasilinear settings, the envelope formula pins down the transfers, for given non-monetary allocation rule. In Markov environments, this formula, jointly with appropriate integral monotonicity conditions on the non-monetary allocation rule, provides a complete characterization of incentive compatibility (Pavan, Segal, and Toikka, 2014).

The approach typically followed in applications to solve for optimal mechanisms consists in disregarding the integral monotonicity conditions and solving a relaxed program in which only the necessary conditions captured by the envelope formulas of the equilibrium payoffs are imposed. This approach, often referred to as the First-Order-Approach (FOA), offers the convenience of bypassing the difficulty of dealing with ironing and bunching, which are notoriously cumbersome even in static settings.

An important question for this literature is the extent to which the predictions identified by restricting attention to settings in which the FOA is valid extend to broader settings. An approach recently introduced in Garrett and Pavan (2015) consists in identifying perturbations of the non-monetary policies that alter payoffs while preserving integral monotonicity. When applied to policies that are incentive compatible, such perturbations preserve incentive compatibility. The perturbations can then be used to identify certain properties of the dynamics of allocations under optimal contracts, without solving for the optimal contracts. For example, in the dynamic managerial compensation model of Garrett and Pavan (2015), such a variational approach permits one to study how risk aversion and type persistence jointly interact in shaping the dynamics of average distortions. In ongoing work, Garrett, Pavan, and Toikka (2016) apply a similar variational approach to study the long-run average dynamics of optimal screening contracts.

Most of the dynamic mechanism design literature assumes the agents' private information is exogenous. In many problems of interest, however, types are endogenous. For example, valuations are endogenous in experimentation settings, and productivity is endogenous in the presence of learning-by-doing. Endogenous processes bring novel effects that qualify (and, in certain cases, overturn) the conclusions obtained assuming exogenous types. For example, in a taxation environment, learning-by-doing may change the predictions the theory delivers for the level, the dynamics, and the progressivity of the marginal tax rates, under optimal tax codes (Makris and Pavan, 2016).

A lot of work remains to be done. One direction is to extend the analysis to settings with partial commitment and/or realistic political economy constraints. The literature on limited commitment has made important progress in recent years (see, for example, Skreta, 2015; Liu et al., 2015; Maestri, 2016; Strulovici, 2016; and Gerardi and Maestri, 2016). However, this literature assumes information is static, thus abstracting from the questions at the heart of the dynamic mechanism design literature. I expect interesting new developments to come out from combining the two literatures.

Most of the dynamic mechanism design literature assumes time-varying information, but a constant population. A conspicuous literature in Operation

Research assumes constant information but a dynamic population. This latter OR literature has been extended in recent years to accommodate for private information (see, for example, the recent manual by Gershkov and Moldovanu, 2014). Combining time-varying information with population dynamics is likely to bring new insights on the structure of optimal contracts and on the dynamics of distortions due to asymmetric information (see Garrett, 2016a, 2016b).

The last few years have also witnessed a renewed interest in information design (see, e.g., Bergemann and Välimäki, 2006; Calzolari and Pavan, 2006a, 2006b; Eső and Szentes, 2007; Li and Shi, 2015; and Bergemann and Wambach, 2015 for models of endogenous disclosure in mechanism design, and Kamenica and Gentzkow, 2011; and Ely et al., 2016, among others, for persuasion in other strategic environments; see also Hörner and Skrzypacz, 2016, for an excellent overview of this literature). I expect interesting results to emerge from dynamic mechanism design models in which part of the endogeneity of the information comes from persuasion.

Lastly, most of the recent developments in the dynamic mechanism design literature have been primarily theoretical. Rich data sets have become available in the last few years about various dynamic contracting environments (insurance, health, consumer recognition, etc.). Most of the empirical contracting literature has confined attention to static problems and only in recent times has started examining dynamic settings (see, for example, Handel, Hendel, and Whinston, 2015; and Einav et al., 2010, 2013). The empirical literature, however, assumes stationary private information. I expect interesting developments will come from this empirical literature as soon as it starts accommodating for time-varying private information.

References

Abdulkadiroğlu, A., and Loertscher, S., (2007). "Dynamic House Allocations," working paper, Duke University and University of Melbourne.

Acemoglu, D., Golosov, M., and Tsyvinski, A., (2011). "Political Economy of Ramsey Taxation." *J. Public Econ.* 95, 467–75.

Aghion P., Fudenberg D., -Holden R., Kunimoto T., and Tercieux. O., (2012). "Subgame Perfect Implementation Under Information Perturbations," working paper, Harvard University.

Akan, M., Ata, B., and Dana, J., (2015). "Revenue Management by Sequential Screening." *J. Econ. Theory* 159 (Part B), 728–74.

Albanesi, S., and Sleet, C., (2006). "Dynamic Optimal Taxation with Private Information." *Rev. Econ. Stud.* 73, 1–30.

Altuğ, S., and Miller, R. (1998). "The Effect of Work Experience on Female Wages and Labour Supply." *The Review of Economic Studies*, 65(1), 45–85.

Alvarez, F., and Jermann, U., (2000). "Efficiency, Equilibrium, and Asset Pricing with Risk of Default." *Econometrica* 68, 775–97.

Armstrong, M., and Zhou, J., forthcoming. "Search Deterrence." *Rev. Econ. Stud.*

Aron-Dine, A., Cullen, M., Einav, L., and Finkelstein, A., forthcoming. "Moral Hazard in Health Insurance: Do Dynamic Incentives Matter?" *Rev. Econ. Stat.*

Athey, S., and Segal, I., (2013). "An Efficient Dynamic Mechanism." *Econometrica* 81, 2463–85.

Atkenson, A., and Lucas, R., (1992). "On the Efficient Distribution with Private Information." *Rev. Econ. Stud.* 59, 427–54.

Ausubel, L. M., and Deneckere, R. J., (1989). "A Direct Mechanism Characterization of Sequential Bargaining with One-Sided Incomplete Information." *Journal of Economic Theory* 48(1), 18–46.

Ausubel, L. M., and Deneckere, R. J., (1993). "Efficient Sequential Bargaining." *The Review of Economic Studies* 60(2), 435–61.

Baron, D., and Besanko, D., (1984). "Regulation and Information in a Continuing Relationship." *Inf. Econ. Policy* 1, 267–302.

Baron, D., and Myerson, R., (1982). "Regulating a Monopolist with Unknown Costs." *Econometrica* 50, 911–30.

Battaglini, M., (2005). "Long-Term Contracting with Markovian Consumers." *Am. Econ. Rev.* 95, 637–58.

Battaglini, M., (2007). "Optimality and Renegotiation in Dynamic Contracting." *Games Econ. Behav.* 60, 213–46.

Battaglini, M., and Lamba, R., (2015). "Optimal Dynamic Contracting: The First-Order Approach and Beyond." Discussion paper, Cornell University and Penn State University.

Bergemann, D., and Hörner, J., (2014). "Should Auctions be Transparent?" Discussion paper 1764R. Cowles Foundation for Research in Economics, Yale University.

Bergemann, D., and Morris, S., (2012). *Robust Mechanism Design: The Role of Private Information and Higher Order Beliefs*, World Scientific, Singapore.

Bergemann, D. and Morris, S., (2016). "Information Design, Bayesian Persuasion, and Bayes Correlated Equilibrium," *Am. Econ. Rev.*, 106, no. 5.

Bergemann, D., and Pavan, A., (2015). "Introduction to JET Symposium on Dynamic Contracts and Mechanism Design." *J. Econ.Theory* 159, 679–701.

Bergemann, D., and Pesendorfer, M., (2007). "Information Structures in Optimal Auctions." *J. Econ. Theory* 137, 580–609.

Bergemann, D., and Said, M., (2011). "Dynamic Auctions: A Survey." In: Cochran, J. (Ed.), *Wiley Encyclopedia of Operations Research and Management Science*. Wiley, New York, pp. 1511–22, no. 1757.

Bergemann, D., and Strack, P., (2015a). "Dynamic Revenue Maximization: A Continuous Time Approach." *J. Econ. Theory 159* (Part B), 819–53.

Bergemann, D., and Strack, P., (2015b). "Stationary Dynamic Contracts." Discussion paper. Yale University and UC Berkeley.

Bergemann, D., and Välimäki, J., (2002). "Information Acquisition and Efficient Mechanism Design." *Econometrica* 70, 1007–33.

Bergemann, D., and Välimäki, J., (2006). "Information in Mechanism Design." In: Blundell, R., Newey, W., Persson, T. (Eds.), *Advances in Economics and Econometrics*. Cambridge: Cambridge University Press, pp. 186–221.

Bergemann, D., and Välimäki, J., (2010). "The Dynamic Pivot Mechanism." *Econometrica* 78, 771–90.

Bergemann, D., and Wambach, A., (2015). "Sequential Information Disclosure in Auctions." *J. Econ. Theory* 159 (Part B), 1074–95.

Berger, A., Müller, R., and Naeemi, S., (2010). "Path-Monotonicity and Truthful Implementation." Discussion paper. Maastricht University.

Besanko, D., (1985). "Multi-Period Contracts Between Principal and Agent with Adverse Selection." *Econ. Lett.* 17, 33–7.

Best, M.C., and Kleven, H.J., (2013). "Optimal Income Taxation with Career Effects of Work Effort." mimeo, LSE.

Bester, H., and Strausz, R., (2000). "Imperfect Commitment and the Revelation Principle: The Multi-Agent Case." *Econ. Lett.* 69, 165–71.

Bester, H., and Strausz, R., (2001). "Contracting with Imperfect Commitment and the Revelation Principle: The Single Agent Case." *Econometrica* 69, 1077–98.

Billingsley, P., (1995). *Probability and Measure*. Wiley Series in Probability and Mathematical Statistics.

Board, S., (2007). "Selling Options." *J. Econ. Theory* 136, 324–40.

Board, S., (2011). "Relational Contracts and the Value of Loyalty." *Am. Econ. Rev.* 101, 3349–67.

Board, S., and Skrzypacz, A., (2016). "Revenue Management with Forward-Looking Buyers." *J. Polit. Econ.* 124(6) 1515–62.

Boleslavsky, R., and Said, M., (2013). "Progressive Screening: Long-Term Contracting with a Privately Known Stochastic Process." *Rev. Econ. Stud.* 80, 1–34.

Börgers, T., (2015). *An Introduction to the Theory of Mechanism Design*. Oxford: Oxford University Press.

Bulow, J., (1982). "Durable Good Monopolists." *J. Polit. Econ.* 90, 314–32.

Burguet, R., and Sákovics, J., (1996). "Reserve Prices Without Commitment." *Games Econ. Behav.* 15, 149–64.

Caillaud, B., and Mezzetti, C., (2004). "Equilibrium Reserve Prices in Sequential Ascending Auctions." *J. Econ. Theory* 117, 78–95.

Calzolari, G., and Pavan, A., (2006a). "Monopoly with Resale." *Rand J. Econ.* 37, 362–75.

Calzolari, G., and Pavan, A., (2006b). "On the Optimality of Privacy in Sequential Contracting." *J. Econ. Theory* 130, 168–204.

Carbajal, J., and Ely, J., (2013). "Mechanism Design Without Revenue Equivalence." *J. Econ. Theory* 148, 104–33.

Carroll, G., (2015). "Robustness and Linear Contracts," *American Economic Review* 105 (2), 536–63.

Carroll, G., and Meng, D., (2016). "Robust Contracting with Additive Noise." Discussion Paper, Northwestern University.

Chassang, S., (2013). "Calibrated Incentive Contracts," *Econometrica*, 81(5), 1935–71.

Che, Y., and Hörner, J., (2015). "Optimal Design for Social Learning." Discussion paper. Columbia University and Yale University.

Chiappori, P.-A., and Salanié, B., (2003). "Testing Contract Theory: A Survey of Some Recent Work." In: Dewatripont, M., Hansen, L., Turnovsky, S. (eds.), *Advances in Economics and Econometrics: Theory and Applications, Eighth World Congress*, Vol. 1. Cambridge University Press, pp. 115–49.

Chiappori, P., Salanié, B., and Valentin, J., (1999). "Early Starters Versus Late Beginners." *J. Polit. Econ.* 107, 731–60.

Clarke, E., (1971). "Multipart Pricing of Public Goods." *Public Choice* 8, 19–33.

Courty, P., and Li, H., (2000). "Sequential Screening." *Rev. Econ. Stud.* 67, 697–717.

Cremer, J., (1995). "Arm's Length Relationships." *Q. J. Econ.* 110, 275–95.

Cremer, J., and McLean, R. P., (1988). "Full Extraction of the Surplus in Bayesian and Dominant Strategy Auctions." *Econometrica*, 56(6), 1247–57.

Dasgupta, P., Hammond, P., and Maskin, E., (1979). "The Implementation of Social Choice Rules: Some General Results on Incentive Compatibility." *Rev. Econ. Stud.* 66, 185–216.

Deb, R., (2014). "Intertemporal Price Discrimination with Stochastic Values." Discussion paper. University of Toronto.

Deb, R., and Pai, M., (2013). "Ironing in Dynamic Revenue Management: Posted Prices and Biased Auctions." In: *Proceedings of the Symposium on Discrete Algorithms (SODA)* 2013, pp. 620–31.

Deb, R., and Said, M., (2015). "Dynamic Screening with Limited Commitment." *J. Econ. Theory* 159 (Part B), 891–928.

Diamond, P.A., (1998). "Optimal Income Taxation: An Example with a U-Shaped Pattern of Optimal Marginal Tax Rates." *American Economic Review*, 88(1), 83–95.

Diamond, P.A., and Mirrlees, J.A., (1978). "A Model of Social Insurance with Variable Retirement." *Journal of Public Economics* 10(3), 295–336.

Doepke, M., and Townsend, R., (2004). "Dynamic Mechanism Design with Hidden Income and Hidden Actions," *Journal of Economic Theory* 126 (1), 235–85.

Doval, L., and Ely, J., (2016). "Sequential Information Design," working paper, Northwestern University.

Dustmann, C., and Meghir, K., (2005). "Wages, Experience and Seniority." *Review of Economic Studies*, 72, 77–108.

Edmans, A., and Gabaix, X., (2011). "Tractability in Incentive Contracting." *Rev. Financ. Stud.* 24, 2865–94.

Edmans, A., Gabaix, X., Sadzik, T., and Sannikov, Y., (2012). "Dynamic CEO Compensation." *J. Finance* 67, 1603–47.

Einav, L., Farronato, C., Levin, J., and Sundaresan, N., (2013). "Sales Mechanisms in Online Markets: What Happened to Internet Auctions?" Discussion paper. Stanford University.

Einav, L., Finkelstein, A., and Levin, J., (2010). "Beyond Testing: Empirical Models of Insurance Markets." *Annu. Rev. Econ.* 2, 311–36.

Ely, J., (2015). "Beeps." *American Economic Review*, forthcoming.

Ely, J., Garrett, D., and Hinnosaar, T., (2016). "Overbooking." *Journal of European Economic Association*, forthcoming.

Ely, J., and Szydlowski, M., (2016). "Moving the Goalposts," working paper, Northwestern University.

Eső, P., and Szentes, B., (2007). "Optimal Information Disclosure in Auctions." *Rev. Econ. Stud.* 74, 705–31.

Eső, P., and Szentes, B., (2015). "Dynamic Contracting: An Irrelevance Result." *Theoretical Economics*, forthcoming.

Eső, P., and Szentes, B., (2017). "Dynamic Contracting: An Irrelevance Theorem," *Theoretical Economics* 12, 109–39.

Farhi, E., and Werning, I., (2013). "Insurance and Taxation Over the Life Cycle." *Rev. Econ. Stud.* 80, 596–635.

Fernandes, A., and Phelan, C., (2000). "A Recursive Formulation for Repeated Agency with History Dependence." *J. Econ. Theory* 91, 223–47.

Fershtman, D., and Pavan, A., (2016). "Matching Auctions." Discussion paper. Northwestern University.

Frankel, A., (2012), "Aligned Delegation," *American Economic Review* 2014, 104(1): 66–83.

Frankel, A., (2016), "Discounted Quotas," *Journal of Economic Theory*, forthcoming.

Freixas, X., Guesnerie, R., and Tirole, J., (1985). "Planning under Incomplete Information and the Ratchet Effect." *Rev. Econ. Stud.* 52, 173–91.

Galperti, S., (2015). "Commitment, Flexibility, and Optimal Screening of Time Inconsistency," *Econometrica*, 83(4) 1425–65.

Garrett, D., (2014). "Robustness of Simple Menus of Contracts in Cost-Based Procurement," *Games and Economic Behavior*, 87, September 2014, 631–41.

Garrett, D., (2016a). "Intertemporal Price Discrimination: Dynamic Arrivals and Changing Values." *Am. Econ. Rev.*, forthcoming.

Garrett, D., (2016b). "Dynamic Mechanism Design: Dynamic Arrivals and Changing Values." Discussion paper. Toulouse School of Economics.

Garrett, D., and Pavan, A., (2012). "Managerial Turnover in a Changing World." *J. Polit. Econ.* 120, 879–925.

Garrett, D., and Pavan, A., (2015). "Dynamic Managerial Compensation: A Variational Approach." *J. Econ. Theory* 159 (Part B), 775–818.

Garrett, D., Pavan, A., and Toikka, J., (2016). "Robust Predictions in Dynamic Screening." Discussion paper. Northwestern University, University of Toulouse, and MIT.

Genesove, D., (1993). "Adverse Selection in the Wholesale Used Car Market." *J. Polit. Econ.* 101, 644–65.

Gentzkow, M., and Kamenica, E. (2015). "Information Environments and the Impact of Competition on Information Provision." University of Chicago mimeo.

Gerardi, D., and Maestri, L., (2016). "Dynamic Contracting with Limited Commitment and the Ratchet Effect." Discussion Paper, Collegio Carlo Alberto.

Gershkov, A., and Moldovanu, B., (2009a). "Dynamic Revenue Maximization with Heterogenous Objects: A Mechanism Design Approach." *Am. Econ. J. Microecon.* 2, 98–168.

Gershkov, A., and Moldovanu, B., (2009b). "Learning About the Future and Dynamic Efficiency." *Am. Econ. Rev.* 99, 1576–88.

Gershkov, A., and Moldovanu, B., (2012). "Optimal Search, Learning and Implementation." *J. Econ. Theory* 147, 881–909.

Gershkov, A., and Moldovanu, B., (2014). "Dynamic Allocation and Pricing: A Mechanism Design Approach." MIT Press, Cambridge, Massachusetts.

Gershkov, A., Moldovanu, B., and Strack, P., (2014). "Revenue Maximizing Mechanisms with Strategic Customers and Unknown Demand: Name-Your-Own-Price." Discussion paper http://ssrn.com/abstract=2527653. Hebrew University and University of Bonn and UC Berkeley

Gershkov, A., and Szentes, B., (2009). "Optimal Voting Scheme with Costly Information Aquisition." *J. Econ. Theory* 144, 1895–1920.

Gibbard, A., (1973). "Manipulation of Voting Schemes." *Econometrica*, 41, 587–601.

Gibbard, A., (1977). "Manipulation of Schemes that Mix Voting with Chance." *Econometrica*, 45, 665–81.

Golosov, M., Troshkin, M. & Tsyvinski, A., (2015). "Redistribution and Social Insurance," *Am. Econ. Rev.*, 106(2), 359–86.

Golosov, M., Troshkin, M., and Tsyvinski, A., (2016). "Optimal Dynamic Taxes." *Am. Econ. Rev.*, 106(2), 359–86.

Golosov, M., Tsyvinski, A., and Werning, I., (2006). "New Dynamic Public Finance: A User's Guide." *NBER Macroeconomic Annual* 2006, MIT Press.

Gomes, R., and Pavan, A., (2016a). "Many-to-Many Matching and Price Discrimination." *Theoretical Economics*, 11, 1005–52.

Gomes, R., and Pavan, A., (2016b). "Matching Plans for Agents with Horizontally and Vertically Differentiated Preferences." Mimeo, Northwestern University.

Green, J., (1987). "'Making Book Against Oneself,' the Independence Axiom, and Nonlinear Utility Theory." *Q. J. Econ.* 98, 785–96.

Green, J., and Laffont, J., (1979). *Incentives in Public Decision Making.* Amsterdam: North-Holland.

Green, J., and Laffont, J., (1987). "Posterior Implementability in a Two-Person Decision Problem." *Econometrica* 55, 69–94.

Groves, T., (1973). "Incentives in Teams." *Econometrica* 41, 617–31.

Grubb, M., and Osborne, M., forthcoming. "Cellular Service Demand: Biased Beliefs, Learning, and Bill Shock." *Am. Econ. Rev.*

Guesnerie, R., and Laffont, J., (1984). "A Complete Solution to a Class of Principal-Agent Problems with an Application to the Control of a Self-Managed Firm." *J. Public Econ.* 25, 329–69.

Gul, F., Sonnenschein, H., and Wilson, R., (1986). "Foundations of Dynamic Monopoly and the Coase Conjecture." *J. Econ. Theory* 39, 155–190.

Guo, Y., and J. Hörner (2016). "Dynamic Contracting Without Money," Discussion paper. Yale University and Northwestern University.

Handel, B., Hendel, I., and Whinston, M., (2015). "Equilibria in Health Exchanges: Adverse Selection vs. Reclassification Risk." *Econometrica*, 83(4), 1261–1313.

Hart, O., and Tirole, J., (1988). "Contract Renogiation and Coasian Dynamics." *Rev. Econ. Stud.* 55, 509–40.

Heathcote, J., Storesletten, K., and Violante, G. L., (2014). "Optimal Tax Progressivity: An Analytical Framework" (Working Paper No. w19899). National Bureau of Economic Research.

Hendel, I., and Lizzeri, A., (2003). The Role of Commitment in Dynamic Contracts: Evidence from Life Insurance." *Q. J. Econ.* 118, 299–327.

Hinnosaar, T., (2016). "Calendar Mechanisms." Discussion paper. Collegio Carlo Alberto.

Holmstrom, B., and Milgrom, P., (1987). "Aggregation and Linearity in the Provision of Intertemporal Incentives." *Econometrica* 55, 303–28.

Hörner, J., and Skrzypacz, A., (2016). "Learning, Experimentation and Information Design." *Adances in Economics and Econometrics. Proceeding of the 2015 World Congress of the Econometric Society*, forthcoming.

Hylland, A., and Zeckhauser, R., (1979). The Efficient Allocation of Individuals to Positions, *Journal of Political Economy*, 87, 293–313.

Jacobson, L. S., LaLonde, R. J., and Sullivan, D. G., (1993). "Earnings Losses of Displaced Workers." *The American Economic Review*, 685–709.

Johnson, T., (2015). "Dynamic Mechanism Without Transfers," working paper, University of Notre Dame.

Kakade, S., Lobel, I., and Nazerzadeh, H., (2013). "Optimal Dynamic Mechanism Design and the Virtual Pivot Mechanism." *Oper. Res.* 61, 837–54.

Kamenica, E., and Gentzkow, M., (2011). "Bayesian Persuasion." *Am. Econ. Rev.* 101(6), 2590–615.

Kapicka, M., (2013a). "Efficient Allocations in Dynamic Private Information Economies with Persistent Shocks: A First Order Approach." *Review of Economic Studies*, 80(3), 1027–54.

Kapicka, M., (2013b). "Optimal Mirrleesean Taxation with Unobservable Human Capital Formation." mimeo, UC Santa Barbara.

Kapicka, M., and Neira, J., (2014). "Optimal Taxation in a Life-Cycle Economy with Endogenous Human Capital Formation." mimeo, UC Santa Barbara.

Kocherlakota, N., (1996). "Implications of Efficient Risk Sharing Without Commitment." *Rev. Econ. Stud.* 63, 595–609.

Kocherlakota, N., (2005). "Zero Expected Wealth Taxes: A Mirrlees Approach to Dynamic Optimal Taxation." *Econometrica* 73, 1587–21.

Kocherlakota, N. R., (2010): *The New Dynamic Public Finance.* Princeton University Press, USA.

Kováč, E., Krähmer, D., and Tatur, T., (2014). "Optimal Stopping in a Principal-Agent Model With Hidden Information and No Monetary Transfers," working paper, University of Bonn.

Krähmer, D., and Strausz, R., (2011). "Optimal Procurement Contracts with Pre-Project Planning." *Rev. Econ. Stud.* 78, 1015–41.

Krähmer, D., and Strausz, R., (2015a). "Optimal Sales Contracts with Withdrawal Rights," *Rev. Econ. Stud.* 82, 762–90.

Krähmer, D., and Strausz, R., (2015b). "Ex Post Information Rents in Sequential Screening," *Games and Economic Behavior* 90, 257–73.

Krähmer, D., and Strausz, R., (2016). "Sequential vs Static Screening – An Equivalence Result." Discussion paper. University of Bonn and Humboldt University of Berlin.

Krause, A., (2009). "Optimal Nonlinear Income Taxation with Learning-by-Doing." *Journal of Public Economics*, 93(9-10), 1098–110.

Krueger, D., and Uhlig, H., (2006). "Competitive Risk Sharing Contracts with One-Sided Commitment." *J. Monet. Econ.* 53, 1661–91.

Kruse, T., and Strack, P., (2015). "Optimal Stopping with Private Information." *J. Econ. Theory* 159 (Part B), 702–27.

Kumar, P., (1985). "Consistent Mechanism Design and the Noisy Revelation Principle." PhD thesis. Stanford University.

Laffont, J., and Tirole, J., (1986). "Using Cost Observation to Regulate Firms." *J. Polit. Econ.* 94, 614–41.

Laffont, J., and Tirole, J., (1988). "The Dynamics of Incentive Contracts." *Econometrica* 59, 1735–54.

Laffont, J., and Tirole, J., (1990). "Adverse Selection and Renegotiation in Procurement." *Rev. Econ. Stud.* 57, 597–625.

Laffont, J., and Tirole, J., (1986). "Using Cost Observation to Regulate Firms." *Journal of Political Economy*, 94, 614–41.

Li, J., Matouschek, N., and Powell, M., (2015). "The Burden of Past Promises," working paper, Northwestern University.

Li, H., and Shi, X., (2015). "Discriminatory Information Disclosure." Discussion paper. University of British Columbia and University of Toronto.

Ligon, E., Thomas, J., and Worrall, T., (2002). "Informal Insurance Arrangements with Limited Commitment: Theory and Evidence from Village Economies." *Rev. Econ. Stud.* 69, 209–44. Discussion paper. University of Rochester.

Liu, H., (2014). "Efficient Dynamic Mechanisms in Environments with Interdependent Valuations," working paper, University of Michigan.

Liu, Q., Mierendorff, K., and Shi, X., (2015). "Auctions with Limited Commitment." Discussion paper. Columbia University and UCL and University of Toronto.

Ljungqvist, L., and Sargent, T., (2004). *Recursive Macroeconomic Theory*, second edition. Cambridge, Massachusetts: MIT Press.

Luz, V., (2015). "Dynamic Competitive Insurance." Discussion paper. University of British Columbia.

Maestri, L., (2016). "Dynamic Contracting Under Adverse Selection and Renegotiation." Discussion paper, Fondacion Gatulo Vergas.

Makris, M., and Pavan, A., (2016). "Incentives for Endogeneous Types: Taxation Under Learning by Doing," Discussion paper. Northwestern University.

Maskin, E., and Riley, J., (1984). "Monopoly with Incomplete Information." *Rand J. Econ.* 15, 171–96.

Maskin, E., and Riley, J., (1989). "Optimal Multi-Unit Auctions." In *The Economics of Missing Markets, Information, and Games*, 312–35. Oxford University Press.

McAfee, R., and Vincent, D., (1997). "Sequentially Optimal Auctions." *Games Econ. Behav.* 18, 24–76.

Miao, J., and Zhang, Y., (2015). "A Duality Approach to Continuous-Time Contracting Problems with Limited Commitment." *J. Econ. Theory* 159 (Part B), 929–88.

Mierendorff, K., (2014). "Optimal Dynamic Mechanism Design with Deadlines." Discussion paper. UCL.

Milgrom, P., and Segal, I., (2002). "Envelope Theorems for Arbitrary Choice Sets." *Econometrica*, 70(2), 583–601.

Miralles, A. (2012). "Cardinal Bayesian Allocation Mechanisms without Transfers," *Journal of Economic Theory*, 147, 179–206.

Miravete, E., (2003). "Choosing the Wrong Calling Plan? Ignorance and Learning." *Am. Econ. Rev.* 93, 297–310.

Mirrlees, J., (1971). "An Exploration in the Theory of Optimum Income Taxation." *Rev. Econ. Stud.* 38, 175–208.

Mueller, C., (2015). "Robust Virtual Implementation under Common Strong Belief in Rationality," *Journal of Economic Theory*, 162, 407–50.

Mussa, M., and Rosen, S., (1978). "Monopoly and Product Quality." *J. Econ. Theory* 18, 301–17.

Myesron, R., (1979). "Incentive Compatibility and the Bargaining Problem," *Econometrica*, 47(1), 61–74.

Myerson, R., (1981). "Optimal Auction Design." *Math. Oper. Res.* 6, 58–73.

Myerson, R. B., (1986). "Multistage Games with Communication," *Econometrica*, 54(2), 323–58.

Myerson, R., and Satterthwaite, M., (1983). "Efficient Mechanisms for Bilateral Trading." *Journal of Economic Theory*, Vol. 29, pp. 265–81.

Nikandrova, A., and Pancs, R., (2015). "An Optimal Auction with Moral Hazard." Mimeo, ITAM.

Pavan, A. (2007). "Long-Term Contracting in a Changing World," Mimeo, Northwestern University.

Pavan, A., Segal, I., and Toikka, J., (2014). "Dynamic Mechanism Design: A Myersonian Approach." *Econometrica* 82, 601–53.

Penta, A., (2015). "Robust Dynamic Implementation," *Journal of Economy Theory*, Vol. 160, 280–316.

Porter, R., (1995). "The Role of Information in U.S. Offshore Oil and Gas Lease Auctions." *Econometrica* 63, 1–27.

Prat, J., and Jovanovic, B., (2014). "Dynamic Contracts when the Agent's Quality is Unknown." *Theoretical Economics* 9, 865–914.

Prendergast, C., (2002). "The Tenuous Trade-Off between Risk and Incentives." *Journal of Political Economy*, 110(5), 1071–102.

Rahman, D., (2011). "Detecting Profitable Deviations." Discussion paper. University of Minnesota.

Rayo, L., and Segal, I., (2010), "Optimal Information Disclosure," *Journal of Political Economy*, 118(5), 949–87.

Riley, J., and Samuelson, W., (1981). "Optimal Auctions." *Am. Econ. Rev.* 71, 381–92.

Riordan, M., and Sappington, D., (1987). "Information, Incentives, and Organizational Mode." *Q. J. Econ.* 102, 243–64.

Rochet, J.-C., (1987). "A Necessary and Sufficient Condition for Rationalizability in a Quasi-Linear Context." *J. Math. Econ.* 16, 191–200.

Rogerson, W., (1985). "Repeated Moral Hazard," *Econometrica*, 53(1), 69–76.

Said, M., (2011). "Sequential Auctions with Randomly Arriving Buyers." *Games Econ. Behav.* 73, 236–43.

Said, M., (2012). "Auctions with Dynamic Populations: Efficiency and Revenue Maximization." *J. Econ. Theory* 147, 2419–38.

Sannikov, Y., (2013). "Contracts: The Theory of Dynamic Principal-Agent Relationships and the Continuous-Time Approach." In: *Advances in Economics and Econometrics: Tenth World Congress*. Cambridge: Cambridge University Press, pp. 89–124.

Satterthwaite, M. (1975). "Strategy-Proofness and Arrow's Condition: Existence and Correspondence Theorems for Voting Procedures and Social Welfare Functions," *J. Econ. Theory* 10, 187–217.

Segal, I., (2003). "Optimal Pricing Mechanisms with Unknown Demand." *American Economic Review*, 93(3): 509–29.

Skreta, V., (2006). "Sequentially Optimal Auctions." *Rev. Econ. Stud.* 73, 1085–111.

Skreta, V., (2015). "Optimal Auction Design Under Non-Commitment." *J. Econ. Theory* 159 (Part B), 854–90.

Skrzypacz, A., and Toikka, J., forthcoming. "Mechanisms for Repeated Trade." *Am. Econ. J. Microecon.*

Stantcheva, S., (2014). "Optimal Income Taxation with Adverse Selection in the Labour Market." *Rev. Econ. Stud.* 81, 1296–329.

Stantcheva, S., (2016). "Optimal Taxation and Human Capital Policies over the Life Cycle." *Journal of Political Economy,* forthcoming.

Stokey, N., (1981). "Rational Expectations and Durable Goods Pricing." *Bell J. Econ.* 12, 112–28.

Strulovici, B., (2016). "Contract Negotiation and the Coase Conjecture." Discussion paper, Northwestern University.

Strulovici, B., and Szydlowski, M., (2015). "On the Smoothness of Value Functions and the Existence of Optimal Strategies in Diffusion Models." *J. Econ. Theory* 159 (Part B), 1016–55.

Thomas, J., and Worrall, T., (1988). "Self-Enforcing Wage Contracts." *Rev. Econ. Stud.* 55, 541–54.

Topel, R., (1991). "Specific Capital, Mobility and Wages: Wages Rise with Seniority." *Journal of Political Economy*, 99(t), 145–76.

Vickrey, W., (1961). "Counterspeculation, Auctions, and Competitive Sealed Tenders." *J. Finance* 16, 8–37.

Williams, N., (2011). "Persistent Private Information." *Econometrica* 79, 1233–74.

Williams, N., (2015). "A Solvable Continuous Time Dynamic Principal-Agent Model." *J. Econ. Theory* 159 (Part B), 989–1015.

Willis, R., (1986). "Wage Determinants: A Survey and Reinterpretation of Human Capital Earnings Functions," in *Handbook of Labor Economics*, ed. by O. Ashenfelter and R. Layard, New York: Elsevier Science Publisher, Vol. 1, pp. 525–602.

Wilson, R., (1993). *Nonlinear Pricing*. Oxford: Oxford University Press.

CHAPTER 2

Learning, Experimentation, and Information Design

Johannes Hörner and Andrzej Skrzypacz

1 INTRODUCTION

The purpose of this paper is to survey recent developments in a literature that combines ideas from experimentation, learning, and strategic interactions. Because this literature is multifaceted, let us start by circumscribing our overview. First and foremost, all surveyed papers involve nontrivial dynamics. Second, we will restrict attention to models that deal with uncertainty. Models of pure moral hazard, in particular, will not be covered. Third, we exclude papers that focus on monetary transfers. Our goal is to understand incentives via other channels – information in particular, but also delegation. Fourth, we focus on strategic and agency problems, and so leave out papers whose scope is decision-theoretic. However, rules are there to be broken, and we will briefly discuss some papers that deal with one-player problems, to the extent that they are closely related to the issues at hand. Finally, we restrict attention to papers that are relatively recent (specifically, we have chosen to start with Bolton and Harris, 1999).

Our survey is divided as follows. First, we start with models of strategic experimentation. These are abstract models with few direct economic applications, but they develop ideas and techniques that percolate through the literature. In these models, players are (usually) symmetric and externalities are (mostly) informational.

Moving beyond the exploitation/exploration trade-off, we then turn to agency models that introduce a third dimension: motivation. Experimentation must be incentivized. The first way this can be done (Section 3) is via the information that is being disclosed to the agent performing the experimentation, by a principal who knows more or sees more. A second way this can be done is

This survey was prepared for the Econometric Summer Meetings in Montréal, 2015. We thank Kostas Bimpikis, Alessandro Bonatti, Daria Khromenkova, Nicolas Klein, Erik Madsen, and Chiara Margaria for detailed comments.

via control. The nascent literature on delegation in dynamic environments is the subject of Section 4.

Section 5 turns to models in which information disclosure is not simply about inducing experimentation, but manipulating the agent's action in broader contexts. To abstract from experimentation altogether, we assume that the principal knows all there is to know, so that only the agent faces uncertainty.

Finally, Section 6 discusses experimentation with more than two arms (Callander, 2011).

2   EQUILIBRIUM INTERACTIONS

2.1   Strategic Bandits

Strategic bandit models are game-theoretic versions of standard bandit models. While the standard "multi-armed bandit" describes a hypothetical experiment in which a player faces several slot machines ("one-armed bandits") with potentially different expected payouts, a strategic bandit involves several players facing (usually, identical) copies of the same slot machine. Players want to stick with the slot machine if and only if the best payout rate makes it worth their time, and learn not only from their own outcomes but also from their neighbors.

Equilibrium strategies are not characterized by simple cutoffs in terms of the common belief. As a result, solutions to strategic bandits are only known for a limited class of distributions, involving two states of the world only. In Bolton and Harris (1999, BH), the observation process (of payoffs) follows a Brownian motion whose drift depends on the state. In Keller, Rady, and Cripps (2005, KRC), it follows a simple Poisson process, with positive lump-sums ("breakthroughs") occurring at random (exponentially distributed) times if and only if the arm is good. Keller and Rady (2015, KR15) solve the polar opposite case in which costly lump-sums ("breakdowns") occur at random times if and only if the arm is bad. Keller and Rady (2010, KR10) consider the case in which breakthroughs need not be conclusive.

These models share in common, in addition to the binary state framework, their focus on symmetric Markov perfect equilibria (MPE).[1] Throughout, players are Bayesian. Given that they observe all actions and outcomes, they share a common belief about the state, which serves as the state variable. They are also impatient and share a common discount rate.

BH and KR10 are the most ambitious models and offer no closed-form solutions for the equilibrium. Remarkably, however, they are able to prove uniqueness and tease out not only their structure, but their dependence on parameters. While it is BH that first develops both the ideas (including the concepts of freeriding and encouragement effects) as well as the methods used

---

[1] KRC and KR15 discuss asymmetric MPE as well, although this remains an open and challenging problem for the Brownian case.

throughout this literature, the most interesting insights can already be gleaned from the simple exponential bandits in KRC and KR15. What makes these two models tractable is that they can be viewed as deterministic: unless a breakdown or breakthrough ("news") occurs, the (conditional) posterior belief follows a known path. If news arrives, the game is over, since if it is commonly known that the state is good (or bad), informational externalities cease to matter, and each player knows the strictly dominant action to take.

Let us consider here a simplified version combining the good and bad news models. The state is $\omega \in \{G, B\}$. Each player $i = 1, \ldots, I$ controls the variable $u_t^i \in [0, 1]$, which is the fraction allocated to the risky arm at time $t \geq 0$ (the complementary fraction being allocated to the safe arm). The horizon is infinite. This leads to a total realized payoff of

$$\int_0^\infty e^{-rt} (h \, dN_{G,t}^i - \ell \, dN_{B,t}^i),$$

where $r > 0$ is the discount rate, $h, \ell > 0$ are the value and cost of a breakthrough or breakdown, and $N_{G,t}^i, N_{B,t}^i$ are Poisson processes with intensities

$$u_t^i \lambda_G \mathbf{1}_{\{\omega=G\}}, \text{ and } u_t^i \lambda_B \mathbf{1}_{\{\omega=B\}},$$

which are conditionally independent across players. Here, $\lambda_G, \lambda_B \geq 0$ are parameters. News is conclusive: if any player experiences a breakthrough (breakdown), all players immediately learn that the state is good (bad) and allocate weight 0 (1) to the risky arm, the alternative having value normalized to 0.

The main distinction in these models hinges on the direction in which updating occurs in the absence of any news. The (conditional) belief $p_t = \mathbf{P}[\omega = G]$ that the state is good evolves according to

$$\dot{p}_t = -\Delta p_t (1 - p_t) \sum_{i=1}^I u_t^i, \text{ where } \Delta := \lambda_G - \lambda_B.$$

Hence, if $\lambda_G > \lambda_B$, then this belief drifts down over time. We call such a model a good news model (because a special case is $\lambda_B = 0$, in which case the only news that might arrive is good). If $\lambda_G < \lambda_B$, the belief drifts up, unless news arrives. This is the bad news model.[2]

The first best, or *cooperative*, outcome is simple. Players should follow a common cut-off (Markov) policy, using the risky arm if and only if the belief p_t is above some threshold (say, $\bar{p}_I$ in the bad news case, and $\underline{p}_I$ in the good news one). Such behavior results in very different dynamics according to the news scenario. In the bad news case, experimentation goes on forever unless (bad) news occurs. In the good news model, experimentation stops unless (good) news occurs. This drastically changes equilibrium predictions.

---

[2] The special case $\lambda_G = \lambda_B$ can be nested in either case.

To understand incentives, let us fix players $-i$'s strategies to what they would do, each on their own (that is, to be the the optimal single-agent policy). Let us start with the bad news case, in which this involves a threshold $\bar{p}_1$ above which they experiment (set $u^i = 1$). This threshold is below the myopic threshold p^m at which the expected reward from taking the risky action is precisely 0, namely,

$$\lambda_G p^m h = \lambda_B (1 - p^m)\ell.$$

This is because the option value from learning via experimentation makes it worthwhile for a lone player to use the risky arm at beliefs slightly below p^m, when the flow loss from doing so is small enough.

Consider now the best reply of a player to such a strategy by the others at beliefs in the neighborhood of this threshold $\bar{p}_1$. Right above $\bar{p}_1$, player i need no longer carry out costly experimentation on his own to learn about the state, because other players are experimenting. Hence, there is a range of beliefs right above $p > \bar{p}_1$ in which his best reply is to use the safe arm only, depressing overall experimentation at such beliefs. This is the *freeriding effect*. See Figure 1. As a result, player i's payoff is boundedly higher than what it would be if he were on his own, given that the value of information is strictly positive.

Consider now beliefs right below $\bar{p}_1$. If player i does not experiment, nothing will happen, given that nobody else does. Yet, getting the belief "over the edge" $\bar{p}_1$ is very valuable, as it will kickstart experimentation by players $-i$. Because player i would be indifferent at $\bar{p}_1$ if he were on his own, without the added benefit provided by others' experimentation, he strictly prefers to do so if this is the prerequisite to get others started. Hence, there is a range of beliefs below $\bar{p}_1$ at which player i's best reply is to experiment. This the *encouragement effect*. Absent freeriding, the encouragement effect is responsible for the monotonicity of the cooperative amount of experimentation to

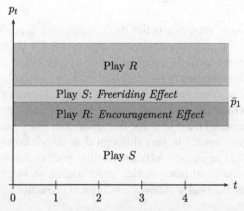

Figure 1 Best reply to the one-player optimal policy under bad news.

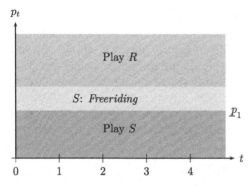

Figure 2 Best reply to the one-player optimal policy under good news.

increase with the number of players (e.g., $\bar{p}_I$ decreasing in I). Of course, for very low beliefs, playing safe is the best reply.

Hence, the best reply to the optimal (single-player) cutoff policy is not a cutoff policy. In fact, it is not monotone. With some work, however, it can be shown that a symmetric monotone (pure-strategy) equilibrium exists, but it involves interior levels of experimentation ($u^i \in (0, 1)$) for some beliefs.

In contrast, consider now the case of good news. Figure 2 illustrates the best reply to the one-player optimal policy, which specifies play of the risky arm if and only if $p \geq \underline{p}_1$. Beliefs are now partitioned into only three intervals. There is no encouragement region for beliefs below $\underline{p}_1$. This is because of the dynamics of beliefs. Here, experimentation at such beliefs does not move the common belief closer to the region at which other players would experiment (unless a breakthrough occurs, obviously). Because the conditional belief absent a breakthrough only drifts down further, a player is on his own, for beliefs below $\underline{p}_1$. Hence, by the definition of this threshold, it is optimal to play safe. This does not imply that the one-player optimal policy is an equilibrium, however, because at beliefs immediately above $\underline{p}_1$, an agent still has incentives to freeride on others' experimentation. Because $\underline{p}_1$ is strictly below the myopic threshold at which playing risky already pays off in the next instant, playing risky at such beliefs is motivated by the option value from learning. Because other players perform this experimentation, it is then best to play safe oneself, at least for beliefs that are sufficiently close to (and above) $\underline{p}_1$.

Hence, here as well, the symmetric equilibrium involves interior levels of experimentation. In this sense, it looks similar to the symmetric equilibrium in the bad news case. But the absence of the encouragement region for beliefs below $\underline{p}_1$ implies that experimentation levels are lower than the socially efficient level, with experimentation ceasing altogether at this threshold independent of the number of players. In particular, independent of I, the total amount of experimentation performed by players over the infinite horizon (which the asymptotic belief precisely measures) is the same as if there was only one player. Delay is higher, as one can show that, unlike with one player, this belief is only asymptotically achieved, as experimentation rates dwindle down when the belief approaches the threshold. Players are better off, of course (they can always ignore the existence of other players, and replicate the one-player policy and payoff), because the cost of experimentation is shared among them. Nonetheless, the outcome is inefficient.

We now provide some details on how these symmetric equilibria can be solved for. Consider the Hamilton–Jacobi–Bellman (HJB) equation for player i's continuation value v, taking as given the aggregate experimentation by other players, $u^{-i}(p) = \sum_{j \neq i} u^j(p)$. It holds that

$$rv(p) = \max_{u^i}\{u^i \pi(p) + (u^i + u^{-i}(p))\underbrace{[(p\lambda_G(\lambda_G h/r - v(p)) - (1-p)\lambda_B v(p))}_{\text{jump in value if news arrives}}$$
$$- \underbrace{\Delta p(1-p)v'(p)]\}}_{\substack{\text{drift in value} \\ \text{if no news arrives}}},$$

where

$$\pi(p) = p\lambda_G h - (1-p)\lambda_B \ell$$

is the expected flow payoff from the risky arm. Over the next instant, $\pi(p)$ is collected by player i at rate u^i. Either one of the players experiences a breakthrough or breakdown, in which case the value jumps from $v(p)$ to either $\lambda_G h/r$ if a breakthrough occurs, or 0 if it is a breakdown. In the absence of news, the value changes at a rate proportional to the belief change $\dot{p}$. We see that the right-hand side is linear in u^i, implying that over a range of beliefs $[p_1, p_2]$ over which player i is indifferent, the coefficient on u^i must be zero, that is,

$$\pi(p) + (p\lambda_G(\lambda_G h/r - v(p)) - (1-p)\lambda_B v(p)) - \Delta p(1-p)v'(p) = 0, \quad (1)$$

a differential equation that can be solved explicitly, given the relevant boundary conditions. Adding and subtracting $u^{-i}(p)\pi(p)$ from the HJB equation (and using (1) to eliminate almost all terms) gives

$$rv(p) = -u^{-i}(p)\pi(p), \quad (2)$$

over such a range.[3]

In a symmetric equilibrium, $u^{-i}(p) = (I-1)u^i(p)$, and the optimal experimentation level follows, as explained next. Equations (1)–(2) are equally valid for good and bad news. The difference appears in the boundary conditions. In the case of bad news, the value drifts up. It is readily verified that u^i increases in p, and so p_2 is determined by $u^i(p_2) = 1$ and $v(p_2) = \bar{v}(p_2)$, which together with (2) imply $r\bar{v}(p_2) = -(I-1)\pi(p_2)$, where $\bar{v}$ is the per-player

[3] Because $v(p) \geq 0$, we see that such a range must be a subset of the beliefs over which π is negative. This should not come as a surprise because above the myopic threshold players certainly use the risky arm.

value from the cooperative solution discussed above. Once this threshold is reached, players achieve the first best. Because of the upward drift, this suffices to determine the candidate value $v(p)$ for all $p < p_2$. Because playing safe is always an option, $v(p) \geq 0$, and finding the solution to $v(p_1) = 0$ then determines p_1, below which indifference no longer holds and the safe arm is exclusively played.

In contrast, with good news, the candidate value function v over the to-be-determined interval of beliefs $[p_1, p_2]$ over which experimentation levels are interior must be solved "bottom-up," starting from p_1. As argued, $p_1 = \underline{p}_1$, the level at which a lone player ceases experimentation. In addition, $v'(\underline{p}_1) = 0$ (smooth-pasting) must hold.[4] This suffices to solve (1) for the candidate value v, and p_2 is determined by $u^{-i}(p_2) = I - 1$. Hence, solving $v(p_2) = -r(I-1)\pi(p_2)$ gives p_2, above which indifference no longer holds and risky is played exclusively.

See Figure 3 and Figure 4 for an illustration of the value functions. The intermediate (dashed) curve is the symmetric equilibrium value function (as a function of the belief), and the lower (dotted) and higher (solid) curves are the single-player and cooperative value ($\bar{v}$) functions. Considering Figure 3 (bad news), the encouragement effect drives the larger range of beliefs at which players experiment (as can be shown), relative to the single-player case, yet the freeriding effect leads to an amount of experimentation that remains too low nonetheless. In Figure 4 (good news), the impact of freeriding has a more dramatic impact, as experimentation stops at the same threshold, as in the single-player case.

To what extent is the solution concept (symmetric MPE) driving these results? As KRC show, symmetry is partly responsible for the inefficiency, and equilibria with higher payoffs can be achieved when players take turns experimenting in a Markov equilibrium, for instance. More generally, Hörner, Klein,

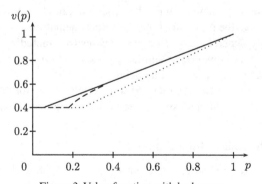

Figure 3 Value function with bad news.

---

[4] This derivative cannot be negative, since, for all $\epsilon > 0$, $v(\underline{p}_1 + \epsilon) \geq 0 = v(\underline{p}_1)$. It cannot be positive either. Otherwise, there is a solution to (1) with $v(\underline{p}_1 - \epsilon) = 0$ as a boundary condition, giving $v(\underline{p}_1) > 0$, a contradiction.

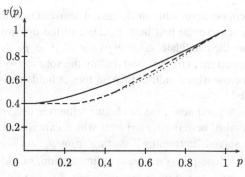

Figure 4 Value function with good news.

and Rady (2015) show that the Markov restriction plays an important role in the inefficiency result, as well as the equilibrium structure. Strongly symmetric equilibrium (SSE), in which all players choose the same continuation strategy after a given history (independent of the identity of a potential deviator, for instance), is a restrictive solution concept in general, yet it is still weaker than symmetric MPE which are automatically SSEs. In the experimentation context, SSE turn out to allow for exactly efficient equilibria for a range of (but not all) parameters. This is the case, in particular, whenever news is bad (whether it is conclusive or not), or in the Brownian case. Furthermore, as far as the total surplus (or the players' average payoff) is concerned, it can be shown that, in all cases, no perfect Bayesian equilibrium outcome outperforms SSE.

Several extensions are worth mentioning, although space does not allow us to discuss them further. Klein and Rady (2011) solve the case of negatively correlated arms (a disease might be either bacterial or viral, but not both). Players might be able to communicate publicly, in the absence of direct monitoring of each others' experimentation, a case considered by Heidhues, Rady, and Strack (2015). Players might be asymmetric (Das, 2015), etc. Nonetheless, open questions remain even for the benchmark models. While Cohen and Solan (2013) solve the problem of optimal experimentation *for a single player* for a reasonably general class of Lévy processes (not including the exponential bad news case, however), a similar analysis that would encompass both the Brownian and the exponential model remains to be done. Also, whereas in the exponential case, KRC (and KR15) were able to solve for the asymmetric MPE, it is unknown whether asymmetric MPE exist in the Brownian case.[5]

2.2   On the Role of Information

What if players do not observe the outcomes of the other players, but only what they do? And what if players don't observe the actions of the other players, but only the outcomes? It is easy to think of examples of either scenario: firms might observe each others' profits, but not techniques; co-authors see

---

[5] As mentioned above, there exist efficient SSE in the Brownian case.

each others' output, not input. On the other hand, consumers see each others' choices, not derived utilities; and firms might see each others' supply chain without being able to evaluate their satisfaction with specific suppliers.

The first problem – observed actions, unobserved outcomes – remains largely unsolved. Rosenberg, Solan, and Vieille (2007) provide a partial answer to it, under the *assumption* that switching to the safe arm is an irreversible choice, while also making clear that this assumption is restrictive: players would like to switch back to the risky arm under circumstances that occur with positive probability. The second problem – unobservable actions, observed outcomes – is better understood, at least in the case of exponential bandits. The answer further underscores the differences between good and bad news bandits.

Rosenberg, Solan, and Vieille (2007) prove that, when the switch to the safe arm is irreversible, the optimal policy remains an index policy (a generalization of a threshold policy defined shortly) under weak distributional assumptions.

Consider the case of two players (the focus of their paper). By round n, assuming player 1 has not switched to the safe arm yet, two possibilities arise. Either player 2 has not either, or he has in round $k < n$. Not observing player 2 stop is a good sign about 2's observed payoffs. As a result, player 1 uses a simple cutoff rule: he compares his private belief, based on his own observations only, to a threshold that is nonincreasing with n. If and only if his belief exceeds this threshold, he continues experimenting. If, instead, player 2 switched to the safe arm in round k, player 1 faces the standard decision problem of a one-armed bandit, for which the solution is an index policy (with a cutoff in terms of his belief). Of course, his belief accounts for the decision of player 2 to quit at time k. Whether an index policy remains optimal when the irreversibility assumption is dropped is an important open question.

Bonatti and Hörner (2011) is based on the good news model, but involves a payoff externality. As soon as a player experiences a breakthrough, the game ends, and every player derives the same utility from it. However, experimenting (effort) is costly and its cost is privately borne. Think of collaborators working on a common project from different locations. Effort is not observable, but the output is automatically reported on Dropbox – if someone cracks the problem, it is immediately common knowledge among players. Importantly, effort is private information. Freeriding is present, but deviations do not lead to changes in the opponents' beliefs, as such deviations are not observed. As a result, the unique symmetric equilibrium, which as in KRC involves interior effort, leads to higher effort provision than with observable effort. This is because unexpected, but observed, shirking leads to a belief that is higher than it would be otherwise, and this optimism leads to more effort. Hence, shirking is more attractive when it is observed, as it leads other players to work harder in the future (relative to how much they would work if shirking was not observed).

What is the ultimate fate of such collaborations? As Bonatti and Hörner show, effort is scaled down over time, so that the asymptotic belief makes agents just indifferent between working and not. The project dwindles over time, but is never abandoned.[6] Gordon, Marlats, and Ménager (2015) consider a variation in which there is a fixed delay $\Delta > 0$ between a player's breakthrough and his collaborator observing it. Remarkably, the unique symmetric MPE exhibits periodic behavior, with players alternating over time phases in which they use the risky and the safe arm exclusively. (These phases are further divided up according to whether a player is likely to hear news from his collaborator or not, depending on whether his collaborator was using the risky arm Δ instants ago.)

With bad news, the logic is reversed, as Bonatti and Hörner (2015) show. Observability leads to more effort because unexpected shirking depresses collaborators, and so leads to lower effort. Hence, such a deviation leads to an automatic punishment, and so mitigates freeriding relative to unobserved effort. Surprisingly, the unique equilibrium is in mixed strategies. That is, players randomize over extremal strategies, with a switching time to the risky arm (if no breakdown has occurred until then) that is chosen at random (this is *not* equivalent to a pure strategy equilibrium with interior levels of experimentation).

The fundamental difference is related to the kind of deviations that are most attractive. Under good news, a player that briefly deviates to the safe arm unbeknown to the other players becomes more optimistic than them, as the lack of a breakthrough is not as statistically significant for him. Hence, his relative optimism strengthens his incentives to revert to experimentation. The deviation "self-corrects" and local first-order conditions suffice, leading to interior but pure strategies. Under bad news, a player that deviates the same way becomes more pessimistic than the other players, as he views the absence of a breakdown as a more likely event. Increased pessimism pushes him further towards the safe arm. Hence, local first-order conditions are no longer sufficient, and so randomization must occur over pure extremal strategies.

2.3   Extensions

Irreversibility.   All but one of the papers mentioned in Section 2.1 involve reversible actions. A player can resume experimentation after playing safe, and vice-versa. This is not innocuous. Instead, Frick and Ishii (2015) assume that using the risky arm (the adoption of a new technology) is an irreversible choice.[7] Their model is not strategic, to the extent that there is a continuum of agents. However, these agents are forward-looking, and learn about the state of the world (whether adoption is profitable or not) from the adoption choices of others. The more others adopt, the more likely it is that an exponentially

---

[6] This inefficiency calls for regulation. Campbell, Ederer, and Spinnewijn (2014) consider the problem of the optimal deadline as a way of alleviating the freeriding. The intervention could be purely informational: Bimpikis, Ehsani, and Mostagir (2016) suggest introducing a "black-out" phase in which no information is shared, a policy that is shown to be optimal within some class of policies. The optimal informational mechanism remains unknown.

[7] Irreversibility presupposes that the unit resource cannot be split across arms.

distributed signal publicly reveals whether the state is good or bad. Opportunities to adopt follow independent Poisson processes, one for each of the agents. Frick and Ishii show that the adoption patterns differ markedly across scenarios. With good news, there cannot be a region of beliefs for which agents are indifferent between adopting or not. This is because, if an agent is willing to invest immediately after t in the absence of news (as would be the case in the interior of such a region, if it existed), then he must strictly prefer to invest at time t. Indeed, the only other event that can occur is good news, in which case adoption is optimal as well. Hence, there is no option value to waiting. As a result, the equilibrium is extremal: all agents that get the chance to adopt do so up to some date t_1. If no breakthrough was observed by that time, agents stop adopting. As a result, the adoption pattern (the fraction of adopters) turns out to be a concave function of time. In contrast, with bad news, there is a region of beliefs (and so, an interval of time) over which agents are indifferent, and so only a fraction of agents that get an opportunity to adopt do so, resulting in an S-shaped adoption pattern.

It is worth mentioning that irreversibility is not necessarily socially costly. But this depends on which action is irreversible. In the models of Section 2.1, the first-best is an equilibrium outcome when switching to the safe arm is irreversible. If switching to the safe arm is irreversible, it is no longer possible to be a bystander while others experiment. And because one still benefits from the accelerated rate of learning that results from others experimenting, it is optimal to follow the first-best strategy when others do so. More generally, we speculate that making the risky action reversible and the safe action irreversible is socially valuable, as it encourages experimentation, which is always too low.[8]

Murto and Välimäki (2011, 2013; hereafter MV11, MV13) consider stopping games (that is, games where switching to the risky arm is irreversible) with observational learning and pure informational externalities.[9] In both papers, stopping corresponds to taking the action whose payoff depends on the state (in this sense, it is the risky one). The models have notable differences. In MV11, the state is binary, values are correlated but not identical, and it is a good news model: if the state is good, agents that have not stopped yet receive a private, independent signal revealing the state at a rate that is exponentially distributed. In MV13, the state space is much richer and is the (common) optimal time to invest. Signals are received at the beginning once and for all, but the signal space is rich (the monotone likelihood ratio property is assumed to impose some discipline). In both models, agents observe the earlier times at which other agents chose to stop, but nothing else. A robust finding across both papers is that, even as the number of players grows large, efficiency is not achieved. Stopping occurs too late, relative to first-best. This is particularly

---

[8] We are not aware of a single model in which strategic interactions lead to over-experimentation. It would be interesting to examine under which conditions this might happen (heterogeneity?).

[9] See also Rosenberg, Salomon, and Vieille (2013) for a related analysis in continuous time for the two-player case.

striking in MV13, as it highlights the role of time passing by, and how it differs from static models, as in common value auctions in which asymptotic efficiency obtains. Further, MV11 show how, with many players and continuous time, exit behavior displays waves of exit interwoven with calm periods of waiting, during which the public belief hardly budges. Exit waves occur because the exit of an agent implies a discrete jump in the public belief, leading with positive probability to the immediate exit of further agents whose belief was nearly the same, which in turn triggers a further cascade of agents leaving.

Payoff externalities. Most of the papers considered so far focus on pure informational externalities. From a theoretical point of view, this allows us to isolate informational incentives. From an economic point of view, it is very restrictive. Other externalities arise in many contexts. For instance, competition in the product market leads to payoff externalities (with more firms "experimenting" in the risky market, profits have to be shared among more firms). Decision-making procedures also lead to externalities, when agents' action cannot be selected of their own free will. Congresspeople do not decide whether they want to experiment in isolation, but rather make decisions by majority voting.

Some papers explore such issues. Cripps and Thomas (2015) consider externalities in terms of congestion costs.[10] Imagine stepping out of an unfamiliar airport, hoping to catch a cab at the curbside. Naturally, there are signs above your head providing potentially critical information for those who can decipher the local alphabet. But you are not one of them. As it turns out, nobody is ahead of you, so this is your lucky day: either the first cab will be for you, or this is not a spot where cabs are authorized to pick up fares. What do you do?

Suppose instead that there are three people in front of you, so that you are fourth in line (your upbringing compelling you to incur the requisite congestion cost if you choose to stay). It is clear to you that their knowledge of the local idiom is as deficient as your own. Yet, having come before you, they might have observed useful data, like a cab picking up somebody ahead of them. Communication would certainly help, but interpersonal skills are not your forte (it may be embarrassing to admit you're standing in line with no assurance this is even a cab stand, so any cheap talk by people in line is likely to be uninformative anyway). What do you do?

This problem looks daunting: incomplete information (a binary state), coarse information sets (the number of people ahead of you in the line), and both informational and payoff externalities. Yet, at least for some range of parameters, Cripps and Thomas (2015) solve for the optimal policy. One of the key insights is that information is nested: the first person in line knows as much as everyone else, since he must have come before. Hence, provided that the queue is not so long that you balk immediately, it is optimal to mimic this first person's behavior. If he ever balks, then so should you, as it reveals that he

[10] See also Thomas (2015).

hasn't seen a cab, and you cannot hope for a higher payoff than his. Yet, it isn't always optimal to stay as long as he does. Cripps and Thomas (2015) do not provide a general solution, unfortunately, but their analysis provides insights into what can go wrong and suggests alternative candidate strategies.

In Strulovici (2010), the externality comes about from the decision-making process. Each player faces an independent one-armed bandit. However, actions are not independent. All players must take the same action at every instant, which gets decided by majority voting. It is a good news model, and outcomes are observed.[11] As a result, players are divided into two groups: those who have found out that their arm is good, and stubbornly cast their vote for the risky arm (which is no longer risky for them), and those who have not yet received a good signal and grow anxious that the safe arm might be the better alternative. If the first group takes over, the uncertain voters will be doomed to use the risky arm, which is most likely bad for them. If instead the second group pre-empts this from happening by voting for the safe alternative while they still can, players from the first group will be frustrated winners. How does this trade-off play out? As it turns out, it leads to under-experimentation. This is not too surprising, as the existence of the first group imposes a cost which the social planner does not account for, on uncertain voters that might be stuck with a bad arm. Strikingly, as the number of voters grows large, experimentation is abandoned as soon as the myopic cutoff is reached.

This analysis suggests interesting questions for future research. What if the bandits are correlated, for instance, when outcomes or information is unobserved? In a jury context, the accused is either guilty or innocent. In such environments, understanding under which conditions information aggregation obtains seems an important problem.

3 MOTIVATION

3.1 Many Options and Coarse Learning

Experimentation is often carried out by a third party whose interests are not necessarily aligned with those of the experimenter. Nobody cares about being a guinea pig, yet it is in society's best interest that some of us are. Consider the example of Waze, as discussed by Kremer, Mansour, and Perry (2014, KMP). Every day, motorists must arbitrage between two routes. Travel time is uncertain, and so is each motorist's payoff π_k, which is shared by the motorists traveling this route that day. Let us assume that it is uniformly drawn from $[a_k, b_k]$, with $k = M, I$ standing for the type of the route: $a_I < a_M < b_M \leq b_I$, so that the Merritt parkway is "safer" than I-95, but also $a_M + b_M > a_I + b_I$, so it is on average faster. Motorists cannot postpone or forward their daily commute, and arrive in a sequence. They do not care about experimenting, as travel times are independently distributed across days,

---

[11] See also Khromenkova (2015) for the analysis of the mixed news case.

and they need to travel only once a day. However, upon taking a route, their cell phone diligently relays travel time to Waze (and hence perfectly resolves uncertainty for that day) unbeknown to the motorist.[12]

Consider first the case in which $a_M = 1$, $b_M = 3$, whereas $a_I = -5$, $b_I = 5$ (with the usual stretch of imagination that negative payoffs demand). Our first motorist, an early bird aware of his position in the line, selects the M-route, as its expected payoff of 2 exceeds zero, I-95's expected payoff. The second motorist's choice is equally simple, *independent* of his knowledge of the first motorist's realized travel time. At worst, it is 1, which still beats the mean payoff from I-95. Hence there is nothing he can be told that would change his mind: route M it is. More generally, if $\mathbf{E}[\pi_I] < a_M$, all drivers take the Merritt parkway, and Waze loses its purpose (not to mention, to the dismay of Waze's innovators, Google's attention). This is captured by Figure 5.

Instead, suppose that $a_M = -1 < b_M = 5$. The early bird selects route M, as before, because its expected payoff exceeds I's expected payoff. Let us first assume that later motorists observe earlier ones' choices and payoffs (if not, they all herd on the M-route). This is what is called transparency here. If the first motorist's realized payoff falls below 0 (say -0.5), then the second motorist selects the I-route, resolving all residual uncertainty as far as the East Coast is concerned.

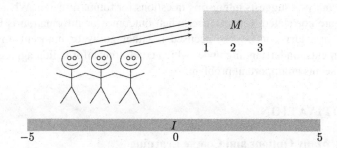

Figure 5 Experimentation cannot start if $\mathbf{E}[\pi_I] < a_M$.

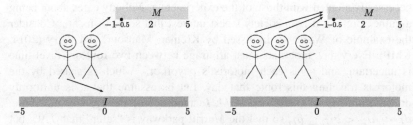

Figure 6 Choices of second and third agent under transparency.

---

[12] As all stories, this one has practical limitations. In particular, choices do not affect travel times. This ignores congestion. But as every user of I-95 or US-101 will attest, there are some things logic cannot explain.

However, if the early bird's realized payoff is 0.5, the second (as well as all later) motorist mimics the first, despite the potential benefits from the I-route. This is where Waze comes into play. Suppose that Waze commits to the following policy: it discloses to the second motorist whether the first motorist's travel time is below or above 1, and nothing more. If the realized payoff is 0.5, the second motorist is willing to experiment with the I-route nonetheless, as, on average, it still does as well as the M-route (0).

What if the first motorist's payoff is 1.5? The second motorist must be told that the early bird did well (more than 1 as a payoff), and so he will follow suit. The third motorist, however, need not be told what the second one was told. In particular, Waze can commit to tell him to take the M-route in one of two events. Either the second motorist took the M-route, as did the first, and their common realized travel time fell short of 2.33; or the early bird's travel time fell short of 1, so that the second experimented with the I-route, and the M-route turns out to be the faster one. Comparing these two possibilities, the choice of 2.33 as a threshold ensures that the third motorist is willing to experiment with the I-route if told so. And if he is not told to experiment (and neither were any of the first three), the fourth is willing to do so, so that, with four motorists or more, all uncertainty can be resolved, while making sure that each motorist remains sufficiently uncertain about the right choice that it is optimal for him to follow Waze's recommendation. See Figure 7 for an illustration.

KMP develop this logic further. With two actions and perfect learning, as in this example, the optimal recommendation mechanism has a simple partitional structure.[13] The partition pertains to the realized value of the interval $[a_M, b_M]$ (the safer action) into a collection of disjoint sets (not necessarily a partition, and not necessarily nonempty) $\mathcal{I}_1, \mathcal{I}_2, \ldots, \mathcal{I}_I$ with the property that, if the realized payoff of the first motorist is in $\mathcal{I}_i$, the i-th agent is the first to experiment with the action with the lower mean (and all later agents make the right choice). Partition strategies need not be optimal under stochastic learning,

Figure 7 Choices of the second and third agent under the optimal recommendation policy.

---

[13] The main focus of KMP is on the case in which the designer maximizes the expectation of the average (undiscounted) payoff of the agents, $I^{-1} \sum_{n=1}^{I} \pi^i$, where I is the number of agents and π^i is agent i's realized utility.

but KMP show that as the number of agents grows large, it does very well nonetheless (it is asymptotically optimal).

3.2   Few Options and Rich Learning

Sometimes once is not enough. Learning takes time, the early bird's reassurances notwithstanding. Let us follow Che and Hörner (2016) and assume that payoffs are coarse – either high (1) or low (0) – but learning is not. Specifically, if the state of the world is good, selecting the risky option is best for everyone, but few of those that have tried bother to let others know. Specifically, assume that, if and only if the state is good, (positive) feedback arrives at a random time, exponentially distributed with an intensity proportional to the (infinitesimal) mass of agents that consume at that point in time. That is, the rate at which feedback arrives is

$$\mathbf{P}[\text{positive feedback}] = \lambda \mu_t \cdot \omega dt,$$

where $\lambda > 0$ is some velocity parameter, μ_t is the fraction that consumes at time t, and $\omega = 0, 1$ is the state. Each consumer consumes at most once. A fraction $\rho > 0$ of consumers have a positive opportunity cost $c \in (p_0, 1)$ (*regular* agents), where p_0 is the probability that $\omega = 1$. The remaining agents (fans) have sufficiently unattractive outside options that they experiment no matter what, although they are just as critical in providing feedback. Because $c > p_0$, these are the only ones experimenting at the start. They are the seeds that jump-start the process. However, if Waze (or its equivalent) simply relays the feedback that these agents provide, if any, the remaining ρ fraction of agents remain on the sideline, unless positive feedback is reported. As a result, experimentation is too slow. To accelerate it, the designer may *spam* these agents, by recommending a fraction α_t of these agents that they try out the product. (Of course, this requires that these agents rely on the designer as their exclusive source of information.) The designer commits to this policy, and selects at random this fraction of guinea pigs. If one of the early consumers has reported that the payoff is high, the designer and consumers have aligned interests. If not, the designer's belief evolves according to

$$\dot{p}_t = -\lambda(1 - \rho + \rho\alpha_t)p_t(1 - p_t). \tag{3}$$

The designer can capitalize on the possibility that he has learnt the state to make spamming credible, provided that spamming is meted out proportionally to the likelihood of this event. Conditional on being told to consume, an agent's expected utility from consuming is

$$\frac{\frac{1-p_0}{1-p_t}\alpha_t p_t + \frac{p_0-p_t}{1-p_t} \cdot 1}{\frac{1-p_0}{1-p_t}\alpha_t + \frac{p_0-p_t}{1-p_t}} = \frac{(1 - p_0)p_t\alpha_t + (p_0 - p_t)}{(1 - p_0)\alpha_t + (p_0 - p_t)},$$

given that $(p_0 - p_t)/(1 - p_t)$ is the probability assigned by this consumer to the designer having learnt the state by time t, and $(1 - p_0)/(1 - p_t)$ is the complementary probability that he has not. Setting this equal to c, and solving for α_t, we obtain

$$\alpha_t = \frac{(1 - c)(p_0 - p_t)}{(1 - p_0)(c - p_t)}. \tag{4}$$

Spamming is not credible at the very beginning ($\alpha_0 = 0$) because it is virtually impossible that the designer has learnt something useful by then. But as time passes by, spamming becomes more credible, and the rate of spamming accelerates. Equations (3) and (4) provide a pair of equations that can be solved for the maximum spamming α, and the corresponding belief p.

However, if the designer is benevolent, spamming has to cease eventually. Persistent lack of feedback from consumers reinforces his belief that the payoff is low, so that experimentation has to stop. When? With only two types of agents, the threshold at which it stops coincides with the cutoff $\underline{p}$ that prevails absent the incentive constraint that constrains the amount of spamming. This is because, at the point at which experimentation with regular agents stops, the continuation game is identical to the one without incentive constraints: only fans experiment. As a result, the first-order condition that dictates when spamming ceases is the same in both problems. Incentives constrain the rate of experimentation from regular agents, but when considering when to stop, this rate is irrelevant for the marginal value of continuing for another instant.[14]

Overall, the pattern of experimentation over time is hump-shaped. Experimentation is most valuable at the start, but this is when the agents' suspicions prevent it from being in full swing. It then rises gradually as the designer's recommendations gain credibility, and finally tapers off as growing pessimism means that high-cost agents should not be carrying out such experimentation. See Figure 8.

An important assumption made so far in our discussion of these two papers is that recommendations are confidential. If spamming is public (reviews, endorsements, etc.), the designer is further constrained. In the last example, it is then optimal for the designer to behave as follows. If he gets feedback at any time, he tells everyone to experiment from that point on. If he fails to, he picks at random a time at which he claims that he did, and gets everyone to experiment from that point on, but only until some later time at which, if he still hasn't heard positive feedback, he concedes that his claim was unwarranted, and experimentation (from regular agents) stops. This spamming occurs at most once. The distribution over the random time is chosen to make experimentation start as early as possible, subject to the claim that he

---

[14] With more than two types, this reasoning carries over to the lowest type among those agents with a positive opportunity cost. But it does not apply to those with a higher cost. Because the rate of experimentation is too slow, the designer optimally chooses to spam such agents a little longer than he would absent incentive constraints. His reduced experimentation "capacity" in the continuation makes their willingness to partially experiment valuable, and he spams at beliefs below those at which they should in the unconstrained problem.

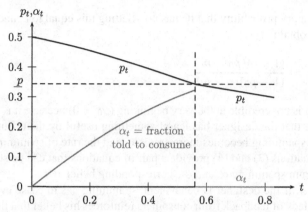

Figure 8 Experimentation rate and belief evolution.

received feedback being sufficiently credible that agents are willing to follow his recommendation over the next phase.

The models we have discussed so far assume that the principal's objective is to maximize social welfare. This may be the right objective for many recommender systems (like Waze, news websites recommending stories to read, or review websites recommending places to visit or apps to download) since the equilibrium with full information disclosure is likely to have inefficiently low experimentation because of the positive externality learning by early consumers has on later ones. That said, if the recommender's objective is to maximize the number of users (for example, because they can monetize traffic to their website) then the objective function can become more complicated, especially in the presence of competition between recommender platforms. That problem has been studied by He (2016). She considers differentiated platforms and agents making single-homing decisions about which one to join based on the experimentation and recommendation policies the platforms follow.

When agents choose platforms without knowing whether they will be early or late in the queue for recommendations, the optimal policy is to maximize efficiency of dynamic learning, consistent with what we have described so far. However, if agents have some information regarding whether they are likely to be early or late, then a new economic force appears. A platform attracts more early users by recommending the myopically optimal product/route instead of the dynamically efficient one (that takes into account the option value of learning and making better recommendations to future agents) in order to attract more early customers. The platform with a larger early market share can obtain a competitive advantage in the future because learning from more early consumers can lead to superior recommendations to future customers. He (2016) shows that a merger of the platforms can make the recommendation system more efficient, because a monopolist can internalize the business stealing effect.

4 DELEGATION

Information is only one of the many tools available to the principal. Authority is another. In two very different environments, Guo (2016) and Grenadier, Malenko, and Malenko (2015, GMM) examine the scope for and the structure of delegation in dynamic problems. In both papers, the direction of the conflict of interest (expressed in terms of timing of the optimal decision) changes the answer drastically. To understand why, we start with a simple example.

4.1　A Simple Example

Consider a simple cheap-talk model based on Crawford and Sobel (1982, CS).[15] We assume that the state is uniformly distributed on $[0, 1]$, and that preferences are quadratic. The receiver is unbiased, with preferences $-(t-y)^2$, where t is the state of the world (the sender's type) and $y \in \mathbf{R}_+$ is the action by the receiver. The sender has preferences $-(t - (y + b))^2$, where $b \in \mathbf{R}$. We distinguish (i) *positive* bias, $b > 0$, and (ii) *negative* bias, $b < 0$. Throughout we assume $|b| < 1/2$, for the problem to be interesting (babbling is the commitment solution otherwise). In CS, this distinction is irrelevant, as it is a matter of normalization. Here, instead, we assume that t also indexes time, and that, as time passes by, opportunities vanish. That is, if the receiver acts at time t, his available actions are elements of $Y_t = \{y \in \mathbf{R} : y \geq t\}$. Delaying is always an option, but acting can only take place once (it ends the game). We ignore any discounting or cost of delay, the possibility of never taking an action (add a large penalty for doing so) and leave aside the technical modeling details regarding continuous-time strategies. Let us think of the sender being able to send a message in $[0, 1]$ at any time t and impose standard measurability restrictions.

Because time flows from "left to right," we will argue that the positive and negative bias cases are very different: that is, admit very different sets of equilibria.

Positive Bias (Bias for Delay).　In that case, we claim that the receiver can do as well as under commitment in the standard model of CS in which types have no temporal meaning. The commitment case has been solved by Holmström (1984) and in greater generality by Melumad and Shibano (1991). It involves setting:

$$y(t) = \begin{cases} t + b & \text{if } t \leq 1 - 2b, \\ 1 - b & \text{if } t > 1 - 2b. \end{cases}$$

See Figure 9. We focus on the equilibrium that is best for the receiver.[16]

---

[15] A related example appears in a preliminary draft by Gordon and de Villemeur (2010).

[16] In CS, ex ante payoffs are aligned and so this also gives the highest payoff to the sender. But this is only true for any allocation in which the receiver takes his preferred action given his

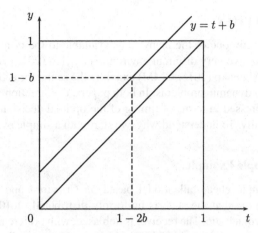

Figure 9 Optimal Delegation.

Why does this require no commitment? Time endows the receiver with the necessary power. When the sender tells him to act at time $t \leq 1-b$, the receiver learns that the state is $t - b$, but this action is no longer available. So the best he can then do is to take action t. Similarly, once time $1 - b$ arrives, he knows that the state is in $[1 - 2b, 1]$, and his expected action $1 - b$ matches what he would do in the next split second had perfect revelation continued – given that it won't, it remains optimal in the absence of information.

Note that (unlike in the commitment case) there are lots of other equilibria. For instance, babbling is always an equilibrium, and so are many other messaging strategies.

Negative Bias (Bias for Action).   With a negative bias, it is clear that the commitment optimum (which now involves a "floor" concerning types in $[0, 2|b|]$, pooled at b, and perfect separation over high types, who obtain $t-|b|$) is no longer incentive compatible. If a type $t \geq 2|b|$ reveals his type, the receiver can take action t if he can take action $t - |b|$, so that sequential rationality prevents him from taking the sender's optimal action.

Does this mean that we are back in the world of CS? In addition to the equilibria of CS, additional ones arise because of the role of time. For instance, consider a two-partition equilibrium, in which types in $[0, t_1]$ get mapped into action $y_1 > t_1/2$ and types in $(t_1, 1]$ get mapped into $y_2 = (1 + t_1)/2$. This can be achieved by waiting till time y_1 (messages are interpreted as "babble" until then), and then senders separating at time y_1 between those whose type is above t_1 and those whose type is below.[17] Type t_1 must be indifferent, which requires

---

information (which is not necessarily the case in our environment, in which there might be a lower bound on the action he can take).

[17] If senders do so by randomizing over $[0, t_1]$ or $(t_1, 1]$ depending on whether their type is above or below t_1 at time y_1, all messages are on path, so that what would happen if the sender

$$t_1 - b - y_1 = y_2 - (t_1 - b), \text{ or } y_1 = 2(t_1 - b) - y_2 = 2(t_1 - b) - (1 + t_1)/2.$$

The receiver must prefer waiting until time t_1 to acting at time $1/2$ (his favorite in the absence of any information), namely,

$$\int_0^1 (t - 1/2)^2 dt \geq \int_0^{t_1} (t - y_1)^2 dt + \int_{t_1}^1 (t - y_2)^2 dt$$

or

$$4t_1^2 - (3 + 16b)t_1 + 8b(1 + 2b) \leq 0,$$

an expression that reduces to $1/2 + 2b$ when $t_1 = (1 + 4b)/2$, the value of t_1 given the partition $\{[0, t_1], (t_1, 1]\}$ in the original CS-model. Hence, for $b < 1/4$ (the usual condition for non-babbling equilibria to exist in CS), we have a range of values of t_1, namely,

$$t_1 \in \left[\frac{1}{2} + 2b, \frac{1}{2} + 2b + \frac{1}{8} \left(\sqrt{9 - 32b} - 1 \right) \right],$$

for which such equilibria exist (this interval is nonempty by our assumption that $b < 1/4$).[18] But note that they are all worse than the original two-partition equilibrium of CS, as the higher value pushes t_1 above what it would have been if $y_1 = t_1/2$. The problem is that the lower interval is already too large, compared to the higher one.

It turns out that in our uniform-quadratic setup, this is a general feature: no pure-strategy equilibrium involving one-way communication improves on the best CS equilibrium.[19] This is because, first, and as in CS, an equilibrium must be partitional. Because the sender's preferences satisfy the single-crossing property, if types $t < t'$ are both mapped into the same outcome y, then so must all types in the interval $[t, t']$. Letting $[t, t']$ be the maximum interval associated with y, either $y = (t + t')/2$ because the receiver finds out about the sender being in that range before this time arrives, or $y > (t + t')/2$ because he learns about it at time y. Surely, the type $y + |b|$ is in the interval $[t, t']$ and so each interval is of length at least $2|b|$, and so there are finitely many intervals, $\mathcal{I}_1, \ldots, \mathcal{I}_K$. The action associated to the highest interval, $\mathcal{I}_K$, must be its midpoint, as it is best for the receiver to take if the time comes. Consider the problem of maximizing the receiver's expected utility over sequences $\{y_1, \ldots, y_K\}$, $t_0 = 0, \ldots, t_K = 1$, such that each y_k is at least as high as the midpoint of $\mathcal{I}_k$, and each $t_k - |b|$ is equidistant from y_k and y_{k-1}. It is easy to see that it is maximized at the midpoints.

---

deviated at time t_1 is irrelevant – the receiver will act at that time. And the receiver has nothing to gain from waiting any longer, if he expects no further meaningful information to be transmitted.

[18] This class of equilibria involves the standard CS equilibrium of partition size 2. The same argument applies to any CS equilibrium, independent of its partition size.

[19] Of course, one can do better with either a randomization device or the receiver talking as well, along the lines of long cheap-talk (Aumann and Hart, 2003), which becomes especially natural in this dynamic environment.

4.2   Economic Applications

Guo and GMM consider two dynamic principal-agent models in which there is uncertainty (an unknown state of the world) and risk (imperfect learning via the observation process, though in GMM the principal only learns via the agent's reports). In both models, the agent has private information that does not evolve over time. The principal and the agent have a conflict of interest. In Guo, it is an experimentation model in which the agent has a vested interest in playing risky or safe (depending on his bias), but also private information at the start regarding the viability of the project. In GMM, the principal faces a problem of real options (an irreversible investment decision) based on a publicly observable signal process (an exogenous geometric Brownian motion) that relates to the project's profitability via a factor that is the agent's private information.[20]

In both models, the principal designs an optimal mechanism, with or without commitment. The principal has authority, and can dictate the agent's choices based on his reports. It matters whether the agent's bias leads him to favor delaying the (optimally, irreversible) decision or not. If he enjoys a longer phase of learning, the principal has to counteract the agent's incentives to act too late; if he enjoys a shorter phase of learning, inefficiently early stopping/investment have to be prevented. This is the dichotomy already present in the simple example of the previous section.

In the case in which for any given prior belief the agent prefers to switch to the safe arm later than the principal, Guo shows that the optimal policy (from the principal's viewpoint) can be implemented by a *sliding rule*: based on the observed history, in which experimentation was pursued throughout by the agent, the principal updates his belief as if the agent was equally uninformed regarding the project's potential. There is a cutoff (in belief space) that he picks at which he dictates the agent to stop. Until then, the agent is free to stop on his own, which might happen if the agent's private information is so bad that earlier termination might be preferable from his point of view despite his bias. The simplicity of this rule is remarkable. Furthermore, as in our example, and for the same reasons, the principal needs no commitment to implement it. If he were free to grant authority to stop or continue experimentation at every moment, he would find it optimal to leave it up to the agent to decide up to the moment at which this threshold is being crossed.[21]

In GMM, the bias is exactly as in CS: upon exercise of the option to invest, the agent receives an additional b to the investment payoff. Positive bias means the agent is biased towards early exercise. As in our example, this implies that delegation dominates communication (at least in the simple class of equilibria with one-way communication, as described above). Indeed, GMM show that

---

[20] The main difference isn't Poisson vs. Brownian uncertainty. Rather, it lies in the updating. In Guo, the public signal is informative about the agent's type, whereas in GMM, it is not, which simplifies somewhat the updating.

[21] Guo also considers the case of bias toward early action, and also finds that the optimal contract with commitment is time-inconsistent and so can't be implemented without commitment.

such (stationary) equilibria involve a partition of the possible values of the signal process into intervals. The agent recommends that the principal invest as soon as the observable process enters a high enough interval, where "high enough" depends on his information. At that point, the principal invests. In contrast, when bias is negative, so that late exercise is favored by the agent, the outcome of delegation, which often involves full revelation, can also be achieved in the game with cheap talk and no commitment.

5 INFORMATION DESIGN

In this section, we abstract from exogenous learning. In the absence of a message by the informed player, the other player does not learn anything. At the same time, we enrich the model by allowing the state to change over time, and by endowing the informed player with a richer set of verifiable messages.

5.1 An Investment Example

A decision-maker (DM) must decide whether to invest ($a = I$) or not ($a = N$) in a project with uncertain returns. Her decision is a function of her belief in the state of the world $\omega = 0, 1$, with a return $r(\omega)$. Doing so is optimal if and only if $p = \mathbf{P}[\omega = 1] \geq p^*$. Accordingly, the invest region is $I = \{p : p \geq p^*\}$, see Figure 10. Unfortunately, the DM does not observe the state, and must rely on an advisor's goodwill to get information. The advisor receives a fixed payoff of 1 from investment. Our players are trained statisticians, not economists: they have no idea about the potential benefits of contractual payments, but know all about statistical experiments à la Blackwell. In particular, the advisor can commit to a splitting of his prior belief into an arbitrary distribution over posterior beliefs (a mean-preserving spread), with the DM only observing the realized posterior.[22] If the game is one-shot, the best experiment from the advisor's point of view is rather immediate. To maximize the probability that the DM invests, it is best to make the posterior belief that leads to an investment to be such that the DM is just indifferent, that is, equal to p^*, and the other posterior equal to 0.[23] See Figure 10. The resulting payoff is p^0/p^* (more generally, $\min\{1, p^0/p^*\}$, as $p^0 \gtrless p^*$). This is the celebrated concavification formula of Aumann and Maschler (1995), which states that the maximum payoff over possible splittings is equal to the smallest concave function no less than the payoff function given a belief (namely, $\min\{1, p^0/p^*\} = \mathrm{cav}\mathbf{1}_{\{p \geq p^*\}}(p^0)$).

We call the corresponding strategy *greedy*. The greedy strategy is the strategy that minimizes information revelation subject to maximizing the one-shot payoff. Formally, it is defined for environments in which there is a binary

---

[22] Note that the advisor need not observe the realized state, but somehow must have access to a technology that generates any posterior distribution.

[23] Such static problems are considered in greater generality by Rayo and Segal (2010), and Kamenica and Gentzkow (2011).

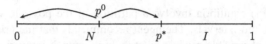

Figure 10 Investment as a function of the belief.

action (such as investing or not) and the payoff to be maximized (the advisor's) is independent of the true state, although it may depend on the action. Let us define the region of beliefs I for which investing is optimal from the DM's point of view (here, $[p^*, 1]$). Then the greedy strategy specifies that no information be disclosed if $p \in I$. Otherwise, it specifies that the DM be told one of two posteriors p_I and p_N, with weights λ and $1 - \lambda$ (so $p = \lambda p_I + (1 - \lambda) p_N$), with $p_I \in I$, in a way that maximizes the weight $\lambda \in [0, 1]$. Such a greedy strategy is generically unique and can be solved using linear programming.

Now suppose that the investment decision is repeated twice, yet the state is persistent: it remains the same with probability $\rho \geq 1/2$, and it switches with probability $1 - \rho$. Hence, the posterior belief, $\phi(p)$ lies somewhere between p and $1/2$, depending on ρ. The advisor's payoff is $\mathbf{1}_{\{a_1 = I\}} + \beta \mathbf{1}_{\{a_2 = I\}}$, where a_n is the action in round n, and $\beta \geq 0$ is the weight assigned to the second round.

To apply Aumann and Maschler's formula, we must compute the payoff $\pi(p)$, where p is the posterior belief of the DM *after* the splitting, but *before* the investment decision in the first round. Because at that stage, the DM invests if and only if $p \geq p^*$, $\pi(\cdot)$ jumps up by 1 at p^*, but this fixed benefit is sunk and simply added to what accrues from the second period. If $p \geq \phi^{-1}(p^*)$, then no information should be disclosed in the second period, because $\phi(p) \geq p^*$. In contrast, disclosing additional information is optimal if $p < \phi^{-1}(p^*)$. As is clear from the left panel in Figure 11, the graph of the resulting payoff differs markedly according to whether $p^* \gtrless 1/2$ (equivalently, $p^* \gtrless \phi^{-1}(p^*)$). In case $p^* > 1/2$ the optimal strategy is greedy for all β. The intuition is as follows. The best case scenario for period 2 payoffs is when the agent reveals nothing in period 1. In that case, since $\phi(p) < p^*$, the optimal disclosure in period 2 is to split the belief between p^* and 0. Now consider the agent following the greedy strategy in the first period, which also induces beliefs 0 and p^*. After that, whatever the interim beliefs, in the beginning of the second stage, the beliefs are less than p^* and in both cases it is optimal to induce posteriors of 0 and p^*. Since in that range the payoff function is linear in beliefs, there is no cost for second-period payoffs if the agent is greedy in the first period. In contrast, if $1/2 > p^*$, greedy is optimal only if β is sufficiently small, because if $p^* < 1/2$ then if the belief at the end of period 1 is p^* then the belief at the beginning of period 2 is above p^* and hence disclosure in period one creates a probability distribution over period-2 beliefs on a concave part of the value function. So in this case there is a trade-off between maximizing period-1 and period-2 payoffs.

Figure 12 shows why the greedy strategy is no longer optimal once β is large enough. For $p < \phi^{-1}(p^*)$, the optimal strategy consists in releasing just enough information for the posterior belief to be equal to $\phi^{-1}(p^*)$. Hence, in

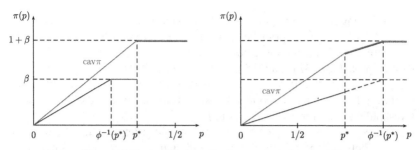

Figure 11 Optimal strategy in the two-period example.

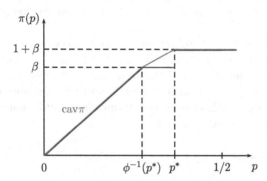

Figure 12 Greedy is not optimal when β is large.

this example, the optimality of the greedy strategy breaks down if the future is important enough, and beliefs drift towards the interior of the investment region. This is easy to understand: if beliefs drift outwards, as on the right panel of Figure 11, then both splittings according to the greedy strategy, and movements due to mean-reversion keep all beliefs inside the region over which π is linear. Given the martingale property of beliefs, this ensures that there is no loss in using the greedy strategy. Once beliefs drift towards the investment region, splitting the belief all the way to p^* leads to a cost for the future, as mean-reversion pushes the posterior belief into a range over which π no longer shares the same slope than in the range where the prior belief lies.

How robust is the optimality of the greedy strategy? Remarkably, Renault, Solan, and Vieille (2015, RSV) show that, in the infinitely (discounted) repeated investment game, the greedy strategy is optimal for an arbitrary two-state irreducible Markov chain. Despite the fact that the future may outweigh the present, stationarity ensures that the scenario depicted in Figure 11 does not occur, or rather that, whenever the intertemporal cost cannot be avoided, the greedy strategy achieves the best trade-off.

Despite this remarkable result, the conditions under which the greedy strategy is optimal are very special. Suppose, for instance, that some extraneous public signal, obtained at the beginning of each of the two rounds, determines whether $p^* = 0.2$ or 0.8, with both being equally likely, but independent across rounds. To simplify, we assume that $\rho = 1$, so that the state is the same in both rounds. Let $p^0 = 0.2$. Suppose that $p^* = 0.8$ in the first round. By not disclosing any information in the first round, the advisor receives a pay-off of $\beta/2$, because the prior belief suffices tomorrow, with probability $1/2$. In contrast, by following the greedy strategy, the advisor splits the prior into 0 (with probability $3/4$) and 0.8 (with probability $1/4$), resulting in a payoff of $(1 + \beta)/4 < \beta/2$ if $\beta > 1$. Hence, the greedy strategy is not optimal if the future is sufficiently important. If the DM invests once and only once, the threshold patience further decreases to $\beta \geq 1/2$.

This example relies on p^* being random, which implies that the relevant distance between the prior belief and the boundary of the investment region might become more favorable by waiting, rather than giving away information. The same phenomenon arises without randomness, by simply considering more states.

Indeed, RSV construct the following three-state counter-example, illustrated in Figure 13. The horizon is infinite, and the discount factor is $\delta < 1$. The DM invests in the light-gray area, the triangle with summits ω^*, ω_1, $\varepsilon\omega_1 + (1 - \varepsilon)\omega_2$, where $\varepsilon > 0$ is a small number. Suppose that the prior is p_1 and the state's persistence is $1/2$, so that given the invariant distribution ω_2, the belief absent any disclosure after one round is

$$\frac{1}{2}p_1 + \frac{1}{2}\omega_2 = \varepsilon\omega_1 + \frac{1}{2}\omega_2 + (\frac{1}{2} - \varepsilon)\omega_3.$$

The greedy strategy calls for a splitting between ω_3, and ω^*, with probability 4ε on ω^*. The resulting payoff is $4\varepsilon\omega^* < 4\varepsilon$. By waiting one round and split-ting the resulting belief between p_2 (with probability $1/(2(1 - \varepsilon)))$ and p_3, the resulting payoff is $1/(2(1 - \varepsilon))$, so that, as long as $4\varepsilon < \delta(1 - \delta)/(2(1 - \varepsilon))$, the latter strategy dominates.

5.2   Beeps

Ely (2015) tells the following relatable story of "beeps" to motivate the optimal design of information disclosure. A researcher clears her email inbox and

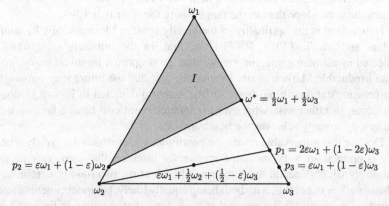

Figure 13 Greedy is not optimal with three states.

begins to work productively at her desk. She believes that emails arrive according to a known stochastic process, and she feels compelled to stop working and check her email when her belief v that a new email has arrived is strictly greater than some threshold $p^* \in (0, 1)$. Assume the researcher gets utility from working but not from checking email since she will become distracted on her computer (so in this stylized example, her compulsion to check email is purely pathological). Her discount rate is $r > 0$.

The researcher can set up her computer to produce an audible beep when an email is received. Perhaps surprisingly, this "distraction" may actually increase the expected time until the researcher checks her email. The beep will compel the researcher to immediately check her email (since her posterior belief μ will jump to 1), but the knowledge that the beep mechanism is enabled (and functional) allows her to work indefinitely with the certainty that no email has arrived, as long as she has not heard a beep. Many other beeping mechanisms are imaginable, so the question naturally arises: What informational filtering policy maximizes the expected discounted time until the agent checks her email?

The set of states is $\Omega = \{0, 1\}$ indicating whether or not an email has arrived, so state 1 is absorbing. Emails arrive at Poisson rate λ, but we work in discrete time with periods of length Δ. Hence, the transition probability from state 0 to state 1 is $m := 1 - e^{-\lambda \Delta}$. Let μ_t (v_t) denote the agent's posterior belief, at time t before (after) receiving the principal's message, that an email has arrived. According to Bayesian updating, when the agent does not receive new information her beliefs obey the following law of motion:

$$\mu_{t+1} = f(v_t) = v_t + m(1 - v_t).$$

In the initial state, we assume no emails have arrived so it is common knowledge that $\mu_0 = v_0 = 0$. The agent checks her email iff $v_t > p^*$. The principal's utility can be expressed directly as a function of the agent's posterior belief:

$$u(v) = \begin{cases} 1 & \text{if } v \leq p^*, \\ 0 & \text{if } v > p^*. \end{cases}$$

The principal's discount factor is $\delta = e^{-r\Delta}$. The principal commits to an information disclosure policy, so the agent always interprets the principal's messages correctly.

The solution to this problem is an immediate corollary of the optimality of the greedy strategy, as established by RSV.[24] Here, it is straightforward to compute.

---

[24] Since this model of beeps satisfies the conditions of Theorem 5 in RSV, it follows that the greedy strategy is optimal for any initial distribution, in particular, for the choice of $\mu_0 = v_0 = 0$. Indeed, this example of beeps is formally equivalent to the investment model in RSV in which the agent's state-dependent payoff from investing $r : \Omega \to \mathbf{R}$ is given by $r(0) = \frac{p^*}{1-p^*}$ and $r(1) = -1$. For then the agent invests and hence the principal receives payoff 1 if and only if $0 \leq r(v) = -v + (1 - v)p^*/(1 - p^*)$, i.e., $v \leq p^*$.

Case 1: $\mu \leq p^*$. Since the agent is taking the desired action (working), the principal releases no information.

Case 2: $\mu > p^*$. The principal chooses the greedy binary splitting at μ, i.e., the agent solves max a_I under the constraints $\mu = a_I p_I + a_N p_N$, over probabilities p_I, p_N, and weights a_I, a_N, with $p_I \leq p^*, a_I, a_N \geq 0, a_I + a_N = 1$. It is easy to see that the maximum is achieved by $p_I = p^*$ and $p_N = 1$, so that

$$a_I = \frac{1 - \mu}{1 - p^*}, \quad a_N = \frac{\mu - p^*}{1 - p^*}.$$

Therefore the principal should release two different messages, one that keeps the agent's beliefs at p^* and one that sends the agent's belief to 1.

Just because the greedy strategy is not robust does not imply that there are no interesting economic settings in which it is optimal. Ely provides a few such examples. More generally, however, little is known on the structure of the optimal strategy. Plainly, the principal's problem is a standard Markov decision problem, where the state variable is the agent's posterior belief, and the control is any splitting over beliefs. Hence, in the discounted case, it suffices to solve the optimality equation

$$V(\mu_t) = \max_{\substack{p \in \Delta(\Delta(\Omega)) \\ E_p v_t = \mu_t}} E_p[(1 - \delta)u(v_t) + \delta V(f(v_t))],$$

or, in Aumann and Maschler's compact notation,

$$V = \text{cav}[(1 - \delta)u + \delta(V \circ f)],$$

with the obvious definitions. Well-known numerical methods exist to solve such a functional equation (e.g., value iteration, the method used by Ely; but also policy iteration, linear programming, etc.). Perhaps structural properties of the optimal policy can be found in some interesting classes of models (supermodular preferences, first-order stochastic dominance on the state transitions).[25]

5.3   Design without commitment

Consider now the game between a firm and a regulator analyzed in Orlov, Skrzypacz, and Zryumov (2016) (OSZ). The firm sells a product (say, a medical device) that is either safe or unsafe. While the product is on the market, the firm and the regulator observe noisy information about user experience, and update their beliefs about the safety of the product. The regulator has the power to recall the product from the market, at which point learning stops (or the reputation of the product is sufficiently tarnished that the firm cannot

---

[25] By now, there are some papers deriving the optimal policy in some specific contexts. Smolin (2015), for instance, considers a related problem, with the twist that the agent's action affect transitions.

reintroduce it to the market without a major redesign). From the regulator's point of view, this is a real options problem. The firm and regulator incentives are partially aligned. They agree that only a safe product should be left on the market. They differ in their patience, or relative costs of type-one and type-two errors. Assume that the optimal stopping belief for the firm would be higher than for the regulator, so that the firm would like to experiment longer than the regulator. While the regulator has the decision power, the firm has control over the collection of additional information. Namely, there is a binary random variable that is correlated with the safety of the product and the firm can perform experiments to reveal information about that additional signal. The information collection technology is as before: the firm freely chooses a posterior distribution over the signal, subject to a martingale constraint. Importantly, whatever the firm learns, it has to disclose, even if it is ex post not in its best interest. As a result, even though information is valuable, the firm may decide not to learn some information (at least for a while) to persuade the regulator to wait a bit longer.

There are several differences between this model and the two discussed previously. First, the firm and the regulator have no commitment power. The paper analyzes Markov Perfect equilibria, with the joint belief about the safety of the drug and the realization of the noisy signal as state variables. Second, the sender's preferred action depends on the state. Third, the regulator's strategy is not a fixed belief cutoff, but a best reply to the firm's information strategy. Finally, beliefs move stochastically in response to public news, even in the absence of disclosure by the receiver.

The resulting equilibrium dynamics depend on the size of the conflict between the firm and regulator. If the conflict is small (as measured by the difference in autarky threshold beliefs, that is, the optimal stopping beliefs when only public news are available), then the firm postpones learning about the additional signal until a belief is reached, at which bad news about the signal moves the posterior belief about the safety to the firm's optimal exercise point. At that belief it is an optimal strategy for the firm to fully reveal the additional information: if the news is bad, it gets its optimal stopping implemented; if it is good, the regulator postpones a recall as much as possible. In equilibrium, the regulator has ex post regret for waiting too long if the news is bad. But if the news is good, the posterior is strictly below his exercise threshold, so waiting is optimal ex post. In equilibrium, information disclosure is inefficiently late from the regulator's viewpoint. The firm manages to make the regulator wait (for some parameters, even pass his autarky threshold) because the discrete full revelation of the signal is credible and valuable to the regulator. In equilibrium, some recalls are forced by the regulator (after good news about the signal followed by bad public news) and some are voluntary (after bad signal realizations), so the firm is able to persuade the regulator into a form of a compromise.

When the difference in preferences between the two players is large, waiting for such full information disclosure is no longer sufficiently valuable to the regulator, and the equilibrium changes dramatically. When the regulator's belief reaches the autarky threshold, the firm "pipets" information about the signal, leading to either a reflection of beliefs at this threshold, or a discrete jump to reveal bad news. That is reminiscent of the greedy strategy above: the firm reveals the smallest amount of information to keep the regulator in the "no-recall" region, an equivalent of the "investment" region in the previous papers. Such persuasion is profitable for the firm (it manages to keep the product longer on the market), but somewhat paradoxically has no value for the regulator (his equilibrium payoff is the same as if no extra signal was available). The intuition comes from the real-options literature: the regulator's autarky value function satisfies smooth pasting condition at the exercise threshold. Since the firm's optimal strategy "pipets" information, it induces beliefs only on the linear part of the regulator's value function and that creates no value.

This stylized model can also reflect internal organization problems in which there is a conflict of interest about timing of exercise of a real option (as in Grenadier, Malenko, and Malenko, 2015 or Guo, 2016) and one agent has decision rights and another one can credibly disclose additional noisy information about the state. In some cases, the agent would like to exercise the option sooner (for example, if it is a decision when to launch a product). OSZ show that the agent then immediately reveals all information about the noisy signal and can be hurt by having access to the information. If the receiver expects full immediate information disclosure, it is rational for him to wait. Hence, an impatient sender is better off revealing the information immediately.

6 RICHER WORLDS

A significant shortcoming of all papers reviewed so far is the restriction to two independent arms. This is probably not the best way to think of the process of discovery and innovation. There are not simply two ways to go, but many, and trying out a new technique close to an existing one is likely to yield similar results. In contrast, trying out a very different technique is risky, but may pay big. Several models attempt to model such environments. These include Akcigit and Liu (2016), Bonatti and Rantakari (2016), Garfagnini and Strulovici (2016), Callander and Matouschek (2015). Here, we showcase Callander (2011).

Callander introduces the following model of learning by trial and error. There is a continuum of products that can be tried, $p \in \mathbf{R}$. Each product is mapped into some outcome, $W(p) \in \mathbf{R}$, and entails a cost $W(p)^2$.

At the start, the value of one and only one product is known, p_0^*, with value $W(p_0^*) > 0$. The player's belief about $W(\cdot)$ is modeled as a two-sided Wiener process. That is, we have two independent one-dimensional Wiener processes $W_- = (W_-(p) : p \geq 0)$ and $W_+ = (W_+(p) : p \geq 0)$, with parameters $(-\mu, \sigma)$ and (μ, σ) respectively, and initial value $W_-(0) = W_+(0) = W(p_0^*)$, and we define

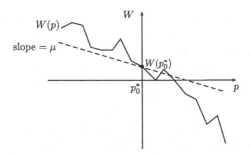

Figure 14 Products and possible outcomes.

$$W(p) = \begin{cases} W_+(p - p_0^*) & \text{if } p \geq p_0^*, \\ W_-(p_0^* - p) & \text{if } p < p_0^*. \end{cases}$$

It is assumed that $\mu < 0$. See Figure 14. Trying out a given p reveals the corresponding value of $W(p)$.

What values of p should be sampled? This is a difficult problem, already interesting when the agent is myopic (a sequence of entrepreneurs, each with one chance only), the focus of Callander's analysis. In a given round n, after history h^n, the entrepreneur chooses p so as to minimize $\mathbf{E}[W(p) \mid h^n]^2 + \mathbf{Var}[W(p) \mid h^n]$.[26] Let $\bar{p}, \underline{p}$ denote the highest and lowest value of p_m for $m < n$ along that history. Because $\mu \leq 0$,

$$p < \underline{p} \quad \Rightarrow \quad \mathbf{E}[W(p) \mid h^n]^2 + \mathbf{Var}[W(p) \mid h^n] > W(\underline{p})^2.$$

Hence, by induction, no value of $p < p_0^*$ is ever chosen. Note that the same argument implies that if $W(\bar{p}) \leq 0$, then choosing a product $p > \bar{p}$ is strictly worse than choosing $\bar{p}$. Hence, if a product p is ever chosen so that $p = \bar{p}$ and $W(p) \leq 0$, no product to the right of $\bar{p}$ will ever be sampled.

Next, notice that $p_m < p_{m'}$ are consecutive products (that is, no product in between their values has been chosen along that history), and sgn $W(p_m) =$ sgn $W(p_{m'})$, then

$$p \in (p_m, p_{m'}) \Rightarrow \mathbf{E}[W(p) \mid h^n]^2 + \mathbf{Var}[W(p) \mid h^n]$$
$$> \min\{W(p_m)^2, W(p_{m'})^2\}.$$

Hence also, if $p_m < p_{m'}$ are tried products, with sgn $W(p_m) =$ sgn $W(p_{m'})$, and all products $p \in (p_m, p_{m'})$ that were ever chosen are such that sgn $W(p) =$ sgn $W(p_m)$. Then, if a product is ever chosen again in the interval $(p_m, p_{m'})$, it must be a known product, namely a product that minimizes the cost among those known products.

This leaves us with two cases: (i) trying a product $p > \bar{p}$, and (ii) trying a product in an interval $(p_m, p_{m'})$ of consecutive products such that sgn $W(p_m) \neq$ sgn $W(p_{m'})$. Note that in that case it must be that $W(p_m) >$

[26] This is because $\mathbf{E}[X^2] = \mathbf{E}[X]^2 + \mathbf{Var}[X]$.

$0 > W(p_{m'})$ (if one is 0 it is clearly optimal to choose it forever). This is because, by our previous observations, products to the right of a product with sgn $W(p) = -1$ are never chosen. Hence, the only configuration that can arise in which there are tried products with both negative and positive values must be such that all products with negative values lie to the right of the products with positive value.

Choosing a product $p > \bar{p}$:   Consider first trying a product at the "frontier," that is, larger than any product tried so far. As discussed, we may assume $W(\bar{p}) > 0$, otherwise such a choice cannot be optimal. We must solve

$$\min_{p \geq \bar{p}} \left\{ \mathbf{E}[W(p) \mid h^n]^2 + \mathbf{Var}[W(p) \mid h^n] \right\}$$
$$= \min_{p \geq \bar{p}} \left\{ (W(\bar{p}) + \mu(p - \bar{p}))^2 + (p - \bar{p})\sigma^2 \right\},$$

clearly, a convex function in p, with first-order condition

$$\mu(p - \bar{p}) = -\frac{\sigma^2}{2\mu} - W(\bar{p}),$$

which is positive if and only if

$$W(\bar{p}) > -\frac{\sigma^2}{2\mu} =: \alpha.$$

(Recall that $\mu < 0$.) Hence, such a choice is only a candidate to optimality if $W(\bar{p}) > \alpha$; if it is chosen, it is set so that

$$\mathbf{E}[W(p)] = W(\bar{p}) + \mu(p - \bar{p}) = \alpha.$$

In particular, this must be the optimal choice p_1^* in the first period $n = 1$ if $W(p_0^*) > \alpha$. (Interestingly, p_1^* is single-peaked in μ.) See left panel in Figure 15. Otherwise, $p_n = p_0^*$ for all $n \geq 1$, as the first outcome is "good enough."

Note that the cost of choosing this candidate is (plugging in the first-order condition into the objective)

$$2\alpha W(\bar{p}) - \alpha^2.$$

Hence the relevant comparison is whether this is larger than the cost of the best alternative so far. In particular, this choice is dominated by the product $p = \arg\min\{W(p_m)^2 : m = 0, \ldots, n - 1\}$ if and only if

$$W(\bar{p}) > \frac{\bar{W}^2 + \alpha^2}{2\alpha},$$

where $\bar{W} = W(p)$.

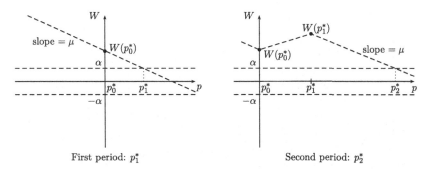

Figure 15 Exploration phase.

Choosing a product $p \in (p_m, p_{m'})$, **where** $\operatorname{sgn} W(p_m) \neq \operatorname{sgn} W(p_{m'})$**:**
Recall that we may assume that no product in the interval $(p_m, p_{m'})$ has ever
been tried so far, and that $W(p_m) > 0 > W(p_{m'})$. This means that we can
assume that

$$\frac{W(p_{m'}) - W(p_m)}{p_{m'} - p_m} < -\mu.$$

That is, the line connecting the points $(p_m, W(p_m))$ and $(p_{m'}, W(p_{m'}))$ is
steeper than the drift line of the Wiener process. This is because of our earlier analysis: when $p_{m'}$ was chosen, it was picked either as the rightest product
so far, in which case the resulting negative value (relative to a positive expected
value of α) means that the slope is indeed steeper. Or it was not the rightest
product, but then it was to the left of the first product that resulted in a negative
value, meaning that the slope is even steeper.

We must minimize

$$\left(W(p_m) + \frac{p - p_m}{p_{m'} - p_m}(W(p_{m'}) - W(p_m)) \right)^2 + \frac{(p - p_m)(p_{m'} - p)}{p_{m'} - p_m}\sigma^2,$$

which gives as candidate the solution to

$$\mathbf{E}[W(p) \mid h^n] = \mu(p_m, p_{m'}) \left(1 - 2\frac{p - p_m}{p_{m'} - p_m} \right),$$

$$\text{where } \mu(p_m, p_{m'}) := -\frac{\sigma^2}{2\frac{W(p_{m'}) - W(p_m)}{p_{m'} - p_m}},$$

which is verified to improve (in expectations) on $p_{m'}$ if and only if

$$-W(p_{m'}) > \mu(p_m, p_{m'}).$$

Of course, one must additionally compare this expected payoff to the payoff
$\bar{W}$ of the best product so far. The specific conditions are tedious, but with
probability one, this process (of "triangulation") stops. See Figure 16.

To summarize, the game always starts with an exploratory phase, in which
new products (to the right of the existing ones) are chosen. This process might
stop, with the agent settling on the one with the best performance (which need

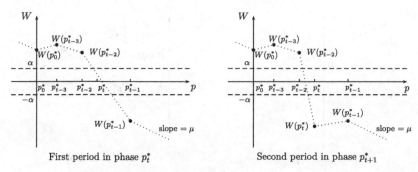

First period in phase p_t^* Second period in phase p_{t+1}^*

Figure 16 Triangulation phase, first and second step.

not be the one furthest to the right). If at some point in the exploratory phase, a negative outcome results, the policy shifts to a triangulation phase, picking either a new product within the unique interval of products over which the realized values change sign, or the best product so far. Eventually, search stops.

It would be interesting to see how these dynamics change when entrepreneurs are forward-looking. Solving Callander's model for patient agents is an important open problem in this area.

References

Akcigit, U., and Q. Liu (2016). "The Role of Information in Innovation and Competition," *Journal of the European Economic Association*, **14**, 828–70.

Aumann, R.J. and S. Hart (2003). "Long Cheap Talk," *Econometrica*, **71**, 1619–60.

Aumann, R.J., and M. Maschler (1995). *Repeated Games with Incomplete Information*, MIT Press.

Bimpikis, K., S. Ehsani, and M. Mostagir (2016). "Designing Dynamic Contests?" working paper.

Bolton, P., and C. Harris (1999). "Strategic Experimentation," *Econometrica*, **67**, 349–74.

Bonatti, A., and J. Hörner (2011). "Collaborating," *American Economic Review*, **101**, 632–63.

Bonatti, A., and J. Hörner (2015). "Learning to Disagree in a Game of Experimentation," working paper, Cowles Foundation for Research in Economics.

Bonatti, A., and H. Rantakari (2016). "The Politics of Compromise," *American Economic Review*, **106**, 229–59.

Callander, S. (2011). "Searching and Learning by Trial and Error," *American Economic Review*, **101**, 2277–308.

Callander, S., and N. Matouschek (2015). "Managing on Rugged Landscapes," working paper, Stanford GSB.

Campbell, A., F. Ederer, and J. Spinnewijn (2014). "Delay and Deadlines: Freeriding and Information Revelation in Partnerships," *American Economic Journal: Microeconomics*, **6**, 163–204.

Che, Y.-K., and J. Hörner (2016). "Optimal Design for Social Learning," working paper, Cowles Foundation for Research in Economics.

Cohen, A., and E. Solan (2013). "Bandit Problems with Levy Processes," *Mathematics of Operations Research*, **38**, 92–107.

Crawford, V., and J. Sobel (1982). "Strategic Information Transmission," *Econometrica*, **50**, 1431–51.

Cripps, M., and C. Thomas (2015). "Strategic Experimentation in Queues," working paper, UCL.

Das, K. (2015). "The Role of Heterogeneity in a Model of Strategic Experimentation," working paper, University of Exeter.

Ely, J. (2015). "Beeps," working paper, Northwestern University.

Frick, M., and Y. Ishii (2015). "Innovation Adoption by Forward-Looking Social Learners," working paper, Harvard.

Garfagnini, U., and B. Strulovici (2016). "Social Experimentation with Interdependent and Expanding Technologies," *Review of Economic Studies*, forthcoming.

Gordon, S., C. Marlats, and L. Ménager (2015). "Observation Delays in Teams," working paper, Paris.

Gordon, S., E.B. de Villemeur (2010). "Strategic Advice on a Timing Decision," draft, Montréal.

Grenadier, S., A. Malenko, and N. Malenko (2015). "Timing Decisions in Organizations: Communication and Authority in a Dynamic Environment," working paper, MIT.

Guo, Y. (2016). "Dynamic Delegation of Experimentation," *American Economic Review*, **106**, 1969–2008.

He, Johanna (2016). "Competition in Social Learning", working paper, Stanford University.

Heidhues, P., S. Rady, and P. Strack (2015). "Strategic Experimentation with Private Payoffs," *Journal of Economic Theory*, **159**, 531–51.

Holmström, J. (1984). "On The Theory of Delegation," in *Bayesian Models in Economic Theory*, eds. M. Boyer and R. Kihlstrom, Amsterdam: North-Holland Publishing Co.

Hörner, J., N. Klein, and S. Rady (2015). "Strongly Symmetric Equilibria in Bandit Games," working paper, Yale University.

Kamenica, E., and M. Gentzkow (2011). "Bayesian Persuasion," *American Economic Review*, **101**, 2590–615.

Keller, G., and S. Rady (2010). "Strategic Experimentation with Poisson Bandits," *Theoretical Economics*, **5**, 275–311.

Keller, G., and S. Rady (2015). "Breakdowns," *Theoretical Economics*, **10**, 175–202.

Keller, G., S. Rady, and M. Cripps (2005). "Strategic Experimentation with Exponential Bandits," *Econometrica*, **73**, 39–68.

Khromenkova, D. (2015). "Collective Experimentation with Breakdowns and Breakthroughs," working paper, Mannheim University.

Klein, N., and S. Rady (2011). "Negatively Correlated Bandits," *Review of Economic Studies*, **78**, 693–792.

Kremer, I., Y. Mansour, and M. Perry (2014). "Implementing the 'Wisdom of the Crowd'," *Journal of Political Economy*, **122**, 988–1012.

Melumad, N., and T. Shibano (1991). "Communication in Settings With No Transfers," *RAND Journal of Economics*, **22**, 173–98.

Murto, P., and J. Välimäki (2011). "Learning and Information Aggregation in an Exit Game," *The Review of Economic Studies*, **78**, 1426–61.

Murto, P., and J. Välimäki (2013). "Delay and Information Aggregation in Stopping Games With Private Information," *Journal of Economic Theory*, **148**, 2404–35.

Orlov, D., A. Skrzypacz and P. Zryumov (2016). "Persuading the Regulator to Wait," working paper, Stanford GSB.

Rayo, L., and I. Segal (2010). "Optimal Information Disclosure," *Journal of Political Economy*, **118**, 949–87.

Renault, J., E. Solan, and N. Vieille (2015). "Optimal Dynamic Information Provision," working paper, arXiv:1407.5649.

Rosenberg, D., A. Salomon, and N. Vieille (2013). "On Games of Strategic Experimentation," *Games and Economic Behavior*, **82**, 31–51.

Rosenberg, D., E. Solan, and N. Vieille (2007). "Social Learning in One-Armed Bandit Problems," *Econometrica*, **75**, 1591–611.

Smolin, A. (2015). "Optimal Feedback Design," working paper, Yale University.

Strulovici, B. (2010). "Learning while Voting: Determinants of Collective Experimentation," *Econometrica*, **78**, 933–71.

Thomas, C. (2015). "Strategic Experimentation with Congestion," working paper, The University of Texas at Austin.

CHAPTER 3

Dynamic Selection and Reclassification Risk: Theory and Empirics

Igal Hendel

This chapter surveys the theory and evidence on contracting under learning and imperfect commitment. We present a simple model of long-term insurance à la Harris and Holmstrom (1982) to show the relevance and insights of the theory. Different variations of the model encompass many situations that have been studied in diverse areas of Economics, including Labor, Finance, and Insurance.

The model is useful for understanding issues such as dynamic selection and reclassification risk. Imperfect commitment is shown to be the source of adverse selection and partial insurance in environments with learning, even when information is symmetric.

The empirical literature has looked at the testable implications regarding selection and optimal contracts. Recent work has focused on the welfare loss from lack of commitment, which has been found to be substantial. The theory offers policy prescriptions on how to contend with the market distortions associated with limited commitment.

1 INTRODUCTION

The provision of insurance is one of the main determinants of how societies organize and regulate economic activity. Since insurance may create perverse incentives, different economic systems – and forms of capitalism – represent distinct alternatives over such trade-offs. The provision of long-term insurance requires commitment to prevent the exclusion of those with the most unfortunate realizations and maintain participation of the most fortunate. Such interactions between insurance provision, incentives, and commitment have been central to the contract theory literature since the 1980s.

Support from NSF grant SES-1259770 and comments from Alessandro Lizzeri, Soheil Ghilli, Victoria Marone, Ariel Pakes, Bernard Salanié, and Steve Tadelis are gratefully acknowledged.

Economists have studied the provision of long-term insurance in the context of labor contracts (Harris and Holmstrom, 1982; Holmstrom, 1983), insurance markets (Pauly, Kunreuther and Hirth, 1995), consumption and savings (Hall, 1978), as well as development economics, where villagers who lack sophisticated financial instruments may rely on mutual insurance within the village (Townsend, 1994). These agency problems arise between firms and customers, firms and employees, or among firms.

This chapter surveys the empirical literature on dynamic contracting. We focus on long-lasting relations between parties, in which the dynamics are driven by information revelation. Evolving information generates gains from long-term contracts to cope with reclassification risk. Reclassification risk is a concern in many markets, such as health or life insurance. The literature is useful for understanding insurance provision and market design.

Empirical work on dynamic contracting is sparse.[1] The typical challenge to empirical work on contracting, even in static situations, is the nature of the agency problem. Agency conflicts arise when critical information on types or actions is not observed by one of the parties. Typically, researchers are only as informed as the least informed party, which renders empirical work difficult. Dealing with dynamic agency relations entails clearing additional hurdles. In dynamic agency problems, the challenge is compounded by the fragility of the theory. Theoretical predictions are quite sensitive to the specific institutions. Commitment, renegotiation, timing, and the extent of information revelation over time have substantial impact on predictions. The theory's sensitivity can help leverage the empirics. For example, the sharply distinct predictions under different forms of learning (more on this in the next paragraph) can guide empirical strategies. However, empirical researchers face the challenge of finding situations and data with clean institutional arrangements that can be properly mapped into the appropriate testable predictions.

The literature has considered situations with symmetric and asymmetric learning. Learning is symmetric when all parties remain equally informed as new information arrives. An example of symmetric learning is health insurance, when all potential insurers have equal access to prior diagnostics and treatment information. This is also typically the case in life insurance; all parties use the same information in underwriting (assuming the risk). Alternatively, learning is asymmetric if only the current insurer has access to such information. This is the case when automobile insurers do not share accident histories. The current insurer, who observes the insuree's record, is at an informational advantage relative to competitors.

---

[1] While empirics lagged behind Contract Theory, there is now a large empirical literature on static contracting, mainly focusing on informational asymmetries. For example, Cardon and Hendel (2001), Chiappori and Salanié (2001), and Cohen (2005) test for asymmetric information in different insurance markets. Later work quantified the welfare costs of adverse selection (Einav et al., 2013 and Handel et al., 2015) in health insurance markets. Handel et al. (2015) studied equilibrium and welfare under different contracting regulations, such as rules on pricing pre-existing conditions.

Evolving information may lead to reclassification risk, dynamic selection, and their respective inefficiencies. Long-term contracts play a critical role in market performance. Consider the example of health insurance coverage at, say, age 50. Spot contracts insure the event risk associated with uncertain health expenses. By the time the spot market opens, however, quite a bit of information might be known about the insuree's expected health expenses. Since premiums depend on expected costs, spot contracts fail to insure the risk associated with the information revealed before the market opens. Premium insurance could be transacted before the type is known – say, at age 25 – only if long-term contracts are feasible. The role and viability of long-term contracts depends on the nature of commitment to the contract by firms and consumers. If information is ex ante symmetric, full commitment (by both parties) yields efficiency. Parties can design a contract that equates marginal utility from consumption over time and states.

For legal and practical reasons, in most markets commitment is at best one-sided (unilateral). Firms can be held accountable, but consumers can walk away from the relationship without penalties (more on this later). The study of optimal unilateral contracts under symmetric learning was pioneered by Harris and Holmstrom (1982), who find that lack of consumer commitment compromises insurance, and thus welfare. Contracts suffer from negative dynamic selection. Adverse selection is the result of consumers' imperfect ability to commit to remain in the pool, rather than being a consequence of asymmetric information. As shown by Harris and Holmstrom, optimal contracts involve delayed reward to customers, which enhances customer retention. The delayed reward is funded through front-loading premiums in the case of insurance, or low initial wages in the case of employment. These mechanisms help alleviate reclassification (premium or wage) risk, at the expense of consumption smoothing.

To highlight the main forces at play, we will present the simplest version of Harris and Holmstrom (1982). After considering the theory and its testable implications, we review the empirical literature.

We look at several pieces of evidence that attest to the theory's relevance. First, we consider the working assumptions. When is learning important? What is the nature of commitment? Second, we review the literature that explores the theory's testable implications. Is selection negative? What is the relation between contractual terms and the likelihood that contracts will lapse? Third, do observed contracts resemble optimal ones? Finally, we move on to more recent work that has looked at welfare. What is the magnitude of the welfare loss from lack of commitment to long-term contracts? What proportion of the welfare loss from lack of commitment is restored by unilateral contracts?

Supporting evidence is found in the life insurance industry by Hendel and Lizzeri (2003). They show that, as predicted, virtually all contracts offered in the USA and Canada were front-loaded in their sample. Front-loading was found to be negatively associated with the likelihood that contracts will be allowed to lapse, which in turn reduces reclassification risk. Further evidence is presented from other insurance markets, such as health (Browne and Hoffmann, 2013 and Atal, 2015), long-term care (Finkelstein, McGarry and Sufi, 2005), labor markets (Chiappori, Salanié and Valentin, 1999), and the evolution of the Kibbutz (Abramitzky, 2008).

We then discuss the literature on asymmetric learning, where outside parties are at an informational disadvantage. As noted previously, competing automobile insurers may not observe accident histories; similarly, potential employers may not observe prior job performance. Informational asymmetries make employers suspicious of new applicants, believing that they must be low types, as high types, presumably, remain at their current jobs. This suspicion lowers outside offers, locking workers into their current jobs, enhancing their commitment to the long-term relationship (Greenwald, 1986; Waldman, 1984). Since lack of commitment compromises welfare, the endogenous lock-in might become a blessing.

The key testable predictions of the model with asymmetric learning are opposite to those under symmetric learning. Instead of negative retention, under asymmetric learning it is the bad draws who drop from the relationship. In turn, good draws who become locked in are profitable to the insurer (or employer). Ex ante competition dissipates those future rents, leading to lowballing in equilibrium, rather than to the front-loaded insurance contracts observed under symmetric learning. Insurers charge less than actuarial premiums to invest in customers, a proportion of whom will turn out to be profitable later on.

These distinct predictions across informational environments enable testing. Cohen (2012) tests for whether learning is asymmetric in the automobile insurance market in Israel, where insurers do not share information. In contrast to the symmetric learning case, Cohen finds positive selection and contract lowballing.

Information sharing between insurers would turn asymmetric learning into symmetric. As shown by de Garidel-Thoron (2005), such a move is welfare-decreasing because asymmetric learning locks the non-committed side, insurees, into the contract. Enhanced commitment (as in Crocker and Moran, 2003) enables the transfer of resources from the best states – i.e., the state in which the individual would otherwise lapse – to less fortunate ones. The transfer lowers consumption variance, and thereby increases welfare. This idea has been studied in the banking literature in the context of borrower–lender relationships (Sharpe, 1990).

This survey starts with a simplified version of Harris and Holmstrom (1982) to explain the main forces at play and motivate the different evidence offered in the literature in the symmetric learning case. We discuss limitations and extensions of the basic framework. Among others, we consider market features such as imperfect competition and switching costs, that have received little attention in this literature. We then present the theoretical predictions in an asymmetric learning environment, and end by reviewing the asymmetric learning literature.

2 SYMMETRIC LEARNING

2.1   A Simple Model

We consider a two-period model with a single risk to insure, suffered in period two. Consumers are healthy (i.e., face no loss) in period one. A signal, λ, that determines the distribution of period 2 medical expense m is observed by all parties prior to period 2 (symmetric learning). Expected medical expenses $E(m|\lambda)$ increase in λ. Consumers are risk-averse, with preferences $u(c_t)$, and generate income y_t for $t = 1$ and 2. The insurance industry is competitive; namely, several firms offer an homogeneous product at each period and state.[2] Competition drives premiums for short- and long-term contracts to expected actuarial costs. For simplicity, we assume no discounting and no borrowing.[3] The timing is shown in Figure 1.

We assume a single period of uncertain expenses to highlight forces in the simplest way. We can interpret $t = 1$ as age 25, when no information has been revealed yet, and $t = 2$ as age 50. A more general model with yearly updates and health expenses is presented later.

Two benchmarks are useful: two-sided commitment and no commitment (spot contracts). The former delivers the first-best allocation, while spot contracts provide no reclassification-risk insurance. We will judge the effectiveness of dynamic unilateral contracts by comparison with these benchmarks.

2.2   Benchmark I: Full Commitment to Long-Term Contracts

Both parties commit to contracts offered at $t = 1$ (age 25), before the health type is known. Because contracting takes place prior to learning λ and the two sides are committed, both the risk associated with m given λ and the risk associated with λ are fully insured, equating marginal utilities, $u'(c)$, across states.

Competition drives the sum (present value) of first- and second-period premiums p_1 and p_2 to $p_1 + p_2 = E_\lambda(E(m|\lambda))$. Since both parties commit to

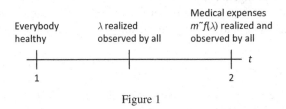

Figure 1

---

[2] Product homogeneity fits a situation in which insurance is purely a financial arrangement, unbundled from healthcare delivery. The delivery of care is differentiated by hospital and physician networks. See Section 5 for a discussion of imperfect competition.

[3] We later elaborate on this assumption. The key is imperfect capital markets that make borrowing costly (not necessarily absent).

the contract, p_1 and p_2 can be timed to smooth consumption, equating $u'(c)$ across periods as well. The allocation is first best.

2.3   Benchmark II: No Commitment

Absent commitment, long-term contracts are not feasible. The spot insurance market opens once λ is known. Under competition, full-event insurance is offered at actuarially fair premiums: $p(\lambda) = E(m|\lambda)$. Thus, uncertainty in m is fully insured in equilibrium, but uncertainty in λ (reclassification risk) is left uninsured.

Lack of commitment prevents eliminating the risk associated with λ. Individuals revealed to be bad risks in period 2 end up paying high premiums.

Reclassification risk represents one of the main motivations behind States' regulation of health insurance markets, specifically the 1996 Health Insurance Portability and Accountability Act (HIPAA) and the Affordable Care Act (ACA). Both States' regulations and HIPAA impose guaranteed renewability of insurance, and most States forbid individualized premium hikes. The ACA goes further in forbidding the pricing of pre-existing conditions, which in effect eliminates both renewability concerns and individualized premium hikes. Lack of commitment might be a reason for the poor performance of unregulated individual insurance markets: if parties committed to future contractual terms (and especially if firms did so), there would be no need for pricing regulations.

2.4   Long-Term Contracts: One-Sided Commitment

With the two benchmarks at hand, we can evaluate the performance of unilateral dynamic contracts. Firms offer long-term contracts $\{p_1, p_2\}$, which entail a first period-premium and commitment to a second-period premium.[4] Consumers do not commit to the policy, and can let the contract lapse without penalty. We assume that the second-period premium is not contingent on the realized λ. We do so without loss of generality; as shown by Hendel and Lizzeri (2003), the competitive allocation can be equally achieved with or without state-contingent contracts.

Since information is symmetric, at $t = 2$ consumers can get coverage for $E(m|\lambda)$ on the spot market. They let the long-term contract lapse in states for which:

$$E(m|\lambda) < p_2.$$

The last inequality implies adverse selection in the second period: better risks are those that lapse the long-term contract.

To find the equilibrium, we can use the fact that the competitive equilibrium contract maximizes consumer welfare subject to (i) the ex ante break-even

---

[4] In principle, a contract could also specify a co-insurance rate. Handel et al. (2017) show that equilibrium unilateral contracts offer full-event insurance, namely, zero co-insurance.

constraint and (ii) the lapsation constraint, which accounts for the states λ in which buyers remain in the pool:

$$p_2 \leq E(m|\lambda). \tag{1}$$

In equilibrium there is full event insurance, namely, all medical expenses are insured (i.e., no out-of-pocket payments). For a proof, see Handel et al. (2017).

To understand how the optimal contract works, notice that the lower p_2 is, the fewer the states in which the insuree lapses. Fewer states in which the lapsation constraint binds means more states across which $u'(c_2)$ is equated. In other words, lower p_2 means more second-period premium insurance.

A low enough p_2 could fully eliminate reclassification risk. However, for the contract to break even ex ante, a low p_2 requires a high p_1; that is, front-loading is necessary. Front-loading is costly in terms of consumption smoothing, and therefore optimal contracts trade off reclassification-risk insurance and consumption smoothing.

The cost of front-loading depends on y_1. Individuals with more limited initial resources, or more limited access to borrowing, prefer less front-loaded contracts, and in turn end up suffering more reclassification risk. More premium uncertainty (namely, fewer states being pooled due to higher lapsation) leads to more intense adverse dynamic selection, which translates into higher present value of premiums. This is formally proved by Hendel and Lizzeri (2003). Intuitively, more front-loading means lower premiums later in the contract. In this example, it means a lower p_2. With a lower second-period premium, fewer types drop coverage. Since it is the good draws who lapse, lower lapsation means a healthier pool is retained. Under competition, firms break even, so that the present value of premiums proxies expected actuarial costs. Thus, the worse pool kept in the long run, when front-loading is low, translates into a higher present value of premiums. To illustrate, if $p_2 = 0$, all types stay with the contract so that $p_1 + p_2 = E_\lambda(E(m|\lambda))$. Instead, absent front-loading, $p_1 = 0$, all but the worse type find a better price on the market and lapse; then $p_1 + p_2 = E(m|\bar{\lambda})$, where $\bar{\lambda}$ represents the worse health state. Naturally, $E(m|\bar{\lambda}) > E_\lambda(E(m|\lambda))$ for all non-degenerate distributions of λ, illustrating the negative link between front-loading and present value of premiums.[5]

It is worth emphasizing that the source of adverse selection is not asymmetric information, but rather lack of commitment. Information is symmetric, but consumers are unable to commit to remain in the contract in good states. Selection, or adverse retention, is driven by the inability to retain good risks.

---

[5] Naturally, perfect capital markets would enable paying all premiums up front, restoring consumer commitment. As we will see later, full insurance would require payments in the tens of thousands of dollars for health or life insurance when the consumer is in her late 20s, which does not seem affordable for most buyers. Pauly, Kunreuther, and Hirth (1995) find the minimum premiums that guarantee no unraveling. Absent capital market imperfections, such an allocation would be first best. Cochrane (1995) discusses a market for premium insurance, which under perfect capital markets achieves full insurance.

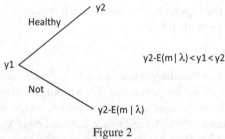

Figure 2

Consumers would be better off ex ante if they could commit to stay with the policy in good states, so that resources in those states could be transferred to the less fortunate ones, up to the point where marginal utility is equated across states.

Figure 2 illustrates the problem in a two-state world, in which the healthy state entails no medical costs. Absent costs, insurees simply walk away in the good state. Transferring resources from the good state to less fortunate ones is not feasible. Up-front payments, however, are feasible. If the first-period income, y_1, is higher than $y_2 - E(m|\bar{\lambda})$, the individual can transfer resources from the first period to the unhealthy state of the second period.

Notice that front-loading differs from saving. Savings transfer resources to all period-2 states. In contrast, the up-front payment goes exclusively to the bad state. As we will see later, with more states, the front-loaded amount goes to those states with higher marginal utility of consumption than the first period. The first-period marginal utility increases as more resources are transferred to the future. The optimal amount of front-loading, and the states pooled, are determined by equating marginal utilities across the first period and the bad second-period states.

In sum, lack of consumer commitment compromises reclassification-risk insurance and creates adverse retention. Optimal contracts resort to front-loading to partially restore consumer commitment. The next section shows the relevance of these simple insights through evidence from different areas of Economics.

3 EMPIRICS

The relevance of the theory can be assessed in several ways. For instance, one can identify the markets in which the main working assumptions of the theory are not only relevant, but actually capture the main forces at play. After identifying those markets, the natural next step is to test the implications of the theory on selection, lapsation, and reclassification risk. We then look at contracts. Do observed contracts resemble those predicted by the model? Finally, we ask: what is the welfare loss associated with limited commitment?

3.1 Main Assumptions

The theory's predictions are very sensitive to the main market characteristics, such as the type of commitment and the nature of learning. Sharply different predictions are in principle a blessing for testing. The challenge for the empirical researcher, given the predictions' sensitivity, is to find institutions that can be reasonably mapped into specific assumptions; such a mapping is complicated when too many forces are at play. It is important, therefore, to identify simple enough situations to isolate the key forces. We concentrate on markets where learning and imperfect commitment are the key determinants of contractual relations.

3.1.1 Symmetric Learning

Learning is prevalent in many economic situations; for example, learning about product quality, worker productivity, or the quality of a match.

Learning might or might not be symmetric. We refer to learning as symmetric when all parties, including competitors, receive the same signals. In many markets, learning might not be symmetric. For instance, signals about workers' performance are revealed over time – yet, work is often done in teams, hindering worker-specific learning. In many situations, supervisors and close co-workers are able to monitor performance, but potential employers cannot. Such asymmetries will discussed in the next section.

An example of a labor market with arguably symmetric learning is academics. Output, both teaching and research, is made public or done in public. Presentations and publications generate observable signals. While coauthoring may interfere with symmetric learning, productivity is to a large extent attributable. As we see later, academics' compensation patterns seem to resemble those predicted by Harris and Holmstrom (1982).

Many lines of insurance involve learning. For example, health status evolves over time. Both existing conditions and prior diagnostics are observable, which make learning arguably symmetric. Life and health insurers can discover such signals prior to underwriting, namely, at the time the insurer assesses and assumes the risk.[6] Regulation often prevents pricing pre-existing conditions, but the underlying information structure is well approximated by symmetric learning.

Accident history in automobile insurance can be public or not, depending on regulation or firms' decision to share information. The USA has a national loss-underwriting database, to which insurers provide information about every home and auto insurance claim. The database can be accessed by all insurance companies at the time of underwriting. In other countries, information is not shared among insurers (Cohen, 2013). While there is learning in the automobile market, whether learning is symmetric or not depends

---

[6] Concealing information at underwriting leads to contestability by life insurers.

on market-specific institutions. As another example, credit-scoring agencies arguably make learning symmetric in credit and mortgage markets.

3.1.2   Unilateral Commitment

In most markets, consumers and workers are free to withdraw from contractual arrangements. Legal considerations make termination fees hard to enforce, thus they are rarely used.[7] Other reasons for partial commitment are discussed by Daily, Hendel and Lizzeri (2008), Fang and Kung (2012), and Bayot (2015). As these authors argue, uncertainty about future need for the product makes commitment costly. Individuals may not want to commit, or to pay health premiums up front, in the private market if they might later switch to an employer who offers more generous health-insurance coverage. Similarly, the possibility of a divorce may detract from the value of committing to life insurance coverage.

Regardless of the reason, we observe contracts with one-sided commitment in many industries: life insurance, health insurance, mortgages, and academics' compensation.

Long-term contracts arise in some markets without intervention, such as US and Canadian life insurance. In other markets – for instance, the health insurance markets in Germany and Chile – government regulation requires that firms offer renewable contracts in a specific format (Atal, 2015; Browne and Hoffmann, 2013), which resembles the theory's prediction. Both regulated and unregulated markets provide evidence on the theory's relevance.

3.2   Testable Implications

Learning and imperfect commitment seem to capture the key forces that shape contracts in many markets. We now turn to empirical work on those markets. One can look at two types of evidence. First, regardless of whether contracts are optimal or not, learning and limited commitment are predicted to have implications on reclassification risk, selection, lapsation, and the link between lapsation and front-loading. Second, one can compare actual and predicted contracts. The distinction between testing the implications of the assumptions, as opposed to the prediction on contracts, is particularly relevant in regulated markets. Regulated contracts need not resemble those predicted by the theory and, if they do, they do not necessarily represent evidence in support of the theory. Even so, regulated markets, such as the Chilean health-insurance market, still help in testing for learning and consumer commitment.

---

[7] The reason termination fees are hard to enforce is that damage due to lapsation is difficult to prove (as a liquidated damage). An example is the infamous early-termination fee for cell phones, which was declared illegal by state courts.

3.2.1 Long-Term Care Insurance

Finkelstein, McGarry and Sufi (2005) study the long-term care insurance market in the USA. It is a thin market, where only a minority of the elderly population with potential long-term care needs buys coverage. The authors present evidence on pricing, which shows that long-term care insurance contracts are front-loaded. Despite the front-loading, a substantial share of insurees lapse.

Under symmetric learning and limited commitment, the theory predicts that the better types are those that lapse. Using data from the Health and Retirement Survey, the authors regress eventual utilization on lapsation to provide evidence of adverse retention. The reported negative relation suggests that, in accordance with the theory, good risks are more likely to lapse.

3.2.2 Health Insurance

Patel and Pauly (2002) discuss contract renewability in the individual health-insurance market in the USA. They argue contracts are dynamic, with renewability guaranteed by the HIPAA. The law is incomplete, however, as it fails to ban individual premium changes within a rating class. Namely, while individual coverage must be renewed, premiums could depend on recently developed health conditions. Patel and Pauly (2002) survey state insurance regulators and find that all but three states forbid individualized premium hikes: the pool can face a premium hike, but not specific individuals within the pool. State law rather than HIPAA makes contracts dynamic. Patel and Pauly conclude that guaranteed renewability works to eliminate premium risk.

Judging by the proportion of the population that was uninsured prior to the ACA, the US individual health-insurance market seemingly did not function properly. Some commentators, including Patel and Pauly (2002), attribute the market's unraveling to state regulation that prevented firms from charging individualized prices at the time of underwriting. Inability to price pre-existing conditions is expected to result in an Akerlof-type unraveling. In other words, while dynamic contracts were offered in the USA, adverse selection generated by restricted underwriting appears to have caused an inefficient level of trade.

Dynamic contracts are also offered in Germany and Chile (Browne and Hoffmann, 2013; Atal, 2015). Government regulation in Germany permits premiums to depend on health conditions when coverage begins, but must remain fixed thereafter. Basically, risk rating is legal at underwriting, but later premiums cannot vary based on new conditions and must remain constant (level premiums). Since health expenses increase with age, level premiums mean that contracts are front-loaded.

Consumers are allowed to switch insurers later in life, and thus these are unilateral contracts. However, the new policy will reflect their increased age and any changes in health conditions. The regulation that forces level premiums, which can only be updated by switching, locks insurees into their policies.

Browne and Hoffmann (2013), using data from a large insurer in the private German health insurance market, report evidence consistent with the model: front-loading lowers lapsation, and better risks are those that lapse.

Atal (2015) studies the costs of lock-in. Regulation in Chile forbids individualized premium increases, thus creating consumer lock-in. Atal shows that actuarial costs divided by premiums increases over time, which confirms front-loading and thus lock-in.

When insurers are differentiated, lock-in may be costly. For example, as their conditions change, insurees may prefer a different hospital network; Atal (2015) quantifies the inefficiency due to inability to change insurers (more details in Section 5).

Another possible hurdle to long-term contracting is uncertainty about future health costs, which is a non-diversifiable risk that firms may be reluctant to take. Basically, if they are unable to predict costs far into the future, they may not want – or be able – to commit to future premiums. German regulation deals with the problem by indexing premiums to the aggregate cost of healthcare. That way, firms insure the idiosyncratic health risk, but do not suffer aggregate shocks to health costs. Indexing to a heathcare price might assist the market in developing elsewhere.

3.2.3   Life Insurance

Hendel and Lizzeri (2003) use data on contract dynamics of term life insurance. Term insurance, unlike whole life, is a simple and homogeneous product that provides coverage for a specified period (often up to age 70) as long as the policy is renewed. The authors use explicit contract data from Compulife (pricing software used by insurance agents). Compulife quotes not only premiums at underwriting for different health statuses, but also future premiums guaranteed by the insurer. Premiums to be paid in the future are, for some contracts, contingent on health status. These health-contingent premiums embed premium risk: namely, individuals will pay different premiums depending on how healthy they remain.

Does the competitive model with symmetric learning and unilateral commitment (as in Harris and Holmstrom, 1982) fit the life-insurance industry? It is a pretty competitive industry, with hundreds of life insurers. Insurers commit to future policy terms, and there are no termination fees. Finally, health type evolves over time (more on health transitions later), while medical examinations and questionnaires at underwriting arguably make learning symmetric.

Learning and Reclassification Risk   Table 1 illustrates a typical term contract, popularized in the 1970s, called Select and Ultimate Annual Renewable Term. The table should be read as follows. The first row shows premiums guaranteed at age 40 to an insuree who has just gone through underwriting (i.e., a medical examination to make sure he qualifies as a preferred risk) as he ages,

Table 1 *Select and Ultimate Annual Renewable Term offered in 7/1997 for $500K coverage to a male non-smoker who qualified as a preferred risk. S&U ART are annual contracts that allow for reclassification by showing good health. Source Compulife Softwars Inc.*

	S&U ART premiums						
Policy Year							
Age	1	2	3	10	11	19	20
40	370	475	640	1,485	2,555	5,680	6,375
41	385	490	660	1,565	2,815	6,375	7,040
42	400	530	690	1,705	3,105	7,040	7,790
49	630	890	1,080	2,725	6,375	13,675	14,785
50	690	945	1,155	2,895	7,040	14,785	15,765
51	735	1,050	1,295	3,230	7,790	15,765	17,230
58	1,245	1,750	2,295	6,420	14,785	33,165	35,445
59	1,340	1,785	2,480	6,945	15,765	35,445	38,715

from the first to the twentieth year of coverage. The insuree would start paying $370 at age 40, and in year 11, at age 50, he is guaranteed to pay no more than $2,555. The second row shows the premiums paid if he remains healthy after a year of coverage: At age 41, he would pay $385 if he is able to produce a letter from his physician attesting to his good health. While he was guaranteed a $475 premium, insurees who requalify as good risks get a discount to $385. At the time of contracting (age 40), the insuree knows what future premiums will cost under different contingencies.

As we move down column 1, we find premiums for an insuree who remains healthy. Once he fails to requalify, horizontal moves depict the premiums that will apply, regardless of how unhealthy he is. For example, the premium to be paid by a 51-year-old who has remained in good health until age 49 is $1,080.

These contracts became popular in the 1970s in response to market competition. Until then, annual renewable term (ART) policies were not state-contingent – that is, premiums depended on age and not health condition; good draws would simply lapse. These contingent contracts were designed to match the better terms offered by competitors, thereby preventing the lapsation of good draws.

Table 1 highlights the role of learning: premiums depend on the information revealed during the contract period. The contract embeds premium risk. At age 59, the insuree could be paying as little as $1,340 or as much as $6,375.

Notice that learning is essentially symmetric, in the sense that the same medical examination that triggers a discount can be used by competitors to generate the outside offers.

Front-Loading Theory predicts that a variety of contracts should be offered that cater to individuals with different income profiles, who find front-loading

Table 2 *Statistics on contracts taken from Hendel and Lizzeri (2003).*
Q(1st)/Q(11th) is the ratio of first to 11th premium, representing (inverse of)
the slope of the premiums. The present value of coverage, PV, represents the
present discounted value of 20 years of coverage at r = 0.08.

	Slope and Cost Dispersion across Contracts			
	Mean	Std Div	Min	Max
Q(1st)/Q(11th)	0.43	0.31	0.11	1.00
PV	16,055	5,245	6,871	28,754

more or less costly. While indeed a variety of contracts are offered in the US
(and Canadian) market, virtually all contracts were front-loaded at the time of
the study.

One can use the slope of premiums over time as a measure of the extent
of front-loading. Actuarially fair premiums, which are expected to arise in a
competitive industry that offers spot contracts, should increase at the same
rate the death probability increases with age. Premiums that increase slower
than death probabilities reflect front-loading. Such contracts do not break even
period by period, which suggests that contracts are dynamic.

The slope of premiums can be proxied by the ratio Q(1st)/Q(11th), the premium in the first year of the contract divided by the premium 10 years later.
Table 2 shows that on average Q(11th) is twice Q(1st). However, the range
of premium slopes is quite wide. Premiums increase as much as ninefold for
some contracts, while premiums remain flat in level-term policies. Naturally,
level-term policies entail substantial front-loading.

It is interesting to note that even the steepest premiums entail front-loading.
In other words, death rates increase faster than even the steepest premiums.
Using US actuarial tables, conditional on being in good health at age 40
(namely, qualifying as a preferred risk), the probability of death at age 59 is
17.2 times higher than at age 40; the steepest premiums are only 9 times larger
at 59 than at 40. Basically, all contracts in the sample are dynamic – that is,
they do not break even period by period.

The row at the bottom of the table displays the present value of 20 years
of coverage starting at age 40. Under competition (zero profits), the present
value of premiums proxies the actuarial cost of covering the respective pools
retained by the different policies. The range of present values of coverage
varies fourfold, from about $6,800 to $28,700.

Because of dynamic adverse selection, we expect a negative relation
between Q(1st)/Q(11th) and the present value of coverage. This prediction is
put to the test in Table 3.

Dynamic Selection The theory's main prediction is that increased commitment through front-loading leads to better dynamic selection. Since good
draws are those predicted to lapse, lower lapsation means a better pool, which

Table 3 *Regression results from Hendel and Lizzeri (2003).*
Dependent Variable log(PV) is the log of the present value
(r = 8%) of the cost to the consumer of 20 years of coverage
starting at age 40.

	log(PV)	
	(1)	(2)
Q(1st)/Q(11th)	−1.06	−
	(−16.79)	−
Other contract		
characteristics	Y	Y
R^2	74.4	16.6
N	125	125

in turn translates into lower costs of coverage. The prediction is tested by regressing the cost of coverage on the premium slope. Hedonic-type regressions, presented in Table 3, show not only that the correlation is negative, but the main determinant of the cost of coverage is premium front-loading. Premium slope accounts for 60 percent of the log variation, while numerous other policy characteristics (convertibility, renewability, etc.) have limited impact on the cost of coverage.

Key Findings Available contracts are state-contingent, which confirms the prevalence of learning and relevance of reclassification risk. All contracts in the USA and Canada were front-loaded at the time of the study, which suggests that front-loading plays an important role in coping with reclassification risk. Lapsation is higher for less front-loaded contracts. More front-loading is associated with lower present value of premiums, which reflects a healthier pool. The increased commitment through front-loading, therefore, seems to reduce dynamic negative selection. Quantitatively, premium slope accounts for the majority of premium variation.

3.2.4 Labor Market

While Finkelstein, McGarry and Sufi (2005) observe long-term care utilization, and Abramitzky (2008) (discussed below) observes workers' types, in many situations, especially in the labor market, types are not observed by the researcher. To overcome this lack of observability, Chiappori, Salanié and Valentin (1999) derive testable implications on promotions rather than productivity. Promotion dynamics reflect the interaction between performance and the optimal contract, and thus help uncover symmetric learning.

Specifically, the authors show that in a situation with symmetric learning and downward wage rigidities, as in Harris and Holmstrom, wages, and thus promotions, display what they term the "late beginner property."

In short, if we compare two individuals currently at the same rank (or wage levels), but one of them rose in the ranks earlier than the other (having both started at the same initial level), the late beginner is expected to do better in the future. Intuitively, the current wage of the early riser, who later slowed down, because of downward rigidities might conceal sufficiently negative information that merits a wage downgrade. In contrast, the late beginner's pay reflects her current performance. In other words, early starters' rank eventually conceal interim bad performance and are therefore expected, other things being equal, to do poorer than late beginners. Chiappori, Salanié and Valentin (1999) test their predictions using data on French public servants' rank and the timing of promotions.

3.2.5   Alternative Forms of Commitment

Looking at alternative forms of commitment, other than front-loading, can attest to the role of imperfect commitment in contracting. Crocker and Moran (2003) study the bundling of health insurance and employment. The idea is that attachment to a job enhances individuals' lock-in to their employer-sponsored health coverage. Commitment is expected to translate into more generous coverage.

Crocker and Moran (2003) use the National Medical Expenditure Survey and information on job attachment to link the nature of insurance offered to the type of job. They show that health insurance generosity (coverage and lifetime limits) is associated with worker immobility.

Their findings are consistent with the pervasiveness of employer-sponsored health insurance coverage in the USA, which suggests that employer-sponsored health insurance may work better than prepayment. As argued by Atal (2015), prepayment can be problematic in health insurance, especially when insurance (i.e., the financial side of coverage) is bundled with healthcare.

On the other hand, employer-sponsored insurance is not ideal either, as it creates job lock-in (Currie and Madrian, 1999) potentially leading to poor worker-employer matches. However, lock-in may also offer benefits. Lock-in to an insurer or an employer may increase incentives to invest in health. Health, as a form of general human capital, delivers immediate as well as future benefits. The lower the turnover, the more the current employer or insurer benefits from future savings. Fang and Gavazza (2010) present evidence of underinvestment during working years in jobs with high turnover, which translates into higher medical expenses after retirement.

Crocker and Moran (2003) interpret their findings as evidence that the key hurdle to the functioning of private health-insurance markets, especially the individual market, is commitment rather than asymmetric information. When commitment is restored by job lock-in, insurance provision improves.

3.2.6   Further Afield: Economic Institutions

Abramitzky (2008) presents a concrete example of how social institutions are designed to provide insurance, by examining economic equality in the Israeli kibbutzim (plural of kibbutz). A Kibbutz is a collective community – originally primarily an agricultural community – that aims to achieve full equality among its members. Equality is understood from an ex ante perspective, before the talent, human capital, and market opportunities of its members are known, as a form of insurance.

Kibbutz formation as an institution started in the early 1900s and reached about 130,000 members at its peak. Participation by kibbutz-born individuals is voluntary (people from the outside must apply to be admitted by the kibbutz); namely, commitment to the institution is unilateral.

For most of their history, kibbutzim offered full equality among its members. However, recent negative financial shocks, such as the loss of government subsidies, decline in world agricultural prices, and bad investments, led them to shift away from full equality toward different, more limited degrees of equality.

Members' earnings go to the kibbutz, which then budgets according to different compensation schemes. Some kibbutzim allocate all members an equal budget; others allocate based on individual earnings.

The theory predicts that higher wealth is associated with a more egalitarian distribution, which, in turn, translates into lower exit levels. Ex ante, members want equality (insurance), but at some point each individual learns their type (including human capital), which determines their market opportunities. At that stage, they may pursue alternative employment, which is mainly in the city. Commitment, in the form of initial resources, achieves partial reclassification-risk insurance.

Abramitzky combines data on about 180 kibbutzim with individual-level census data to test whether the wealth of the kibbutz worked as a lock-in mechanism. The key information on the kibbutz is their wealth, how egalitarian their budgeting is, as well as their ideology. Census data are used to track migration to and from the kibbutz, by profession.

The main findings are that wealthier kibbutzim retained higher equality. Entry and exit are associated with negative selection; namely, those that leave for the city are the individuals with higher talent, measured by their wages.

More specifically, evidence on the talent of those leaving the kibbutz is supported by the finding that less educated former kibbutz members earn more than similar individuals in the city; that is, the good draws (in terms of talent) are those that depart. In addition, more educated former kibbutz members earn less than similar individuals: for instance, most MBAs leave, not just the good ones. Entering members have lower wages than similarly educated individuals had before entering.

4 THE WELFARE IMPLICATIONS OF LONG-TERM CONTRACTS

The papers just reviewed provide evidence on the relevance of the theory. A natural next step is to assess the impact of the identified distortions on welfare. In short, how painful is reclassification risk in the absence of dynamic contracts? How effective are long-term contracts for eliminating reclassification risk?

4.1   Regulation of Health Insurance Premiums

Understanding the performance of different contractual arrangements in contending with reclassification risk is important for policy design. Reclassification risk is one of the key motivations behind health insurance market regulation. The ACA bans pricing health conditions. One of the goals of HIPPA, the ACA and numerous state regulations was to eliminate reclassification risk and coverage denials.

While effective in eliminating premium risk, banning the pricing of health conditions comes at a cost. By imposing a uniform price on a heterogeneous population, the ban results in adverse selection, and possibly the full collapse of the market. This concern is supported by the findings of Handel et al. (2015). They simulate the functioning of health exchanges using data from a large employer. They compute the actuarial risk of every person in the population using Adjusted Clinical Group software (described in the next section). Preferences towards risk are recovered through a choice model that fits observed coverage choices. Using preference estimates and the distribution of risk types, they simulate the equilibrium of a market in which high and low coverage policies are offered by multiple insurers. The Nash equilibrium is then computed for numerous populations and different pricing rules. Unraveling is pervasive even when age is priced. The equilibrium involves full unravelling to the minimum coverage, 60 percent actuarial value.

As an alternative to the ban on pricing health conditions, long-term contracts may permit addressing reclassification risk without inducing adverse selection. For instance, the contracts described in Browne and Hoffmann (2013) avoid adverse selection by allowing for the pricing of pre-existing conditions at underwriting, while at the same time eliminating premium risk by forcing constant premiums over time. The welfare gains delivered by long-term contracts, in particular vis-à-vis ACA regulation, is studied by Handel et al. (2017).

The first step in assessing welfare is to characterize contracts under different regimes. The model described in the next section is used by Handel et al. (2017) jointly with an individual-level panel of workers at a large employer (25,000 covered lives) to simulate equilibria and compare welfare in different situations.

The key component of the data is the detailed information on health realizations: all medical claims, including the ICD-9 diagnostic codes. The diagnostic codes are used in conjunction with Adjusted Clinical Group (ACG) software (which was developed at the Johns Hopkins Medical School to assess the actuarial risk of individuals) to generate a risk score for each individual in the population. In turn, the score is used to compute health state transition matrices. All those parameters are fed into the following model, to predict the shape of optimal dynamic contracts.

4.1.1 Model

The model in Handel, Hendel, and Whinston (2017) is a T-period version of the one described in Section 2.1. The T-period model is meant to capture a population aged 25 to 65, from college to medicare. The model predicts optimal history-contingent premiums for a given income profile $\{y_t\}$, parametrized by risk preferences, the distribution of health costs, and transitions across states.

Consumer preferences are: $U = E\left[\sum_t \delta^t u(c_t)\right]$. Health state λ_t (ACG) determines expected health costs, $E[m_t|\lambda_t]$. Information is symmetrically revealed: m_t and λ_t are commonly observed by consumers and firms. The insurance industry is competitive, firms are risk-neutral, and the discount factor is δ. Capital markets are imperfect: savings or borrowing.

As in the simple model, full commitment delivers the first best allocation. No commitment leads to full event insurance at actuarial premiums $E[m_t|\lambda_t]$, so that insurees are fully exposed to the information revealed by λ_t. The ex ante welfare of a representative consumer under these benchmarks is immediate to compute.

4.1.2 Equilibrium under Unilateral Commitment

Handel et al. (2017) show that equilibrium contracts involve full insurance against medical risk and are front-loaded, and their premiums are such that consumption is downward rigid.

Premiums, at the start of a contract, are designed to guarantee a minimum consumption level. No matter how bad the health state turns out to be later in life, consumption is guaranteed never to decline. This guarantee is funded by the upfront premiums.

The consumption guarantee is bumped up to match the outside offers that arise every time the consumer receives good news – that is, when her type improves. The newly guaranteed consumption level is the first-period consumption of an optimal contract that would start at that date and improved state. Basically, the consumption level of the outside offer is matched.

The consumption guarantee parallels the downward rigid wages in Harris and Holmstrom (1982). Optimal wages increase when the worker's productivity is upgraded, but do not decline after bad news. These bad states are subsidized with low initial wages. Like front-loading, the delayed reward generates worker lock-in.

While first-best involves equating marginal utilities across all states and periods, under unilateral commitment only states and periods without tempting outside offers can be pooled. Why is reclassification risk left uninsured? Insurees would like to transfer resources from the healthier states to the less fortunate ones, but lack of commitment implies that they will exit the contract when a more attractive offer comes. Since resources can be sent costlessly forward, at actuarial value, consumption is not expected to decrease even if health deteriorates.

Table 4 *First period consumption, premiums and front-loading for an individual with flat income net of health expenses under the optimal dynamic one-sided contract. The premiums and consumption depend on the realized health state. See Handel et al. (2017).*

State	1	2	3	4	5	6	7
Consumption	52, 548	51, 143	49, 642	49, 168	46, 414	43, 408	37, 294
Premium	2, 750	4, 155	6, 008	6, 130	8, 885	11, 890	18, 554
Front-loading	1, 619	1, 864	2, 228	2, 155	3, 035	1, 235	–

Table 5 *CE_x represents the certainty equivalent of being in a specific contractual regime. Welfare is evaluated using risk preference CARA parameter $r = 0.0004$. See Handel et al. (2017).*

	Certainty Equivalents			
	TS	D	S	ACA
CE_x	53.67	52.77	46.27	51.30

4.1.3 Optimal Contract for Flat Net Income

Optimal contracts are recursively computed to find consumption guarantees. Table 4 presents first period consumption, premiums, and front-loading for a consumer with flat net income, namely, constant $y_t - E[m_t]$. The main interest in such income profile is that gains from long-term contracting are not driven by life cycle considerations (saving and borrowing), since individuals with flat disposable income do not want to borrow or save.

Except for state 7, in which the individual is as unhealthy as she will ever be, premiums are well above actuarial value. Front-loading is substantial in all but the worse state. Those savings are used to guarantee future consumption in those states in which bad news arrives. Subsequent premiums (not shown here) are contingent on more complex histories. Should good news arrive, consumption is upgraded. Otherwise, initial promises are kept in all future periods.

4.1.4 Welfare

Table 5 presents certainty equivalents CE_X. CE_X is the constant monetary amount that makes the individual indifferent to scenario X. The following contracting scenarios are considered: D denotes dynamic contracts with one-sided commitment, S denotes spot contracts, and TS denotes two-sided commitment.

CE_{TS} reflects welfare under the optimal allocation. The gap between CE_{TS} and CE_S represents the welfare loss from reclassification risk due to lack of commitment. The loss is about 14 percent of welfare. As expected, CE_D is between CE_S and CE_{TS}. One-sided commitment recaptures almost 90 percent of the gains from full commitment relative to spot contracts. Handel et al. (2017) study how these gains depend on risk aversion, switching costs, and income profiles.

Handel et al. (2017) also compute welfare under the ACA, to assess the effectiveness of dynamic contracts relative to alternative ways of contending with reclassification risk.

5 EXTENSIONS AND LIMITATIONS

Several additional market features deserve attention, especially for applied work. Switching costs have been documented to be substantial in insurance markets (Handel, 2013). We also consider non-health-related determinants of lapsation. For example, employment-related insurance may render participation in the individual market unnecessary. We look at imperfect competition, which is quite relevant in the exchanges; in many exchanges only a couple of insurers compete.

5.1   Switching Costs

Handel (2013) shows the importance of switching costs in health insurance demand, using the data described in the previous section. He does so in the context of static choices, studying the link between inertia and adverse selection. When switching costs are high, individuals are less likely to act on the information they learn, thus attenuating adverse selection.

Switching costs are typically associated with back-loading. Consumers are attracted with low prices, which are then raised to exploit lack of price responsiveness. It is thus important to consider how switching costs are expected to affect dynamic contracts, especially front-loaded ones.

In the context of dynamic contracts, switching costs induce commitment, reducing lapsation. The model described above predicts that good draws will lapse. Bad risks stay with the contract, as they find no better deals on the market. Thus, adding inertia to the model affects mostly the behavior of good risks: it becomes easier to retain good risks in the pool. Handel, Hendel, and Whinston (2017) show welfare increases in switching costs, as in de Garidel-Thoron (2005). In de Garidel-Thoron, lock-in is endogenous, due to asymmetric learning. Keeping good risk in the pool enables the transfer of resources from states with low to states with high marginal utility from consumption, which lowers consumption variance. We present more details in Section 6.1.

5.2   Non-Health-Related Lapsation

Insurees lapse for many reasons besides being in good health. For instance, a divorce may render a life insurance policy unnecessary or a new job may offer health insurance. Those events might generate the lapsation of types that are expected to remain in the pool, namely, the bad risks; good risks are expected to lapse regardless.

Lapsation has conflicting effects on the willingness to commit to long-term contracts through front loading. On the one hand, uncertain about their future needs, buyers may be less willing to front-load future payments. On the other hand, the lapsation of bad risks reduces the front-loaded amount necessary for the policy to break even ex ante.[8] The main features of the predicted contracts remains unchanged.

5.3   Imperfect Competition

Most of the literature assumes that insurance is a purely financial product. As such, one would expect little product differentiation – which, jointly with the assumption of many sellers, justifies looking at the industry as competitive as a first approximation. One can argue that competition is a reasonable assumption for the life insurance industry, in which the product itself is a monetary transfer and hundreds of insurers compete.

This assumption is less realistic in other contexts. Most health insurance products available in the exchanges are bundled with healthcare provision (Dafny, 2015), and plans are differentiated by the hospital and physician networks they offer. In addition, only a few insurers compete in most states' exchanges. For health insurance markets, and especially in the exchanges, pure competition is not a good approximation.

Imperfect competition is harder to model. Characterizing the equilibrium dynamic contracts under competition entails maximizing consumer utility subject to the break-even and lapsation constraints. Instead, finding the equilibrium under imperfect competition requires finding the dynamic contract that maximizes each seller's profits subject to the lapsation constraints, given the contracts offered by other sellers. Namely, one has to find the fixed point of the contracts that best respond to each other, which is much more complicated than finding the competitive outcome.

How would optimal contracts look in an imperfectly competitive market? The easiest set-up to consider involves two competitors, two periods, and the following preferences:

$$U_t(c_t, j) = u(c_t) + \varepsilon_{jt}, \quad j = a, b.$$

Product differentiation enters through a brand-specific shock that is additive to the utility from the financial terms of the policy. Consider stable preferences by assuming $\varepsilon_{j1} = \varepsilon_{j2}$.

---

[8] Interstingly, in the life insurance industry the term "lapsation-based products" is quite common. It refers to firms' expectation that they will not fully compensate bad risks, under the assumption they are likely to lapse: if they did not, the product would not be profitable (Daily, 1989).

As the second period spot market opens, for consumers in every state s, firms can poach customers currently covered by their competitor's long-term contract. Due to product differentiation, firms face downward-sloping demand for second-period coverage. Unlike the competitive case, firms charge a second-period spot premium above actuarial costs. Thus, the lapsation constraints of the first-period contracts are relaxed relative to the competitive solution, in which outside offers are at actuarial costs. In other words, spot market markups reduce incentives to lapse. Contracts still display front-loading to enhance long-term insurance, and the good risks are those expected to lapse, but it appears that by relaxing the lapsation constraints, market power enhances commitment to the long-term contract.

5.4   Lock-In and Changing Needs

In many situations – and health insurance in particular – needs may change, so that $\varepsilon_{j1} \neq \varepsilon_{j2}$. Thus, committing to a policy may be far from optimal. That is the question studied by Atal (2015). Atal uses choice and utilization data from Chile to estimate preferences for different health insurance plans, taking into account preferences for specific hospital networks and how those preferences change as the health status of the insuree changes. Using the estimated preferences and health-state transitions, he assesses the cost of being stuck with a given hospital network. He finds that consumers would be willing to pay an additional 13 percent in premiums to avoid the lock-in.

How are optimal contracts affected by changing needs? When tastes change, $\varepsilon_{j1} \neq \varepsilon_{j2}$, some consumers regret their commitment to a policy and they may prefer to lapse, rendering the benefits of front-loading more limited. On the other hand, as in Section 5.2, the front-loading necessary for the contract to break even ex ante is more limited, since some bad risks will lapse as well. It is not clear that the gains from dynamic contracting are compromised by changing needs.

Interestingly, Atal (2015) reports that most of the lock-in in the Chilean case comes from fear of future denials, rather than from front-loading. Namely, consumers in good health remain insured – even, perhaps, temporarily over-insured – because lapsing entails the risk of not being able to return to the private market. Good draws could purchase cheaper insurance, or switch to the public system (which is cheaper and lower quality), but they may later be denied coverage once they develop a health condition.

5.5   Aggregate Risks

So far we have considered insurance against idiosyncratic risks. In some markets, consumers suffer aggregate risks. For example, borrowers suffer a common risk associated with the evolution of the interest rate. Risk-neutral lenders can offer fixed rates to insure the risk of rising interest rates. Fixed rates, or at least temporary locks, are common in mortgages.

Learning is symmetric in mortgage markets: everybody observes the evolution of the interest rate and commitment is unilateral, since borrowers can prepay their balances, typically without penalty. Lenders suffer from dynamic selection. When the interest rate declines, borrowers refinance. If interest rates increase, lenders are stuck, unable to shift their capital to higher-yield opportunities. Front-loading in the form of points attenuates dynamic selection.

The problem with aggregate risk and symmetric learning has been considered in the context of employment by Beaudry and DiNardo (1991). The state of the economy is likely to affect workers' productivity, making employers willing to pay more for workers when the economy is in good shape. Absent long-term contracts, workers would suffer uncertainty in wages due to the business cycle. With long-term contracts, risk-neutral employers are expected to insure workers, at least partially, against productivity shocks.

Using individual data from the Current Population Survey and the Panel Study of Income Dynamics, Beaudry and DiNardo (1991) study the link between wages and the state of the economy, specifically unemployment. Several contractual arrangements are considered. Under spot contracts, wages should depend on contemporaneous unemployment. Under two-sided commitment, wages are expected to be fixed at a level determined by unemployment at the time the worker was hired. Under one-sided commitment, wages should depend on the lowest unemployment rate realized since the worker was hired. Namely, wages are downward rigid, and get upgraded every time the worker finds better opportunities on the market.

In line with the one-sided commitment model's predictions, wages are found to be negatively related to the lowest unemployment rate realized since the worker started his or her present job. Interestingly, controlling for labor market conditions since the employment began, the contemporaneous unemployment rate no longer significantly affects wages.

6 ASYMMETRIC LEARNING

In many markets, outsiders have inferior information; learning is not symmetric. Current employers arguably observe workers' performance better than competitors. Similarly, insurers observe their customers' accident histories while competitors may not.

Interestingly, the information structure has stark implications on equilibrium contracts and market performance. These distinct implications permit us to identify the kind of learning present in the market.

In some markets, the information structure is a matter of choice – for example, by forcing insurers to share (or forbidding them from sharing) customers' claims histories. The European Commission debated the legality of sharing accident information among automobile insurers in France and Belgium, which would have switched the market from one with asymmetric learning into one with symmetric learning. De Garidel-Thoron, 2005) studies the welfare implications of making accident information public.

To ease exposition, let's call the insurers in the spot market "competitors," and the incumbent insurer who sold coverage in the first period "the insurer."

6.1   Theory

To study the role of dynamic contracts under asymmetric learning, we modify the model in de Garidel-Thoron (2005) to align the analysis with that of Section 2.1, so that the only difference between this section and Section 2.1 is the nature of learning.

De Garidel-Thoron (2005) presents a two-period model with symmetric priors, asymmetric learning, and one-sided commitment. Ex ante identical risk-averse consumers with income y in both periods can suffer a financial loss m.

Unlike de Garidel-Thoron, for simplicity and consistency with Section 2.1, we assume there is no loss in the first period. The probabilities of a second-period loss are p_A and p_N, depending on the signal received between periods. The signal $\lambda = \{A, N\}$ can be interpreted as having a first-period accident or not (a costless accident, since we assume no first-period loss, for simplicity), so that $p_A > p_N$.[9] Unlike Section 2.1, we capture asymmetric learning by assuming the signal is exclusively observed by the insuree and the insurer. We allow for changing income, $y_1 \neq y_2$.

Let's consider the two benchmarks presented in Section 2.1, but now with asymmetric learning in which competitors do not observe λ.

6.1.1   Benchmark I: Two-Sided Commitment

Because of commitment, insurance is sold before the signal is observed. Competitive premiums break even ex ante, so that $p_1 + p_2 = E_\lambda(E(m|\lambda))$. Premiums are independent of λ: both event risk and premium risk are fully insured, equating $u'(c)$ across period-2 states.

Premiums p_1 and p_2 are timed to smooth consumption, equating $u'(c)$ across periods as well. The allocation is first best, as it is under two-sided commitment with symmetric learning. The asymmetry of information is immaterial for the allocation because parties commit before the information is revealed.

6.1.2   Benchmark II: No Commitment

Absent commitment, the spot market plays an active role. When the spot market opens, competitors are at an informational disadvantage relative to the insurer who observed λ. This asymmetry is the key shaping contracts under no commitment as well as under unilateral commitment (discussed next).

---

[9] It seems strange that we assume there is no first-period risk, despite signals being observed. We do so for simplicity and to mimic the analysis in Section 2.1.

Because of the informational disadvantage, competitors must offer Roth-schild – Stiglitz-type contracts to separate buyers. Notice separation is neces-sary in equilibrium. If a pooling contract were offered, the insurer would retain N and let A go, making the pooling contract unprofitable.

The period-2 separating spot contracts screen A by offering partial coverage to N. A gets full insurance at actuarially fair premiums, while N's premium is set so that A is indifferent between the two contracts.

The insurer, having observed λ, can offer full coverage to both types of customers. Having full information means it does not need to screen buyers.

The insurer enjoys an informational rent from N, whose outside option involves partial coverage. Although the market is competitive, unable to show her type in the spot market, N is locked into the insurer, paying more than actuarially fair premiums.

In the first period, insurers compete to attract customers, charging premiums below cost in anticipation of future rents. Insurers invest in customers to enjoy the second-period rent from those who end up becoming good drivers, N. First-period competition dissipates the rent ex ante.

Interestingly, despite consumers' lack of commitment, N is stuck with the insurer. The lock-in enables the transfer of resources away from the most for-tunate state – the state with the lowest marginal utility of consumption – to the first period. Asymmetric learning creates consumer commitment in the state in which it is valuable to commit to remain with the insurer, namely, in the good state.

By taking resources away from state N, the lock-in lowers consumption variance. Thus, as shown by de Garidel-Thoron (2005), welfare is higher under asymmetric learning than under symmetric learning when parties cannot commit.

6.1.3   One-Sided Commitment

Similar forces are at play under unilateral contracts. N finds herself locked in with the insurer, who enjoys a second-period rent. The main distinction is that the insurer is now able to commit to the future terms of the contract, and promises to transfer resources to state A. The combination of lock-in to extract resources away from N and insurer commitment to send resources to state A improves welfare, relative to no commitment, as well as relative to one-sided commitment with symmetric learning.

More specifically, second-period competitors offer separating contracts with full insurance for A and partial coverage for N. The terms offered differ from those under no commitment, since the inside option of each type depends on the long-term contract offered by the insurer in period 1.

The long-term contract offers full insurance to both A and N. As in the non-commitment case, lock-in generates an informational rent from N. Com-petition in the first period dissipates the rent in the form of a transfer to period 1 and to state A in the second period, equating marginal utility across period 1 and state A in period 2. Absent commitment, such a promise is not feasible.

Relative to symmetric learning, N finds herself locked in; committed to stay in the state, she is tempted to lapse, enabling the transfer of resources to period 1 and state A, reducing consumption variance.

6.2 Policy Implications

What are the welfare consequences of disclosing accident information? As noted previously, the question was debated by the European Commission in the context of automobile insurance. On the plus side, symmetric information eases switching, perhaps increasing second-period competition. On the other hand, locking in good types enhances commitment (as in Crocker-Moran, 2003).

De Garidel-Thoron (2005) shows that the extra commitment induced by asymmetric learning locks in type N drivers, which reduces consumption variance and is thus welfare-improving. He does so by comparing market performance in the situation described in Section 2.4 under symmetric learning with the one with asymmetric learning in Section 6.1.3. In this stylized two-period world, banning information sharing is preferable.

6.3 Testable Implications

The two environments, symmetric and asymmetric learning, deliver starkly opposite predictions on premium profiles, lapsation, and selection.

Under asymmetric learning, good draws are unable to show their type and do not generate attractive offers. The insurer enjoys an informational rent, which is competed away through first-period premiums below actuarial costs, known in the literature as lowballing. Moreover, since good types are locked in, we expect advantageous selection. Under symmetric learning, in contrast, we expect the good draws to get the best outsider offers and lapse from the contract, leading to adverse selection. These predictions were tested by D'Arcy et al. (1990) and Cohen (2012).

There is one important caveat to these theoretical results. While the symmetric learning predictions are derived from multi-period models (Harris and Holmstrom, 1982; Handel et al., 2017), we are not aware of any work showing the robustness of de Garidel-Thoron's (2005) predictions to horizons longer than two periods. While it is not clear if predictions would change, more work is needed to understand asymmetric learning in multiple periods.

6.4 Labor Markets

Employment relations are natural situations in which asymmetric learning may arise. Performance might be monitored within the confines of the workplace, but is not easy to follow by outsiders. Not surprisingly, the earliest interest in asymmetric learning came from the work of Labor Economists.

Greenwald (1986) studied the frictions created by the asymmetry of information between current and potential employers. Similar to the analysis above, outsiders expect movers to be of lower quality and thus offer low wages, so that good draws remain in their current jobs, and the initial employer enjoys an informational rent.

Waldman (1984), and Ricart I Costa (1988) address a similar situation to Greenwald's, but assume that while worker performance is not observed by competitors, rank and promotions are. In equilibrium, promotions are delayed to prevent dilution of the informational rent enjoyed by current employers.

6.5   Insurance

Work on insurance includes Kunreuther and Pauly (1985) and D'Arcy et al. (1990). These papers, unlike de Garidel-Thoron (2005), assume initial asymmetry in information between insurers and drivers. Nevertheless, predictions are similar to those derived above. The eventual asymmetry vis-à-vis competitors creates customer lock-in: good draws cannot prove their type in order to get better quotes from competitors. Locked-in drivers become profitable customers for their current insurers. These models predict lowballing: competition drives initial premiums below actuarial costs, due to later profits once good drivers become locked in.

6.6   Credit Markets

Starting with Sharpe (1990), the banking literature has looked at the advantage banks have in ongoing relationships with repeat borrowers. Observing their performance over time, they enjoy an informational rent over new lenders. Rajan (1992) studies the impact banks' bargaining power, due to lock-in, has on firms' portfolio choice of borrowing sources. He shows that differential treatment due to lock-in can lead to inefficient capital allocation. Dell'Ariccia, Friedman, and Marquez (1999) study the impact of superior information by the incumbent lender on entry, which blockades entrants.

6.7   Evidence

Gibbonś and Katz (1991) is the first empirical paper to use labor data to assess the presence of asymmetric information between current and potential employers. They compare wages and unemployment duration under two different scenarios: when individuals are individually laid off versus layoffs due to plant closings. Plant closings convey no information about the individual worker's type, while an individual layoff might be attributed to low performance. The authors find shorter unemployment spells and higher subsequent wages for workers displaced by a plant closing than those individually laid off. While the findings do not directly speak to issues of dynamic contracting, they do attest to the association of switchers with poor performance and worker lock-in.

D'Arcy and Doherty (1990) present evidence of lowballing in the US automobile insurance market. Loss ratios (losses over premiums) in their sample of seven insurers decline in the age of the policy, consistent with lowballing and lock-in of good types.

Cohen (2012) presents evidence from an automobile insurer in Israel. There is no information sharing among insurers in Israel, so learning is asymmetric. Cohen finds that drivers with a good record (good types) are less likely to lapse, and over time good types become more profitable. More precisely, drivers get a discount for their good driving record, but the discount does not fully account for the loss differential. The cost reduction is not fully passed to the insuree, which is consistent with the insurer having an informational advantage. Namely, good drivers are unable to fully convey their type to competitors.

In D'Arcy and Doherty (1990) and Cohen (2012), as well as in the model presented by Kunreuther and Pauly (1985), there is initial asymmetric information between the driver and the insurer. While the initial asymmetry departs from the basic setup presented above, as well as from that of de Garidel-Thoron, predictions are to a large extent similar. We can think of the initial informational asymmetry as arising from a prior driving history under a different insurer – that is, as if the initial period in those models is the second stage of de Garidel-Thoron. A multi-period version of the latter might provide additional insights into the function of markets with asymmetric learning.

7 CONCLUSIONS

This chapter surveys the theory and evidence on contracting under learning à la Harris and Holmstrom (1982) and its variations. Models of learning and imperfect commitment are useful for understanding dynamic selection and reclassification risk. Imperfect commitment can be the source of adverse selection, even when information is symmetric. We draw from diverse areas of economics to show the relevance of the theory.

The empirical literature has looked at testable implications on selection and on optimal contracts, and more recently has estimated the welfare loss from lack of commitment to be substantial. The theory offers policy prescriptions on how to overcome the market distortions associated with limited commitment, mainly to prevent the lapsation of good draws.

References

Abramitzky, R. (2008) "The Limits of Equality: Evidence from the Israeli Kibbutz," *Quarterly Journal of Economics* 123(3): 1111–59.

Akerlof, G. (1970) "The Market for 'Lemons' Quality Uncertainty and the Market Mechanism," *Quarterly Journal of Economics* 84(3): 488–500.

Atal, J. P. (2015) "Lock-In in Dynamic Health Insurance Contracts: Evidence from Chile."

Bayot, D. (2015) "Why Do Markets Fail to Fully Insure Against Reclassification Risk? Contract Incompleteness v. Limited Commitment in the Life Insurance Industry."

Beaudry, P. and J. DiNardo. (1991) "The Effect of Implicit Contracts on the Movement of Wages Over the Business Cycle: Evidence from Micro Data," *Journal of Political Economy*, 99(4), 665–88.

Browne, M. and A. Hoffmann. (2013) "One-Sided Commitment in Dynamic Insurance Contracts: Evidence from Private Health Insurance in Germany," *Journal of Risk and Uncertainty*, February 2013, 46(1), 81–112.

Cardon, J. and I. Hendel. (2001) "Asymmetric Information in Health Insurance: Evidence from the National Medical Expenditure Survey," *RAND Journal of Economics* 32, 408–27.

Cochrane, J. (1995) "Time-Consistent Health Insurance," *Journal of Political Economy* 103, 445–73.

Cohen, A. (2005) "Asymmetric Information and Learning in the Automobile Insurance Market," *Review of Economics and Statistics*, 87, 197–207.

Cohen, A. (2012) "Asymmetric Learning in Repeated Contracting: An Empirical Study," *Review of Economics and Statistics,* 94(2), 419–32.

Crocker, K. and J. Moran. (2003) "Contracting with Limited Commitment: Evidence from Employment-Based Health Insurance Contracts," *RAND Journal of Economics*, 694–718.

Currie, J. and B. Madrian. (1999) "Health, Health Insurance and the Labor Market," *Handbook of Health Economics*, 3, Part C, 3309–416.

Dafny, L., I. Hendel, and N. Wilson. (2015) "Narrow Networks on the Health Insurance Exchanges: What Do They Look Like and How Do They Affect Pricing? A Case Study of Texas," *American Economic Review* P&P 105(5), 110–14.

Daily, G. (1989) *The Individuals Investor's Guide to Low-Load Insurance Products* (Chicago, IL: International Publishing Corporation).

Daily, G., I. Hendel, and A. Lizzeri. (2008) "Does the Secondary Life Insurance Market Threaten Dynamic Insurance?" *American Economic Review,* 98(2), 151–6.

D'Arcy, Stephen P. and Doherty, Neil A. (1990) "Adverse Selection, Private Information, and Lowballing in Insurance Markets." *Journal of Business,* 63, April, 145–64.

De Garidel-Thoron, T. (2005) "Welfare-Improving Asymmetric Information in Dynamic Insurance Markets," *Journal of Political Economy*, 113(1), 121–50.

Dell'Ariccia, C., E. Friedman, and R. Marquez. (1999) "Adverse Selection as a Barrier to Entry in the Banking Industry," *RAND Journal of Economics* 30, 515–34.

Fang, H. and A. Gavazza. (2010). "Dynamic Inefficiencies in an Employment-Based Health-Insurance System: Theory and Evidence," *American Economic Review*, 101(7), 3047–77.

Fang, H., and E. Kung. (2012) "Why Do Life Insurance Policyholders Lapse? The Roles of Income, Health and Bequest Motive Shocks."

Finkelstein, A., K. McGarry, and A. Sufi. (2005) "Dynamic Inefficiencies in Insurance Markets: Evidence from Long-Term Care Insurance," *The American Economic Review, Papers and Proceedings*, 95(2), 224–8.

Gibbons, R. and L.F. Katz. (1991) "Layoffs and Lemons," *Journal of Labor Economics*, 9(4), 351–80.

Greenwald, B. (1986) "Adverse Selection in the Labor Market," *Review of Economic Studies* 53, 325–47.

Hall, R. (1978) "Stochastic Implications of the Life Cycle-Permanent Income Hypothesis: Theory and Evidence." *Journal of Political Economy*. 86(6) 971–87.

Handel, B. (2013) "Adverse Selection and Switching Costs in Health Insurance Markets: When Nudging Hurts," *American Economic Review,* 103(7), 2643–82.

Handel, B., I. Hendel, and M. Whinston. (2015) "Equilibria in Health Exchanges: Adverse Selection vs. Reclassification Risk" *Econometrica*, 83(4), 1261–313.

Handel, B., I. Hendel, and M. Whinston. (2017) "The Welfare Impact of Long-Term Health Insurance Contracts," Working paper.

Harris, M. and B. Holmstrom. (1982) "A Theory of Wage Dynamics," *Review of Economic Studies,* XL, 315–33.

Hendel, I. and A. Lizzeri. (2003) "The Role of Commitment in Dynamic Contracts: Evidence from Life Insurance," *Quarterly Journal of Economics* 118, 299–327.

Herring, B. and M. Pauly. (2006) "Incentive-Compatible Guaranteed Renewable Health Insurance Premiums," *Journal of Health Economics* 25, 395–417.

Holmstrom B. (1983) "Equilibrium Long-Term Labor Contracts," *Quarterly Journal of Economics*, 98, Supplement, 23–54.

Koch, T. (2011) "One Pool to Insure Them All? Age, Risk, and the Price(s) of Medical Insurance," UC-Santa Barbara Working Paper.

Kunreuther, H. and M. Pauly. (1985) "Market Equilibrium with Private Knowledge: An Insurance Example," *Journal Public Economics* 26 April, 269–88.

Ligon, E., J. Thomas, and T. Worrall. (2002) "Informal Insurance Arrangements with Limited Commitment: Theory and Evidence from Village Economies," *Review of Economic Studies* 69, 209–44.

Patel, V. and M. Pauly. (2002) "Guaranteed Renewability and the Problem of Risk Variation in Individual Health Insurance Markets," *Health Affairs*, pp. 280–9.

Pauly, M., H. Kunreuther and R. Hirth. (1995) "Guaranteed Renewability in Insurance," *Journal of Risk and Uncertainty,* 10, 143–56.

Pauly, M., A. Percy, and B. Herring. (1999) "Individual vs. Job-Based Health Insurance: Weighing the Pros and Cons," *Health Affairs* 18(6), 28–44.

Rajan, R. (1992) "Insiders and Outsiders: The Choice between Informed and Arm's Length Debt," *Journal of Finance* 47, 1367–1400.

Ricart I Costa, J. (1988) "Managerial Task Assignment and Promotions," *Econometrica* 56(2), 449–66.

Sharpe, S. (1990) "Asymmetric Information, Bank Lending and Implicit Contracts: A Stylized Model of Customer Relationships," *Journal of Finance* 45, 1069–87.

Waldman, M. (1984) "Job assignments, signalling, and efficiency." *RAND Journal of Economics* 15, 255–67.

CHAPTER 4

Discussion of "Agency Problems"

Bernard Salanié

Apart from their high quality, these two papers share a common thread: they emphasize learning. Now learning can take place in a wide variety of ways. It can be a purposeful and costly activity; or information can flow in exogenously. One can learn from one's own experiments, as well as from observing others' experimenting and its results; or learning can be informed by recommendations from experts. In a market situation, one can learn from competitors, in ways that are shaped both by their strategies and by regulations. Learning also builds on what one already knows; in modelling terms, some information about the world must be assumed to be known. I will return to this perhaps obvious point in my conclusion.

In the models surveyed by Hörner and Skrzypacz, learning is costly, as experimenting with a risky choice forgoes the benefits of safer options. In so far as each agent can also learn from what (s)he observes on other agents experiments, this opens the door to free riding. But since other agents' payoffs to experimenting depend on their current beliefs, it is sometimes useful to experiment in order to change these beliefs – "nudging" others to experiment. This strategic interaction between agents in turn opens the door for other parties to attempt to manipulate information accrual. The seller of a new experience good, for instance, can design the way it rewards early adopters for their reviews, or simply how it chooses to publish them.

Hendel's chapter builds on a long tradition in contract theory: it has principals learning about agents' types over time. The main focus of the chapter is on the case when each agent's type changes exogenously over time, so that learning occurs on both sides of the relationship. Learning can still be asymmetric, both because the agent learns his type privately and/or because other principals may not observe what one principal has learnt. Unlike much of the theoretical literature on dynamic contracting, Hendel focuses on learning that is symmetric between the two parties in a relationship, but may be asymmetric between the various principals: my insurer learns my risk at the same time that I do, but her competitors may be equally well-informed ("symmetric learning" in the chapter) or not ("asymmetric learning".) Given limited commitment, changes in the agent's type may give rise to reclassification risk: insurers are tempted to index premia to risk. Even if my health insurer can commit not to increase my premia if my health deteriorates, I won't commit not to look for a better deal if my health improves – provided that I can prove to other insurers that I have become a better risk. This introduces a stark difference between the predictions of models with symmetric and with asymmetric learning between competitors. It also gives regulations on information disclosure a crucial role.

I will discuss the chapter by Hörner and Skrzypacz first, and then turn to Hendel's. Finally I will attempt to offer concluding remarks that apply to both papers.

1 LEARNING AND EXPERIMENTATION

Hörner and Skrzypacz discuss a wide variety of papers and topics; this literature is so rich and develops so fast that it is not entirely clear (yet) what its dominant themes are. As an applied economist, I am especially keen on robust predictions of theoretical models. It would be churlish to complain about the specific assumptions that theorists rely on to generate solutions – the Brownian motions and linear payoff structures of the strategic experimentation literature, for instance. It is more important to "break the bone and suck the substantific marrow" (Rabelais, 1534).

The encouragement effect in the models of strategic experimentation is a case in point. While free-riding is an obvious enough phenomenon when one can benefit from others' costly experimenting, the encouragement effect is more subtle; and in fact it only exists in the "bad news model." Remember that in these strategic bandits games, information accrues randomly as a function of the effort spent on experimenting. Information can be bad news (the risky payoff is low) or good news (it is high); and it fully reveals the state of the world. In more succinct terms,

> with good news no news is bad news
> with bad news no news is good news;
>
> and all news is conclusive news.

The News Rap (anonymous, 2015)

Experimenting in order to encourage others to experiment can only be relevant if others observe my experimenting when it generates no news. Moeover, it only works if the experiment does not generate any news (since all news is conclusive) and if this absence of news is good news (otherwise it will discourage rather than encourage further experiments in the risky arm.) This is why the encouragement effect only appears in the bad news model.

The paragraph above applies to the basic model, in which, once the state of the world is revealed, all players choose the best arm and receive the same payoff. Consider several firms researching a new technology. The intensity of their research effort may be more easily observed by their competitors than the results of their research, so that the encouragement effect could play a role. The basic model suggests that if the new technology is highly speculative (which I loosely interpret as bad news being more likely than good news), it may pay to invest research money in order to nudge others to do so; and that firms are more likely to free-ride if the new technology is a reasonably safe bet.

In real-world competitive situations one would expect payoffs to be interdependent, with an advantage accruing to the first player who receives conclusive news – in the R&D example, the first firm to innovate will reap a temporary monopoly, and/or the first firm to find out that the new technology is a dud can let its competitors waste their efforts. What does it suggest about the encouragement effect? With bad news more likely, it may be even more tempting to do a little experimenting so as to push others into doing more. On the other hand one could imagine a "discouragement effect" whereby firms reduce their (visible) experimenting so as to reduce the likelihood that others get to the prize first. I confess that I have little intuition concerning the features of the solution – but I am eager to read about it.

Let me also note here that the conclusive feature of news in this model is quite restrictive for this application. Innovation often occurs in stages, each standing on the shoulders of the previous one. If firm A was successful with stage 1, should it disclose its results, as it must if it wants to patent stage 1? Or does the "winner takes all" character of such contests push players into hiding their progress? And how would early success modify later experimentation? There is a wealth of fascinating questions for applied theorists to explore.

Finally, a common feature of most models discussed in this chapter is that agents are homogenous ex ante. My gut feeling is that, in many applications of learning and experimentation, differences in prior beliefs matter, perhaps even more than different preferences. There is convincing evidence that CEOs who invest more in innovation tend to be overconfident (see, e.g., Galasso and Simcoe, 2011); not to mention individual innovators. Theorists are understandably reluctant to drop the common prior assumption, but we may lose much by imposing it in studying innovation contests. This again raises a host of new questions. It should be possible to use hierarchical priors to model "meta-learning," by which agent A learns also about the priors of agent B by observing her experimenting.

Even the case when it is known that some agents are more optimistic than others (and they agree to disagree) presents interesting possibilities. How would known differences in priors shape the incentives of each to experiment? Do large firms rely on smaller innovators just because they are more nimble, or perhaps also because the law of averages makes it more likely that small groups have more extreme beliefs?

2 (EMPIRICS OF) DYNAMICS OF SELECTION

Debates on health insurance policies and in particular around the 2010 Affordable Care Act (hereafter ACA) in the United States have made "reclassification risk" almost a household name; but it goes much beyond insurance. Agents face reclassification risk when other parties' perception of their type changes over time in ways that they do not fully control, and their future payoff is type-dependent. In this broad sense, other examples can be drawn from labor economics as in the paper, or indeed from the "new dynamic public finance" – uninsurable shocks to the value of human capital drive reclassification risk just as health shocks do. I will focus most of my remarks on insurance under symmetric learning, as the paper does; but I will return to the labor market in 2.3.

While the process that drives shocks may respond to agents' actions, Hendel's paper stresses "exogenous" reclassification risk. To return to health insurance, the quality of past care and/or prevention efforts has no impact on current health shocks. This simplifies the analysis; but any welfare evaluation of the ACA should also take into account the "preventive care" argument – that more affordable insurance can have positive effects on the dynamic of health shocks. I should note here that the early results of the Oregon Health Insurance Experiment are not very encouraging in that regard (see, e.g., Baicker and Finkelstein, 2014).

The simplest model of reclassification risk assumes that the insurer and all insurees observe health shocks symmetrically and that insurees cannot commit beyond the current insurance period (typically a year.) Its predictions are clear: consumers who have a positive health shock will switch insurers ("lapse" their current policy) unless premia decrease enough. Assuming away barriers to switching insurers, consumers who lapse are better risks than those who do not. The contractual second-best front-loads premia ("highballing"), in so far as the liquidity of insurees allows it. This generates a rich set of testable predictions, since the strength of these effects depends on income profiles, on switching costs, and on the distribution of risks. The chapter makes a strong case that empirical studies have generally found a high degree of support for these predictions.

Handel, Hendel, and Whinston (2015) show that the market equilibrium depends a great deal on policy towards reclassification risk. They study the "community rating" clause of the ACA, which banned varying premiums according to individual health status. Community rating only allows pricing to depend on age and tobacco use, within limited bands. As such, it essentially removes reclassification risk; but it generates adverse selection. Health plans with better coverage become much less profitable, causing a partial unraveling of the market at the higher end. Remember that community rating prevents front-loading of premia, which is particularly harmful to individuals whose incomes rise over time. Since those individuals tend to have higher lifetime income, community rating benefits the better off – surely a case of unintended consequences.

As I already mentioned, reclassification risk could be "endogenous" in that insurees can influence the perception of their type by insurers. In particular, insurers attempt to learn about any *persistent* component of insuree risk. Dionne and Doherty (1994) characterized the optimal insurance contracts under repeated adverse selection with one-sided commitment. They showed that they also involve highballing; moreover, insurees whose persistent risk is lower choose more experience-rated contracts. While community rating now rules out these contracts in US health insurance, Dionne and Doherty tested their predictions on Californian automobile insurance data. They also found support for the theory.

2.1   Imperfect Competition

If I may cite myself (Chiappori and Salanié, 2014),

> [...] perfect competition does not approximate insurance markets that well. Fixed costs, product differentiation, price stickiness, switching costs, and cross-subsidization are common; oligopoly is probably the rule rather than the exception.

Cross-subsidies and switching costs are particularly relevant to this discussion. Handel (2013) has shown how surprisingly high switching costs can be in employer-provided health insurance. By the very logic of dynamic selection, switching costs should attenuate it, or perhaps even reverse it since insurers would find it profitable to charge low initial premia and to raise them over the course of a relationship. It would be interesting to check whether insurance markets with lower switching costs are less subject to highballing and lapsation of good risks.

The role of cross-subsidies is a bit less obvious. Most models of cross-subsidies in insurance have low risks subsidizing high risks, à la Miyazaki–Spence–Wilson. Cross-subsidization may therefore reduce unraveling of high coverage contracts in equilibrium. If this were confirmed by a more rigorous analysis, it would again point the way to further tests.

2.2   Exclusive and Nonexclusive Insurance

Hendel's chapter is entirely focused on *exclusive* insurance, in which each insuree can only buy one contract. Automobile insurance is a classic case of exclusive insurance, as most companies will refuse to pay out if an insuree is covered by another insurer. Life insurance, on the other hand, is nonexclusive: there is no limit to how many contracts a person can buy. Health insurance sits somewhere in between. It is generally possible to buy additional health coverage, for instance to cover other risks; but regulation often constrains how much supplementary insurance a person can buy, so as to limit demand for care.

The distinction between exclusive and nonexclusive insurance has been underemphasized in empirical work, but it is hugely important. Nonexclusivity severely constrains price discrimination. While dealing with adverse selection normally requires price schedules that are convex (unit prices that increase with the quantity bought), agents can always defeat convexity by buying small contracts from several insurers. Without exclusivity, prices must be linear in quantity in equilibrium[1].

When all agents face the same unit price, low-risk agents subsidize high-risk agents; and high-risk agents will be overrepresented among buyers. In addition, they will buy more insurance. This is a different form of market unraveling than the one studied in the chapter. It is also harder to test, as with nonexclusive insurance we must obtain data on *all* insurance contracts held by each insuree in the sample.

More generally, agents derive insurance from many sources. They can simply expend effort to reduce their exposure, either by self-precaution or self-prevention, by precautionary saving, or by building up social networks. They can resort to private insurance markets, or rely on a public safety net. In that sense, nonexclusive insurance seems to be the rule rather than the exception. It is clear that even in a static framework, if factor supply responds to taxation, or if private insurance generates moral hazard, then private and public insurance have externalities (e.g. Chetty and Saez, 2010). How do we deal with dynamic selection *across* all these sources of insurance? This is a topic that cries for more research.

2.3   Learning in the Labor Market

All of the phenomena that Hendel's chapter describes are pervasive in the labor market. Workers' performance varies over time, and they learn about its persistent component too, as does their employer and its competitors. As the chapter suggests, there have been few empirical studies on dynamic selection in the labor market. Moral hazard considerations have figured more prominently in the empirical literature; and our understanding of dynamic moral hazard has not made much progress beyond simple exponential or linear models. I would still like to point to the remarkable contribution of Gayle, Golan, and Miller, (2015), which incorporates selection as well as moral hazard in a very ambitious study of executive compensation and career dynamics.

2.4   Concluding Remarks

As I mentioned in the introduction, all learning models must start by assuming that, while agents may have different information, each agent knows some basic features of the world, and has some prior belief about what it does not

---

[1] I refer the reader to Attar, Mariotti, and Salanié (2011; 2014) for more rigorous and nuanced versions of this statement.

know. In addition, they characterize the optimal strategies of fully rational agents.

These are of course shared features of most economic models, and they have been questioned by the literature on bounded rationality among others. But when the emphasis is on learning, they should perhaps be probed with an even more critical eye. I already suggested that the common prior assumption may detract from important and interesting phenomena in models of experimentation. When agents play a game repeatedly, or at least can observe past instances of the game, it is reasonable to assume that they have learned its basic structure and perhaps simple heuristics; and bad heuristics may have been weeded out by selection over time. It is not clear to me that either of these arguments apply in the R&D example, for instance. It would be interesting to explore learning with agents who play simple and relatively detail-free rules; this may lead to more robust solutions.

The insurance market also exhibits some surprising behavior. For one thing, price elasticities across policies are often low; and the high price of increases in coverage is hard to reconcile with standard estimates of risk aversion. I already mentioned the relevance of switching costs. In addition, the stakes in car insurance for instance are fairly small. With a yearly risk of an accident at-fault of 5 percent or so, choosing a $500 or a $1,000 deductible only represents an expected value difference of $25. Health insurance is a much more consequential choice, and the increased transparency mandated by the ACA may change the competitive picture. This contrast suggests that we should approach different markets in a pragmatic manner, taking into account informational resources available to agents. Such an approach may require more cautious welfare evaluations, as choices may not reveal preferences as straightforwardly as we would like them to.

References

Attar, A., T. Mariotti and F. Salanié (2011), "Nonexclusive Competition in the Market for Lemons," *Econometrica*, 79, 1869–918.

Attar, A., T. Mariotti and F. Salanié (2014), "Non-Exclusive Competition under Adverse Selection," *Theoretical Economics*, 9, 1–40.

Baicker, K. and A. Finkelstein (2014), "Insuring the Uninsured," www.povertyac tionlab.org/sites/default/files/publications/Insuring_the_Uninsured.pdf.

Chetty, R. and E. Saez (2010), "Optimal Taxation and Social Insurance with Endogenous Private Insurance," *American Economic Journal: Economic Policy*, 2, 85–114.

Chiappori, P.-A, and B. Salanié (2001). "Testing for asymmetric information in insurance markets." *Journal of political Economy*, 108, 56–78.

Chiappori, P.-A. and B. Salanié (2014), "Asymmetric Information in Insurance Markets: Predictions and Tests", ch. 14 in *Handbook of Insurance*, G. Dionne, ed.

Chiappori, P.-A, B. Salanié, and J. Valentin (1999), "Early starters versus late beginners." *Journal of Political Economy*, 107, 731–60.

Dionne, G. and N. Doherty (1994), "Adverse Selection, Commitment and Renegotiation: Extension to and Evidence from Insurance Markets," *Journal of Political Economy*, 102-2, 210–35.

Galasso, A. and T. Simcoe (2011), "CEO overconfidence and innovation," *Management Science*, 57, 1469–84.

Gayle, G.-L., L. Golan and R. Miller (2015), "Promotion, Turnover and Compensation in the Executive Labor Market," *Econometrica*, 83, 2293–369.

Handel, B. (2013), "Adverse Selection and Switching Costs in Health Insurance Markets: When Nudging Hurts," *American Economic Review*, 103, 2643–82.

Handel, B., I. Hendel and M. Whinston (2015), "Equilibria in Health Exchanges: Adverse Selection vs. Reclassification Risk," *Econometrica*, 83, 1261–313.

Rabelais, F. (1534), prologue of *Gargantua*.

CHAPTER 5

Recent Developments in Matching Theory and Their Practical Applications
Fuhito Kojima

In recent years, many developments have been made in matching theory and its applications to market design. This paper surveys them and suggests possible research directions. The main focus is on the advances in matching theory that tackle market design problems in practical markets where the classical theory is inapplicable. Specifically, I discuss the recent theory of matching in large markets and "approximate market design," and a new theory of "matching with constraints," as well as their applications.

1 INTRODUCTION

Matching theory has made considerable progress since the seminal theoretical contribution by Gale and Shapley (1962) and its economic application by Roth (1984). The theory has been used to guide designs of medical match (Roth and Peranson, 1999) and other entry-level labor markets (Roth, 2002), school choice (Abdulkadiroğlu and Sönmez, 2003), course allocation in education (Sönmez and Ünver, 2010; Budish and Cantillon, 2012), and organ donation (Roth, Sönmez, and Ünver, 2004, 2005, 2007), just to name a few examples.

Theory has been put to practical use with much success, but the interaction between theory and practice is not unidirectional. On the contrary, as more practical applications have been found, the accompanying experiences have

This paper was prepared for an invited talk at the 2015 World Congress of Econometric Society in Montréal. I am especially grateful to Federico Echenique, who gave an excellent discussion at the World Congress. I benefited from discussions with Yeon-Koo Che and Parag Pathak, as well as comments from Bryan Cheong, Bobak Pakzad-Hurson, Michi Kandori, Shengwu Li, Giorgio Martini, Indira Puri, Son To, Akhil Vohra, Michael Wang, and seminar participants at Oxford, Santa Clara, Stanford, Tokyo, Waseda, and the World Congress. Stephen Nei and Eric Fanqi Shi provided excellent research assistance. Special thanks go to Al Roth, who not only gave comments but also kindly shared figures from one of his papers, which I included in this paper. I gratefully acknowledge financial support from the Sloan Foundation, as well as financial support from the National Research Foundation through its Global Research Network Grant (NRF-2013S1A2A2035408).

also uncovered limitations of existing theory. This has opened up opportunities for researchers to not only deepen the analysis of existing models but also generalize the standard model or introduce new models, thereby enabling us to address challenges that arise in applications.

Much of recent development in matching theory has been guided by our desire to solve practical problems with features that are absent from the standard model but are important in practice. New models that incorporate some of these features lead to sharp predictions while still being general enough to enrich our understanding of the markets beyond one specific example.

This paper describes recent developments in matching theory and its applications. The survey by Abdulkadiroğlu and Sönmez (2013), based on their lectures at the last World Congress, offers an excellent introduction to the basic models as well as applications.[1] Thus, in this piece, I will focus on several specific topics that represent the kind of recent interaction between theory and practice I alluded to above. More specifically, my focus will be on how the features of some real markets deviate from the classical models, and how the theory has been modified or expanded to tackle these problems.

In this paper, I will focus on two topics that share the above general theme. The first topic is the analysis of an approach for design that could be called "approximate market design." Classical theory has found that it is often impossible to satisfy some desirable properties, no matter how hard one tries to design a matching mechanism. For example, there exists no two-sided matching mechanism that is strategy-proof and produces a stable matching for every given input. Another example is a result that if a labor-matching market includes a married couple who desire a pair of positions for them, then even the existence of a stable matching is not guaranteed. There are many impossibility results like these in the matching literature. For practical design, however, it is not clear if these negative results pose a big concern. I explore the idea of relaxing the desirable properties by requiring them only approximately: in matching with couples, for instance, I will only require the existence of a stable matching "with high probability." In order to formalize such approximate statements, I typically study the asymptotic behavior of the economy as it becomes large. This modeling approach appears to be especially fit for representative applications such as labor markets for medical residents and school choice in large school districts.

The other topic covered in this paper is the burgeoning literature of "matching with constraints." In the standard theory of matching, the only constraints for an allocation are those given by each agent's ability to consume at most a fixed number (in many cases, one) of goods and supply constraints such as limited positions in a firm or limited space in a school. However, many

---

[1] Other surveys include Roth (2007, 2008) and Sönmez and Ünver (2009). Roth and Sotomayor (1990) provide a comprehensive account of the early literature.

matching markets are subject to other kinds of constraints.[2] For example, medical markets are often constrained by regulations that limit the number of doctors practicing in certain medical specialties. Regulations on geographical distributions of doctors, teachers, and other kinds of workers are widespread. School districts may require each school in the district to maintain a certain diversity of socio-economic status or academic skill. The classical theory is not applicable in such situations, but recent advances in matching with constraints have generalized the theory to analyze these more complicated situations.

These specific topics are of interest by themselves, but I believe that they also enable us to learn a more general lesson. On the one hand, many models in these lines of research are highly tailored to very specific situations so that they can be directly applied to them: this paper offers a lot of discussions of American, British, and Japanese medical residency markets, school choice programs in New York City and Boston, and US clinical psychologist matching, for example. On the other hand, many of the models are also general enough to guide the direction of analysis and design beyond any one application. I believe that a good economic theory, or at least good economic theory of matching, is both detailed enough to make a sharp prediction or recommendation in specific applications *and* general and tractable enough to provide general insights and guide our thinking when facing new problems. Thankfully, I think that the effort of the research community has been successful in achieving both of these goals.

The rest of this paper proceeds as follows. Section 2 presents the basic matching model and classical results. Section 3 describes the research on large matching market models and approximate market design. Section 4 discusses research in matching with constraints. Section 5 concludes.

2 BASIC MODEL

This section introduces a simple two-sided matching model. I describe the model in terms of matching between doctors and hospitals because the theory has been extensively applied to that type of markets. Needless to say, one can use the same model to analyze many other situations, such as worker–firm matching or heterosexual marriage or school choice (i.e., matching between students and schools) among other things.

Let there be a finite set of doctors and a finite set of hospitals. Let me denote a generic doctor by i, j, and so forth, and a generic hospital by A, B, and so forth. Each doctor i has a strict preference relation $\succ_i$ over the set of hospitals and an exogenously given outside option (denoted by $\emptyset$) which represents being unmatched. For any doctor i and any pair of hospitals (or the outside option)

---

[2] Of course, constraints are important in other contexts as well. In the upcoming auction for reallocating spectrum rights in the US, there are numerous interference constraints that need to be handled (Milgrom and Segal, 2014). See also Milgrom (2009) who proposes an auction based on the "assignment messages" that can express various preferences and constraints.

A, B, I write $A \succeq_i B$ if and only if $A \succ_i B$ or $A = B$. I say that hospital A is **acceptable** to doctor i if $A \succ_i \emptyset$.

Notations and terminologies introduced for doctors in the last paragraph are also used for hospitals in analogous manners. I assume each doctor can work for at most one hospital, while allowing for a hospital to hire multiple doctors (a model with this property is called a many-to-one matching model). Thus, naturally I assume that each hospital has a preference relation over the set of subsets of doctors. Although in principle the preferences can be quite arbitrary, throughout this paper I assume that hospital preferences satisfy a condition called **responsiveness**: this condition requires that the hospital has a capacity (i.e., the number of positions) and a linear order over the doctors plus the outside option, and its optimal choice from any set of applicants to it is its most preferred acceptable doctors (with respect to the aforementioned linear order) up to its capacity.

Let us introduce further notation for preferences. Thanks to the responsiveness assumption, it turns out that only the ranking over acceptable partners matters for our analysis. Given this observation, I denote preferences by writing an ordered list of only acceptable partners. For example, the notation $\succ_i$: A, B represents a preference relation of doctor i such that she likes hospital A best, hospital B second, and the outside option third, and finds all other hospitals unacceptable. A **matching** μ is a mapping that specifies which doctor is assigned to which hospital (or the outside option). A matching μ is **individually rational** if (i) no agent is matched with a partner who is unacceptable to her, (ii) no doctor is matched with more than one hospital, and (iii) no hospital is matched with more doctors than its capacity. Given a matching μ, a **blocking pair** to it is a doctor – hospital pair that prefer to be matched with each other (while possibly rejecting some or all of their partners at μ) rather than being matched according to μ. A matching is **stable** if it is individually rational and there is no blocking pair to it.

A **mechanism** is a function from the set of preference profiles to the set of matchings. A mechanism is said to be **strategy-proof** if reporting the true preferences is a weakly dominant strategy for each agent. Strategy-proofness is regarded as an important property for a mechanism's success. However, it is well known that strategy-proofness and stability are incompatible with each other. More specifically, there is no strategy-proof mechanism that produces a stable matching for all possible preference profiles (Roth, 1982). Given this impossibility result, it is customary to consider incentive compatibility for doctors only. A mechanism is said to be **strategy-proof for doctors** if truthful preference reporting is a weakly dominant strategy for each doctor.

In this problem, the following **(doctor-proposing) deferred acceptance algorithm** due to Gale and Shapley (1962) plays a crucial role:

- Step 1: Each doctor applies to her first choice hospital. Each hospital rejects its least-preferred doctors in excess of its capacity and all unacceptable doctors among those who applied to it, keeping the remaining doctors tentatively.

In general, for any $t = 1, 2, \ldots$

- Step t: Each doctor who is not tentatively kept by a hospital applies to her next highest choice (a doctor does not apply to any hospital if she has been rejected by all hospitals acceptable to her). Each hospital considers these doctors *and* doctors who are tentatively kept from the previous step together, and rejects its least-preferred doctors in excess of its capacity and all unacceptable doctors, keeping the remaining doctors tentatively.

This algorithm terminates at the first step in which no rejection occurs (clearly, it terminates in a finite number of steps). Gale and Shapley (1962) show that the resulting matching is stable. This algorithm plays an important role throughout, and I discuss it many times, so I refer to it as DA for brevity (the *hospital-proposing* version of the deferred acceptance algorithm can be defined in an analogous manner, but in this paper I use DA to refer to only the doctor-proposing version of the algorithm).

Even though there exists no strategy-proof mechanism that produces a stable matching for all possible inputs, DA is strategy-proof for doctors (Dubins and Freedman, 1981; Roth, 1982).

3 LARGE MARKETS AND APPROXIMATE MARKET DESIGN

3.1   Manipulating stable mechanisms

As already mentioned, the stability requirement for a matching mechanism necessarily leads to manipulation possibilities, because there is no stable mechanism that is strategy-proof for both sides of the market. Below is a simple example illustrating this point for DA.[3]

Example 1   Consider the following market with two hospitals A, B, and two doctors i, j. Suppose that each hospital has only one position, and the hospital and doctor preferences are

$$\succ_A : i, j, \qquad\qquad \succ_i : B, A,$$
$$\succ_B : j, i, \qquad\qquad \succ_j : A, B.$$

With this input, at the first step of DA, i and j apply to B and A, respectively, and both of them are accepted. Hence, DA terminates at the first step, and the resulting matching is

---

[3] This example is not necessarily meant to be realistic. Rather, my intention is to present the simplest example possible to convey the main point. Similarly, many of the examples of this survey are made simple at the cost of realism.

$$\mu = \begin{pmatrix} A & B \\ j & i \end{pmatrix},$$

where this matrix notation means A is matched to j while B is matched to i.[4]

Now, suppose that hospital A misreports its preferences by declaring that only i is acceptable to it (hence j is unacceptable to it). Then, at the first step of DA, j's application to A is rejected, while i's application to B is tentatively accepted. The algorithm proceeds to step 2, j applies to B, and B tentatively accepts j while rejecting i. Then, at step 3, i applies to A, and this application is accepted. DA terminates at this step, and the resulting matching is:

$$\mu' = \begin{pmatrix} A & B \\ i & j \end{pmatrix}.$$

Comparing matchings μ and μ', one can verify that hospital A is made better off by misreporting its preferences, implying that DA is not strategy-proof. □

As mentioned earlier, the manipulability of DA in the above example can be extended to the general impossibility of strategy-proof and stable mechanisms. This finding has a profound implication for matching theory. It provides a sense in which a desirable market design is impossible for the two-sided matching problem if its participants behave strategically. However, whether this impossibility result has a "bite" in a given application or not is far from obvious. This is because the result is based on a highly stylized example under complete information, and it is silent about whether DA or other stable mechanisms are easily manipulable in reality. If anything, there are many real markets that employ stable matching mechanisms despite its incentive incompatibility, and evidence suggests that stable mechanisms work without much problem while unstable ones often fail (Roth, 1991, 2002). A question for economists is to understand why stable mechanisms appear to be working despite the failure of strategy-proofness.

To tackle this problem, Roth and Peranson (1999) conduct a series of simulations on data from the NRMP and other medical matching markets as well as randomly generated data. In their analysis of NRMP data, they find that very few agents had any profitable misreporting of preferences. Among the key features of the NRMP data is that there are many participants. For the randomly generated data, Roth and Peranson (1999) find that the proportion of agents who can profitably misreport preferences is smaller in large markets than in small markets, as shown in Figure 1. These findings lead them to conjecture that the proportion of participants who can profitably misreport preferences decreases and tends to zero as the size of the market grows.[5]

---

[4] I use similar notation throughout this paper.

[5] Similar empirical observations have also been made for other markets such as APPIC, which is an American market for clinical psychologists (Kojima, Pathak, and Roth, 2013), and Boston Public School's student assignment system (Pathak and Sönmez, 2008).

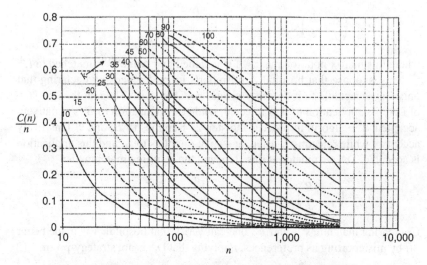

Figure 1 The vertical axis measures the proportion of hospitals that have a profitable unilateral manipulation in DA (denoted $C(n)/n$). There are n doctors and n hospitals, each doctor finds a constant number k of hospitals acceptable, each firm ranks all doctors who apply to it, and preferences are uniformly i.i.d. Reproduced from Roth and Peranson (1999).

Theories have been developed to account for this regularity found in simulations, and formalized a sense in which the above conjecture holds. I follow Immorlica and Mahdian (2005) and Kojima and Pathak (2009) to illustrate the main forces behind this phenomenon. Consider a growing sequence of markets indexed by the number of hospitals, which can be interpreted as representing the market size (the number of doctors are allowed – although not required – to grow at the same rate as the hospitals). Each agent's preference is his or her private information. Doctors and hospitals simultaneously report their preferences given their private information. Under certain regularity conditions (which I discuss in Section 3.1.1), Kojima and Pathak (2009) show approximate incentive compatibility of DA as formalized in the following statement.

Theorem 1 *Consider a sequence of markets. For any $\varepsilon > 0$, there exists a positive integer n such that truthtelling is an ε-Bayes Nash equilibrium in the game of preference reporting under DA for each market with at least n hospitals.*[6]

Instead of presenting the formal proof, let us describe an intuition here. To do so, recall first that DA is strategy-proof for doctors, so it suffices to show approximate incentive compatibility for hospitals. More specifically, I

---

[6] I say that a strategy profile is an ε-Bayes Nash equilibrium if no agent gains more than ε in expectation by any unilateral deviation from that strategy profile.

shall establish that, for each hospital, truth-telling of its preferences is an approximate best response if everyone else is truthful. For this purpose, I first note that the intuitive reason for a successful misreporting by hospitals is by way of a "rejection chain," which is a chain reaction of applications and rejections that occur during the execution of the algorithm. More specifically, a rejection chain is a sequence of applications and rejections initiated by a strategic rejection which causes the rejected doctor to apply to her next choice hospital, which may displace another doctor, who applies to her next choice hospital, and so forth. Some of the rejected doctors along the rejection chain may apply to the misreporting hospital, and this hospital may be made better off if these new applicants are desirable.[7] In the context of the previous example, hospital A initiates a rejection chain by rejecting j; the rejected doctor j applies to her next choice hospital B, causing it to reject doctor i; and this in turn causes i to apply to the original manipulating hospital A, making it better off.

The above observation helps obtain the intuition for the approximate incentive compatibility result in Theorem 1. In a large market (in the sense of having a large number of participants), there are many hospitals with at least one vacant position at the DA outcome under truthtelling (with high probability).[8] This implies that the doctors who are strategically rejected by a misreporting hospital or the doctors who are rejected later in the rejection chain are likely to apply to one of the hospitals with those vacant positions. Once a doctor applies to a vacant position, she is accepted and the rejection chain terminates because no new doctor is rejected. When this happens, the misreporting hospital loses the original doctor because of strategically rejecting her, but it does not get any new doctor. Therefore, in a large market the misreporting hospital is unlikely to be made better off at all, which implies approximate incentive compatibility as stated in the theorem.

Remark 1   Theorem 1 has an implication for a structural property of the set of stable matchings. It is well known that if there are two stable matchings such that a hospital is matched to different sets of doctors between them, then there is a profitable preference misreporting for that hospital under DA (the converse holds for one-to-one matching, although not in many-to-one matching). Hence Theorem 1 implies a "core convergence" property in the sense that if the market is large, then for most agents, their stable matching partner(s) is/are unique.

3.1.1   How robust is approximate incentive compatibility?

While it may be tempting to summarize the aforementioned findings as that "incentive problems go away for DA in large markets," such a general

---

[7] This intuition turns out to be precise. More specifically, Kojima and Pathak (2009) show that if there exists profitable misreporting for a hospital, then that hospital receives an application by some doctor at some step of the rejection chain.

[8] A number of regularity conditions play important roles to guarantee that there are many vacant positions. This point is discussed in some detail in Section 3.1.1.

statement can be misleading. In particular, the result of Kojima and Pathak (2009), as well as earlier analyses by Roth and Peranson (1999) and Immorlica and Mahdian (2005), relies on a number of regularity conditions.

Among other things, let me discuss the so-called "limited acceptability" assumption.[9] This assumption requires that each doctor finds only a small fraction of hospitals acceptable among the many hospitals in the market. In its simplest and perhaps most restrictive form, this notion is formalized as the assumption that there is a fixed number k such that all doctors find only k hospitals acceptable even as the number of the hospitals, n, grows without a bound.

Limited acceptability is widely assumed in the literature despite its restrictiveness, so it warrants discussion here. Roth and Peranson (1999) motivate this assumption by an empirical observation. Specifically, they note that the numbers of employers listed as acceptable in most applicants' submitted preferences are very small in practice. For example, most applicants in NRMP apply to 15 or fewer hospital residency programs out of about four thousand programs (Roth and Peranson, 1999); in the Japanese Residency Matching Program, the average number of programs listed by applicants is between 3 and 4 out of more than 1000 residency programs (Kamada and Kojima, 2015); in an NYC high-school match, more than 70 percent of the students list 11 or fewer school programs out of about 500 (Kojima and Pathak, 2009); in APPIC (an American matching market for clinical psychologists), both the median and mean number of programs listed in the applicants is between 7 and 8 out of just over 1000 programs.

Another motivation for this assumption is that under *un*limited acceptability (i.e., the assumption that every doctor finds every hospital acceptable and vice versa), predictions from large market models do not match stylized facts. Roth and Peranson (1999) conduct simulations in markets in which the numbers of doctors and hospitals are equal to each other, and they find that the average proportion of hospitals that have a profitable misreporting opportunity *increases* under unlimited acceptability, as shown in Figure 2. In fact, Knuth, Motwani, and Pittel (1990) have shown earlier that the expected proportion of such hospitals converges to 100 percent as the market size goes to infinity.[10] These results cast some doubts on the external validity of the above approximate incentive compatibility results: Does it hinge on very restrictive assumptions or is it a robust feature of most markets in practice?

To my knowledge, Lee (2012) is the first to make a significant theoretical advance to shed light on this issue. He sets up a model of one-to-one matching[11] where the numbers of doctors and hospitals are equal to each other, and

---

[9] To my knowledge, the term "limited acceptability" was coined by Lee (2012).

[10] Kojima and Pathak (2009) note that the extreme form of limited acceptability such as constant k is not needed for their conclusion and show sufficient conditions for the growth rate of k as a function of n, but the growth rate that is allowed in their analysis is as slow as $o(\ln(n))$.

[11] Appendix E of Lee (2012) extends his results to the many-to-one matching model, but the analysis for this case is significantly more complicated, and it does not fully establish approximate incentive compatibility for the many-to-one case.

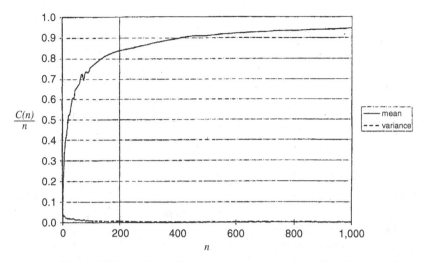

Figure 2 The vertical axis measures the proportion of hospitals that have a profitable unilateral manipulation in DA (denoted $C(n)/n$). There are n doctors and n hospitals, each doctor finds each hospital acceptable and vice versa, and preferences are i.i.d. uniformly distributed. Reproduced from Roth and Peranson (1999).

each doctor finds each hospital acceptable and vice versa – an environment where each hospital has a profitable misreporting under DA with high probability. Agents are ex ante identical and draw cardinal utility functions from a certain distribution. Lee (2012) shows that, for any stable matching mechanism, the expected cardinal utility gain from optimal preference misreporting becomes vanishingly small as the market becomes large. Note that this result does not contradict the earlier manipulability results under unlimited acceptability by Knuth, Motwani, and Pittel (1990) and Roth and Peranson (1999). This is because what these earlier papers show is that there is a large probability that a misreporting results in some strictly positive utility gain, whereas what Lee (2012) shows is that for most instances of profitable manipulation, the cardinal utility gain from a manipulation is very small. His result shows that, even with unlimited acceptability, there is a sense in which stable mechanisms are hard to exploit by preference misreporting.

Another major advance has been made by a recent contribution by Ashlagi, Kanoria, and Leshno (2015). They consider one-to-one matching markets with unlimited acceptability, just as earlier studies such as Knuth, Motwani, and Pittel (1990), Roth and Peranson (1999), and Lee (2012). In contrast to these contributions, however, they assume that the market is unbalanced in the sense that the numbers of doctors and hospitals are different from each other.[12] Surprisingly, they find that unbalanced markets behave very differently

---

[12] Some other studies such as Immorlica and Mahdian (2005) and Kojima and Pathak (2009) allow for balanced as well as unbalanced markets, and their results hold in both cases.

from balanced ones. They establish that in an unbalanced market, the expected number of hospitals who can profitably misreport becomes small as the market becomes large, just as in the markets with limited acceptability studied by Kojima and Pathak (2009). In other words, the manipulability problem under unlimited acceptability may be a knife-edge phenomenon for balanced markets, and in a "typical" market (even with a small imbalance between the demand and supply of doctors), stable mechanisms are robust to strategic manipulations.

3.2   Existence with complementarity

Another problem that a labor matching organizer often faces is caused by preferences that exhibit complementarity. A canonical example is preference complementarity of married couples who need two jobs, one for each member. For most couples, many pairs of positions are complements because they want to have two jobs close to each other.

Match organizers such as NRMP and APPIC try to accommodate couples by letting them submit preferences over pairs of hospital positions and treating them differently from singles in the algorithm.[13] Couples pose a more fundamental problem, however, because their presence in the market can lead to nonexistence of stable matchings. This, of course, implies that it is impossible to find a mechanism that produces a stable matching for all possible preferences. To see these facts clearly, consider the following simple example.

Example 2   There are two hospitals A and B with one position each, one single doctor s and one couple (m, w) composed of the man m and the woman w. Their preferences are

$$\succ_A : m, s, \qquad\qquad \succ_s : A, B,$$
$$\succ_B : s, w, \qquad\qquad \succ_{(m,w)} : (A, B),$$

where the notation for the couple (m, w) means that the only acceptable outcome for this couple is for m to be matched to A and w to be matched to B, and everything else is less preferred to the outside option (the outcome in which both members of the couple are unmatched). To show that there exists no stable matching in this market, consider the following (exhaustive) cases.

    (1) Suppose m and w are matched to A and B, respectively. Then s is unmatched because the seats of both hospitals are filled by the couple. Given this, s and B block this matching because s prefers

---

[13] Other match organizers such as Scottish Foundation Allocation Scheme (the medical matching market in Scotland) do not ask couples to submit preferences over pairs of positions, but have the algorithm follow an exogenously given rule to guarantee that the two positions for each couple are not too far away from each other.

B to her current outcome (the outside option) and B prefers s to its current match, w.

(2) Suppose m and w are both unmatched.

   (a) If s is matched to A, then the couple (m, w) and hospitals A, B block this matching since the couple prefers (A, B) to the current outcome (the outside option), A prefers m to its current match s, and B prefers w to its current outcome (the outside option).

   (b) Suppose that s is matched to B or s is unmatched. Then s and A block this matching because A is the first choice for s while A prefers s to its current outcome (the outside option).

(3) Every other matching is individually irrational for the couple (m, w), so it is unstable.

Cases (1)–(3) are exhaustive, so this establishes that there exists no stable matching in this market.

This conclusion immediately implies that there exists no algorithm which is guaranteed to produce a stable matching in the presence of couples. To get intuition, however, consider an algorithm that tries to modify the doctor-proposing DA to accommodate couples. More specifically, imagine that the algorithm lets doctors apply as in DA, but lets each couple apply to pairs of positions, and if one member of the couple is rejected, then it lets its remaining member withdraw her application to her tentative partner, and lets other applicants withdraw their current applications to apply to the newly open position, and so on (these features are important for addressing preference complementarity). If one applies such a modified algorithm to the present example, then it would proceed as follows. In the first step, s applies to A while m and w apply to A and B, respectively. Given these applications, A rejects s in favor of m. Then, in the second step, s applies to his second choice, B. Now, given the new application, B rejects w and keeps s. Because w has been rejected, the couple withdraws the application of m to A. This withdrawal creates a vacancy at A, so now s withdraws the application to B and applies to A. Finally, m and w apply to A and B, respectively, which results in the same situation as in the very first step of the algorithm. Thus, this heuristic algorithm follows a cycle of applications and rejections and fails to terminate, never producing a stable matching in this market.   □

Despite this theoretical possibility, some matching clearinghouses in practice regularly enjoy high rates of participation and produce matchings that are honored by participants. In fact, these clearinghouses have almost always found stable matchings. For instance, Roth and Peranson (1999) run several variants of DA on submitted preferences from 1993, 1994 and 1995 in NRMP and find that these algorithms produce a stable matching for each of these years. Kojima, Pathak, and Roth (2013) similarly study data from APPIC during 1999–2007 and find a stable matching for each of these years.

These observations raise the question: why do these matching clearing-houses produce stable matchings even though the standard theory suggests there may exist no stable matchings when couples participate? Kojima, Pathak, and Roth (2013) suggest that the market size may again be the answer. More specifically, under certain regularity conditions similar to those in Kojima and Pathak (2009), the probability of the existence of a stable matching is high in large markets:

Theorem 2 *Consider a sequence of markets. For any $\varepsilon > 0$, there exists a positive integer n such that the probability that a stable matching exists is at least $1 - \varepsilon$ for each market with at least n hospitals.*

This result can be shown using a constructive algorithm, which shows not only the existence of a stable matching, but also how to find it. The algorithm is a close variant of the one used in NRMP and works as follows. First, I run DA for a market composed of hospitals and single doctors only, while excluding couples. Then I add couples to the market one by one, allowing them to apply to pairs of positions from their top choices as described in Example 2. The additional applications by a couple may displace some doctors, creating rejection chains just as those created by a strategic rejection analyzed in Section 3.1. If a rejection chain reaches a hospital which a member of some couple is tentatively matched to, then he or she may be dislocated and cause withdrawal of an application by the remaining member of the couple, which may lead to a failure of an algorithm, as I have observed in Example 2. In a large market with many hospitals, however, it is with high probability that the rejection chains created by the couples are terminated as a doctor applies to a hospital with a vacant position, just like the rejection chain created by strategic manipulation in the last section. Therefore, in large markets with a relatively small number of couples, the probability of the existence of a stable matching is high.

3.2.1   How robust is approximate existence?

As in the case of the approximate incentive compatibility, it is important to note that the proof of asymptotic existence by Kojima, Pathak, and Roth (2013) depends on a number of assumptions such as limited acceptability. One of the most important – and perhaps the most restrictive – assumptions is that the number of couples is very small compared to the market size. More specifically, the authors assume that the number of couples grows at a rate that is strictly smaller than the square root of the number of the hospitals (whereas the number of single doctors can grow at the same rate as the number of hospitals), and this assumption plays a crucial role in their proof. Roughly speaking, this assumption requires that the proportion of couples becomes vanishingly small, and does so fast enough. This is unfortunate, because there is no obvious reason why a large market size makes most applicants singles. Kojima, Pathak, and Roth (2013) complement their theoretical results using data from APPIC and simulations on randomly generated data, verifying that in these markets, the probability of finding a stable matching is indeed close to one. Still, the reason for such high probability of existence remained somewhat unresolved.

Ashlagi, Braverman, and Hassidim (2014) address this issue. They demonstrate that if the number of couples increases strictly more slowly than the market size – not the square root of the market size – then the probability that a stable matching exists converges to one as the market size grows.[14] The proof is based on a novel modification of the algorithm used in Kojima, Pathak, and Roth (2013), which enables them to declare failure for fewer instances and find a stable matching more often than Kojima, Pathak, and Roth (2013). In addition, the authors find that if the number of couples increases at the same rate as the market size, then the nonexistence probability can stay bounded away from zero even in large markets. Therefore, for the guaranteed existence of a stable matching, it is *necessary* for the couple population to grow more slowly than the market as a whole. Given this necessity result, we still do not seem to fully understand whether matching markets work well in real large markets when the proportions of couples are high.[15]

3.2.2 Complementarity

Married couples offer a leading example of complementarity, but they are not the only source of it. To the contrary, complementarities are prevalent in various markets. Firms often seek to hire workers with complementary skills. Professional sport teams demand athletes that complement one another in skills or in their positions. Public schools may need to satisfy diversity of their student bodies in terms of skill levels or socio-economic statuses.

Che, Kim, and Kojima (2015) and Azevedo and Hatfield (2015) study this problem and find that, similarly to the case of matching with couples, there is a sense in which the market size helps establish the existence of a

---

[14] Strictly speaking, there are some other differences in assumptions between Ashlagi, Braverman, and Hassidim (2014) and Kojima, Pathak, and Roth (2013), so a direct comparison is not obvious. However, these differences appear to be unimportant for the main mechanics of the model and analysis, so I do not elaborate on them here.

[15] In that regard, a series of studies in computer science have made notable advances. Biró, Irving, and Schlotter (2011) consider a certain matching problem with couples that is motivated by medical matching in Scotland, and compare various algorithms including the one used in Scotland as well as the one used in NRMP. Biró, Fleiner, and Irving (2016) and Biró, Manlove, and McBride (2014) provide algorithms which are based on Scarf's algorithm and integer programming, and show that stable matchings are found by these algorithms with high probability even when the proportion of couples is high. For these contributions, see an interdisciplinary survey by Biró and Klijn (2013).

stable matching.[16] Both papers study a model of continuum of agents and find that a stable matching exists in the continuum economy.[17] Based on that result, these papers study markets with a large but finite number of participants. While the existing impossibility results in the literature (Hatfield and Milgrom, 2005; Hatfield and Kojima, 2008; Sönmez and Ünver, 2010) imply that a stable matching does not always exist in any finite market, there exists a matching that is "almost stable" in the sense that the utility gain from blocking it is negligibly small, and in addition the blocking activity leads to only a small change in the overall matching pattern of the economy.

In addition to the substantive contribution, a novel methodology may be worth mentioning. In Che, Kim, and Kojima (2015), existence of a stable matching is shown based on two findings: (i) a stable matching is characterized as a fixed point of a certain mapping over a function space that, like the classical tâtonnement process in general equilibrium theory, adjusts demand and supply of positions, and (ii) such a fixed point exists given the continuity of the tâtonnement mapping, where the continuum population assumption plays a crucial role for establishing the continuity property.[18] The existence of a fixed point is established by the Kakutani–Fan–Glicksberg fixed point theorem, a generalization of Kakutani fixed point theorem to function spaces. While this type of technique is not uncommon in economics and game theory, it appears to be new to the matching literature.

A recent paper by Nguyen and Vohra (2014) explores another approach. They consider a situation in which the social planner can force some hospitals to accommodate an excessive number of applicants by increasing their capacities. The authors provide a bound on the increase of positions such that the existence of a stable matching is guaranteed. In the case of couples, even if a given instance has no stable matching, there is another instance with a small change of seats – at most 2 seats in each hospital and at most 4 seats in total – where a stable matching exists. Thus, as long as the social planner can change the number of positions of some hospitals, say through mandate or subsidy, then a stable matching exists.[19]

---

[16] There are several differences between the models of Che, Kim, and Kojima (2015) and Azevedo and Hatfield (2015), so their results are independent of each other. I do not go into detail here and discuss the main features that are common to both papers unless otherwise noted.

[17] It is worth mentioning the preceding research by Azevedo and Leshno (2015). They, like Che, Kim, and Kojima (2015), set up a model with a finite number of hospitals and a continuum of doctors. The main difference is that Azevedo and Leshno (2015) assume that hospitals have responsive preferences, which implies the absence of complementarity.

[18] The construction of the tâtonnement-like mapping is inspired by those in the literature such as Adachi (2000), Hatfield and Milgrom (2005), and Echenique and Oviedo (2006), but some modifications are needed to account for the continuum population.

[19] Nguyen, Peivandi, and Vohra (2016) use a similar idea of violating feasibility in a random object allocation setting and obtain a result of a similar flavor.

3.3   Object allocation

I now turn our attention to the object allocation setting, i.e., the problem in which the social planner has a number of indivisible objects and aims to allocate them to the members of the society. In this setting, the "hospitals" are mere objects to be consumed, and they have no intrinsic preferences. Given this assumption, stability is not the main requirement because no agent has a resource with which she can block the prescribed assignment.[20] Instead, other properties such as efficiency, fairness, and incentive compatibility are of primary importance.

In this setting, one of the most well-known mechanisms is the **random priority** (also known as random serial dictatorship) mechanism, **RP** henceforth. In this mechanism, a serial order over all the applicants is determined by a fair lottery. Then, under the realized serial order, the first applicant receives her stated first choice object, the second applicant receives his stated first choice among the remaining objects, and so forth. In addition to being very simple to describe and easy to implement, RP has desirable properties. First, it is strategy-proof. Second, this mechanism satisfies the "equal treatment of equals" property, a form of fairness which means that two applicants whose stated preferences are identical to each other receive the same random assignment. Third, it is ex post efficient in the sense that the final (deterministic) outcome after the lottery has been resolved is Pareto efficient.

However, despite its ex post efficiency, the RP mechanism may produce a random assignment that is inefficient from an *ex-ante* point of view. To see this point, consider the following example due to Bogomolnaia and Moulin (2001) with a slight modification.

Example 3   Let there be four applicants with preferences given by

$$\succ_{i_1} : A, B,$$
$$\succ_{i_2} : A, B,$$
$$\succ_{i_3} : B, A,$$
$$\succ_{i_4} : B, A,$$

and two hospitals A and B, each with only one seat to be allocated. As I am considering the object allocation setting in this section, let these hospitals be mere objects to be consumed by the applicants, and thus have no intrinsic preferences.[21]

---

[20] However, note that stability can be interpreted as a fairness property if the objects are endowed with priorities over the agents as in the case of the school choice problem (Abdulkadiroğlu and Sönmez, 2003).

[21] Although hospitals have their own preferences in many doctor–hospital matching markets, I keep using the term "hospital" here for convenience. Note also that in some markets, such as the UK, hospitals' preferences are not elicited and hospitals are treated as mere objects to be

Let me now describe how RP works in this example. If the realized serial order is i_1, i_2, i_3, i_4, then i_1 receives A, i_2 receives B, and i_3 and i_4 receive the outside option. If the realized order is i_4, i_3, i_2, i_1, then i_4 receives B, i_3 receives A, while i_2 and i_1 receive the outside option. Observe that, under the first serial order, doctor i_2 receives the seat at B although it is her less preferred hospital. Also observe that, under the second serial order, doctor i_3 receives the seat at A although it is his less preferred hospital. Moreover, B is the first choice for i_3 while A is the first choice for i_2. Therefore, if they could exchange probability shares of receiving these hospitals with each other at the ex ante stage, then both doctors would be better off. In other words, RP leaves some room for mutually beneficial trades in probability shares (although not in the final pure outcomes), and thus it is not ex ante efficient.   □

To improve efficiency in this problem, Bogomolnaia and Moulin (2001) propose a new mechanism. It is called the **probabilistic serial (PS)** mechanism, and is based on the following "simultaneous eating algorithm". Imagine that each doctor reports her preferences, and the doctors (or more precisely, proxies on the doctors' behalf) simultaneously engage in "eating" at the speed of one in time interval $[0, 1]$. What do the doctors eat? Each doctor eats an infinitesimal amount of probability shares to get into a hospital of her choice. That is, at each point in time interval $[0, 1]$, each doctor increases the probability to receive her first choice hospital by a unit speed. If many doctors desire the same hospital, the sum of the probability shares of that hospital eaten away may reach its supply of seats before the ending time of the algorithm, i.e., time one. If such a situation occurs, then the algorithm prohibits doctors from eating further from that hospital, and has them eat from their most preferred remaining hospitals. At time one, each doctor has eaten probability shares from various hospitals. These probability shares indeed specify a valid probability distribution over the objects because by construction each of them is nonnegative and they sum up to one. The PS mechanism returns this probability share profile as its output.

Bogomolnaia and Moulin (2001) show that PS eliminates the kind of inefficiency of RP we saw in Example 3. At the PS outcome in the above example, doctors i_1 and i_2 are admitted to hospital A with probability $1/2$ while the other two doctors get into hospital B with probability $1/2$. These probabilities are more preferred to the RP assignments by all doctors, and it is efficient in the sense that no further improvement for everyone is possible. More generally, Bogomolnaia and Moulin (2001) show that the PS assignment always satisfies an efficiency property called ordinal efficiency (or sd-efficiency), which is the property that it is not first-order stochastically dominated by any other random assignment.[22] Moreover, the PS assignment is fair in the

---

assigned to doctors (Biró, Irving, and Schlotter, 2011). In other applications such as school choice, it is common for schools to be treated as objects (Abdulkadiroğlu and Sönmez, 2003).

[22] The term "sd-efficiency" is an abbreviated expression for stochastic-dominance efficiency.

sense that an agent's own random assignment (weakly) first-order stochastically dominates those of others with respect to her own preference. This property is called envy-freeness, and it implies equal treatment of equals, the main fairness property of RP (by contrast, RP does not necessarily satisfy envy-freeness).

PS has one major drawback, however: this mechanism is not strategy-proof. Unfortunately, Bogomolnaia and Moulin (2001) demonstrate that there is no mechanism that satisfies strategy-proofness, ordinal efficiency, and equal treatment of equals. Therefore, while both RP and PS satisfy two of these three properties, there is no way to improve upon them to satisfy all of these desiderata.

Given this impossibility result, it is important to study the trade-offs between RP and PS in the kind of applications that are of practical interest. Pathak (2007) conducts simulations based on the data from New York City's high-school match. He computes the RP and PS assignments under the submitted preferences in NYC's supplementary round of school seat assignment. He finds that the PS assignment places more applicants to their preferred choices than RP, but the difference is very small: for example, out of the total of 8,255 students, 4,999 receive their top choice in RP, while 5,016 receive their top choice in PS, a difference of only 17. Based on this finding and the fact that PS is not strategy-proof, he recommends using RP rather than PS in this application.

On the other hand, Kojima and Manea (2010) show that PS becomes non-manipulable in large markets. More specifically, given any doctor and her preferences, if hospital capacities are sufficiently large, then PS makes it a dominant strategy to report her true preferences (note that truth-telling is an exact, as opposed to approximate, dominant strategy in this statement). To get an intuition for this result, observe that misreporting in PS has two effects. First, given the same set of available hospitals, reporting false preferences may prevent a doctor from eating her most preferred available hospital. Second, reporting false preferences can delay the expiration date of some hospital (that is, the period at which the hospital gets completely eaten away) by affecting the overall eating schedules of the doctors. The first effect always weakly hurts the misreporting doctor because it may prevent her from eating her most preferred remaining hospital, but the second effect can benefit the doctor by allowing her to eat probability shares of her preferred hospital later in the algorithm than under truthtelling. But the second effect becomes small in large markets because the expiration dates of the hospitals are pinned down by eating behavior of many doctors. Meanwhile, the cost of eating suboptimally does not become small. Thus, the first negative effect dominates the second (potentially positive) effect, which establishes the large-market incentive compatibility of PS.

These studies are aimed at understanding the trade-offs between RP and PS and, interestingly, they show that shortcomings of both mechanisms become small in large markets. A natural question is why this is the case, and whether one can still make a recommendation between these mechanisms on the basis of some other properties.

Che and Kojima (2010) study this issue and show that the trade-offs between these mechanisms vanish in large markets. More precisely, they demonstrate that RP and PS assignments converge to the same limit as the market size becomes large. Therefore, in the school choice application, as long as the district is large as in the case of NYC, there is little difference between RP and PS. In fact, this result implies that both mechanisms approximately achieve all the desirable properties mentioned above, i.e., an ordinal notion of efficiency, incentive compatibility, and fairness. Just as in the two-sided matching case, market size helps the social planner achieve desirable properties that are impossible in an exact form for markets of arbitrary sizes. For instance, consider replica economies of Example 3, where in the q-fold replica economy, there are supplies of q seats in each hospital, as well as q copies of each doctor in the base economy. The probability that a doctor is matched to her less preferred hospital is positive for all q but approaches zero as $q \to \infty$, as can be seen in Figure 3.

3.3.1   Further developments

While the above contributions have identified some senses in which RP and PS mechanisms both achieve desirable properties in certain large markets, they are far from being the last word on this problem.

A notable contribution is made by Manea (2009). He considers allocation of n different types of objects to n agents, where each agent should be allocated exactly one object. In this setting, he shows that the proportion of preference

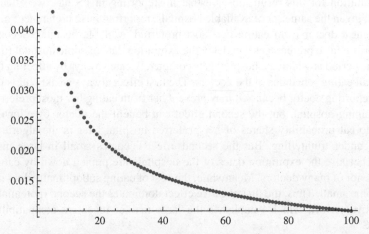

Figure 3 Horizontal axis: Market size q. Vertical axis: probability for each doctor to be matched to her second choice hospital. Reproduced from Che and Kojima (2010).

profiles under which the RP random assignment is ordinally inefficient converges to one as n goes to infinity. This result may sound contradictory to Che and Kojima (2010), so two points are worth some discussion in order to understand these results better. First, there are different ways in which one can model large markets: in Kojima and Manea (2010) and Che and Kojima (2010), the number of the types of the objects are fixed and the supply of each type of object increases, while in Manea (2009), it is the *types* of objects that increases while the supply of each type of good is fixed at one. Which of the "large markets" describes a given market better depends on the application in question, and thus the policy implication should be derived with some caution. Second, the notion of ordinal efficiency used by Manea (2009) is binary in the sense that a random assignment is judged to be efficient if and only if there is *no room for improvement at all*, while the other contributions such as Pathak (2007) and Che and Kojima (2010) use approximate efficiency, i.e., they judge a random assignment to be close to being efficient as long as the room for an improvement is small.

Another recent contribution is related to the asymptotic equivalence result of Che and Kojima (2010). Their approach leaves unanswered the question of whether the equivalence depends crucially on the algorithmic features of these mechanisms or there is a deeper reason for the equivalence. Moreover, from a practical point of view, it is reasonable to ask whether there are other mechanisms that satisfy good finite-market properties in efficiency, incentives, and fairness (or at least some of them) and behave differently from RP or PS in large markets, which may leave some scope for improvements over RP and PS. A recent study by Liu and Pycia (2013) investigates this issue. They demonstrate that asymptotically efficient, symmetric, and asymptotically strategy-proof mechanisms converge to the same limit as the market size becomes large. Therefore, mechanisms such as RP and PS exhaust most of the good properties, and at least in large markets, little room for further improvement is left. Theoretically, it also shows that the asymptotic equivalence as identified by Che and Kojima (2010) is not an isolated coincidence for these two mechanisms, but an instance of a more general phenomenon.

3.4   Discussion on the "large market methodology"

As detailed in the previous sections, considering large markets allows us to overcome many existing impossibility results by establishing approximate properties in various contexts, ranging from incentives to existence and efficiency. Given that so many positive results hold in large markets, some researchers have raised the following concern to me: isn't the large market approach "too permissive," such that this methodology will result in a theory with the "anything goes" property, i.e., any conclusion can be drawn? I think that these criticisms are unfounded. This section explains why.

The above two criticisms are closely related to each other, but for the sake of argument, let me begin with the first criticism that the large market modeling strategy is "too permissive." This criticism appears to suggest that there are "too many" positive results in large markets given the pervasiveness of negative results in finite markets. I do not think that this is a valid criticism because there is no reason that there should be a "right proportion" of positive or negative results except for the amount dictated by reality. If many problems of matching mechanisms in small markets indeed vanish in large markets, then that fact simply uncovers the nature of reality, and not any drawback of the modeling approach. Unless the positive results in those large market studies are shown to depend on unrealistic assumptions or contradict data, this line of criticism does not have any ground.

This leaves us with the second concern, which may be summarized as the "anything goes" claim. That is, the degree of freedom in modeling choice is too high, and any positive result one wishes to obtain can be obtained by choosing a model in a clever manner.

While this claim could be valid in principle, it does not appear to be supported by research in large matching markets so far. For instance, take a claim that strategic misreporting vanishes in large markets. As we have seen before, this claim has been shown to be true for stable mechanisms in various settings. However, this statement highly depends on the nature of the mechanism (stability), and thus it is not a blanket claim that incentives are unimportant in large markets. To see this point, I consider the so-called **Boston mechanism**, which was used in Boston for student placement before it was replaced by DA. The mechanism proceeds as follows:

- Step 1: Each doctor applies to her first choice hospital. Each hospital rejects the lowest-ranking doctors in excess of its capacity and all unacceptable doctors.

In general, for any $t = 1, 2, \ldots,$

- Step t: Each doctor who was rejected in the last step proposes to her next highest choice. Each hospital considers these doctors, *only as long as* there are vacant positions not filled by doctors who are already matched by the previous steps, and rejects the lowest-ranking doctors in excess of its capacity and all unacceptable doctors.

This algorithm terminates when every unmatched doctor (if any) has been rejected by every hospital acceptable to her. The main difference of this mechanism from DA is that in each step of the algorithm, doctors who are not rejected are accepted *immediately* rather than in a deferred manner.[23]

Under this mechanism, doctors may have incentives to misrepresent their preferences even in large markets. To see the reason for this, consider a situation where a doctor's first choice is so popular that she is unlikely to be matched

[23] Due to this difference from the deferred acceptance algorithm, the Boston mechanism is sometimes referred to as the immediate acceptance algorithm.

if she truthfully ranks it as her top choice in her reported preference. Also assume that her second choice is reasonably popular and thus she is unlikely to be matched to it if she applies to it as her second choice, but there is a significantly better chance to be accepted if she applies to it in the first step of the algorithm (note that this is a likely scenario under the Boston mechanism while not in DA). Then she is made better off by misreporting her preference by listing her true second choice as her stated first choice.

Note that in order to make an inference just illustrated above, the doctor only needs to know the overall popularity of the hospitals. Such aggregate information is often available to each doctor even in large markets, if with some noise. And note that the argument presented above holds even if the doctor's information is noisy. Indeed, an example of Kojima and Pathak (2009) shows that this argument goes through with preferences being private information of each doctor, showing that manipulation incentives do not vanish even as the market size goes to infinity.

The preceding discussion demonstrates that it is *not true* that all problems go away in large markets. On the contrary, the large market modeling approach allows us to *distinguish mechanisms* based on approximate desiderata. By contrast, if a researcher is constrained to use only traditional binary criteria such as exact strategy-proofness or exact efficiency, too many mechanisms fail such stringent requirements, and the researcher may end up being unable to capture the crucial difference between mechanisms that are close to achieving good properties and those that are far from doing so. Failing to capture such difference is problematic because the distinction between good and bad mechanisms seems to be as important as (if not more important than) the distinction between perfect and less-than-perfect ones. Therefore, contrary to the view that the large market methodology makes market design irrelevant (i.e., all problems go away anyway), this methodology helps us tell apart good mechanisms from bad ones.

A recent paper by Hatfield, Kojima, and Narita (2016) makes this point in a different context. The question studied is how the design of a school choice mechanism affects the competitive pressure on schools for improving themselves. They investigate whether a matching mechanism has the property that a school is matched to a weakly more preferred set of students whenever it becomes more preferred by students.[24] This concept formalizes the requirement that a mechanism should never punish a school for becoming more desirable to students. They find that all standard mechanisms, including all stable mechanisms as well as the Boston and the top trading cycles (TTC) mechanisms, fail this property. In a sharp contrast to this negative result, they then consider an approximate version of this property in the large markets and establish that all stable mechanisms satisfy this approximate property, while both the Boston and the TTC mechanism fail even this property. Their result is

---

[24] This concept is called respecting improvements of school quality. It is an adaptation of a notion due to Balinski and Sönmez (1999) who consider respecting improvements of student quality.

another case in point, suggesting that considering approximate properties in the large market setting enables us to make sharper statements about desirability of competing mechanisms.

More generally, modeling a market with a large number of participants can serve as a useful modeling device. In studies of decentralized matching markets by Avery and Levin (2010) and Che and Koh (2015), for instance, models with a continuum of students facilitate equilibrium characterization. Echenique and Pereyra (2014) analyze a finite population model for decentralized markets, but analyze its limit behavior as the market size converges to infinity, which allows the authors to tell which predictions of the finite population model are robust and remain relevant in large markets. For these papers, a large market assumption is a natural modeling approach.

For all these reasons, criticisms toward the large market methodology seem to be unfounded. For market design, this approach allows us to distinguish good mechanisms from bad ones based on their approximate performances. More generally, it allows researchers to tell which of the properties found in stylized finite markets are likely to be relevant in real markets. As such, I think that the large market approach should be regarded as a standard tool in matching theory.

4   MATCHING WITH CONSTRAINTS

Another major issue in matching theory is also related to the fact that the standard model is not always applicable in practical problems of interest. In this section, I discuss recent research in matching with constraints. As in the last section, the issue arises in both two-sided matching and object allocation settings.

4.1   Two-sided matching with constraints

Real matching markets are often subject to constraints. Medical residency programs may be subject to regulations which restrict the number of positions for different medical specialties. In school choice, it is a common practice to impose certain balance requirements on the student composition in terms of socio-economic status or academic achievement (Abdulkadiroğlu and Sönmez, 2003).

A leading example of matching with constraints is the medical residency match in Japan. The Japanese government introduced a centralized matching mechanism for medical residents in 2003, and the initial mechanism was the doctor-proposing DA. However, some critics asserted that DA placed too many doctors with hospitals in urban areas such as Tokyo while causing doctor shortages in rural areas. In order to address this complaint, the government introduced a new regulation, which I call a "regional maximum quota" policy. Under this policy, for each region of the country, the number of residents who are placed in that region is required to be at most the regional maximum quota

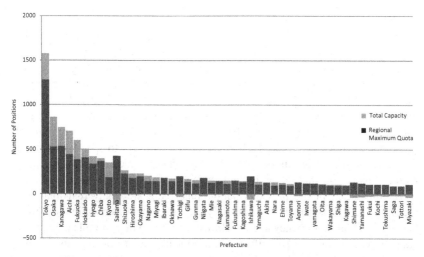

Figure 4 For each prefecture, the total capacity is the sum of advertised positions in hospitals located in the prefecture in 2008. The regional maximum quotas are based on the government's plan in 2008 (Ministry of Health, Labour and Welfare, 2009). Negative values of total capacities in some prefectures indicate the excess amount of regional maximum quotas beyond the advertised positions. Reproduced from Kamada and Kojima (2015).

granted for that region. The idea of this regulation is to restrict the number of doctors matched in urban areas such as Tokyo, thereby preventing what some see as too much imbalance of doctor distributions.

In the Japanese application, each region corresponds to one of the 47 prefectures that partition the country, such as Tokyo, Kyoto, and Osaka. Figure 4 presents the magnitude of the regional maximum quota policy. Urban areas suffer from stringent constraints under the policy. For instance, the total numbers of positions advertised by hospitals in Tokyo and Osaka were 1,582 and 860 positions in 2008, respectively, while the government set the regional maximum quotas of 1,287 and 533. Kyoto received an even larger proportional reduction of positions, which offered 353 positions in 2008 while receiving the regional maximum quota of 190, which is almost a 50 percent decline.[25] In total, 34 out of the country's 47 prefectures are subject to binding regional maximum quotas in the sense that the imposed regional maximum quotas are smaller than the total numbers of advertised positions in 2008.

Policies that are mathematically isomorphic to regional maximum quotas exist in various contexts beyond the Japanese medical match example. For example, Chinese graduate admission is regulated by a policy that imposes

---

[25] In fact, the magnitude of the planned changes were so large that the government implemented a temporary provision that limited per-year reductions within a certain bound in the first few years of operation.

a maximum quota on academically oriented masters programs, which is part of an attempt by the government to increase masters educated in professionally oriented programs. In many countries, there are state-sponsored college seats which are subject to the state's budget constraint, so the "region" of the state-sponsored college seats is subject to a maximum quota constraint (examples of Hungary and Ukraine are documented by Biró, Fleiner, Irving, and Manlove, 2010 and Kiselgof, 2012). Medical match in the UK works in two rounds, the first of which is an allocation of doctors to different regions of the country while the second is the allocation of doctors to specific hospitals within the region. The number of doctors matched in each region is bounded by the capacity for that region in the first round of the allocation scheme.

As illustrated in the previous paragraphs, there are many real matching problems with constraints. Unfortunately, existing solutions used in those markets suffer from inefficiency and instability. The following example taken from Kamada and Kojima (2015) illustrates a typical problem of existing mechanisms in the constrained matching problem, using the Japanese mechanism as a concrete case (they also find similar drawbacks for mechanisms in other constrained matching markets in practice).

Example 4   (An existing mechanism may lead to inefficiency and instability) The Japanese mechanism, called Japan Residency Matching Program (JRMP: a term coined by Kamada and Kojima, 2015), is perhaps the simplest and the most prevalent mechanism aimed at addressing regional maximum quotas. The mechanism runs the doctor-proposing DA except that it replaces the actual hospital capacity with an exogenously given artificial capacity, called the target capacity, which is weakly smaller than each hospital's real capacity and, for each region, sums up to the regional maximum quota.

To see the shortcomings of the JRMP mechanism, consider the following (overly simplified) example. Let there be one region, and its regional maximum quota be 10 positions. There are two hospitals, A and B, each with a capacity of 10. Suppose that there are 10 doctors, $i_1, \ldots, i_{10}$. Both hospitals prefer i_1 to i_2 to $\ldots$ to i_{10} to the outside option. Doctors i_1, i_2, and i_3 prefer A to the outside option to B while all other doctors prefer B to the outside option to A.

Now consider the JRMP mechanism, assuming the target capacities for each hospital to be 5. At the first step of the algorithm, doctors i_1, i_2 and i_3 apply to hospital A, and all the remaining doctors apply to hospital B. Hospital A rejects no one at this round, because the number of applicants is less than its target capacity and all the applicants are acceptable to it. By contrast, hospital B rejects i_9 and i_{10} while accepting other applicants, because the number of applicants exceeds the *target capacity* while not the actual hospital capacity. Given that i_9 and i_{10} find A unacceptable, this algorithm terminates at this point. Thus, the the the outcome of this algorithm is given by

$$\mu = \begin{pmatrix} A & B & \emptyset \\ i_1, i_2, i_3 & i_4, i_5, i_6, i_7, i_8 & i_9, i_{10} \end{pmatrix}.$$

Consider a matching μ' defined by,

$$\mu' = \begin{pmatrix} A & B \\ i_1, i_2, i_3 & i_4, i_5, i_6, i_7, i_8, i_9, i_{10} \end{pmatrix}.$$

Since the regional maximum quota is still respected, μ' is feasible. Moreover, every agent is weakly better off with i_9, i_{10}, and B being strictly better off than at μ. Hence I conclude that the JRMP mechanism results in an inefficient matching in this example.[26]   □

Remark 2   In the above example, the outcome of JRMP is unstable in a certain sense as well. For instance, hospital B and doctor i_9 form a blocking pair while the regional maximum quota is not binding at μ. That is, even after i_9 is matched with B, the total number of doctors in the region is 9, which is fewer than the regional maximum quota of 10. Although it is beyond the scope of this paper to provide and analyze a formal definition of stability under constraints, the outcome of the JRMP mechanism clearly violates any reasonable notion of stability. See Kamada and Kojima (2015, 2014b) for detail.

As mentioned earlier, Kamada and Kojima (2015) study other examples such as graduate school admission in China, medical match in the United Kingdom, and teacher matching in Scotland. They find that all these environments are isomorphic to the problem with regional maximum quotas and mechanisms used in these markets fail efficiency and stability.

The problem with the existing solutions is that they modify a standard mechanism such as DA in one way or another, but they do not appropriately maintain desirable properties of the original mechanism. Thus, instead of making a modification in an undisciplined manner, it is useful to formalize normative properties that need to be satisfied and seek a mechanism that satisfies those properties. Kamada and Kojima (2015) take this approach and present a new mechanism that, for any given input, achieves efficiency, stability, and incentive compatibility, among others. To do so, they define the **flexible deferred acceptance (FDA) algorithm**. This algorithm resembles DA and in fact it is identical to JRMP except that it has a kind of "wait list processing" phase during each step of the algorithm, where the target capacities allocated across hospitals in a region are modified in a flexible manner. More specifically,

[26] In this example, not all hospitals are acceptable to all doctors. One may wonder whether this is an unrealistic assumption because doctors may be so willing to work that any hospital is acceptable. However, the example can be easily modified so that all hospitals are acceptable to all doctors while some doctors are unacceptable to some hospitals (which may be a natural assumption because, for instance, typically a hospital only lists doctors who they interviewed). Also, in many markets doctors apply to only a small subset of hospitals. In JRMP, for instance, a doctor applies to only between three and four hospitals on average (Kamada and Kojima, 2015).

the FDA algorithm proceeds in multiple steps of doctors' applications and hospitals' acceptances/rejections like DA. The algorithm begins with the empty matching, and each step $t = 1, 2, \ldots$ proceeds as follows:

- Step t: Each doctor who is not tentatively kept by a hospital applies to her next highest choice (if any).
    - Phase 1: Each hospital considers both new applicants and doctors who are temporarily held from the previous step together, and tentatively accepts its most-preferred acceptable doctors up to its target capacity, put the next preferred acceptable doctors on its wait list up to its true capacity, and rejects every other doctor.
    - Phase 2: Take the first hospital with respect to an exogenously fixed order. If there is any applicant on its wait list and the total number of doctors tentatively matched in the hospital's region is strictly smaller than its regional maximum quota, then let the hospital tentatively accept its most preferred applicant from its wait list. Apply the same procedure to the second hospital (again, with respect to the exogenously fixed order), and so forth (and after the last hospital, return to the first hospital). When there is no further applicant to be processed, reject all the remaining doctors on the wait list and proceed to the next step.

The algorithm terminates at a step in which no rejection occurs (it is straightforward to verify that this algorithm terminates in a finite number of steps). I define the **FDA mechanism** to be the mechanism which produces the matching at the termination of the above algorithm.

FDA is similar to DA, but guarantees a feasible outcome in the presence of constraints. It differs from the JRMP mechanism in that it lets hospitals accept doctors in a flexible manner, using the idea of wait lists. Note that Phase 1 of the FDA algorithm is identical to a phase of JRMP, but it is followed by Phase 2, where hospitals can tentatively accept additional doctors from the wait list as long as the region's maximum quota is not full. This phase helps FDA correct the efficiency loss of the JRMP mechanism while still following DA closely. In fact, Kamada and Kojima (2015) demonstrate that this algorithm finds a stable and constrained efficient matching. In Example 4, for instance, the source of inefficiency in JRMP was that doctors i_9 and i_{10} are rejected from hospital B because of the artificially specified target capacity even though neither the hospital's capacity nor the regional maximum quota necessitates rejection. The FDA algorithm eliminates this inefficiency by allowing hospital B to accept doctors i_9 and i_{10} from the wait list in Phase 2.

Efficiency and stability are arguably among the most important goals for matching market design, but they are by no means the only ones. As discussed in previous sections, incentive compatibility is important given that the matching organizer needs to elicit preference information from the participants. In that regard, Kamada and Kojima (2015) show that FDA is strategy-proof for doctors just as the original DA is.

Finally, when considering changing practical mechanisms, the effect of different mechanisms needs to be carefully traded off, because most policy changes do not cause Pareto improvement. It turns out that the outcome of FDA is a Pareto improvement over JRMP for doctors, although not necessarily for all hospitals. That is, each doctor weakly prefers the outcome of FDA to the outcome of JRMP. A corollary of this result is that the total number of unmatched doctors will weakly decrease if the mechanism is changed from JRMP to FDA.

One important question is whether the magnitude of improvement by a better mechanism is substantial, and whether the loss from the constraints are significant enough to warrant attention in the first place. As it seems elusive to establish a sharp and general prediction on this question by theory alone, Kamada and Kojima (2015) supplement their theoretical analysis with simulations. In their simulations, preferences of market participants are randomly generated, with the model parameters calibrated to closely match the publicly available data for Japanese medical match. One of their simulations, reproduced in Figure 5, reports the number of matched and unmatched doctors under the unconstrained DA (i.e., DA with no regional maximum quotas), JRMP, and FDA. The simulation shows that the existence of regional maximum quotas can cause substantially more doctors to be unmatched: About 800 out of roughly 8300 doctors are unmatched in DA while the corresponding number is about 1400 in JRMP. Meanwhile, FDA alleviates many of the additional unmatched doctors. FDA leaves about 1000 doctors unmatched, which is a mere increase of 200 additional doctors compared to the case with no constraints, as opposed

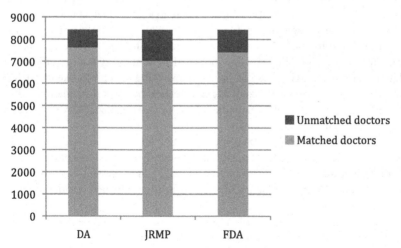

Figure 5 The numbers of matched and unmatched doctors under different mechanisms. "DA" refers to the DA outcome under no regional maximum quota constraints.

to 600 additional unmatched doctors in JRMP. See Kamada and Kojima (2015) for more detail including the simulation methods and additional numerical results.

4.1.1   Further contributions

Systematic studies in matching with constraints are still in an early stage of development, so there are various unsolved topics.

One of the basic questions in this area is: what matching should be deemed "desirable"? For efficiency, this question is pretty straightforward because the standard concept of constrained Pareto efficiency is well defined and has an obvious appeal. For stability, however, the answer to this question is not trivial at all: on the one hand, the standard notion of stability is too demanding because there are cases in which every stable matching in the standard sense violates a constraint; on the other hand, ignoring stability completely seems to be very unappealing given existing evidence that stability is important for the success of matching markets (Roth, 2002). Is there a reasonable weakening of stability that takes constraints into account while maintaining the spirit of the original concept?

Kamada and Kojima (2014b) study this issue. They define two concepts of stability under constraints. The first concept, which the authors call strong stability, requires (in addition to feasibility and individual rationality) that for any blocking pair, satisfying that blocking pair by letting them match with each other will result in a violation of a constraint. This definition is based on the requirement that when a blocking pair exists, it is "inevitable" because satisfying them would result in infeasibility.

Although this is perhaps the most natural definition of stability under constraints, the authors find that a strongly stable matching does not always exist: in fact, a strongly stable matching can be guaranteed to exist *if and only if* the constraints are trivial.[27] Motivated by this result, they define a less demanding concept: weak stability.[28] They show that weak stability implies efficiency, that it is strong enough to exclude some unappealing matchings like the JRMP outcome in Example 4, and that it is characterized by several standard axioms. In addition, a weakly stable matching always exists: indeed, FDA produces a weakly stable matching.[29]

Although weak stability has some normative appeal, this concept may still be too permissive for some applications. In fact, FDA satisfies not only weak stability, but also certain distributional balance among hospitals in the same region. Motivated by this fact, Kamada and Kojima (2014a) consider a model

---

[27] More specifically, the necessary and sufficient condition is that each constraint involves just one hospital or the associated regional maximum quota is zero.

[28] We omit the formal definition of weak stability here. See Kamada and Kojima (2014b) for detail.

[29] The weak stability concept can be defined under more general constraint structures. In the general case, FDA is not defined, but the authors show the existence of a weakly stable matching using a different method.

in which the social planner has a policy goal on distributional balance of doctors beyond the hard regional maximum quota constraints. They define an intermediate requirement called stability and show that a generalization of FDA is strategy-proof for doctors and finds a stable matching.

Although matching with constraints is a new research topic, related models have been studied in the literature in several contexts. In the medical match in the twentieth-century United Kingdom, some hospitals preferred to hire exactly one female doctor, and an algorithm used there accommodated such hospital preferences (Roth, 1991). In school choice, schools are often subject to diversity constraints in terms of socio-economic status and academic performance (Abdulkadiroğlu and Sönmez, 2003; Abdulkadiroğlu, 2005; Westkamp, 2013; Kojima, 2012; Hafalir, Yenmez, and Yildirim, 2013; Ehlers, Hafalir, Yenmez, and Yildirim, 2014; Echenique and Yenmez, 2013). Models with constraints on *sets* of agents have also been explored in the context of student-project allocations (Abraham, Irving, and Manlove, 2007; Sönmez and Ünver, 2006) and college admission (Biró, Fleiner, Irving, and Manlove, 2010). Kojima, Tamura, and Yokoo (2014) provide a framework based on discrete convex analysis, a branch of discrete mathematics, to obtain various results in these related but different models with a unified technique.

An important and actively studied problem with constraints is the case with *minimum quotas*. Clearly, there are many matching problems in which the constraints take the form of minimum quotas rather than maximum quotas. For example, school districts may require at least a certain number of students are assigned to each school (Biró, Fleiner, Irving, and Manlove, 2010). The cadet–branch matching program organized by United States Military Academy imposes minimum quotas on the number of cadets who must be assigned to each branch (Sönmez and Switzer, 2012; Sönmez, 2013). Minimum quotas are studied by recent contributions such as Ehlers, Hafalir, Yenmez, and Yildirim (2014), Ueda, Fragiadakis, Iwasaki, Troyan, and Yokoo (2012), Goto, Hashimoto, Iwasaki, Kawasaki, Ueda, Yasuda, and Yokoo (2014), Goto, Kojima, Kurata, Tamura, and Yokoo (2016), and Fragiadakis and Troyan (2016). A stable matching does not always exist in the presence of minimum quotas, but these studies have found various mechanisms that improve upon existing mechanisms while satisfying desirable incentive compatibility properties.

4.1.2 Connection with matching with contracts

There is a connection between matching with constraints and matching with *contracts* as defined by Hatfield and Milgrom (2005).[30] This section illustrates how they are related.

---

[30] Fleiner (2003) considers a framework that is more general than Hatfield and Milgrom (2005), although he does not consider some results of interest for our purposes such as strategy-proofness. See also Crawford and Knoer (1981) and Kelso and Crawford (1982), who consider matching with wages, which is a form of contracts. Importantly, Echenique

Given the additional complications caused by constraints, it is often difficult to see which of the desirable properties in the standard model can be generalized to the model with constraints. Even if a generalization is possible, it may still be unclear to see what kind of mechanism achieves those properties. In the context of matching with regional maximum quotas, it proves useful to consider a hypothetical matching model where doctors are matched with *regions* rather than hospitals. In such a model, the choice pattern implied by hospital preferences and constraints is interpreted to be the result of a "region's preferences." The main advantage of this approach is that it enables us to treat a regional maximum quota as a usual capacity of an agent, i.e., region, and apply results from existing matching models *without* constraints. Then one can show that a stable allocation in the hypothetical model corresponds to a stable matching in the original model with constraints. Moreover, some other desirable properties in the hypothetical model can be translated to corresponding properties in the original model of matching with constraints.

However, this approach requires us to use a model of matching with contracts, because the model needs to distinguish between matchings of the same doctor to two different hospitals even if these hospitals are in the same region. More specifically, we treat these two matchings as *different contracts between the same doctor–region pair*. The model of matching with contracts provides a useful language to describe such a distinction. With this technique, Kamada and Kojima (2015, 2014a) show that results such as the existence of a stable matching and strategy-proofness of FDA for doctors follow from corresponding results in matching with contracts.[31] Kojima, Tamura, and Yokoo (2014) use a similar technique to derive results in various models of matching with constraints such as regional maximum quotas, regional minimum quotas, diversity constraints in schools, and the cadet-branching problem, all by way of associating them to models of matching with contracts.

4.2   Object allocation with constraints

Object-allocation problems are often subject to constraints as well. I return to the model of the object allocation problem which I described in Section 3.3, but now I allow for constraints to restrict feasible allocations.

As illustrated earlier, randomization is a leading approach to restore fairness when allocating objects, especially if monetary transfer is not allowed due to legal or ethical or other reasons. However, a major problem with randomization

---

(2012) shows that in many-to-one matching with contracts, if preferences of all hospitals are substitutable, then the model is isomorphic to matching with wages. The models of Kamada and Kojima (2015, 2014a) do not reduce to matching with wages, however, because their models need to use *many-to-many* matching with contracts (Kominers, 2012, finds a correspondence similar to Echenique's in many-to-many matching under an additional condition, but his condition is not satisfied in their setting).

[31] They use results from Hatfield and Milgrom (2005), Hatfield and Kojima (2009, 2010), and Hatfield and Kominers (2009, 2014).

is that even if deterministic mechanisms under consideration have desirable properties such as Pareto efficiency, a randomization over them can lose those properties. The RP mechanism is a case in point, which is a uniform randomization over serial dictatorships with different serial orderings: although serial dictatorship is Pareto efficient for any serial order, RP can produce an ordinally inefficient random allocation. To remedy such a drawback, a mechanism that directly produces a random assignment is promising (PS is such an example). More generally, consider a random assignment matrix $P = (P_{iA})$ indexed by doctors and hospitals, where entry P_{iA} specifies the probability that doctor i obtains a seat at hospital A. Working directly with such a matrix is useful because it makes it easy to define and study efficiency, fairness, and incentive properties.

It is not clear, however, that such a method is justified. That is, given a random assignment matrix, does there always exist a way to realize it as a lottery over feasible deterministic outcomes?

Budish, Che, Kojima, and Milgrom (2013) tackle this question. They provide a necessary and sufficient condition for this method to be justified. First, using well-known results in the combinatorial optimization literature, they identify a condition on the structure of the constraints that is sufficient to guarantee that every random assignment that satisfies the constraints in expectation can be implemented as a lottery over feasible pure assignments. That condition, called the "bihierarchy" condition, states that the entire structure can be partitioned into two hierarchical sets (aka laminar families) of constraints. Then they demonstrate that the same condition is not only sufficient, but also necessary for guaranteeing the implementation in two-sided assignment and matching environments.

Remark 3 As stated above, there is a sense in which the bihierarchy structure is necessary for implementation. The necessity statement, however, is formulated *in terms of the structures of the constraints* for guaranteeing the implementation for all possible random assignments and constraint values. There are cases in which implementation of a given random assignment under particular constraint values are possible even without the bihierarchy structure. A sufficient condition based on this idea is given by Che, Kim, and Mierendorff (2013).

Budish, Che, Kojima, and Milgrom (2013) apply the above implementation result to several object allocation problems with constraints. First, the implementation result enables them to generalize PS to various cases with maximum constraints, such as the school choice problem with diversity constraints. Just as the original eating algorithm, their generalized algorithm has each agent continuously "eat" her favorite available object over a unit time interval; the only modification to this algorithm is to declare an object "unavailable" to an agent whenever allowing her to eat more of that object will result in a violation of a constraint. The above implementation result implies that the outcome of this eating algorithm can be implemented as a lottery over feasible pure outcomes. In addition, efficiency and fairness properties of the eating algorithm in the original setting extend to their more general environment. In a similar spirit, the implementation result allows generalizing other random assignment mechanisms such as the pseudo-market mechanism by Hylland and Zeckhauser (1979).

4.2.1   Approximate implementation

As illustrated above, some types of constraints can be readily accommodated by the bihierarchy condition of Budish, Che, Kojima, and Milgrom (2013), enabling fairly straightforward generalizations of desirable mechanisms from simple settings to environments with those constraints. However, there are also natural constraints that violate their condition. For instance, two maximum constraints that partially overlap with each other cannot be part of one hierarchy, so examples such as school diversity constraints on race and gender cannot be handled by the above approach.[32] Because the bihierarchy condition is not only sufficient but also "necessary" for guaranteeing implementation of lotteries, it seems elusive to find a more general sufficient condition.

Akbarpour and Nikzad (2014) tackle this question from a perspective closer to the approach of "approximate market design," described in Section 3. They presume that the constraints are divided into *hard* constraints that must always be satisfied and *soft* goals that can be slightly violated if necessary. In school choice, for instance, the physical capacity of a school may be a hard constraint that cannot be changed, while the diversity constraints for different socio-economic classes could be violated by a small amount if necessitated by other requirements. Akbarpour and Nikzad (2014) demonstrate that if the hard constraints have the bihierarchical structure of Budish, Che, Kojima, and Milgrom (2013), and the set of soft constraints satisfies certain conditions, then any given random assignment can be implemented as a lottery over pure assignments that satisfy all the hard constraints while violating soft constraints by a large amount only with small probabilities. Nguyen, Peivandi, and Vohra (2016) take a similar approach to study random assignment problems when the agents have limited preference complementarities.

5   CONCLUSION

This paper surveyed some of the recent advances in matching theory and its applications to market design. I emphasized the influence of theory to applications and vice versa. In particular, I described the way that recent development of theory has produced positive results in problems in which traditional theory has been negative.

---

[32] For this statement, I assume that there is another (natural) hierarchy that includes constraints on the number of schools that any one student can attend (typically just one school).

As I mentioned at the outset, I restricted attention to a small subset of topics in matching theory. Inevitably, there are many exciting topics I had to omit. One such topic is dynamic matching. Akbarpour, Li, and Oveis Gharan (2014) and Anderson, Ashlagi, Gamarnik, and Kanoria (2015) study dynamic matching when preferences are dichotomous as in the case of kidney exchange.[33] They find that the benefit from waiting and making the market thick depends on the agents' discount factor and information structure in very striking manners. Baccara, Lee, and Yariv (2015) consider two-sided matching over time with vertically differentiated types and derive an optimal policy. These papers have started to formally study trade-offs between thickening the market and matching agents quickly, a topic that the standard static matching models did not have a tool to analyze with.

Matching theory plays an increasingly important role in economic theory while also influencing policies in a fruitful manner. I think that the literature has been advancing with a healthy mix of abstract theory and practical considerations. I hope that this trend will continue and help us understand how to improve our institutions.

References

Abdulkadiroğlu, A. (2005): "College Admissions with Affirmative Action," *International Journal of Game Theory*, 33(4), 535–49.

Abdulkadiroğlu, A., and T. Sönmez (2003): "School Choice: A Mechanism Design Approach," *American Economic Review*, 93, 729–47.

(2013): "Matching Markets: Theory and Practice," *Advances in Economics and Econometrics*, 1, 3–47.

Abraham, D. J., R. W. Irving, and D. F. Manlove (2007): "Two Algorithms for the Student-Project Allocation Problem," *Journal of Discrete Algorithms*, 5(1), 73–90.

Adachi, H. (2000): "On a Characterization of Stable Matchings," *Economics Letters*, 68(1), 43–9.

Akbarpour, M., S. Li, and S. Oveis Gharan (2014): "Dynamic Matching Market Design," mimeo.

Akbarpour, M., and A. Nikzad (2014): "Approximate Random Allocation Mechanisms," mimeo.

Anderson, R., I. Ashlagi, D. Gamarnik, and Y. Kanoria (2015): "A Dynamic Model of Barter Exchange," in *Proceedings of the Twenty-Sixth Annual ACM-SIAM Symposium on Discrete Algorithms*, pp. 1925–33. SIAM.

Ashlagi, I., M. Braverman, and A. Hassidim (2014): "Stability in Large Matching Markets with Complementarities," *Operations Research*, 62(4), 713–32.

Ashlagi, I., Y. Kanoria, and J. Leshno (2015): "Unbalanced Random Matching Markets: the Stark Effect of Competition," forthcoming, *Journal of Political Economy*.

Avery, C., and J. Levin (2010): "Early Admissions at Selective Colleges," *American Economic Review*, 100, 2125–56.

---

[33] See also an earlier contribution of Ünver (2010), who studies the optimal design of kidney exchange in a dynamic environment.

Azevedo, E. M., and J. W. Hatfield (2015): "Existence of Equilibrium in Large Matching Markets with Complementarities," mimeo.

Azevedo, E. M., and J. D. Leshno (2015): "A Supply and Demand Framework for Two-Sided Matching Markets," forthcoming, *Journal of Political Economy*.

Baccara, M., S. Lee, and L. Yariv (2015): "Optimal Dynamic Matching," mimeo.

Balinski, M., and T. Sönmez (1999): "A Tale of Two Mechanisms: Student Placement," *Journal of Economic Theory*, 84, 73–94.

Biró, P., T. Fleiner, and R. Irving (2016): "Matching Couples with Scarf's Algorithm," *Annals of Mathematics and Artificial Intelligence*, pp. 1–14.

Biró, P., T. Fleiner, R. Irving, and D. Manlove (2010): "The College Admissions Problem with Lower and Common Quotas," *Theoretical Computer Science*, 411(34-36), 3136–53.

Biró, P., R. W. Irving, and I. Schlotter (2011): "Stable Matching with Couples: An Empirical Study," *Journal of Experimental Algorithmics*, 16, 1–2.

Biró, P., and F. Klijn (2013): "Matching with Couples: A Multidisciplinary Survey," *International Game Theory Review*, 15(02).

Biró, P., D. F. Manlove, and I. McBride (2014): "The Hospitals/Residents Problem with Couples: Complexity and Integer Programming Models," in *Experimental Algorithms*, pp. 10–21. Springer.

Bogomolnaia, A., and H. Moulin (2001): "A New Solution to the Random Assignment Problem," *Journal of Economic Theory*, 100, 295–328.

Budish, E., and E. Cantillon (2012): "The Multi-Unit Assignment Problem: Theory and Evidence from Course Allocation at Harvard," *American Economic Review*, 102, 2237–71.

Budish, E., Y.-K. Che, F. Kojima, and P. Milgrom (2013): "Designing Random Allocation Mechanisms: Theory and Applications," *American Economic Review*, 103(2), 585–623.

Che, Y.-K., J. Kim, and F. Kojima (2015): "Stable Matching in Large Economies," mimeo.

Che, Y.-K., J. Kim, and K. Mierendorff (2013): "Generalized Reduced-Form Auctions: A Network-Flow Approach," *Econometrica*, 81(6), 2487–520.

Che, Y.-K., and Y. Koh (2015): "Decentralized College Admissions," forthcoming, *Journal of Political Economy*.

Che, Y.-K., and F. Kojima (2010): "Asymptotic Equivalence of Probabilistic Serial and Random Priority Mechanisms," *Econometrica*, 78(5), 1625–72.

Crawford, V., and E. M. Knoer (1981): "Job Matching with Heterogeneous Firms and Workers," *Econometrica*, 49, 437–50.

Dubins, L. E., and D. A. Freedman (1981): "Machiavelli and the Gale-Shapley algorithm," *American Mathematical Monthly*, 88, 485–94.

Echenique, F. (2012): "Contracts Versus Salaries in Matching," *The American Economic Review*, pp. 594–601.

Echenique, F., and J. Oviedo (2006): "A Theory of Stability in Many-to-Many Matching," *Theoretical Economics*, 1, 233–73.

Echenique, F., and J. S. Pereyra (2014): "Strategic Complementarities and Unraveling in Matching Markets," forthcoming, *Theoretical Economics*.

Echenique, F., and M. B. Yenmez (2013): "How to Control Controlled School Choice," forthcoming, *American Economic Review*.

Ehlers, L., I. E. Hafalir, M. B. Yenmez, and M. A. Yildirim (2014): "School Choice with Controlled Choice Constraints: Hard Bounds versus Soft Bounds," *Journal of Economic Theory*, 153, 648–83.

Fleiner, T. (2003): "A Fixed-Point Approach to Stable Matchings and Some Applications," *Mathematics of Operations Research*, 28, 103–26.

Fragiadakis, D., and P. Troyan (2016): "Improving Matching under Hard Distributional Constraints," forthcoming, *Theoretical Economics*.

Gale, D., and L. S. Shapley (1962): "College Admissions and the Stability of Marriage," *American Mathematical Monthly*, 69, 9–15.

Goto, M., N. Hashimoto, A. Iwasaki, Y. Kawasaki, S. Ueda, Y. Yasuda, and M. Yokoo (2014): "Strategy-Proof Matching with Regional Minimum Quotas," in *Thirteenth International Conference on Autonomous Agents and Multiagent Systems (AAMAS-2014)*, pp. 1225–32.

Goto, M., F. Kojima, R. Kurata, A. Tamura, and M. Yokoo (2016): "Designing Matching Mechanisms under General Distributional Constraints," forthcoming, *American Economic Journal: Microeconomics*.

Hafalir, I. E., M. B. Yenmez, and M. A. Yildirim (2013): "Effective Affirmative Action in School Choice," *Theoretical Economics*, 8(2), 325–63.

Hatfield, J. W., and F. Kojima (2008): "Matching with Contracts: Comment," *American Economic Review*, 98, 1189–94.

——— (2009): "Group Incentive Compatibility for Matching with Contracts," *Games and Economic Behavior*, pp. 745–9.

——— (2010): "Substitutes and Stability for Matching with Contracts," *Journal of Economic Theory*, 145(5), pp. 1704–23.

Hatfield, J. W., F. Kojima, and Y. Narita (2016): "Improving Schools Through School Choice: A Market Design Approach," forthcoming, *Journal of Economic Theory*.

Hatfield, J. W., and S. D. Kominers (2009): "Contract Design and Stability in Matching Markets," mimeo.

——— (2014): "Contract Design and Stability in Many-to-Many Matching," Discussion paper, Unpublished mimeo.

Hatfield, J. W., and P. Milgrom (2005): "Matching with Contracts," *American Economic Review*, 95, 913–35.

Hylland, A., and R. Zeckhauser (1979): "The Efficient Allocation of Individuals to Positions," *Journal of Political Economy*, 87, 293–314.

Immorlica, N., and M. Mahdian (2005): "Marriage, Honesty, and Stability," *SODA 2005*, pp. 53–62.

Kamada, Y., and F. Kojima (2014a): "General Theory of Matching under Distributional Constraints," mimeo.

——— (2014b): "Stability Concepts in Matching with Distributional Constraints," forthcoming, *Journal of Economic Theory*.

——— (2015): "Efficient Matching under Distributional Constraints: Theory and Applications," *The American Economic Review*, 105(1), 67–99.

Kelso, A., and V. Crawford (1982): "Job Matching, Coalition Formation, and Gross Substitutes," *Econometrica*, 50, 1483–504.

Kiselgof, S. (2012): "Matching Practices for Universities–Ukraine," www.matching-in-practice.eu/index.php/matching-in-practice/universities/ukraine.

Knuth, D. E., R. Motwani, and B. Pittel (1990): "Stable Husbands," *Random Structures and Algorithms*, 1, 1–14.

Kojima, F. (2012): "School Choice: Impossibilities for Affirmative Action," *Games and Economic Behavior*, 75(2), 685–93.

Kojima, F., and M. Manea (2010): "Incentives in the Probabilistic Serial Mechanism," *Journal of Economic Theory*, 145(1), 106–23.

Kojima, F., and P. A. Pathak (2009): "Incentives and Stability in Large Two-Sided Matching Markets," *American Economic Review*, pp. 608–27.

Kojima, F., P. A. Pathak, and A. E. Roth (2013): "Matching with Couples: Stability and Incentives in Large Markets," *Quarterly Journal of Economics*, 128, 1585–632.

Kojima, F., A. Tamura, and M. Yokoo (2014): "Designing Matching Mechanisms under Constraints: An Approach from Discrete Convex Analysis," mimeo.

Kominers, S. D. (2012): "On the Correspondence of Contracts to Salaries in (Many-to-Many) Matching," *Games and Economic Behavior*, 75(2), 984–9.

Lee, S. (2012): "Incentive Compatibility of Large Centralized Matching Markets," Unpublished mimeo.

Liu, Q., and M. Pycia (2013): "Ordinal Efficiency, Fairness, and Incentives in Large Markets," Unpublished mimeo.

Manea, M. (2009): "Asymptotic Ordinal Inefficiency of Random Serial Dictatorship," *Theoretical Economics*, 4(2), 165–97.

Milgrom, P. (2009): "Assignment Messages and Exchanges," *American Economic Journal: Microeconomics*, 1(2), 95–113.

Milgrom, P., and I. Segal (2014): "Deferred-Acceptance Auctions and Radio Spectrum Reallocation," mimeo.

Ministry of Health, Labour and Welfare (2009): "On Opinions Expressed in the Public Comment Procedure (in Japanese)," www.mhlw.go.jp/shingi/2009/04/dl/s0423-8a.pdf.

Nguyen, T., A. Peivandi, and R. Vohra (2016): "Assignment Problems with Complementarities," *Journal of Economic Theory*, 165, 209–41.

Nguyen, T., and R. Vohra (2014): "Near Feasible Stable Matchings with Complementarities," mimeo.

Pathak, P. A. (2007): "Lotteries in Student Assignment," PhD thesis, Harvard University.

Pathak, P. A., and T. Sönmez (2008): "Leveling the Playing Field: Sincere and Sophisticated Players in the Boston Mechanism," *The American Economic Review*, 98(4), 1636–52.

Roth, A. E. (1982): "The Economics of Matching: Stability and Incentives," *Mathematics of Operations Research*, 7, 617–28.

(1984): "The Evolution of the Labor Market for Medical Interns and Residents: A Case Study in Game Theory," *Journal of Political Economy*, 92, 991–1016.

(1991): "A Natural Experiment in the Organization of Entry-Level Labor Markets: Regional Markets for New Physicians and Surgeons in the United Kingdom," *American Economic Review*, pp. 415–40.

(2002): "The Economist as Engineer: Game Theory, Experimentation, and Computation as Tools for Design Economics," *Econometrica*, 70, 1341–78.

(2007): "Repugnance as a Constraint on Markets," *Journal of Economic Perspectives*, 21, 37–58.

(2008): "Deferred Acceptance Algorithms: History, Theory, Practice, and Open Questions," *International Journal of Game Theory*, 36, 537–69.

Roth, A. E., and E. Peranson (1999): "The Redesign of the Matching Market for American Physicians: Some Engineering Aspects of Economic Design," *American Economic Review*, 89, 748–80.

Roth, A. E., T. Sönmez, and U. Ünver (2004): "Kidney Exchange," *Quarterly Journal of Economics*, 119, 457–88.

(2005): "Pairwise Kidney Exchange," *Journal of Economic Theory*, 125, 151–88.

(2007): "Efficient Kidney Exchange: Coincidence of Wants in Markets with Compatibility-Based Preferences," *American Economic Review*, 97, 828–51.

Roth, A. E., and M. A. O. Sotomayor (1990): *Two-Sided Matching: A Study in Game-Theoretic Modeling and Analysis*. Cambridge University Press.

Sönmez, T. (2013): "Bidding for Army Career Specialties: Improving the ROTC Branching Mechanism," *Journal of Political Economy*, 121(1), 186–219.

Sönmez, T., and T. Switzer (2012): "Matching with (Branch-of-Choice) Contracts at United States Military Academy," forthcoming, *Econometrica*.

Sönmez, T., and M. Ünver (2006): "School Choice with Aggregate Capacity Constraints," mimeo.

Sönmez, T., and U. Ünver (2009): "Matching, Allocation, and Exchange of Discrete Resources," forthcoming, in: *Handbook of Social Economics*, eds. J. Benhabib, A. Bisin, and M. Jackson, Elsevier.

(2010): "Course Bidding at Business Schools," *International Economic Review*, 51(1), 99–123.

Ueda, S., D. Fragiadakis, A. Iwasaki, P. Troyan, and M. Yokoo (2012): "Strategy-Proof Mechanisms for Two-Sided Matching with Minimum and Maximum Quotas," in *AAMAS*, pp. 1327–8.

Ünver, M. U. (2010): "Dynamic Kidney Exchange," *The Review of Economic Studies*, 77(1), 372–414.

Westkamp, A. (2013): "An Analysis of the German University Admissions System," *Economic Theory*, 53(3), 561–89.

CHAPTER 6

What Really Matters in Designing School Choice Mechanisms
Parag A. Pathak

In the last decade, numerous student assignment systems have been redesigned using input from economists in the large American cities and elsewhere. This article reviews some of these case studies and uses practical experiences to take stock on what has really mattered in school choice mechanism design so far. While some algorithm design details are important, many are less practically important than initially thought. What really matters are basic issues that market operators in other contexts would likely be concerned about: straightforward incentives, transparency, avoiding inefficiency through coordination and well-functioning aftermarkets, and influencing inputs to the design, such as applicant decision-making and the quality of schools.

1 INTRODUCTION

In recent years, there has been a great deal of research activity and excitement among economists who study the design of systems used to assign students to schools. Motivated by Turkish college admissions, Balinski and Sönmez (1999) first defined the student placement problem, and Abdulkadiroğlu and Sönmez (2003) defined the closely related school choice problem, motivated by K-12 public school admissions in the United States. Both articles showed how insights from matching theory could be used to re-engineer and potentially

Prepared for the 2015 World Congress of the Econometric Society in Montreal. I'm particularly grateful to Federico Echenique, my discussant, and Fuhito Kojima for helpful feedback. I would also like to thank Atila Abdulkadiroğlu, Nikhil Agarwal, Alonso Bucarey, Umut Dur, Arda Gitmez, Peter Hull, Yusuke Narita, Cara Nickolaus, and Tayfun Sönmez for comments and Miikka Rokkanen for his assistance with Tables 4 and 5. Many of the ideas in this paper developed from long-standing collaborations with Atila Abdulkadiroğlu, Alvin Roth, and Tayfun Sönmez, for which I'm grateful. I've also benefitted from interactions with Neil Dorosin, Gabriela Fighetti, and many other school assignment practitioners. Financial support was provided by the National Science Foundation. I'm on the scientific advisory board of the Institute for Innovation in Public School Choice, a nonprofit 501(c) that provides assistance to school districts on the implementation of school choice systems.

improve existing centralized school assignment systems. Abdulkadiroğlu and Sönmez (2003) proposed two alternative mechanisms, which are adaptations of widely studied mechanisms in the literature on matching and assignment markets, following seminal contributions by Gale and Shapley (1962) and Shapley and Scarf (1974). Since that article was published, I have been involved in a number of efforts to redesign school choice systems, including those in New York City (2003), Boston (2005), New Orleans (2012), Denver (2012), Washington DC (2013), and Newark (2014).[1] New systems have also been developed in England, Amsterdam, a number of Asian cities, and elsewhere.

The purpose of this article is to review some facts from the field about these redesign efforts and to take stock on what I think has been important in practice so far. This article is not a survey of research on school choice market design (for surveys see, e.g., Pathak, 2011 and Abdulkadiroğlu and Sönmez, 2013). My inspiration comes from Klemperer (2002), who presents his views on what matters for practical auction design based on his experience in designing auctions and advising bidders. Klemperer concludes that "in short, good auction design is mostly good elementary economics," whereas "most of the extensive auction literature is of second-order importance for practical auction design."

My argument in this paper proceeds along similar lines. I argue that what really matters for school choice market design are basic insights about straightforward incentives, transparency, avoiding inefficiency through coordination of offers and well-functioning aftermarkets, and influencing inputs to the design, including applicant decision-making and the quality of schools. Some of the issues examined in the extensive theoretical literature on school choice matching market design are less important for *practical* design. However, my conclusion is not as pessimistic as that of Klemperer (2002), and I will discuss a handful of issues examined in the theoretical literature on matching mechanisms that have proven to be first-order. It's worth emphasizing that it is only with the benefit of several design case studies that we're beginning to understand which issues are quantitatively important.

This paper is organized as follows. Section 2 introduces and reviews the literature on algorithms to match demand and supply, with a focus on some theoretical issues that have emerged from the field. Section 3 reviews the role of strategy-proofness, transparency, offer coordination, aftermarkets, and participation across a variety of field settings. Section 4 discusses work on inputs to a school choice market design. The last section concludes.

2 CLEARING THE MARKET

The initial literature on school choice mechanisms compared the properties of assignment algorithms given the demand and supply in the market, as

---

[1] Abdulkadiroğlu, Pathak, Roth, and Sönmez (2005) and Abdulkadiroğlu, Pathak, and Roth (2005) report details on Boston and New York City, respectively.

expressed via student preferences, school priorities, and school capacities. This literature theoretically shows that classic economic trade-offs between fairness, efficiency, and incentives are unavoidable in the allocation of school seats. With the benefit of datasets from districts using strategy-proof mechanisms, it is now possible to revisit the quantitative magnitudes of these trade-offs. I begin by reviewing the theoretical background.

2.1   Efficiency vs. Fairness

Abdulkadiroğlu and Sönmez (2003) proposed two strategy-proof student assignment mechanisms. The first is based on the celebrated deferred acceptance (DA) algorithm of Gale and Shapley (1962) and is defined as follows:

Step 1) Each student proposes to her first choice. Each school tentatively assigns seats to its proposers one at a time, following their priority order. Any remaining proposers are rejected.

In general, at

Step k) Each student who was rejected in the previous step proposes to her next best choice. Each school considers the students it has been holding together with its new proposers and tentatively assigns its seats to these students one at a time following the school's priority order. Any remaining proposers are rejected.

The algorithm terminates either when there are no new proposals or when all rejected students have exhausted their preference lists.

The second mechanism builds on the Gale's top trading cycles (TTC) algorithm described in Shapley and Scarf (1974). Several authors have extended this algorithm and substantially broadened its use for potential applications including Abdulkadiroğlu and Sönmez (1999) and Papai (2000). I will refer to the version that Abdulkadiroğlu and Sönmez (2003) define for school choice as TTC.[2] First, assign a counter for each school that keeps track of how many seats are still available at the school. Initially set the counters equal to the capacities of the schools. The mechanism works as follows:

Step 1) Each student points to her favorite school. Each school points to the student who has the highest priority. There is at least one cycle. Every student can only be part of one cycle. Assign every student in a cycle to the school she points to, and remove the student. The counter of each school in a cycle is reduced by one and if it is zero, remove the school.

In general, at

---

[2] Recent literature examines alternate versions of TTC for school assignment (e.g., Abdulkadiroğlu, Che, Pathak, Roth, and Tercieux (2017), Dur (2014), and Morrill (2016)).

Step k) Each remaining student points to her favorite school among the remaining schools, and each remaining school points to the student with the highest priority. There is at least one cycle. Every student in a cycle is assigned the school she points to and the student is removed. The counter of each school in a cycle is reduced by one, and if it is zero, remove the school.

The procedure terminates when either all students are assigned a school or unassigned students have exhausted their preference lists.

Balinski and Sönmez (1999) and Abdulkadiroğlu and Sönmez (2003) observed the close relationship between fairness concepts in the student placement problem and stability in an associated college admissions problem. The following well-known example illustrates how these two mechanisms resolve the trade-off between efficiency and fairness:

Example: Consider an economy with three students i_1, i_2, and i_3 and three schools s_1, s_2, and s_3, each with one seat. Student preferences, P, are:

$$i_1 : s_2 - s_1 - s_3$$
$$i_2 : s_1 - s_2 - s_3$$
$$i_3 : s_1 - s_2 - s_3,$$

and priorities are given by the following orderings:

$$s_1 : i_1 - i_3 - i_2$$
$$s_2 : i_2 - i_1 - i_3$$
$$s_3 : i_3 - i_1 - i_2.$$

The matching produced by DA is:

$$\mu_{DA} = \begin{pmatrix} i_1 & i_2 & i_3 \\ s_1 & s_2 & s_3 \end{pmatrix}.$$

In this matching, none of the students obtains their top choice. The matching is not Pareto efficient, but since there are no blocking pairs, it is stable. The matching produced by the TTC is:

$$\mu_{TTC} = \begin{pmatrix} i_1 & i_2 & i_3 \\ s_2 & s_1 & s_3 \end{pmatrix}.$$

This matching is Pareto efficient for students and both student i_1 and i_2 obtain their top choice. However, student i_3 prefers school s_1 and has higher priority than student i_2, who is assigned there. Therefore, student i_3 has *justified envy* at s_1, or in the language of two-sided matching models, student i_3 and school s_1 form a blocking pair.

Abdulkadiroğlu and Sönmez (2003) framed the debate between these two alternatives in terms of the interpretation of priorities: when elimination of justified envy is a more important goal than efficiency, DA should be used because it Pareto dominates any other fair outcomes; when efficiency is paramount, they argued for TTC.

In Boston, this article led to one of the first school choice market design efforts in the field after it was featured prominently in a local newspaper (Cook, 2003). Boston has a long-standing but controversial school choice system following court-ordered busing in the 1970s. From 2003 to 2005, a Student Assignment Task force, led by civic leaders, evaluated possible improvements to the choice system. While they mostly debated the merits of alternative school zone configurations, which determine the schools a student can rank, they ended up recommending no change to Boston's three-zone system. However, they did recommend changing the student assignment algorithm. Their recommendation favored TTC over DA. The description of the trade-offs involved between the algorithms illustrates how these two alternatives were perceived (Landsmark, Dajer, and Gonsalves, 2014):

> [T]he Gale-Shapley algorithm [...] cuts down on the amount of choice afforded to families. The Top Trading Cycles algorithm also takes into account priorities while leaving some room for choice. [...] [C]hoice was very important to many families who attended community forums...

Based on this report and further consultation with the community and academic experts, the official recommendation was for DA. TTC was faulted for allowing students to trade as stated in the final school committee report (BPS, 2005):

> [TTC's] trading shifts the emphasis onto the priority and away from the goals BPS is trying to achieve by granting these priorities in the first place.

Since the debate between DA and TTC sparked by Abdulkadiroğlu and Sönmez (2003) came to such prominence in Boston's deliberations, it is natural to ask about the extent of differences between the two systems using data from Boston. A major advantage of both mechanisms is that it is a weakly-dominant strategy for applicants to report their true preferences. The strategy-proofness property motivates using preferences from applicants under DA to compute counterfactual assignments, holding the submitted preferences fixed.

Table 1 shows relatively little difference between DA and TTC for applicants in Boston's choice plan. I use data from four school years when BPS employed DA and examine outcomes for roughly 6,000 elementary, middle and high school applicants per year. The fraction who are assigned their top choice is 65.4 percent under TTC, compared to 64.8 percent under DA. The fractions are similar comparing the number who obtain one of their top k choices for $k = \{2, \ldots, 10\}$. The similarity of the aggregate rank distribution suggests that in practice, the choice between the two mechanisms does not involve large differences in overall efficiency. The table also tabulates the fraction of students who have justified envy under TTC. A small percentage of total applicants, 6.8 percent, prefer a school seat over what they are assigned and have higher priority for it.

Table 1 *Comparing Deferred Acceptance and Top Trading Cycles*

| | Boston Elementary, Middle and High School | | New Orleans OneApp (All Grades) | |
Choice Assigned	TTC (1)	DA (2)	TTC (3)	DA (4)
1	65.4%	64.8%	73.2%	72.0%
2	17.9%	18.8%	11.7%	13.1%
3	7.8%	8.1%	3.3%	3.9%
4	3.3%	3.4%	1.0%	1.2%
5	1.3%	1.3%	0.4%	0.4%
6	0.4%	0.4%	0.1%	0.1%
7	0.2%	0.2%	0.0%	0.0%
8	0.1%	0.1%	0.0%	0.0%
9	0.0%	0.0%	0.0%	0.0%
10	0.0%	0.0%	0.0%	0.0%
Unassigned	3.5%	2.9%	10.3%	9.3%
Number of Students	5,927	5,927	7,789	7,789
Percentage of Students with Justified Envy	6.8%		10.0%	

Notes. Data covers four schools years, 2009–10 to 2012–13, from Boston Public Schools and one year, 2012–13, from the New Orleans Recovery School District. Boston data are from grades K2, 6, and 9, while New Orleans data are from grades PK-9. DA is the student-proposing deferred acceptance algorithm. TTC is Gale's Top Trading Cycles algorithm as defined by Abdulkadiroğlu and Sönmez (2003). The same lottery number is used for TTC and DA.

Table 1 reports on a similar comparison of DA and TTC using data from the Recovery School District (RSD) in New Orleans. The RSD was formed in 2003 and came to oversee the majority of schools in New Orleans following Hurricane Katrina. In 2012, Louisiana state and district officials launched a pioneering universal enrollment process, known as OneApp, which coordinated admissions across traditional and charter school sectors.[3] In the first year of OneApp, the assignment process was based on TTC, the first time to my knowledge that TTC was used in a real-life application (for more details, see Abdulkadiroğlu, Che, Pathak, Roth, and Tercieux, 2017). The RSD was initially a perfect test bed for TTC since the priority structure involves a mix of sibling and neighborhood priorities, much like Boston, and did not involve any schools that screened applicants via test scores or some other criteria.

After one year with TTC, the Recovery School District switched the assignment mechanism to one based on DA. Officials adopted a new algorithm largely based on three reasons: 1) the desire to attract participation from

---

[3] A charter school is a publicly funded school that operates with more autonomy than a traditional district school. Since the 2014–15 school year, the RSD consists entirely of charter schools. Abdulkadiroğlu, Angrist, Hull, and Pathak (2016) conduct an evaluation of RSD takeover charter schools.

schools in the neighboring Orleans Parish School Board district, many of which involve screened admissions criteria; 2) the need to include private scholarship schools in the system, which by law cannot allow for situations of justified envy;[4] and 3) the simplicity of explaining results from DA relative to TTC. To investigate whether the switch from TTC to DA in RSD resulted in a large change in the aggregate distribution of ranks, Table 1 reports the ranks from TTC and DA for grades Pre-K through 9. As with Boston, slightly more students are assigned their top choice under TTC than DA, but slightly fewer are assigned their second choice. However, the overall distribution of top choices is similar across both mechanisms. 10 percent of students have justified envy under the TTC allocation, which is larger than in Boston.

Given that TTC and DA may generate substantially different allocations in theory, one question motivated by the results in Table 1 is what features of preferences and school priorities in the Boston and New Orleans school districts result in such similar aggregate outcomes. Ergin (2002) identified an acyclicity condition under which the outcome of DA with strict school priorities is Pareto efficient, and Kesten (2006) identified conditions for when two mechanisms are equivalent. Ehlers and Erdil (2010) generalized this result when school priorities have indifferences. Given that these conditions are not likely to be satisfied in practice (and are not in Boston and New Orleans), some have interpreted these results as negative ones (e.g., Abdulkadiroğlu and Sönmez, 2013). It seems more likely that the relatively small tension between efficiency and the elimination of justified envy is driven by aspects of preferences and priorities in those cities that are not captured by the Ergin (2002) and Ehlers and Erdil (2010) conditions. One conjecture involves the role of neighborhood priority, which exists in both cities. All else being equal, families prefer schools closer to home, so many students rank schools for which they obtain a high priority. The correlation between preferences and priorities induced by proximity may in turn result in less scope for Pareto-improving trades across priority groups that involve situations of justified envy. This pattern may then result in a small degree of inefficiency in DA, though such an intuition remains to be formalized.[5]

---

[4] Louisiana's Department of Education's Act 2 expanded Louisiana's Student Scholarships for Excellence Program statewide, a program that provided state-funded scholarships for low-income students who attend a C, D, or F school to enroll in state-approved non-public schools. The state's legal counsel advised that blocking pairs potentially produced by TTC might be in violation of Act 2. Abdulkadiroğlu, Pathak, and Walters (2015) evaluate the effect of the program on student achievement.

[5] Table 2 of Abdulkadiroğlu, Pathak, and Roth (2009) compares a student-optimal stable matching to an efficient matching, computed by applying TTC to the economy where the student-optimal stable matching is treated as the students' endowments. Just over 5 percent of applicants obtain a more preferred assignment under TTC, whereas 44 percent of applicants are involved in a blocking pair, suggesting a larger efficiency and equity trade-off in New York than in Boston and the RSD. Since high schoolers appear to be more willing to travel for schools than students in earlier grades, this pattern is consistent with those in Boston and New Orleans, which have many more applicants in earlier grades. It's also worth emphasizing that New York City's assignment

2.2   Student Optimality in DA

A second widely studied issue with DA for school assignment involves turning coarse school priorities into strict ones. Unlike matching applications for labor markets, coarse priorities, such as neighborhood or sibling priority, are widespread. In such an environment, the mechanism must adjudicate claims for school seats between same-priority applicants. In footnote 14, Abdulkadiroğlu and Sönmez (2003) suggest using a single tie-breaker, in which each applicant receives a random number, may be a better idea under DA, and there are now several papers exploring this issue in much greater depth.

To illustrate the issue, consider the earlier example, but now suppose that schools s_1 and s_2 give equal priority to all applicants. That is, the priorities are:

$$s_1 : \{i_1, i_2, i_3\}$$
$$s_2 : \{i_1, i_2, i_3\}$$
$$s_3 : i_3 - i_1 - i_2,$$

where the notation indicates that schools s_1 and s_2 are indifferent between pupils, but pupils are ordered in a strict way at s_3. If DA uses lotteries to convert these indifferences into strict orderings, and the resulting orderings are as in the earlier example, then both students i_1 and i_2 are assigned to their second choice, when each would be better off trading their placements with one another. If the priorities at s_1 had been strict, then one might justify prohibiting this trade because student i_3 forms a blocking pair with school s_1 after the trade. However, this is not a blocking pair in the traditional sense because s_1 is indifferent between applicants. This example shows that DA does not always produce a student-optimal stable matching, and therefore allows for efficiency loss even among stable allocations.

The issue of how best to break ties is a theoretical issue that arose from practical experiences with school districts. Pathak (2011) describes an intuition from policymakers in New York City, where the issue was a central part of designing the rules of the new mechanism. Questions related to tie-breaking have reappeared in nearly every city I have interacted with using DA. For instance, in Washington DC, where DA was used in 2013 and 2014 as part of their universal enrollment system, MySchoolsDC, there has been widespread skepticism over the use of a single lottery number for each applicant. For instance, a parent on a popular online forum summarized the concern (urbandcmoms.com, 2014):

> Man would it SUCK to get a crappy number for all 12 choices. Wouldn't that essentially knock you out of the whole lottery because, at least for the most

system involves a mix of screened and unscreened schools, which places it outside of the original Abdulkadiroğlu and Sönmez (2003) school choice model because screened schools submit rankings over pupils as in a two-sided matching model for labor markets. Therefore, TTC-based mechanisms were never initially considered in New York's design.

popular schools, there is guaranteed to be more people with better numbers who ranked it high enough to be competing with you?

Abdulkadiroğlu, Pathak, and Roth (2009) show that any student-optimal stable matching can be produced by a single lottery draw, so that school-specific lotteries only generate additional matchings that are not student-optimal relative to a single lottery draw. Their results represent an ex post perspective, and, as far as I know, there is no stronger ex ante argument for single versus multiple tie-breaking based on the distribution of matchings. Erdil and Ergin (2008) show that there is no strategy-proof mechanism that produces a student-optimal matching when there is coarse priority ordering at schools. They also construct a mechanism that computes a student-optimal stable matching in polynomial time. Kesten (2010) defines an enhanced version of deferred acceptance, where students consent to waive certain priorities. Kesten and Ünver (2015) examine how definitions of fairness with deferred acceptance change from an ex ante view and propose two new mechanisms that produce fair allocations.[6]

How much do these issues matter in practice? Table 2, from Abdulkadiroğlu, Pathak, and Roth (2009), reports on the aggregate distribution of choices assigned under DA with single tie-breaking (DA-STB) compared to DA with school-specific tie-breaking (DA-MTB). For both Boston's elementary schools and New York City's high schools, 3 percent more applicants obtain their top choice from single tie-breaking than multiple tie-breaking, but slightly more students obtain their second or lower choice under DA-MTB. This phenomenon is also seen in a similar exercise in data from Amsterdam (de Haan, Gautier, Oosterbeek, and van der Klaauw, 2015).

In column 3, I report the difference between DA-STB and a student-optimal matching computed via the stable improvement cycles algorithm for Boston. There is virtually no difference between the two assignments in the case of Boston; that is, deferred acceptance with single tie-breaking produces an allocation that is nearly student-optimal. Column 6 shows that, for New York City, there is a slight improvement compared to DA-STB, where 1,488 students (or 1.9 percent of applicants) obtain a more preferred assignment. It's worth emphasizing that any potential gain from a student-optimal stable matching requires using a mechanism that is no longer strategy-proof.

Quantitatively, multiple tie-breaking appears to result in a larger difference in allocations relative to computing a student-optimal stable matching using the Erdil and Ergin (2008) procedure, but the magnitudes of both exercises seem modest. Though understanding the effects of tweaks to DA is a worthwhile

---

[6] A related literature examines the question of tie-breaking in the context of TTC-based mechanisms. See Abdulkadiroğlu and Sonmez (1998), Pathak and Sethuraman (2011), Carroll (2014), and Lee and Sethuraman (2014).

Table 2 *Tie-Breaking with Deferred Acceptance*

	Boston Elementary			NYC High Schools		
Choice Assigned	DA-STB (1)	DA-MTB (2)	Student Optimal (3)	DA-STB (4)	DA-MTB (5)	Student Optimal (6)
1	77%	74%	77%	41%	38%	42%
2	11%	12%	11%	18%	18%	18%
3	5%	6%	5%	12%	13%	12%
4	2%	3%	2%	8%	8%	8%
5	1%	1%	1%	5%	6%	5%
6	0%	0%	0%	3%	4%	3%
7	0%	0%	0%	2%	2%	2%
8	0%	0%	0%	1%	2%	1%
9	0%	0%	0%	1%	1%	1%
10	0%	0%	0%	1%	1%	1%
11	0%	0%	0%	0%	0%	0%
12	0%	0%	0%	0%	0%	0%
Unassigned	4%	4%	4%	7%	7%	7%
N	2927	2927	2927	78729	78728	78729

Notes. Extracted from Abdulkadiroğlu, Pathak, and Roth (2009). Boston and NYC data are from 2006–07. Boston data is for Elementary (K2), while NYC is for high school applicants. DA-STB is the student-proposing deferred acceptance algorithm with single tie breaking, DA-MTB is the student-proposing deferred acceptance algorithm with school-specific tie-breaking, and Student-Optimal Stable Matching is the result of the Erdil-Ergin (2008) Stable Improvement Cycles from the DA-STB allocation. Each colum reports the average from 250 lottery draws.

pursuit, there may be little reason to employ them in the field ahead of deferred acceptance with single tie-breaking.

2.3   Constrained Rank Order Lists

The initial theory of school choice mechanisms was based on the assumption that applicants can rank as many choices as they wish. In practice, applicants are usually not allowed to rank all choices, and mechanisms that are strategy-proof without constraints are no longer strategy-proof with this constraint. Pathak and Sönmez (2013) report on a number of systems based on DA, and in all cases aside from Boston, the mechanisms in the field do not allow participants to submit a complete rank order list.

The widespread presence of constraints inspired a theoretical and experimental literature examining what happens to popular mechanisms when applicants cannot submit a complete rank order list. Haeringer and Klijn (2009) analyze the properties of the DA and TTC, showing that in DA, when a student may rank only k schools, (1) if a student prefers at most k schools, then she can do no better than submitting her true rank order list; (2) if a student prefers more than k schools, then she can do no better than employing a strategy that selects k schools among the set she prefers to being unassigned and ranking

Table 3 *Constrained Rank Order Lists*

Application Year	Constraint (1)	Number of Options (2)	Fraction at Constraint (3)
	A. New York City High Schools		
2006	12	777	22.85%
2007	12	795	20.67%
2008	12	781	17.70%
	B. Chicago Public Schools		
2009	4	9	84.60%
2010	6	10	56.80%
2011	6	10	49.50%
2012	6	10	46.60%
2013	6	10	46.02%
	C. Denver Public Schools		
2012	5	78	26.80%
2013	5	81	26.60%
	D. New Orleans RSD		
2013	8	41	4.97%

Notes. Denver applicants are from major transition grades (EC, K,6,9). RSD applicants are from transition grades (PK-9). The number of possible choices is equally-weighted across these applicant grades. Chicago Public Schools applicants are non-special education applicants in Chicago Public Schools in 8th grade.

them according to her true preference ordering (Proposition 4.2). Pathak and Sönmez (2013) propose an ordering on manipulability and show that for $\ell > k$, DA when applicants can rank k schools is more manipulable than DA when applicants can rank ℓ schools. This result implies that Chicago's 2010 reform to allow applicants to rank six choices rather than four has made their mechanism less manipulable. Calsamiglia, Haeringer, and Kljin (2010) report results from laboratory experiments showing that constraints do lead to preference manipulations, the most common of which involves participants including a "safety school" among their choices.

Since an applicant can only rank 12 schools in New York's high school match, if the applicant ranks all 12 choices, then the applicant may potentially prefer more choices, and hence his incentives to truthfully rank schools is affected by this constraint on the number of choices. On the other hand, if an applicant ranks fewer than 12 choices (he could have ranked more choices but opted not to), so his preference submission problem was not constrained by the mechanism. This observation motivates tabulating the fraction of applicants who submit a rank order list equal to the maximum allowed in systems with constraints. Table 3 reports on New York City, Chicago, Denver and New Orleans, for years where each city used a mechanism that would be strategy-proof in the absence of a constraint.

The table shows that when there are few options, many more applicants rank the same number of schools as the constraint. In districts with many options, a relatively smaller fraction are at the constraint. For instance, in 2009, when students at Chicago's exam high schools were allowed to rank four out of nine choices, more than 80 percent of applicants ranked all four schools. In 2010, the district allowed students to rank six choices, and roughly half of applicants listed all six choices. In contrast, in New York City, roughly one fifth of participants rank all 12 choices, but 12 choices represents a very small percentage of the choice set. Denver's constraint of five choices is about 6 percent of all possible rankable schools, and about 25 percent of students rank five schools. Finally, the constraint in New Orleans seems least severe, with fewer than 5 percent of students ranking all eight possible choices.

Given how a constraint interferes with the incentive properties of mechanisms, it continues to be a puzzle why it is much more common for system operators to restrict the number of choices a participant can rank rather than having no constraint on what can be ranked. It seems unlikely that technical constraints prevent a system that allows participants to rank many choices. For instance, in the National Residency Matching Program, there is no limit on the number of choices an applicant can rank in the Main residency match, though applicants may have to pay a fee to rank more programs than on the standard form. However, that market involves an important interview stage where a fair amount of sorting takes place, and a similar phase is not present in most school choice settings, in which applicants most often apply to a program without the need to interview or visit.

Market operators have made three different arguments to me about constraining rank order lists. First, they are concerned about the perceived complications involved in ranking many choices, but it's not clear that the costs of information acquisition motivate capping the number of choices for everyone. Second, they are reluctant to advertise that an applicant received their 20th choice because it makes salient that there is a shortage of desirable options. However, this hardly seems better than advertising that an applicant is unassigned. Finally, operators have emphasized that take-up rates would be lower when applicants can rank more choices. They are concerned that applicants would submit less "serious" choices, only to not take them up after the main assignments are announced, leaving those seats vacant. One simple response is to over-book schools accounting for less than full yield. Abdulkadiroğlu, Agarwal, and Pathak (2015) report that take-up of main round assignment in New York City is largely invariant to the length of an applicant's rank order list. For instance, the fraction of students who rank five choices (who are assigned on average their 2.5th choice) who enroll in the school assigned in their main round is 91.2 percent, while the fraction of students who rank 12 choices (who are assigned on average their 3.9th choice) is 94.3 percent. The take-up rates tend to be lower for students who have ranked few choices, though these students are much more likely to enroll in private schools. It's possible that these patterns would change if participants were able to rank more choices, but there is no direct evidence of that.

Overall, despite the fact that so many systems place ad hoc constraints on the number of schools an applicant can rank, it does not seem to be a pressing concern for operators even in cities where the constraint appears to bind more severely. This suggests that either there are aspects of the constraint that existing models don't capture or this design issue is less central in practice than initially thought.

2.4   Ranking Behavior in New Mechanisms

Abdulkadiroğlu and Sönmez (2003) emphasize that many popular assignment schemes do not encourage participants to truthfully report their preferences. During initial meetings in Boston, officials referenced results on preference manipulation in Boston, DA, and TTC in laboratory experiments in Chen and Sönmez (2006). The paper reports that there is a higher degree of preference manipulation under Boston than either alternative. For instance, in one of the treatments, less than 30 percent of applicants report their true preferences under the Boston mechanism, while over half of applicants report their true preferences under DA. They report that a common strategy in the Boston mechanism involves ranking a district school, for which they obtain priority, in a higher position than the true preference order.

Using field data from Boston from 1999–2005, Abdulkadiroğlu, Pathak, Roth, and Sönmez (2006) report that about 20 percent of applicants ranked two popular schools as top and second choices. They argued that this ranking behavior was a mistake because an applicant stands no chance of getting assigned their second choice if it is heavily oversubscribed because its seats will have been depleted by first choice applicants in the Boston mechanism. Not all applicants submit preferences naively, however. Without quantifying the fraction of strategic players, Abdulkadiroğlu, Pathak, Roth, and Sönmez (2006) collect anecdotes on strategic heuristics from parent groups who appear to understand incentive properties of the mechanism. Following this work, it's remained an open question about how many applicants understand and react to the incentives to manipulate preferences in non-strategy proof mechanisms. I next turn to field data from policy changes in Boston and Chicago to examine how families might be responding to mechanisms.

2.4.1   Before and After DA in Boston

It's clear that the extent of any behavioral response will depend crucially on outreach efforts and whether participants believe and react to the advice given by those who run the mechanism. School officials in Boston who studied the Chen and Sönmez (2006) experiment observed that in the laboratory experiment, descriptions of the alternative mechanisms did not indicate that truthful reporting is an optimal strategy. This experimental design decision was intended to isolate the actual incentive properties of the mechanism as experienced by laboratory subjects, not how participants responded to advice about mechanisms. In the experimental instructions, the authors went to great lengths to limit the variation in how the three mechanisms were described.

The absence of advice was notable to policymakers, given that BPS had been giving recommendations to participants in their school brochures. Prior to 2005, the Boston school brochure recommended (emphasis in original):

> For a better chance of obtaining your "first" choice, consider choosing less popular schools.

Under a strategy-proof mechanism, it is no longer necessary to rank schools based on their popularity. Following the change in the mechanism, from 2006 through 2010, DA was described in school brochures as follows (emphasis in original):

> Assignments are made by a computer that is programmed with a **mathematical formula**. The computer programs tries to assign students to their highest listed **choice** for which they have the highest **priority.**

The brochure also stated (BPS, 2008):

> List your school choices in your true order of preference. There is no need to "strategize." If you list a popular school first, you won't hurt your chances of getting your second choice school if you don't get your first choice.

Aside from changes in how the mechanism was described in written communications, there were also outreach activities from BPS that trained family resource center staff members, who field questions on how school choice works in Boston. Of course, counselors in these centers are not necessarily algorithm experts, so it seems likely some of the intended effects of the Boston change would be gradual as information disseminates and families gained experience with the new system over time.

To focus our discussion on what happened after Boston's algorithm change, I recount the deliberations prior to the vote to change the mechanism in official hearings. First, Boston officials conjectured that (BPS, 2005):

> selection habits will change, and fewer students are expected to receive their first choice school if more people are vying for seats in over-demanded schools.

Second, they speculated that:

> the number of school choices made by families is likely to increase, as parents will be more inclined to list all schools they are interested in, not just those to which they are more likely to gain admittance.

Using data from years before and after the mechanism change, Figure 1 shows that applicants ranked more schools following the adoption of DA. The figure reports the fraction of applicants ranking four or more choices

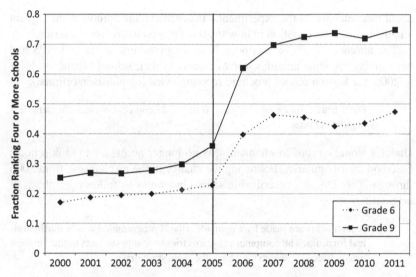

Figure 1 Length of Applicant Preference Lists in Boston.

from 2000 to 2011 for grades 6 and 9.[7] Applicants are therefore being more expressive by listing more schools, suggesting that under the Boston mechanism, applicants had less of an incentive to consider choices beyond their top one.

Figure 2 shows that there is a reduction in the number of students who obtain their stated top choice. For both grades 6 and 9, when the Boston mechanism was used, roughly 70 percent of students obtained their top choice, while in the following years, the number decreases to between 50–60 percent. Since the Boston mechanism prioritizes first choices, this outcome likely represents a best-case scenario for assigning as many as possible to their top choice, holding fixed applicant behavior.

While a more through investigation of the effects of Boston's new mechanism is beyond the scope of this paper, the patterns in both figures illustrate that two of the conjectured effects of the new mechanism occurred in Boston. Of course, attributing all of these changes solely to the new mechanism does not take into account the possibility that other aspects of the market may also have changed. Moreover, there is a different set of applicants participating across years, so some of the variation in the submitted reports may reflect the preferences of these new applicants. I therefore turn to an examination of an unusual experiment in Chicago's Public Schools.

[7] I do not report numbers for the elementary school entry point because alongside the new algorithm, there was an expansion of the number of kindergarten programs in the city. In particular, in early years grade K2 was the main entry point, but this shifted to K1, which caused a number of applicants at K2 to be effectively guaranteed their choice.

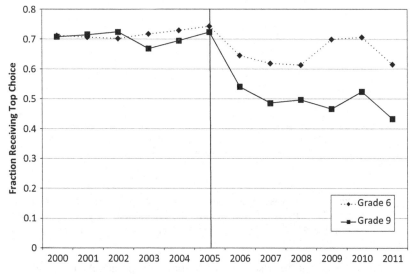

Figure 2 Fraction Receiving Top Choice in Boston.

2.4.2   Chicago

Pathak and Sönmez (2013) report on a stunning midstream change in Chicago's assignment system for its elite exam schools in 2009. After eliciting preferences from over 13,000 8th graders, CPS officials announced a new system and allowed any 8th grader to re-rank preferences if they wished. Prior to this reform, Chicago's school system placed children to exam schools using a version of the Boston mechanism, where schools were allowed to make uncoordinated offers and a racial quota was in place. Following the reform, the system was based on a version of DA, and the racial quota changed to an affirmative action system based on a socioeconomic index.[8] We therefore can observe the same participants submitting rankings under two different assignment mechanisms. Submissions occurred about two months apart, allowing for the possibility that preference changes reflect new information, so the magnitude of potential changes can be attributed to both the new mechanism and time elapsing between preference submissions. Nonetheless, unlike the comparisons I reviewed in Boston, the set of participants are fixed in Chicago.

Before reporting on applicant responses, it's worth noting the type of advice given to participants about the new system. After their initial preference submission, each applicant received a letter stating:

> ...the original application deadline is being extended to allow applicants an opportunity to review and re-rank their Selection Enrollment High School

---

[8] For more details on the socioeconomic index, see Ellison and Pathak (2015) and Dur, Pathak, and Sönmez (2015).

Table 4 *Chicago Preference Changers*

Applicants who:	Change Choice (1)	Change School (2)
1	1.33%	5.29%
2	3.48%	1.62%
3	3.74%	0.38%
4	2.38%	0.04%
No change	89.07%	92.68%

Notes. N=13,121. This table tabulates the fraction of applicants to Chicago's selective enrollment high schools who change a listed choice in 2009.

choices, if they wish. It is recommended that applicants rank their school choices honestly, listing schools in the order of their preference, while also identifying schools where they have a reasonable chance of acceptance.

Table 4 shows that the vast majority of applicants do not change their rank order list at all after receiving this letter. 89 percent of applicants continue to apply to the same set of schools in the same order, whereas 93 percent of applicants continue to list the same four schools, though not necessarily in the same order. It's possible that large switching costs are responsible for the fact that most applicants did not change their preferences, though I think that is unlikely because each participant received a new application form. Instead, I think that the 11 percent of applicants who changed their preferences are either reacting to new information obtained since making their initial preference submission or responding to the new mechanism's incentives.

Chicago's midstream change may be the best case so far for measuring how participants respond to the incentives of a mechanism in the field. However, our ability to draw inferences from this policy change comes with an important weakness: under both the old and new mechanisms, an applicant can apply to at most four different schools. An applicant's incentives to change their rank ordering may be dominated by the fact that he can only rank four choices. In other words, it is possible that a preference manipulation under the old mechanism still remains a manipulation under the new mechanism. Pathak and Sönmez (2013) formally demonstrate that Chicago's new mechanism is less manipulable than the old one, and that the old mechanism was highly manipulable. That is, the old mechanism is the most manipulable among a large class of mechanisms. Therefore, it seems unlikely that an applicant's report under the old mechanism is still their the best strategy under the new mechanism.

In light of earlier theoretical work that distinguishes between sincere and sophisticated players, it is worthwhile to examine the attributes of the 11 percent of applicants who reported a different rank order list. In Table 5, I report on correlates of preference changers and applicant covariates. For instance, applicants who change at least one choice tend to have higher admissions test points

Table 5 *Attributes of Preferences Changers*

	Change at least one choice(1)	Change at least one school(2)
Admission test points	55.157***	28.481***
	(4.683)	(5.496)
Baseline Math	0.178***	0.082***
	(0.026)	(0.030)
Baseline Reading	0.122***	0.028
	(0.022)	(0.026)
White	−0.007	−0.031***
	(0.008)	(0.008)
Black	0.047***	0.078***
	(0.014)	(0.017)
Hispanic	−0.060***	−0.056***
	(0.014)	(0.016)
Lowest SES Census Tracts	−0.016	−0.006
	(0.012)	(0.014)
Second Quartile Census Tracts	−0.018	−0.008
	(0.012)	(0.015)
Third Quartile Census Tracts	0.026**	0.007
	(0.013)	(0.015)
Highest SES Census Tracts	0.009	0.007
	(0.012)	(0.014)
Days Absent	−1.108***	−0.669***
	(0.161)	(0.200)

Notes. N=13121. Baseline Math is from grade 8 ISAT Math. Baseline Reading is grade 8 ISAT Reading. Baseline scores and days absent are not available for all applicants. Standard errors in parentheses, $^*p < 0.1$, $^{**}p < 0.0.5$, $^{***}p < 0.1$.

and baseline scores. They tend to be more black and Hispanic, and they are less likely to be absent from school. There is almost no relationship between whether students are from high- or low-SES census tracts, where I define census tract characteristics using the same six-factor model that is used by CPS in their assignment system.[9]

It therefore appears that the policy change in Chicago induced a modest response in how applicants ranked schools. The magnitude of the behavioral response is swamped, for instance, by the mechanical change in how applicants are processed by the mechanism now that an applicant with a higher test score can no longer be rejected from a school due to an application from someone with a lower score who ranked that school higher.

The findings from Chicago contribute to an ongoing debate in the literature on the extent of preference manipulations in data. Hastings, Kane, and Staiger (2009) show that an applicant's preferences for school quality did not react to a change in neighborhood boundaries in Charlotte North Carolina, and they use this fact to motivate treating reported preferences as truthful even though

---

[9] For more details on this affirmative action scheme, see Ellison and Pathak (2015) and Dur, Pathak, and Sönmez (2015).

Charlotte employs a variant of the Boston mechanism. This study, like the Chicago evidence, is based on observing participant reactions to changes in the assignment mechanism. Other work develops methods to quantify preference manipulations using variation within a particular assignment mechanism. Agarwal and Somaini (2014) report discontinuities in preferences at the proximity priority boundaries that they attribute to preference manipulation. They then develop a method to recover preferences from potentially manipulated reports and find that more than half of participants find it optimal to report their true preferences. Calsamiglia, Fu, and Guell (2014) estimate a mixture model with sincere and sophisticated applicants and find that the overwhelming majority of participants are responding strategically in Barcelona's adaption of the Boston mechanism. He (2012) considers the empirical implications of assuming that applicants do not submit strictly dominated rankings using data from Beijing, which employs a version of the Boston mechanism, though without any priorities. Hwang (2015) is another similar effort.

If we interpret the Chicago evidence as suggesting that only a small fraction of applicants respond to the incentives in manipulable mechanisms by manipulating their preferences, then it begs the question of why it was cited as a factor in Chicago's decision to abandon the mechanism midstream. I next turn to describe some other experiences in the field, which show how participants perceive and reject highly manipulable mechanisms. These episodes suggest some new rationales for mechanisms with straightforward incentives.

3   CONSIDERATIONS FROM THE FIELD

3.1   Straightforward Incentives

Abdulkadiroğlu and Sönmez (2003) describe existing manipulable assignment schemes as ones where "students and their parents are forced to play very complicated admissions games...[which] is confusing to students and their parents, but also results in inefficient allocation of school seats." The aspect of Boston's scheme that most strongly resonated with BPS officials in policy discussion was not the possibility of inefficiency, but rather that their manipulable mechanism might stand in the way of allowing for equal access to high-quality schools across the district. Differential knowledge about manipulation opportunities could exacerbate inequalities as sophisticated players benefit from understanding algorithmic details at the expense of those who were not aware. In public hearings, Boston school officials articulated this rationale as follows (BPS, 2005):

> a strategy-proof algorithm 'levels the playing field' by diminishing the harm done to parents who do not strategize or do not strategize well. [...] [T]he need to strategize provides an advantage to families who have the time, resources, and knowledge to conduct the necessary research.

Pathak and Sönmez (2008) present a formal investigation of this "equal access" argument for strategy-proof mechanisms in a model with sincere and sophisticated players in the preference revelation game induced by the Boston mechanism. Sincere players do not react to the incentives for preference manipulation, while sophisticated players best respond in the model. The paper shows that sophisticated players prefer the manipulable mechanism because they can exploit their knowledge about how the mechanism works. In particular, compared to the equilibrium outcome of the student-proposing deferred acceptance algorithm, sophisticated students weakly prefer their outcome under the Pareto-dominant Nash equilibrium of the Boston game. Even though sincere players lose priority to sophisticated players in equilibrium, it is sometimes possible that they prefer their outcome under the Boston mechanism. It's interesting to note that when the consequences of manipulation are modeled in this way, they imply distributional effects across player sophistication, which are not present if everyone is assumed to play strategically as in Ergin and Sönmez (2006). Dur, Hammond, and Morrill (2015) identify sophistication by tracking applicants who log in to the online application portal and revise their preferences in response to feedback on existing demand. They then show how strategic sophistication allows applicants to get admissions into higher quality schools than sincere participants.

The idea that a manipulable mechanism frustrates participants and creates inequities for sincere participants is a theme that I have seen in cities other than Boston. Even if only a small fraction of participants manipulate their preferences, these players appear to bear substantial costs, with potentially uncertain benefits. Even in the context of the model of Pathak and Sönmez (2008), the benefit that a sophisticated player obtains from manipulation still requires coordination at the Pareto-dominant equilibrium. Moreover, the perception that the mechanism encourages "gaming" suggests that the mechanism and its operator cannot be trusted. I believe these two aspects – not the potential for allocative inefficiency resulting from manipulation – are central for rationalizing stunning dismissals of highly manipulable mechanisms.

I've already described how Chicago abandoned its mechanism after eliciting rankings from thousands of participants. Another indication of how society perceives highly manipulable mechanisms comes from England, where a manipulable mechanism was outlawed by an Act of Parliament (Pathak and Sönmez, 2013). The 2007 English School Admissions Code, which regulates "National Offer Day" for hundreds of thousands of 10- and 11-year-olds looking for school seats throughout England, outlawed a particular class of mechanisms (in Section 2.13):

In setting oversubscription criteria the admission authorities for all maintained schools must not:

> give priority to children according to the order of other schools named as preferences by their parents, including 'first preference first' arrangements.

More specifically, a first preference first system is any "oversubscription criterion that gives priority to children according to the order of other schools named as a preference by their parents, or only considers applications stated as a first preference" (DfES, 2007). The Boston mechanism is probably the most famous example of a first preference first system. Both the 2007 and 2010 Admissions Code outlaws use of first preference first systems at more than 150 Local Authorities in England.

What is remarkable about this revision of the admissions code is that, to my knowledge, it occurred without any direct involvement of matching theorists or economists. Unlike in Boston, where economists played an active role lobbying against the mechanism, there is no evidence that academic research on school assignment either directly inspired rejections of the old mechanisms or led to the development of the new ones. Nonetheless, the arguments made by English authorities bear an uncanny resemblance to points discussed in the Boston debate. For instance, England's Department for Education and Skills viewed first preference first arrangements as making the system "unnecessarily complex" (DfES, 2007). Newspaper accounts alleged that first preference first arrangements "force many parents to play an 'admissions game' with their children's future" (Smith, 2007).

Even prior to this nationwide ban, numerous regions across England had already done away with first preference first arrangements. The Pan-London Admissions scheme adopted variants of DA known as "equal preference systems," where all preferences were considered without reference to the rank order made by parents (Pennell, West, and Hind, 2006). The report of the Pan-London Board and London Inter-Authority Admissions Group states that equal preference scheme was designed to "make the admissions system fairer" and "create a simpler system for parents" (Association of London Government, 2005). The Newcastle Admissions Forum recommended that "the equal preference system was more parent-friendly as it would reduce anxiety among parents as they can set out their ranked preferences without having to calculate the chances of their getting a place" (Young, 2003). As with Chicago, the poor incentive properties of the assignment mechanism appears to be central for its dismissal.

Pathak, Song, and Sonmez (2015) recount similar turmoil driven by a highly manipulable mechanism used for school assignment in Taiwan, which appear unrelated to concerns about allocative efficiency. In June 2014, more than five hundred parents and teachers marched in downtown Taipei, Taiwan, protesting the deduction point system used for senior high school placement largely because it encourages strategic ranking. Fiercely protesting parents held placards stating, "fill out the preference form for us," while others complained that the process was akin to "gambling" (I-chia, 2014). These protests were inspired by the 2014 Senior–High School Education Act, which changed both exam scoring and the assignment mechanism.

In Taiwan's new assignment system, students obtain points or priority based on the order in which preferences are ranked. For instance, in Jibei, the largest district with over 60,000 applicants, a student obtains thirty points on top of their maximum possible score of 90 points for their first choice. For their second choice, only 29 points are added to their test score. Compared to the first choice, the next ten choices experience a deduction of one point from the test score relative to one choice immediately higher. In other districts, the points are the same for a group of choices. In the limit where deduction points are large, the Taiwanese system is equal to a special version of the Boston mechanism, where the priorities are the same at each school. Therefore, protests in Taiwan represent yet another situation where a variant of the Boston mechanism generated public outcry and reproach.

The widespread condemnation of variations of the Boston mechanism from Chicago, England, and Taiwan involved participants themselves protesting and reorganizing market designs (and not matching theorists). In this respect, the school admissions reforms parallel changes in marketplace rules for the placement of medical residents in the early 1950s documented by Roth (1984). However, while reforms of the residency market were motivated in part by concerns about the inefficiency of unraveling, the school choice design efforts were motivated by concerns about excessive vulnerability to "gaming." In that respect, these efforts challenge a traditional mechanism design paradigm that treats incentive compatibility only as a constraint and not as a direct design objective. That is, in the discussions about these new policies there is almost no attempt to establish a direct link between preference manipulation and the inefficiency of outcomes, suggesting that the rationales for new mechanisms are in part inspired by non-consequentialist objectives.

Roth (1991) recounts the history of regional markets for physicians in the UK and argues that stable marketplaces were more likely to succeed than centralized markets that produced unstable outcomes. He therefore attributes a positive interpretation to stability as a governing principle of market design in addition to its traditional normative rationale. Likewise, when interpreted through the lens of the public and policymaker's revealed preferences, it is clear that strongly manipulable mechanisms are perceived as undesirable and inequitable, even absent overwhelming evidence that they generate widespread inefficiencies and that large numbers manipulate their preferences.

3.2   Transparency

Another property that shapes actual school choice market designs in the field involves transparency, or the ability to explain how the assignment process works. This aspect of admissions is particularly important when a new centralized scheme replaces a largely unregulated market, where both students and schools must trust the system operator, as was the case in New Orleans, Denver, and Washington DC.

Transparency is paramount even for modifications of algorithms within existing centralized systems. For instance, in Boston, the new mechanism was touted as one that (BPS, 2005):

Adds transparency and clarity to the assignment process, by allowing for clear and straight forward advice to parents regarding how to rank schools.

Similarly, Abdulkadiroğlu, Pathak, and Roth (2009) describe how NYC school officials preferred a simple mechanism with straightforward incentive properties over one that might allow for strategic manipulation because of the ability to give advice. While hard to formalize, the idea that a mechanism is transparent and simple to understand plays as important a role in choosing mechanisms as the algorithmic properties of mechanisms. It has even played a role in decisions between strategy-proof mechanisms, as I describe next.

3.2.1   Aversion to TTC

Transparency and the ability to explain the process were two main reasons why Boston officials opted for DA over TTC, despite the fact that DA may not be efficient. Quoting BPS officials (BPS, 2005):

> ... trading of priorities [under TTC] could lead families to believe they can still benefit from strategizing, as they may be encouraged to rank schools to which they have priority, even if they would not have put it on the form if the opportunity for trading did not exist. The behind the scenes mechanized trading makes the student assignment process less transparent.

Given that TTC is strategy-proof, it would be possible to advise participants that reporting references truthfully is the best course of action. However, BPS officials were concerned that when TTC was described, participants may perceive preference manipulations to be advantageous, even though it would be possible to provide a clear recommendation that reporting the truth is best for applicants. The BPS position has some support in the laboratory experiments of Chen and Sönmez (2006), where the rates of preference manipulation under TTC are higher than under DA.

The difficulty in explaining TTC compared to DA is also a reason that Recovery School District in New Orleans switched mechanisms after one year with DA. Those overseeing the OneApp process frequently fielded questions from parents and schools on how TTC worked and why it produced a particular outcome, which they often found challenging to handle. In particular, under DA, when an applicant is not admitted to a school, they could explain that there was another applicant who applied to the school who had higher priority. Under TTC, such an explanation is not as simple, because lack of admittance is due to a higher priority applicant trading away his seat with someone who wanted the school (and may have in fact had lower priority than the rejected applicant). I believe that the difficulty of explaining TTC, together with the precedent set by New York and Boston's choice of DA, are more likely explanations for why TTC is not used in more districts rather than the fact that it allows for justified envy, while DA does not.

3.2.2   Demise of Walk Zones in Boston

The reforms to the Boston choice system in 2013 are another setting where the desire for increased transparency led to dramatic changes in assignment mechanisms. Until 2013, Boston Public Schools used walk zone priority to assign students for half of each school's seats. For the other half of the school seats, walk zone priority did not apply. BPS's 50:50 seat split was official policy starting in 1999, following the end of racial and ethnic tie-breakers. At that point, there was a citywide debate, with a faction pushing for the elimination of the choice system and a return to neighborhood schools. Motivated by concerns that such a system would increase segregation across schools, the school committee chose to reduce the fraction of seats where walk zone priority applies from 100 percent to 50 percent of seats within each school. When an applicant with a high lottery number also has walk zone priority, they can be assigned either to a walk zone slot or a non-walk slot.

Dur, Kominers, Pathak, and Sönmez (2014) theoretically and empirically examine the performance of DA in a matching model with slot-specific priorities motivated by Boston's problem. The paper shows that because of how the 50:50 split was implemented, the outcome of the BPS mechanism is not at the midpoint of the allocation with no walk zone priority and the allocation when all seats use walk zone priority. Instead, the allocation produced by Boston's implementation of DA is nearly the same as the allocation when none of the seats use a walk zone priority. The reason is that BPS's choice of precedence – the order in which seats are depleted by the mechanism – undermined the priority policy. Boston's implementation ensured that any applicant with walk zone priority who did not qualify for a walk zone slot had little chance of being assigned a school seat at the other half. While there was active debate about the priority structure, the precedence, a much more arcane aspect of the assignment mechanism, was a detail left to the system operator. This detail ended up having significant implications for the final allocation.

Once the findings of Dur, Kominers, Pathak, and Sönmez (2014) were made public, there was widespread confusion about how walk zone priority could matter little due to precedence. Many thought that walk zone applicants had been advantaged by the current 50:50 rule, even though in practice they appear to have had little advantage. The discovery about how precedence became a central part of the fight between those favoring neighborhood assignment and those favoring increased choice (Additional details are in Dur, Kominers, Pathak, and Sönmez (2014)).

After drawn-out deliberations, policymakers decided that simply eliminating walk zone priority may be the best solution, especially in light of the observation that it played a relatively small role in practice. Moreover, getting rid of walk zone priority altogether avoids the (false) impression that applicants from the walk zone are receiving a boost under the mechanism. In March 2013, the Superintendent recommended eliminating walk zones entirely, overturning an earlier recommendation (Johnson, 2013):

Leaving the walk zone priority to continue as it currently operates is not a good option. We know from research that it does not make a significant difference the way it is applied today: although people may have thought that it did, the walk zone priority does not in fact actually help students attend schools closer to home. The External Advisory Committee suggested taking this important issue up in two years, but I believe we are ready to take this step now. We must ensure the Home-Based system works in an honest and transparent way from the very beginning.

The quote emphasizes that lack of transparency with the previous implementation of walk zone priority was a major reason for its demise. Alongside the elimination of walk zone priority, the city also adopted a new procedure, known as the Home-Based system, to determine where applicants can apply; see Pathak and Shi (2014) for more details. This policy change was inspired by a desire to reduce the district's busing costs, while still ensuring equitable access across the district.

Boston's recent experience also illustrates how the criteria used to allocate seats – taken as given by much of the literature – are just as important as how the mechanism processes applicants' claims. The public process that led to the new system in 2013 followed many similar attempts that resulted in stalemates. One consequence of the increasing adoption of strategy-proof mechanisms is that the role of students' property rights in determining the distribution of school access becomes more transparent. A small but growing body of research directly addresses how these property rights interact with the mechanism beyond considerations of justified envy, which is emphasized in the earlier literature (see, e.g., Calsamiglia and Miralles, 2014; Echenique and Yenmez, 2015; Shi, 2014; and Dur, Pathak, and Sönmez, 2015).

3.2.3   Seattle's Setback

Notwithstanding concerns for transparency-motivated policymakers to consider simplifications of existing mechanisms, the lack of transparency allows system operators to achieve certain ends through indirect channels. One example of this phenomenon is the policy of "principal's discretion," used for assignment at Chicago's exam schools. This policy allows principals of exam schools to handpick applicants for 5 percent of incoming seats. The application process considers criteria aside from those used in the centralized mechanism and has led to accusations of special assignments for politically connected applicants. A 2010 Audit reported that nearly all high school principals routinely received telephone calls and inquiries from politicians, CPS staff members, and others seeking preferential treatment for enrollment in schools, and there have been calls to eliminate this practice (Inspector-General, 2010). Principals defend the policy as necessary for ensuring a diverse student body or to give students another chance for admissions. It is of course possible to accommodate some concerns for diversity within centralized choice plans (see, e.g., Erdil and Kumano, 2012; Hafalir, Yenmez, and Yildirim, 2013; Kojima,

2012; Kominers and Sönmez, 2016; and Echenique and Yenmez, 2015), but doing so in a opaque way, such as principal's discretion, appears to undermine participants' trust in the system.

Seattle Public School's experience with school choice provides another example of the dangers of the lack of transparency. In 1999, Seattle switched from the Boston mechanism to DA, but called it the Barnhart–Waldman (BW) amendment in honor of two school board members who proposed the modification. Given that this change predated academic work on school choice mechanism design, it is not surprising that it was not widely understood. For instance, in a court challenge to the Seattle choice plan by *Parents Involved in Community Schools*, a case eventually decided by the US Supreme Court, confusion about the mechanism came up in the school board president's deposition (US District Court of Appeals, 2001):

> Q: Can you explain for me what the Barnhart/Waldman Amendment is and how it works?
> A: If I could I'd be the first. The Barnhart/Waldman – this is my understanding. The Barnhart/Waldman Amendment affects the way that choices are processed. Before we adopted that amendment, all the first choices were processed in one batch and assignments made. If you did not get your first choice, it is my understanding that all the students who did not get the first choice fell to the bottom of the batch processing line, and then they would process the second choices, et cet[e]ra. Barnhart/Waldman says that after all the first choices are processed, in the next batch, if you don't get your first choice, you don't fall to the bottom of the list but you are then processed, your second choice, with all the other second choices together. The result is that instead of a high degree of certainty placed – or of value placed on first choice, people can list authentically their first, second and third choices and have a higher degree of getting their second and third choice if they do not get their first choice. Now, was that clear as mud?

In 2007, a parent obtained the computer code and verified that the BW amendment actually corresponds to the student-optimal stable mechanism (McGregor, 2007). Interestingly, researchers did not learn about the change until Seattle returned to the Boston mechanism in 2009.[10]

Pathak and Sönmez (2013) present evidence that lack of understanding about the mechanism was exploited by some who wanted to reduce transportation costs in the current mechanism. I corresponded with some of the school committee members involved in this decision. While they mentioned a few hard-to-square reasons (such as computer implementation costs), one suggested that the BW amendment encouraged mobility among students since parents could freely express their choices, without having to take their geographic priority into account. By forcing families to adopt more conservative strategies such as ranking their neighborhood schools, the return to

---

[10] The first reference to Seattle is in Abdulkadiroğlu, Che, and Yasuda (2011), who describe the episode as the "clock turning back."

the Boston mechanism discouraged student movement and therefore reduced transportation costs. My impression from these interviews is that the absence of a transparent design was exploited by a faction that was uncomfortable with the idea of school choice in the first place. Returning to the Boston mechanism was a politically attractive alternative to decrease mobility across neighborhood zones while still maintaining the illusion of choice, even though that goal could have been achieved in a more transparent manner by simply changing priorities and choice menus within the deferred acceptance algorithm.

3.3   Coordinating Offers

Some of the largest allocative improvements due to new market designs are from relatively simple ideas. One important example involves eliminating multiple offers in favor of systems that produce a single offer for each applicant. Proponents of multiple-offer systems believe that parents value the added flexibility of investigating their options following assignment, but this comes at the cost of making sure extra offers percolate to those initially not offered. There's often not enough time for the market to clear in multiple-offer systems, and managing yields through over-booking of school seats requires lots of experience and fine-tuning. In the labor market context, Roth and Xing (1997) highlighted that congestion can generate inefficiencies, and automation of the offer process can go a long way towards improving the market's performance.

Abdulkadiroğlu, Agarwal, and Pathak (2015) measure the effects of coordinating admissions by examining the change in New York City's high school assignment system in 2003. Prior to 2003, roughly 80,000 aspiring high school students applied to five out of more than 600 school programs; they could receive multiple offers and be placed on wait lists. Students in turn were allowed to accept only one school and one wait list offer, and the cycle of offers and acceptances repeated two more times. Students initially expressed their preferences on a common application, but admissions offers were not coordinated across schools, allowing some students to obtain more than one offer. In Fall 2003, the system was replaced by a single-offer assignment system based on DA for the main round. Applicants were allowed to rank up to 12 programs for enrollment in 2004–05, and a supplementary round placed those unassigned in the main round.

Abdulkadiroğlu, Agarwal, and Pathak (2015) document how few rounds of offer processing and a limited number of applications make it difficult for schools to make enough offers to assign to clear the market. In the uncoordinated mechanism, more than 25,000 applicants were assigned in the administrative round. Roughly one-fifth of applicants received more than one first round offer, generating about 17,000 extra offers in the first round. However, the second and third rounds only processed 10,000 applicants, and this led to the large number of unassigned students after the main round. Students assigned administratively are placed at schools with attributes that differ from what they initially ranked. They are also more likely to enroll in schools other than where they are assigned and more likely to leave the public schools altogether.

Using preference estimates from econometric models of school demand, Abdulkadiroğlu, Agarwal, and Pathak (2015) compare the aggregate utility associated with several alternative allocations. On one extreme is neighborhood assignment, where pupils are allotted to schools closest to their home, given capacity constraints. The other extreme is the utilitarian optimal assignment, computing by taking estimated cardinal utility parameters and finding the allocation that maximizes the sum. This interval provides a way to gauge the magnitude of different aspects of school choice market design. The paper identifies large allocative gains from a choice system, given substantial heterogeneity in student preferences. It also investigates the effects of relaxing mechanism design constraints and finds that they are much smaller than the gains from moving from the uncoordinated to the coordinated assignment scheme. This finding suggests that the gains from fine-tuning algorithmic details are swamped by simply moving from multiple to single offers.

It's important to note that the automation that comes from market design inspired solutions is not necessarily always beneficial. For instance, another growing trend in school assignment involves the adoption of a common application, where an applicant can apply to all schools in one place, and then schools make offers in an uncoordinated way. A large fraction of US colleges participate in a common application, and these systems are often intended to streamline the process of applying to colleges. The fact that offers are not coordinated suggests that it will be necessary to develop a way to ensure that offers percolate through the system to avoid congestion problems like those experienced in New York City. For colleges, there may be more experience with yield management and smaller costs for either over- or under-booking (see Che and Koh, 2015 for an analysis of yield management when there is uncertainty over student preferences).

3.4   Aftermarkets

Another issue brought to light by experiences in the field involves how applicants who are unmatched or who wish to change their assignment are processed. Some cities operate wait lists, while others conduct second round matches. For instance, in Boston Public Schools, DA is actually run four separate times, with adjustments to priorities in each round that give applicants the highest priority at the school (if any) that they were assigned in the previous round. This approach allows applicants to resubmit preferences if they wish, but also does not switch the assignment of applicants who do not wish to move. Most applicants in rounds after the first are not in the main transition grades and therefore have not participated in the first round. But there are a handful who have changed their mind after the first round, and BPS's system tries to mimic the continuation of DA for these applicants. This well-functioning process for handling applicants after the main round contrasts with that in place in Denver's school choice system. Currently, Denver runs an ad hoc school-by-school application process, which is unrelated to what occurred in the match.

Most models of school assignment are static, even though circumstances change and students who were not assigned need to be placed at the conclusion of the assignment process. A major lesson of the reform of New York City's assignment mechanism is that it is undesirable to be placed in the administrative round. Abdulkadiroğlu, Agarwal, and Pathak (2015) show welfare gains are larger for populations of students who are more likely to have been assigned administratively. This fact raises the question of what can be done to improve the administrative round or assignments following the initial match.

One approach is to develop a centralized procedure for applicants who are unassigned or who wish to change assignments. Before the adoption of DA in NYC, those unassigned were simply manually placed to schools that had extra capacity after the main round. Aware of the fact that there were going to be unassigned applicants, in the new mechanism, NYC officials developed a supplementary round where unassigned applicants could re-express preferences. But even after this round, students could be unassigned, and they were placed manually. Why not simply elicit preferences from these applicants again? Narita (2015) investigates properties of schemes that take evolving preferences into account. He shows that a two-stage mechanism potentially improves welfare over a static mechanism.[11] Interestingly, he finds that the effects of his dynamic mechanism are much larger when combined with efforts to speed up learning about school choices. Given the mismatch associated with the administrative round, there are likely large returns to efforts to place students who are left over after the match or to reduce the fraction who need to be assigned post-match.

4 MAKING THE MARKET WORK

The two ingredients of any school assignment problem are the students and schools. Much of the recent school choice market design literature focuses on market clearing algorithms because there are not enough desirable schools available to accommodate the demand of all applicants. There is growing interest in understanding the relationship between the assignment process and what is being assigned. I start by reviewing research that focuses on the student side before turning to an examination of the school side.

---

[11] There have been similar proposals for a two-stage match in the National Residency Matching Program, the main clearinghouse for US doctors.

4.1   Families as Consumers

Starting with Abdulkadiroğlu and Sönmez (2003), models of the school choice market design take preferences of families as given. All else being equal, families tend to prefer schools that are closer to home. The relationship between the housing market and school assignment rules is widely documented (see, e.g., Black, 1999; Bayer, Ferriera, and McMillan, 2007), and a central aspiration of school choice plans is to delink residential location from access to schools. It is therefore important to consider how residential choices might be influenced by school assignment when comparing market designs.

Avery and Pathak (2015) develop a model to compare neighborhood and school choice when households make a simultaneous decision about schools and residential choices.[12] Though their model of school choice abstracts away from many market design elements, it highlights a counterintuitive force underlying school choice when also considering residential choices. Compared to neighborhood assignment, choice results in a compression of school qualities in a city, which is reflected in housing prices. This compressed distribution generates incentives for both the highest and lowest types to move out of cities with school choice, typically producing worse outcomes for low types than neighborhood assignment rules. Paradoxically, even when choice results in improvement in the worst performing schools, the lowest type residents may not benefit. By incorporating feedback between residential and school choices, the model suggests that analysis of school assignment that does not account for the possibility of residential resorting may lead to an incomplete understanding about the consequences of school choice.

Aside from proximity to schools, recent work has started to investigate the extent to which student preferences reflect productive dimensions of school quality. Proponents of school choice as a reform strategy embrace the market paradigm: when families act like consumers when choosing schools, it can unleash valuable competitive forces as schools compete to attract parents. Rothstein (2006), on the other hand, argues that parental demand may reflect peers rather than value added, and such sorting may not generate productivity improvements. MacLeod and Urquiola (2015) show that with imperfect information schools may have incentives to invest in their reputation, which may not enhance their productivity. The extent to which preferences reflect what a system operator might value for productive reasons (such as school value-added) remains an open question.

In the context of high-performing charter schools, Walters (2014) shows that the applicants who are most likely to benefit are actually those who are

---

[12] This paper builds on an earlier literature that is not focused on market design aspects of school assignment, but does integrate housing and school choices, such as Epple and Romano (2003) and Nechyba (2003). These papers incorporate multidimensional student types, define school quality as functions of tax funding and peers, and allow for property taxes and the housing market to be determined endogenously, often relying on computational methods.

the least likely to apply. This evidence comes from a decentralized application process, so it's possible that a centralized system may make it easier for disadvantaged applicants to access higher-quality providers. Abdulkadiroğlu, Angrist, Hull, and Pathak (2016) compare applicants who arrive at high-performing charter schools passively to those who apply via lottery and find larger gains for the former, suggesting large potential gains from making it easier to exercise choice. However, datasets from centralized market designs consistently show that more disadvantaged families place more weight on proximity than various measures of school quality (see, e.g., Hastings, Kane, and Staiger, 2009; Pathak and Shi, 2014; and Abdulkadiroğlu, Agarwal, and Pathak, 2015). Such a finding implies that choice reforms might exacerbate inequalities.

While many design initiatives aspire to make school selections easier, the ranking decision still remains complex for many families, even in strategy-proof mechanisms. Hastings and Weinstein (2008) report on a field experiment showing that small information queues can change how parents rank schools in Charlotte's variant of the Boston mechanism. Efforts to improve how participants interact with market designs, including decision aids and other informational interventions, hold great promise to complement research on market clearing algorithms.

4.2   Improving School Quality

On the school side, encouraging participation of highly-desired schools diminishes the importance of a market clearing algorithm. Participation by schools in a centralized system, however, is not always an easy issue to navigate in practice. Charter and other autonomous schools often view centralized assignment as a threat to their autonomy. For instance, in New Orleans, there are two school districts: the Recovery School District (RSD), and the Orleans Parish School Board (OPSB). OPSB schools have been reluctant to join the RSD's OneApp process because school administrators like the ability to screen applicants, including groups of applicants (for arts and music and sports programs). There is an on-going debate about participation of OPSB schools, and OPSB charter schools are currently mandated to participate in the system upon reauthorization (Dreilinger, 2013). Ekmekci and Yenmez (2014) study participation by schools in a centralized clearinghouse. After showing that schools may have an incentive not to participate, they propose modifications to current mechanisms that encourage greater participation. Relatedly, Hatfield, Kojima, and Narita (2014) study which market clearing algorithms influence a school's incentive for improving quality.

Market design schemes hold great potential to influence the portfolio of schools in a district indirectly through the data they generate. First, centralized systems systematically elicit preferences for schools, which may be used to guide enrollment and planning. For instance, if a school is perennially undersubscribed, then a district might consider intervening in the school, either by changing staff, educational programming, or by closing the school altogether. Often efforts to reconstitute schools require the district to decide which schools to target (see, e.g., Abdulkadiroğlu, Angrist, Hull, and Pathak, 2016, who report on charter school takeovers of traditional district schools in New Orleans and in Boston). The ranking data available from strategy-proof mechanisms provides complementary information about perceived school desirability that may allow for more sophisticated systems of school accountability and portfolio planning. When school supply decisions do not reflect any information on school demand, it seems like a missed opportunity to harness competitive forces that could generate productivity improvements.

Second, the data generated by centralized systems allow for more effective ways to measure the performance of schools or school sectors. Research exploiting this aspect of school choice market designs has become increasingly popular. A centralized assignment system not only generates systematic admissions data, but it often lends itself to natural research designs. Abdulkadiroğlu, Angrist, Dynarski, Kane, and Pathak (2011) exploit random assignment embedded in DA to measure the effects of attendance on student achievement at one Boston's pilot schools. Such schools have some of the independence of charter schools, but they are regulated by Boston Public schools and are covered by some of its collective bargaining provisions. The paper reports mixed results for pilots compared to results for Boston's charter schools, which generate impressive achievement results on statewide assessments. Using the DA-induced variation in New York City's centralized match, Abdulkadiroğlu, Hu, and Pathak (2013) estimate the effects of New York's small schools, more than 200 of which were created in the 2000s. The paper shows that small schools created as part of the NYC's *Children's First Initiative* in 2002 produce significant achievement gains on standardized assessments and lead to more high schoolers attending college. Abdulkadiroğlu, Angrist, and Pathak (2014) use data from a centralized exam school assignment mechanism to construct regression discontinuity estimates of value added of New York and Boston's elite exam schools. Even though these schools are heavily over-subscribed, the estimates show little evidence of value-added. These three studies are examples of how evidence on the performance of particular school sectors generated via a centralized assignment mechanism can yield new information that system operators can use for decisions about what schools to expand or contract.

Centralized school market designs also allow researchers to sidestep a major difficulty that has hindered evaluations in decentralized systems in the past: poor record-keeping on how students were admitted into schools. For instance, Abdulkadiroğlu, Angrist, Dynarski, Kane, and Pathak (2011) collected admissions records individually from Boston's charter schools, since each runs their own admissions lottery with large variation in record-keeping.[13] If these schools were part of a unified enrollment system, it would be relatively simple to understand how a given applicant was assigned to a particular school. Understanding the admissions process in this precise way, then, allows for quasi-experimental approaches to measuring the performance of schools. Examples of papers exploiting data from centralized systems include Dobbie and Fryer (2014), Ajayi (2014), Lucas and Mbiti (2014), Pop-Eleches and Urquiola (2013), Jackson (2010), Bergman (2014), Hastings, Neilson, and Zimmerman (2013), Kirkeboen, Leuven, and Mogstad (2016), Angrist, Hull, Pathak, and Walters (2017) and Abdulkadiroğlu, Pathak, and Walters (2015).

Abdulkadiroğlu, Angrist, Narita, and Pathak (2015) develop econometric techniques to use data from a DA match to measure school effectiveness by fully exploiting all randomly assigned variation. Since assignments depend on both nonrandom student preferences and school priorities, centralized assignment schemes generate complex stratified random assignments to schools. After developing easily-implemented empirical strategies that fully exploit the random assignment embedded in DA, the paper estimates large achievement gains from charter school attendance in Denver, which uses DA to assign both charter and traditional district schools. Compared to ad hoc methods that fail to exploit the full richness of the lotteries generated by centralized assignment with random tie-breaking, the new method results in substantial efficiency gains. This paper therefore shows how market design feeds into powerful research designs for credible impact evaluation.

In summary, school choice market design has had a positive spillover on work that seeks to understand the impact of schools on student outcomes. Although this work has not been explicitly linked to the actual assignment algorithm, it has the potential to guide the district's offering of schools by exploiting the data emerging from well-designed assignment schemes. This feedback may ultimately lead to improved educational outcomes.

5 CONCLUSION

Much of the school choice market design literature evaluates different ways to assign students given student preferences, school priorities, and school capacities. This literature has generated numerous insights on the tension between efficiency and fairness, the role of incentives, the implications of coarseness in school priorities, and constraints on rank order lists. Experiences from the field highlight new issues that have not been the focus of this earlier literature such as non-consequentialist rationales for straightforward incentives, the importance of transparency and simplicity in influencing designs,

---

[13] Lack of systematic record-keeping was also a significant hurdle for charter school evaluations in Angrist, Dynarski, Kane, Pathak, and Walters (2012) Angrist, Dynarski, Kane, Pathak, and Walters (2012) and Angrist, Pathak, and Walters (2013).

the value of single-offer systems over multiple-offer alternatives, the need to streamline aftermarkets, and the importance of participation on the school and student side. It is my hope that further interaction between theory and practice will sharpen focus on these and potentially other significant issues that have received relatively little attention from the theoretical literature.

While much of the market design literature has taken student preferences and schools as given, I believe there is great potential for work that examines the feedback between market clearing algorithms and these aspects of demand and supply. Without a deeper investigation of these broader aspects of school choice markets, our understanding of what really matters in designing school choice mechanisms will be incomplete.

References

Abdulkadiroğlu, A., N. Agarwal, and P. Pathak (2015): "The Welfare Effects of Coordinated Assignment: Evidence from the NYC HS Match," NBER Working Paper 21046.

Abdulkadiroğlu, A., J. D. Angrist, S. M. Dynarski, T. J. Kane, and P. A. Pathak (2011): "Accountability and Flexibility in Public Schools: Evidence from Boston's Charters and Pilots," *Quarterly Journal of Economics*, 126(2), 699–748.

Abdulkadiroğlu, A., J. D. Angrist, P. Hull, and P. Pathak (2016): "Charters Without Lotteries: Testing Takeovers in New Orleans and Boston," *American Economic Review*, 106(7), 1878–1920.

Abdulkadiroğlu, A., J. D. Angrist, Y. Narita, and P. Pathak (2015): "Research Design Meets Market Design: Using Centralized Assignment for Impact Evaluation," NBER Working Paper 21705.

Abdulkadiroğlu, A., J. Angrist, and P. Pathak (2014): "The Elite Illusion: Achievement Effects at Boston and New York Exam Schools," *Econometrica*, 82(1), 137–96.

Abdulkadiroğlu, A., Y.-K. Che, P. Pathak, A. Roth, and O. Tercieux (2017): "Minimizing Justified Envy in School Choice: The Design of New Orleans' OneApp," NBER Working Paper 23265.

Abdulkadiroğlu, A., Y.-K. Che, and Y. Yasuda (2011): "Resolving Conflicting Preferences in School Choice: The 'Boston Mechanism' Reconsidered," *American Economic Review*, 101(1), 399–410.

Abdulkadiroğlu, A., W. Hu, and P. Pathak (2013): "Small High Schools and Student Achievement: Lottery-Based Evidence from New York City," NBER Working Paper 19576.

Abdulkadiroğlu, A., P. A. Pathak, and A. E. Roth (2005): "The New York City High School Match," *American Economic Review, Papers and Proceedings*, 95, 364–7.

(2009): "Strategy-Proofness versus Efficiency in Matching with Indifferences: Redesigning the New York City High School Match," *American Economic Review*, 99(5), 1954–78.

Abdulkadiroğlu, A., P. A. Pathak, A. E. Roth, and T. Sönmez (2005): "The Boston Public School Match," *American Economic Review, Papers and Proceedings*, 95, 368–71.

(2006): "Changing the Boston School Choice Mechanism," NBER Working Paper 11965.

Abdulkadiroğlu, A., P. A. Pathak, and C. Walters (2015): "School Vouchers and Student Achievement: First-Year Evidence from the Louisiana Scholarship Program," NBER Working Paper 21839.

Abdulkadiroğlu, A., and T. Sonmez (1998): "Random Serial Dictatorship and the Core from Random Endowments in House Allocation Problems," *Econometrica*, 66(3), 689–701.

Abdulkadiroğlu, A., and T. Sönmez (1999): "House Allocation with Existing Tenants," *Journal of Economic Theory*, 88, 233–60.

(2003): "School Choice: A Mechanism Design Approach," *American Economic Review*, 93, 729–47.

(2013): "Matching Markets: Theory and Practice," in: D. Acemoglu, M. Arellano, and E. Dekel (eds), *Advances in Economics and Econometrics*, Econometric Society, vol. 1, 3–47.

Agarwal, N., and P. Somaini (2014): "Demand Analysis Using Strategic Reports: An Application to a School Choice Mechanism," NBER Working Paper 20775.

Ajayi, K. (2014): "Does School Quality Improve Student Performance? New Evidence from Ghana," Working paper, Boston University.

Angrist, J. D., S. M. Dynarski, T. J. Kane, P. A. Pathak, and C. R. Walters (2012): "Who Benefits from KIPP?," *Journal of Policy Analysis and Management*, 31(4), 837–60.

Angrist, J., P. Hull, P. Pathak, and C. Walters (2017): "Leveraging Lotteries for Value Added: Testing and Estimation," *Quarterly Journal of Economics*, 132(2), 871–919.

Angrist, J. D., P. A. Pathak, and C. R. Walters (2013): "Explaining Charter School Effectiveness," *American Economic Journal: Applied Economics*, 5(4), 1–27.

Avery, C. N., and P. A. Pathak (2015): "The Distributional Consequences of Public School Choice," NBER Working Paper 21525.

Balinski, M., and T. Sönmez (1999): "A Tale of Two Mechanisms: Student Placement," *Journal of Economic Theory*, 84, 73–94.

Bayer, P., F. Ferriera, and R. McMillan (2007): "A Unified Framework for Measuring Preferences for Schools and Neighborhoods," *Journal of Political Economy*, 588–638.

Bergman, P. (2014): "Educational Attainment and School Desegregation: Evidence from Randomized Lotteries," Working paper.

Black, S. (1999): "Do Better Schools Matter? Parental Valuation of Elementary Education," *Quarterly Journal of Economics*, 114(2), 577–99.

BPS (2005): "Recommendation to Implement a New BPS Assignment Algorithm," Presentation to the Boston School Committee by Carleton Jones, May 11.

(2008): "Introducing the Boston Public Schools: A Guide for Parents and Students," Available from Boston Public Schools.

Calsamiglia, C., C. Fu, and M. Guell (2014): "Structural Estimation of a Model of School Choices: The Boston Mechanism vs. Its Alternatives," Working paper, University of Wisconsin.

Calsamiglia, C., G. Haeringer, and F. Kljin (2010): "Constrained School Choice: An Experimental Study," *American Economic Review*, 100(4), 1860–74.

Calsamiglia, C., and A. Miralles (2014): "Catchment Areas and Access to Better Schools," Working paper, Universitat Autonomy de Barcelona.

Carroll, G. (2014): "A General Equivalence Theorem for Allocation of Indivisible Objects," *Journal of Mathematical Economics*, 51, 163–77.

Che, Y.-K., and Y. Koh (2015): "Decentralized College Admissions," forthcoming, *Journal of Political Economy*.

Chen, Y., and T. Sönmez (2006): "School Choice: An Experimental Study," *Journal of Economic Theory*, 127, 202–31.

Cook, G. (2003): "School Assignment Flaws Detailed," *Boston Globe*, pp. Metro Desk, September 12.

de Haan, M., P. A. Gautier, H. Oosterbeek, and B. van der Klaauw (2015): "The Performance of School Assignment Mechanisms in Practice," Working paper.

DfES (2007): "School Admissions Code, Department for Education and Skills," Available at: www.dcsf.gov.uk/sacode/, Last accessed: January 31, 2011.

Dobbie, W., and R. G. Fryer (2014): "Exam High Schools and Academic Achievement: Evidence from New York City," *American Economic Journal: Applied Economics*, 6(3), 58–75.

Dreilinger, D. (2013): "Orleans Parish School Board Pulls Back on OneApp, Lets Schools Choose Students," *Times-Picayune*, June 18.

Dur, U. (2014): "A Characterization of the Top Trading Cycles Mechanism in the School Choice Problem," Working paper, NC State.

Dur, U., R. Hammond, and T. Morrill (2015): "Identifying the Harm of Manipulable School Choice Mechanisms," Working paper, NC State.

Dur, U., S. Kominers, P. Pathak, and T. Sönmez (2014): "The Demise of Walk Zones in Boston: Priorities vs. Precedence in School Choice," NBER Working Paper 18981.

Dur, U., P. Pathak, and T. Sönmez (2015): "Equity vs. Merit in Affirmative Action: Explicit and Statistical Preferential Treatment at Chicago's Exam Schools," Unpublished working paper, MIT.

Echenique, F., and B. Yenmez (2015): "How to Control Controlled School Choice?," *American Economic Review*, 105(8), 2679–94.

Ehlers, L., and A. Erdil (2010): "Efficient Assignment Respecting Priorities," *Journal of Economic Theory*, 145(3), 1269–82.

Ekmekci, M., and M. B. Yenmez (2014): "Integrating Schools for Centralized Admissions," Working paper, Carnegie-Mellon.

Ellison, G., and P. Pathak (2016): "The Inefficiency of Race-Neutral Affirmative Action: Evidence from Chicago's Exam Schools," NBER Working Paper 22589.

Epple, D., and R. Romano (2003): "Neighborhood Schools, Choice, and the Distribution of Educational Benefits," in *The Economics of School Choice*, ed. by C. Hoxby. University of Chicago Press.

Erdil, A., and H. Ergin (2008): "What's the Matter with Tie-Breaking? Improving Efficiency in School Choice," *American Economic Review*, 98, 669–89.

Erdil, A., and T. Kumano (2012): "Prioritizing Diversity in School Choice," Unpublished working paper, Washington University.

Ergin, H. (2002): "Efficient Resource Allocation on the Basis of Priorities," *Econometrica*, 70, 2489–98.

Ergin, H., and T. Sönmez (2006): "Games of School Choice under the Boston Mechanism," *Journal of Public Economics*, 90, 215–37.

Gale, D., and L. S. Shapley (1962): "College Admissions and the Stability of Marriage," *American Mathematical Monthly*, 69, 9–15.

Haeringer, G., and F. Klijn (2009): "Constrained School Choice," *Journal of Economic Theory*, 144, 1921–47.

Hafalir, I., B. Yenmez, and M. A. Yildirim (2013): "Effective Affirmative Action in School Choice," *Theoretical Economics*, 8(2), 325–63.

Hastings, J., T. J. Kane, and D. O. Staiger (2009): "Heterogenous Preferences and the Efficacy of Public School Choice," Working paper, Yale University.

Hastings, J., C. Neilson, and S. Zimmerman (2013): "Are Some Degrees Worth More than Others? Evidence from College Admission Cutoffs in Chile," NBER Working Paper 19241.

Hastings, J., and J. M. Weinstein (2008): "Information, School Choice and Academic Achievement: Evidence from Two Experiments," *Quarterly Journal of Economics*, 123(4), 1373–414.

Hatfield, J. W., F. Kojima, and Y. Narita (2014): "Promoting School Competition Through School Choice: A Market Design Approach," *Journal of Economic Theory*, 166, 186–211.

He, Y. (2012): "Gaming the Boston School Choice Mechanism in Beijing," Unpublished working paper, Toulouse School of Economics.

Hwang, S. I. (2015): "A Robust Redesign of High School Match," Working paper, University of Chicago.

I-chia, L. (2014): "Parents, Teachers Protest Senior-High Entrance Process," *Taipei Times*, Front Page, June 22.

Inspector-General (2010): "Office of the Inspector General: Chicago Board of Education, Annual Report, July 1, 2009 – June 30, 2010," City of Chicago.

Jackson, K. (2010): "Do Students Benefit from Attending Better Schools? Evidence from Rule-Based Student Assignments in Trinidad and Tobago," *Economic Journal*, 120(549), 1399–1429.

Johnson, C. R. (2013): "Speech to Boston School Committee, March 13," Available at: http://bostonschoolchoice.files.wordpress.com/2013/03/3-13-13-superintendent-sc -memo-on-assignment.pdf, last accessed: April 14, 2013.

Kesten, O. (2006): "On Two Competing Mechanisms for Priority-Based Allocation Problems," *Journal of Economic Theory*, 127, 155–71.

——— (2010): "School Choice with Consent," *Quarterly Journal of Economics*, pp. 1297–1394.

Kesten, O., and U. Ünver (2015): "A Theory of School Choice Lotteries," *Theoretical Economics*, 10, 543–95.

Kirkeboen, L., E. Leuven, and M. Mogstad (2016): "Field of Study, Earnings, and Self-Selection," *Quarterly Journal of Economics*, 131(3), 1057–1111.

Klemperer, P. (2002): "What Really Matters in Auction Design," *Journal of Economic Perspectives*, 16(1), 169–89.

Kojima, F. (2012): "School Choice: Impossibilities for Affirmative Action," *Games and Economic Behavior*, 75(2), 685–93.

Kominers, S. D., and T. Sönmez (2016): "Matching with Slot-Specific Priorities: Theory," forthcoming, *Theoretical Economics*, 11(2), 683–710.

Landsmark, T., H. Dajer, and L. Gonsalves (2014): "Report and Recommendations of the Boston Public Schools Student Assignment Task Force," Report to the Boston School Committee, September 22.

Lee, T., and J. Sethuraman (2014): "Equivalence Results in the Allocation of Indivisible Objects: A Unified View," Working paper, Columbia University.

Lucas, A., and I. Mbiti (2014): "Effects of School Quality on Student Achievement: Discontinuity Evidence from Kenya," *American Economic Journal: Applied Economics*, 6(3), 234–63.

MacLeod, W. B., and M. Urquiola (2015): "Reputation and school competition," *American Economic Review*, 105(11), 3471–88.

McGregor, C. (2007): "The REAL Truth about Seattle Public Schools Kindergarten Assignments," Available at www.cybermato.com/projects/school-assignments/, Last accessed: December 12, 2011.

Morrill, T. (2016): "Making Just School Assignments," *Games and Economic Behavior*, 92, 18–27.

Narita, Y. (2015): "Match or Mismatch: Learning and Inertia in School Choice," Working paper, MIT.

Nechyba, T. (2003): "Introducing School Choice into Multi-District Public School Systems," in *The Economics of School Choice*, ed. by C. Hoxby. University of Chicago Press.

Papai, S. (2000): "Strategyproof Assignment by Hierarchical Exchange," *Econometrica*, 68, 1403–33.

Pathak, P. A. (2011): "The Mechanism Design Approach to Student Assignment," *Annual Reviews*, 3, 513–36.

Pathak, P. A., and J. Sethuraman (2011): "Lotteries in Student Assignment: An Equivalence Result," *Theoretical Economics*, 6(1), 1–17.

Pathak, P. A., and P. Shi (2014): "Demand Modeling, Forecasting, and Counterfactuals, Part I," NBER Working Paper 19859.

Pathak, P., F. Song, and T. Sonmez (2015): "Turmoil in Taiwan: Preference-Driven Priority Mechanisms in School Choice," Working paper, MIT.

Pathak, P. A., and T. Sönmez (2008): "Leveling the Playing Field: Sincere and Sophisticated Players in the Boston Mechanism," *American Economic Review*, 98(4), 1636–52.

—— (2013): "School Admissions Reform in Chicago and England: Comparing Mechanisms by their Vulnerability to Manipulation," *American Economic Review*, 103(1), 80–106.

Pennell, H., A. West, and A. Hind (2006): "Secondary School Admissions in London," Centre for Educational Research, Department of Social Policy, LSE, Clare Market Papers, No. 19.

Pop-Eleches, C., and M. Urquiola (2013): "Going to a Better School: Effects and Behavioral Responses," *American Economic Review*, 103(4), 1289–24.

Roth, A. E. (1984): "The Evolution of the Labor Market for Medical Interns and Residents: A Case Study in Game Theory," *Journal of Political Economy*, 92, 991–1016.

—— (1991): "A Natural Experiment in the Organization of Entry Level Labor Markets: Regional Markets for New Physicians and Surgeons in the U.K.," *American Economic Review*, 81, 415–40.

Roth, A. E., and X. Xing (1997): "Turnaround Time and Bottlenecks in Market Clearing: Decentralized Matching in the Market for Clinical Psychologists," *Journal of Political Economy*, 105, 284–329.

Rothstein, J. (2006): "Good Principals or Good Peers: Parental Valuation of School Characteristics, Tiebout Equilibrium, and the Incentive Effects of Competition Among Jurisdictions," *American Economic Review*, 96(4), 1333–50.

Shapley, L., and H. Scarf (1974): "On Cores and Indivisibility," *Journal of Mathematical Economics*, 1, 23–8.

Shi, P. (2014): "Guiding School-Choice Reform through Novel Applications of Operations Research," *Interfaces*, 45(2), 117–32.

Smith, A. (2007): "Schools Admissions Code to End Covert Selection," The *Guardian*, Education section, January 9.

urbandcmoms.com (2014): "More Info on Common Lottery Algorithm," URL:
     www.dcurbanmom.com/jforum/posts/list/354001.page#4517696, January 8.
The US Court of Appeals, T. U. S. C. (2001): "Parents Involved in Community Schools
     vs. Seattle School District," Page 58 of the U.S. Court of Appeals for the Ninth
     Circuit, No. 01-35450, No. 1.
Walters, C. R. (2014): "The Demand for Effective Charter Schools," UC Berkeley,
     Working paper.
Young, P. (2003): "First Choice for Schools May Go," *Evening Chronicle*, Newcastle,
     November 26.

CHAPTER 7

Networks and Markets

Sanjeev Goyal

Networks influence human behavior and well-being, and, realizing this, individuals make conscious efforts to shape their own networks. Over the past decade, economists have combined these ideas with concepts from game theory, oligopoly, general equilibrium, and information economics to develop a general framework of analysis. The ensuing research has deepened our understanding of classical questions in economics and opened up entirely new lines of enquiry.

1 INTRODUCTION

Our life takes place at the intersection of the global and the local: we function in a world dominated by large firms and international markets, but we also inhabit small and overlapping neighborhoods of friends and family, colleagues and collaborators. Game theory is well suited for the study of behavior in small exclusive groups while general equilibrium theory provides a sophisticated approach to the understanding of large anonymous systems. Networks offer us a framework that combines local interactions within large interconnected populations. In doing so, they fill an important gap in the toolkit of economists.

The key methodological innovation of the early research on networks in the 1990s was the introduction of graph theory alongside purposeful agents. Two ideas were central: the study of how the network architecture shapes human behavior and the study of how purposeful individuals form links and thereby create networks. Over the past decade, economists have developed models that include networks, alongside the familiar notions of strategy, information, prices and competition. These models are now being applied to address an

This is the background paper for an Invited Lecture at the 2015 World Congress of the Econometric Society in Montreal. I would like to thank Matt Elliott, Julien Gagnon, Andrea Galeotti, Edoardo Gallo, Rachel Kranton (the discussant), David Minarsch, Gustavo Paez, and Anja Prummer for helpful comments on an earlier draft. Financial support from a Keynes Fellowship and the Cambridge-INET Institute is gratefully acknowledged.

215

increasingly ambitious range of questions in economics. I see here a close analogy with the spread of game theory in economics, during the 1980s and 1990s, in one applied field after another.[1]

I begin by developing notation and basic concepts on networks in Section 2.

Section 3 outlines a framework that combines individual choice, networks and markets, while Section 4 introduces the elements of an economic theory of network formation.[2]

The rest of the paper is devoted to a discussion of economic applications. There has been very rapid growth in research in this field over the last decade. In my presentation, I will favor lines of work that explicitly combine network ideas with familiar models of markets.

Section 5 deals with macroeconomic fluctuations. An understanding of their origins remains a fundamental question in economics. The dominant view is that aggregate fluctuations cannot be caused by sector specific shocks as we would expect that there are many such shocks taking place, and that they would cancel each other out. This section develops a model in which profit maximizing firms are located on nodes and the links reflect production linkages across sectors. Production decisions of firms are coordinated through prices in competitive markets. I show how sector-specific shocks may be amplified by the network structure – viz. the existence of general purpose technologies – to generate aggregate fluctuations.

Sections 6 and 7 turn to the study of trading and market power. In Section 6, I study direct trade between buyers and sellers (with no resale). In the real world, buyers typically trade only with a subset of sellers. By contrast, in the standard Walrasian model, all agents can trade with each other at a common price. The first goal is to understand how this "incompleteness" of direct trading relations affects economic activity. I study price formation in a network of buyers and sellers. The analysis provides an elegant network foundation for Walrasian competitive outcome: local trading relations must mirror the global buyer/seller surplus. The analysis also tells us how network structure shapes the distribution of earnings. As individuals are aware of the network in shaping their earnings, they seek to form links to create the "right" networks. I show that linking activity among traders is rich in externalities. The discussion then moves on to conditions under which trading networks thus created are efficient.

Section 7 studies intermediation, a defining feature of the modern economy. Intermediation is prominent in agriculture, in transport and communication, in

---

[1] For an overview of the early work on networks, see the previous invited lecture on networks, delivered at the 2005 Econometric Society World Congress (Jackson, 2006). The present paper focuses on developments in the theory of networks; for a survey of empirical work, see the companion piece by de Paula (2016).

[2] For a more systematic and extensive exploration of these two general themes (the effects of networks on behavior and on how individuals create networks), see Goyal (2016). Easley and Kleinberg (2010) offer a general introduction to networks; Bramoulle, Galeotti, and Rogers (2016) provide an overview of recent research on the economics of networks.

international trade, and in finance. I begin with a study of pricing games on intermediation networks and discuss how the pricing protocol and the network jointly shape pricing and define market power. The discussion highlights the role of critical nodes – nodes that lie on all paths in a network – in shaping behavior. I then turn to link formation by individuals who seek to extract intermediation rents. The analysis once again highlights the role of externalities and provides a theoretical foundation for the empirically salient core–periphery networks.

Section 8 takes up the role of social networks in labor, product and financial markets. Information asymmetries are an important feature of these markets. I begin with the empirical observation that a large fraction of jobs at all levels of the economy are obtained through social connections. This leads me to study the role of networks in shaping wages, unemployment and inequality. I then turn to product markets: social connections shape tastes and provide access to information. This motivates the introduction of social networks in traditional models of advertising and pricing. The analysis allows me to study the ways in which governments and firms can use social networks to further their own goals. The section ends with a brief discussion on social networks in financial markets.

Section 9 takes up transport networks. The state and private firms set up a variety of transport networks and then price access to these networks. Traditionally, research has focused on pricing issues. The discussion here focuses on network design issues. I begin with the monopoly problem: what is the best way to design a network to transport passengers across a collection of cities? This sets the stage for a discussion of competition between two networks. Hub–spoke networks economize on linking costs and on path length: they are salient both under monopoly and in the duopoly setting.

Section 10 discusses the nature of the firm. It is customary to partition economic activity between firms (based on hierarchy) and markets (based on anonymous arms length relations). In practice, economic activity often takes place outside markets and hierarchy; prominent examples are research alliances and capacity sharing. I discuss behavior of firms in these two contexts and then explore incentives to form networks. The discussion brings out the importance of the two-way flow of influence: networks are shaped by competitive forces in markets, but the formation of networks also significantly alters the functioning of the "market".

In Section 11, I turn to the dynamic interaction between social networks and markets. Markets are traditionally associated with the erosion of social relations, but empirical work also provides us with notable instances where markets strengthen social interaction. I present a framework where individuals can choose exchange through networks *and* in (frictionless) anonymous markets. The analysis shows how social structure and the strategic relation between networks and markets – whether they are substitutes or complements – jointly shape individual choice, inequality and aggregate welfare.

Section 12 concludes.

2 NETWORKS

I begin by introducing some notation and a few basic concepts about networks that will be used throughout the paper. For a general overview of graph theory, see Bollobás (1998); for introduction of network concepts to economics, see Goyal (2007), Jackson (2008) and Vega-Redondo (2007).

A network g comprises a collection of nodes $N = \{1, 2, \ldots n\}$ with $n \geq 2$, and the links (g_{ij}), $i, j \in N$, between them. A node may be an individual, a firm, a project, a city or a country, or even a collection of such entities. A link between them signifies a relation. In some instances it is natural to think of the link as bidirectional; examples include friendship, research collaboration, and defence alliance. In other instances, a link is unidirectional: examples include investment in a project, citation, a web link, listening to a speech or following a tweet.

Given a network g, $g + g_{ij}$ and $g - g_{ij}$ have the natural interpretation. In case $g_{ij} = 0$ in g, $g + g_{ij}$ adds the link $g_{ij} = 1$, while if $g_{ij} = 1$ in g then $g + g_{ij} = g$. Similarly, if $g_{ij} = 1$ in g, $g - g_{ij}$ deletes the link g_{ij}, while if $g_{ij} = 0$ in g, then $g - g_{ij} = g$. Let $N_i(g) = \{j | g_{ij} = 1\}$ denote the nodes with whom node i has a link; this set will be referred to as the *neighbors* of i. Let $\eta_i(g) = |N_i(g)|$ denote the number of connections/neighbors of node i in network g. Moreover, for any integer $d \geq 1$, let $\mathcal{N}_i^d(g)$ be the d-neighborhood of i in g: this is defined inductively, $\mathcal{N}_i^1(g) = N_i(g)$ and $\mathcal{N}_i^k(g) = \mathcal{N}_i^{k-1}(g) \cup (\cup_{j \in \mathcal{N}_i^{k-1}} N_j(g))$.

There is a path from i to j in g either if $g_{ij} = 1$ or there exist distinct nodes $j_1, \cdots, j_m$ different from i and j such that $g_{i,j_1} = g_{j_1,j_2} = \ldots = g_{j_m,j} = 1$. A component is a maximal collection of nodes such that there is a path between every pair of nodes. A network g is said to be connected if there exists one component, i.e., there is a path from any node i to every other node j.

Let $\mathbf{N}_1(g), \mathbf{N}_2(g), \ldots, \mathbf{N}_{n-1}(g)$ be a partition of nodes: two nodes belong to the same group if and only if they have the same degree. A network is said to be *regular* if every node has the same number of links, i.e., $\eta_i(g) = \eta \; \forall i \in N$ (and so all nodes belong to one group in the partition). The *complete* network, g^c, is a regular network in which $\eta = n - 1$, while the *empty* network, g^e, is a regular network in which $\eta = 0$. Figure 1 presents regular networks.

A *core–periphery* network contains two groups: the periphery, $\mathbf{N}_1(g)$, and the core, $\mathbf{N}_2(g)$. Nodes in the periphery have a link only with nodes in the core; nodes in the core are fully linked with each other and have links with a subset of nodes in the periphery. The star (or hub–spoke) network is a special case in which the core contains a single node. The *interlinked star* or *multi-hub* network is a special case of the core–periphery network in which every node in the core is linked to all other nodes. Figure 2 presents core–periphery networks.

Exclusive groups is an architecture with a group of isolated nodes $D_1(g)$ and $m \geq 1$ distinct groups of completely linked nodes, $D_2(g), \ldots, D_{m+1}(g)$. Thus $\eta_i(g) = 0$, for $i \in D_1(g)$, while $\eta_j(g) = |D_x(g)| - 1$, for $j \in D_x(g)$,

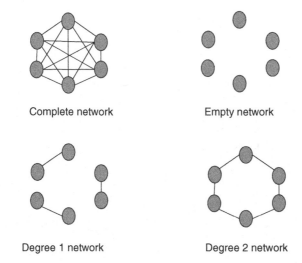

Complete network   Empty network

Degree 1 network   Degree 2 network

Figure 1 Regular networks.

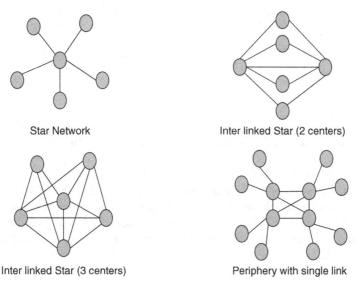

Star Network   Inter linked Star (2 centers)

Inter linked Star (3 centers)   Periphery with single link

Figure 2 Core–periphery networks.

$x \in \{2, 3, \ldots, m + 1\}$. A special case of this architecture is the *dominant group* network in which there is one complete component with $1 < k < n$ nodes, while $n - k > 0$ nodes are isolated. Figure 3 illustrates exclusive group networks.

It is important to note that networks allow for a very rich range of possibilities in relationships, that go beyond degrees. To bring out this point in a simple

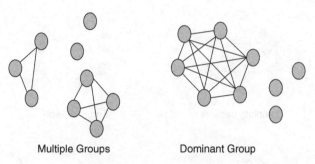

Multiple Groups   Dominant Group

Figure 3 Exclusive group networks.

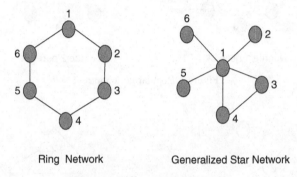

Ring Network   Generalized Star Network

Figure 4 Differences in networks.

way, consider a degree-2 regular connected network and a corresponding generalized star network with the same number of links. This is illustrated in Figure 4.

Observe that as the nodes increase, "distance" between the nodes is unbounded in the ring; distance is bounded above by 2 in the latter network. In the regular network, all nodes are essentially symmetric, while in the multi-hub network the hub nodes clearly have many more connections and are more "central" than the other nodes. Finally, observe that in the ring, no two neighbors are linked, while in the latter network one pair of periphery nodes is linked (the frequency of "connected" triads is measured by the "clustering" coefficient).

3   INDIVIDUAL CHOICE, NETWORKS, AND MARKETS

This section develops the elements of a framework for individual choice at the intersection of networks and markets. I will present three economic examples.

The first example concerns social learning and diffusion. The diffusion of new ideas and technologies in a society is a classical theme in the social sciences. In economics, the traditional models of diffusion examine the role of individual heterogeneity in explaining differential rates of adoption (Griliches, 1957). By contrast, there exists a long tradition of empirical work in sociology and related disciplines on the role of social connections in shaping adoption and individual behavior (Coleman, 1966; Katz and Lazarsfeld, 1955; Rogers, 1983; Ryan and Gross, 1943). Drawing on the early work of Bala and Goyal (1998, 2001), I present a model for the analysis of the dynamics of choice of technology among socially connected individuals.

Example 1 *Learning and Diffusion*

Individuals – e.g., farmers, consumers, doctors, firms – are located on nodes of a network and the links between the nodes reflect information flows between them. They choose between alternatives whose relative advantages are imperfectly known. Since rewards are uncertain, individuals use their own past experience and also gather information from their *neighbors*. The goal is to understand if information gathered from one neighbor spreads through connections to other neighbors and if everyone eventually adopts the optimal action.

There are two alternatives, a_0 and a_1. Action a_0 yields 1 and 0 with equal probability. Action a_1 is an unknown technology. Its payoffs may be High or Low. In High state it yields 1 with probability 0.75 (and 0 with probability 0.25), and in Low state it yields 1 with probability 0.25 (and 0 with probability 0.75). So action a_0 is optimal in Low state and action a_1 is optimal in High state.

At the start, individual i believes that action a_1 is High with probability $\mu_i \in (0, 1)$ and Low with probability $1 - \mu_i$. Given the belief μ_i, the one period expected utility from action a_1 is given by

$$u(a_1, \mu_i) = \mu_i \pi_H + (1 - \mu_i)\pi_L. \tag{1}$$

An individual chooses an action to maximize (one-period) expected payoffs (I abstract from the information value of actions). So he chooses a_1 if $\mu_i > 1/2$ and a_0 if $\mu_i < 1/2$. At the end of the first period, every individual i observes the outcome of his own actions and those of his neighbors, $N_i(g)$ and then updates his prior μ_i, to arrive at the prior for period 2, μ_i'.[3] He then makes a decision in period 2, and so forth.

Let the passing of time be denoted by $t = 1, 2, ...$ The goal is to understand how the network g, shapes the evolution of individual actions and beliefs $(a_{i,t}, \mu_{i,t})_{i \in N}$, over time.

Bala and Goyal (1998, 2001) first draw out a general implication of network connections: in a (strongly) connected society, all agents choose the same

---

[3] In this example, a link is taken to be directed: so, for instance, $g_{ij} = 1$ means that i observes j, but it does not say anything about whether j observes i. Formally, a directed link model allows for $g_{ij} \neq g_{ji}$. All the concepts introduced in Section 2, for undirected networks, carry over in a natural way to directed networks.

action and obtain the same utility, in the long run. They then examine the conditions on the network under which social learning ensures choice of the efficient action.

To fix ideas, suppose individuals are arranged around a circle and observe their immediate neighbors and in addition observe a common set of individuals (referred to as the "Royal Family"). Bala and Goyal (1998) show that there is a strictly positive probability that everyone chooses action a_0 (even when a_1 is the optimal action), in the long run, *irrespective of the size of the population*. On the other hand, in a large society with only local neighbors (thus with no Royal Family), everyone chooses the optimal action with probability 1 in the long run. More generally, if there is an upper bound on the in-degree, then everyone will eventually choose the optimal action in a large (strongly) connected society. □

This example shows how concepts from graph theory (directed graphs, connectedness, heterogeneities in connections), taken together with results from statistical decision theory and probability theory, illuminate the dynamics of diffusion. In recent years, the study of diffusion and social learning has attracted a great deal of interest; see, e.g., Banerjee, Chandrasekhar, Duflo, and Jackson (2013), Acemoglu, Dahleh, and Ozdaglar (2011), Gallo (2014), and Golub and Jackson (2010). For overviews of the research in this field, see Goyal (2012, 2016).

This example also draws attention to a very general finding in the research on networks: inequality in connections (reflected here in the presence of the highly connected Royal Family) can have large economic implications.

The second example combines choice, networks and markets within a common framework. The concept of neighbors plays a key role. An action that I take may raise or lower payoffs of neighbors: actions are said to create *positive externality* if an increase in their value raises the rewards of neighbour and they are said to create *negative externality* otherwise. If an increase in others' actions raises the marginal returns from own actions, the actions are *strategic complements*, while if an increase in others' actions lowers the marginal returns from own actions then we say that the actions are *strategic substitutes*. The effects of others' actions can have different effects depending on network location. So, for instance, actions of neighbors may generate positive effects while actions of non-neighbors may generate negative effects, and vice versa. This draws attention to the rich and potentially complex interplay between action externalities and network location.

The goal is to understand how network location and structure shapes individual behavior and well being: do better connected individuals earn larger rewards as compared to poorly connected individuals? What is the best design of a network? For a general introduction to games on networks, see Goyal (2007).[4] I present an early model, taken from Goyal and Moraga-Gonzalez (2001), that introduces networks in an oligopolistic market.

---

[4] The study of games on networks remains an active field of research; see, e.g., Bramoulle and Kranton (2007), Ballester, Calvo-Armengol, and Zenou (2006) and Galeotti, Goyal, Jackson,

Example 2   *Collaboration in Oligopoly*

Suppose demand is linear and given by $Q = 1 - p$. There are $n \geq 2$ firms. The initial marginal cost of production in a firm is $\bar{c} > 0$ and assume that $n\bar{c} < 1$. Each firm i chooses a level of research effort given by $s_i \in \mathbb{R}_+$. Collaboration between firms involves sharing of research efforts that lower costs of production. The marginal costs of production of a firm i, in an network g, facing a profile of efforts s, are given by:

$$c_i(s|g) = \bar{c} - (s_i + \sum_{j \in N_i(g)} s_j). \tag{2}$$

Note that $N_i(g)$ refers to the (undirected) neighbors. Let $\eta_i(g) = |N_i(g)|$. Research effort is costly: $Z(s_i) = \alpha s_i^2/2$, where $\alpha > 0$. Given costs $c = \{c_1, c_2, \ldots c_n\}$, firms choose quantities ($\{q_i\}_{i \in N}$), with $Q = \sum_{i \in N} q_i$. Using standard methods, it is possible to compute the Cournot equilibrium quantities for any cost profile c. Thus the payoffs of firm i, located in network g, and faced with a research profile s are:

$$\left[\frac{1 - \bar{c} + s_i[n - \eta_i] + \sum_{j \in N_i(g)} s_j[n - \eta_j(g)] - \sum_{l \in N \setminus \{i\} \cup N_i} s_l[1 + \eta_l(g)]}{n + 1} \right]^2 - \frac{\alpha s_i^2(g)}{2}.$$

There is a positive externality across neighbors and negative externality across non-neighbors actions. Moreover, (due to the quadratic term) in the payoffs expression, actions of neighbors are strategic complements, while the actions of non-neighbors are strategic substitutes.

Goyal and Moraga-Gonzalez (2001) focus on regular networks (everyone has the same degree). They show that research effort is decreasing, production costs are initially declining and then increasing, and profits are initially increasing but eventually falling in degree.

They also consider the case where firms are local monopolists: in this situation, research efforts of neighbors and non-neighbors exhibit positive externalities and are strategic complements: consequently research efforts and profits are increasing in degree.   □

Example 2 illustrates how concepts from game theory (strategic substitutes and complements), oligopoly theory, and concepts from the theory of graphs (increasing density of links) can be brought together to understand firm behavior in a textbook economic setting.

The third example takes up individuals embedded in communities who participate in competitive exchange markets. The example is drawn from Ghiglino and Goyal (2010).

Vega-Redondo, and Yariv (2010). For recent surveys of the research in this field, see Bramoulle and Kranton (2016) and Jackson and Zenou (2014).

Example 3   *Communities and Competitive Exchange*

Consider a pure exchange competitive economy with individuals located on nodes of an (undirected) network. There are two goods, x and y. Individuals have Cobb–Douglas preferences; the novel feature is that the good y is a relative consumption good. In particular, assume that utility of individual i, facing a consumption profile $(x_i, y_i)_{i \in N}$, is:

$$u_i(x_i, y_i, y_{-i}) = x_i^{\sigma} [y_i - \alpha \eta_i (y_i - \frac{1}{\eta_i} \sum_{j \in N_i(g)} y_j)]^{1-\sigma}, \tag{3}$$

where $\sigma \in (0, 1)$ and α measures the strength of social comparisons, $N_i(g)$ refers to the set of neighbors, and η_i to the number of neighbors of i.

Let good x be the numeraire and sets its price equal to 1. A general equilibrium is defined as a price p_y (for good y) that clears all markets given that individuals optimally allocate their budgets across x and y. Our interest is in understanding how the structure of the network affects individual consumption and market prices.

Building on the work of Ballester, Calvo-Armengol, and Zenou (2006), the authors show that general equilibrium prices and consumption are a function of a single network statistic: (Bonacich) centrality. An individual's "centrality" is given by the weighted sum of paths of different lengths to all others in a social network. Individual consumption is proportional to its node centrality and the relative price of good y is proportional to the average network centrality of all agents in the network. Adding links to a network pushes up centralities and this, in turn, pushes up the price of good y. □

This example shows how a key concept from social networks and graph theory – centrality – helps us understand prices and consumption in a textbook competitive economy.[5]

Centrality is a key concept in the literature on networks; the research over the past decade has shown that the relevant notion of centrality depends on the specific economic application. For an introduction to centrality in networks, see Goyal (2007) and Jackson (2008); for a survey of key player problems in economics, see Zenou (2016).

4 LINKING AND NETWORK FORMATION

The finding that network structure can have large and systematic economic effects suggests that individuals will seek to form and dissolve links and create networks that are advantageous. At the very outset, it is worth emphasizing the novelty of the approach: the traditional approach in sociology and other social sciences focuses on the effects of social structure on behavior

---

[5] I have focused on the case where the absolute difference in consumption of a good matters. In a recent paper, Immorlica, Kranton, Manea and Stoddard (2016) explore behavior of individuals who seek status – higher "ranks" – in their neighborhood. For a general introduction to the role of the social comparisons, see Frank (1993).

(Granovetter, 1985; Smelser and Swedberg, 2005). In contrast, the economic approach to network formation locates the origins of networks in individual choice.

The beginnings of the theory of network formation can be traced to the work of Boorman (1975), Aumann and Myerson (1988) and Myerson (1977, 1991). In recent years, the theory of network formation has been a very active field of research. Broadly speaking there are two approaches: unilateral linking and bilateral linking.

The model of unilateral link formation was introduced in Goyal (1993) and systematically studied in Bala and Goyal (2000). Consider a collection of individuals, each of whom can form a link with any subset of the remaining players. A link with another individual allows access, in part and in due course, to the benefits available to the latter via his own links. As links are created on an individual basis, the network formation process can be analyzed as a noncooperative game. Bala and Goyal (2000) assumed that the payoffs of individuals are increasing in the number of people accessed and declining in the number of links formed.

There are important practical examples of this type of link formation – investments in a project, loans/borrowing, hyperlinks across web pages, citations, (following links in) Twitter. But the principal appeal of this model is its simplicity.

The set of individuals is given by $N = \{1, ..., n\}$, where $n \geq 2$. The strategy of person $i \in N$ is $s_i = (s_{i,1}, ..., s_{i,i-1}, s_{i,i+1}, ..., s_{i,n})$ where $s_{i,j} \in \{0, 1\}$ for each $j \in N\backslash\{i\}$. Player i has a *link* with j if $s_{i,j} = 1$. A strategy profile for all players is denoted by $s = \{s_1, s_2, s_3, .., s_n\}$, with the set of all strategies being given by $\mathcal{S} = \prod_{i=1}^{n} \mathcal{S}_i$. There is an equivalence between the set of strategies and the set of all directed networks $\mathcal{G}$. So I use g to refer to a strategy profile and also to the directed network, thus created.

Abusing terminology slightly, I shall say that $N_i^d(g) = \{j \in N | g_{i,j} = 1\}$ is the set of players with whom player i forms a link; let $n_i^d(g) = |N_i^d(g)|$. In the directed network g, let $\mathcal{N}_i(g) = \{k \mid i \xrightarrow{g} k\}$ be the set of individuals to whom i has a directed path. I follow the convention that a player accesses herself, and so the number of players accessed by player i in network g, is given by $n_i(g) \equiv |\mathcal{N}_i(g)| + 1$.

Example 4   *One-way and two-way flow models*

Consider a setting of information sharing. The model reflects the idea that more information is valuable, that a link with another person allows access to information that this person in turn accesses from her links, and that links are costly to form. In the one-way flow model, given a strategy profile g, the payoff of player i is

$$\Pi_i(g) = \phi(n_i(g), \eta_i^d(g)). \tag{4}$$

The function ϕ is strictly increasing in the first argument and strictly declining in the second argument. I interpret $n_i(g)$ as the "benefit" that player i

receives from the network, while $\eta_i^d(g)$ measures the "cost" associated with maintaining her links. This is known as the one-way model.

The two-way flow model describes a network formation game in which links are unilaterally formed but where the benefits flow in both directions. Define $\hat{\eta}_i(g)$ as the number of people accessed by i in the undirected graph induced by g.

In the two-way flow model, the payoff to player i under strategy profile g is

$$\hat{\Pi}_i(g) = \phi(\hat{n}_i(g), \eta_i^d(g)). \tag{5}$$

The function ϕ is increasing in the first and decreasing in the second argument.   □

Following the convention in this literature, let welfare in a network be given by the sum of individual payoffs. Denoting $W(g)$ as welfare in network g, it follows that

$$W(g) = \sum_{i \in N} u_i(g). \tag{6}$$

A network g is said to be efficient if $W(g) \geq W(g')$, for all $g' \in \mathcal{G}$.

Bala and Goyal (2000) develop a characterization of the architecture of equilibrium networks. They show that the network externalities in the linking process imply that equilibrium networks are either (strongly) connected or empty. Moreover, equilibrium networks have simple architectures: star (hub–spoke) networks (in the two-way flow model) and the cycle (in the one-way flow model). They also find that externalities have major effects: equilibrium networks are typically inefficient and the welfare costs can be very large.

I turn next to two-sided or bilateral link formation. A link between two players requires the approval of both the players involved. This is a good description of friendships, co-authorships, collaborations between firms, and free trade agreements between nations.

Following Myerson (1991) suppose that all players announce a set of *intended* links. An intended link is a binary variable, $s_{i,j} \in \{0, 1\}$ where $s_{i,j} = 1$ ($s_{i,j} = 0$) means that player i intends to (does not intend to) form a link with player j. Define $g_{i,j} = \min\{s_{i,j}, s_{j,i}\}$. Every strategy profile $s = \{s_1, s_2, \ldots, s_n\}$ therefore induces a corresponding *undirected* network $g(s)$. Define $\Pi_i : S \to \mathcal{R}$ as the payoff function of a player i in network g.

What is the architecture of networks that are "stable" and what are their welfare properties. Jackson and Wolinsky (1996) introduce the concept of pairwise stability.

Definition 1   *A network g is pairwise stable if:*

1. *For every $g_{i,j} = 1$, $\Pi_i(g) \geq \Pi_i(g - g_{i,j})$ and $\Pi_j(g) \geq \Pi_j(g - g_{i,j})$*
2. *For $g_{i,j} = 0$, $\Pi_i(g + g_{i,j}) > \Pi_i(g) \implies \Pi_j(g + g_{i,j}) < \Pi_j(g)$.*

Pairwise stability looks at the attractiveness of links in a network g, *one at a time*. The *first* condition requires that every link that is present must be (weakly) profitable for the players involved in the link. The *second* condition requires that for every link which is not present in the network it must be the case that if one player strictly gains from the link then the other player must be strictly worse off.

Jackson and Wolinsky (1996) develop a number of interesting economic examples. They also establish a general tension between pairwise stable and efficient networks. The theory of network formation remains a vibrant field of research; for overviews of this work, see Goyal (2007), Jackson (2008), Bloch and Dutta (2012), Chandrasekhar (2016), Choi, Gallo, and Kariv (2016).

5 MACROECONOMIC FLUCTUATIONS

Modern economies exhibit significant fluctuations that have large scale welfare implications. An understanding of their origins remains a fundamental question in economics. The dominant view is that large scale aggregate fluctuations cannot be caused by local/sector-specific shocks: the reason is that in a complex large economy, one would expect that there are many shocks taking place and that they would cancel each other out. Long and Plosser (1983) and Acemoglu, Carvalho, Ozdaglar, and Tahbaz-Salehi (2012) provide a framework to illustrate how local sector specific shocks may be amplified by the production network structure to generate large scale aggregate fluctuations. Therefore, understanding the empirical structure can deepen our understanding of the origins of aggregate fluctuations and thereby help the design of appropriately targeted policies.[6]

By way of motivation, consider the 2011 earthquake in Japan: this set in motion the ensuing tsunami and led to the meltdown problems at the nuclear plant in Fukushima, Japan. These three events resulted in the destruction of human and physical capital, but they were amplified by the disruption of national and global supply chains.

> *When the linkage structure in the economy is dominated by a small number of hubs supplying inputs to many different firms or sectors, aggregate fluctuations may arise for two related, but distinct, reasons. First, fluctuations in these hub-like production units can propagate throughout the economy and affect aggregate performance, much in the same way as a shutdown at a major airport has a disruptive impact on scheduled flights throughout a country . . . the presence of these hubs provides shortcuts through which these supply chain networks become easily navigable.* (Carvalho, 2014, page 24).

Acemoglu, Carvalho, Ozdaglar, and Tahbaz-Salehi (2012) study a production economy. There are n distinct firms, each specializing in a different good.

---

[6] For an early study of the implications of local network based complementarities on aggregate growth patterns, see Durlauf (1993).

These goods are a final good for consumption by the consumer but they also serve potentially as inputs in the production of other goods. For simplicity suppose that the consumer values all goods equally, and that she supplies labor inelastically and that she spends the wage income on consumption of the n goods. The output of sector i is given by:

$$x_i = (z_i l_i)^{1-a} (\prod_{i=1}^{n} x_{ij}^{\omega_{ij}})^a. \tag{7}$$

where x_{ij} is the input from sector j to sector i. The amount of labor hired by sector i is given by l_i, while $(1 - a)$ is the share of labor in production. The sector specific productivity shock is captured by the term z_i. It is natural to start with the assumption that these productivity shocks are independent across producers of goods in the economy. The coefficients a and the ω_{ij} reflect the technological relations in the economy. Putting together the nodes and the technological relations then gives us the production network of the economy. Price taking firms (in the sectors) seek to maximize profits. The authors study the general equilibrium of this production economy.

The analysis in Acemoglu, Carvalho, Ozdaglar, and Tahbaz-Salehi (2012) yields:

Observation 1 *In equilibrium, (the logarithm of) aggregate value added, y, is a weighted sum of the (logarithm of) sector level productivity shocks, ϵ_i:*

$$y = \sum_{i=1}^{n} v_i \epsilon_i \tag{8}$$

where the weights, v_i, are given by the Leontief inverse matrix, and reflect the centrality of a sector in the production network, and $\epsilon_i = \log z_i$. This sets the stage for a study of how network topology affects the propagation of sector specific shocks.

I take up three networks to illustrate how network structure matters; see Figure 5. Consider first the simplest baseline case: an empty network with no intermediate input trade in the economy. So all sectors only use labor for production. In this economy, shocks to any given sector will not affect any other sector: there is no amplification of micro-level volatility.

Next consider a supply chain with six nodes, where inputs flow unidirectionally from a well-defined upstream sector through intermediate stages to a final downstream sector. In network parlance, this is a tree or line structure with a single source. Productivity fluctuations at the most upstream source, sector 1, now have a first-round effect on its immediate downstream customer, sector 2; a smaller, second-round effect on sector 3 and so forth. The presence of these indirect effects means that the production network amplifies the shock to sector 1.

Finally, consider the (directed) hub–spoke network with a single general purpose technology. The hub is used as the sole intermediate input in all other

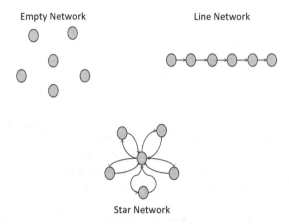

Figure 5 Simple Production Networks.

sectors and each of these sectors is necessary for the general purpose technology. The general purpose technology reflects features of real world sectors such as real estate and construction, finance, energy and information technology. It can be shown that this network generates the highest volatility. There are two reasons for this. One, fluctuations in the hub sector now have a large first order impact on every sector in the economy and two, the hub brings all sectors close to each other and therefore raises the power of second order effects.

This observation reinforces an important finding in Example 1 (in Section 2 above): the key role of highly connected hubs in shaping aggregate outcomes.

To close the circle, I note some facts about the production network of the US economy: this is a relatively sparse graph that contains a small collection of highly connected hub sectors – the general purpose technologies – making the production economy a typical "small world" (Acemoglu et al., 2012; Blochl, Theis, Vega-Redondo, and Fisher, 2011). Thus sector-specific shocks can potentially be amplified by the network structure to generate large aggregate shocks. The study of network amplification is a major field of research currently: for a survey of some of the general themes, see Acemoglu, Ozdaglar, and Tahbaz-Salehi (2016). In a related line of work, global supply chains have motivated the study of the role of production networks in international trade (Antras, 2015; Costinot, Vogel, and Wang, 2012).

In the discussion above, it was assumed that firms are price takers and the network is exogenously given. In real world markets, firms often have stable relationships with small subsets of the market. A deeper understanding of price formation and market power in networks is thus clearly important in these settings. The study of market power is also a first step in developing a theory of the how the production economy itself evolves over time. The next section takes up the theory of price formation in networks.

6 EXCHANGE AND MARKET POWER

In the standard Walrasian model, individuals – be they consumers, producers or traders – are anonymous: they can all trade with each other and this trade takes place at a common price. Empirically, individuals have clear identities and develop durable and personal relations of exchange, and there are definite limitations on who can trade with whom. Moreover, the terms of trade – between the buyers and sellers for the same good – often differ and these differences are related to the structure of relationships among the individuals (Uzzi, 1996; Kirman and Vignes, 1991). There is thus a need to move beyond the Walrasian framework and develop a systematic understanding of exchange networks: their antecedents and their implications for pricing, allocation of surplus and aggregate efficiency.

I start with a simple two-sided market comprising of buyers (numbering B) and sellers (numbering S). Each seller has a single indivisible good (which she values at 0) and every buyer has a known valuation for the good (which he values at 1). The trading relationships are represented by a bipartite network. A network in which all sellers can trade with all buyers (and vice versa) is a special case of this setting. Suppose that an auctioneer announces prices with the aim of equating demand and supply. A price of p between a pair of traders means the buyer's payoff is $1 - p$ while the seller makes p. It is easy to see that if $B > S$ then the equilibrium price must be 1, while if $B < S$ then the price must be 0. Thus there is a single price for all trade and the outcome is efficient. I will denote this as the Walrasian benchmark.

I now turn to the more general networks where some buyers and sellers cannot trade with each other. Our interest is in the role of the network and so I use a price formation protocol that is close to the centralized Walrasian auctioneer. Following Corominas-Bosch (2004), I consider a model of price formation through bargaining. The bargaining process proceeds as follows. In period 1 and all subsequent odd periods, sellers make offers, which are observed by the connected buyers. Buyers who wish to trade at the prices they see, propose a price. Given these offers and counter-offers, a maximal matching is picked (this is a matching that maximizes the number of trades). Those who have an agreed trade, exchange at the agreed price and leave the market (without replacement). In round 2, and all subsequent even numbered rounds, buyers make offers, and connected sellers respond. Suppose all traders discount the future at rate $\delta \in [0, 1]$. This completes the description of a game on a network.[7] Our aim is to understand how network structure affects prices and the efficiency of trading.

There are broadly three types of outcomes: a buyer gets most of the surplus (p close to 0), a seller gets most of the surplus (p close to 1), and traders split

---

[7] The bargaining protocol in Polanski (2007) also has a centralized structure though it differs in some details. The analysis there also exploits the Gallai–Edmonds decomposition and the results of the two papers are closely related.

the surplus (price close to $1/2$). If two buyers are linked to a single seller then p is equal to 1; traders in disjoint pairs agree on a price $p = 1/1 + \delta$, as in the original Stahl–Rubinstein bilateral bargaining model. I now turn to more general networks.

The Marriage Theorem (Hall, 1935) provides us with conditions for a perfect matching: where all traders can in principle trade. It says that there exists a matching that covers a set of buyers B if and only if every subset of buyers in B is connected to a set of sellers of equal or larger cardinality.

The key to understanding trading in these networks is the idea of "local" market dominance. Following Manea (2016a), let us say that a node i is under-demanded if there exists a maximal matching in which it is unmatched. Let U be the set of under-demanded nodes. Correspondingly, the set of over-demanded nodes $\mathcal{O}$ consists of nodes that do not belong to U and have at least one link to an under-demanded node. The set of perfectly matched nodes is simply the complement of the set of under-demanded and over-demanded nodes.

Corominas-Bosch (2004) exploits the Gallai–Edmonds Decomposition Theorem to establish the following striking result.

Observation 2 *Fix a network g. For every δ there exists a sub-game perfect equilibrium, in which under-demanded and over-demanded traders earn respectively 0 and 1. Sellers in the perfectly matched set earn $z = 1/1 + \delta$, while buyers get $1 - z$.*

In this model all trade occurs in the first period and so the outcome is efficient. However, the terms of trade can differ widely, depending on local market conditions.

The idea behind this result is simple: consider the profile in which all over-demanded sellers propose 1 and all buyers accept it. Suppose that a buyer rejects this proposal. Then in equilibrium the trade will take place among the remaining buyers and sellers in the sub-graph. So the buyer will be disconnected from all sellers in the original sub-graph. So his only hope is a possible payoff from connections across in other sub-graphs. But the decomposition theorem tells us that this buyer is only linked to sellers in other over-demanded sets. In such a sub-graph, sellers propose 1 and the buyers linked to them agree to the proposal. So the buyer cannot hope to earn anything positive by deviation. Given Observation 2, it follows that if $S > B$, then G will support the competitive outcome if and only if every seller is under-demanded. Likewise, if $S < B$, then G will support the competitive outcome if and only if every seller is over-demanded. Finally, if $S = B$, then G will support the competitive outcome if and only if all traders are perfectly matched.

This paper provides an elegant micro-foundation for the Walrasian benchmark: in particular, it tells us that the law of one price obtains only when all local markets reflect the global balance of buyer vs sellers. So, in a "market" with surplus sellers there may be an outcome in which subsets of sellers make large sums of money because they are "locally" in a buyer surplus market. In a follow-up paper, Charness, Corominas-Bosch, and Frechete (2007) show that the behavior of experimental subjects in a laboratory conforms to the predictions of the model.

In the Corominas-Bosch (2004) and Polanski (2007) models, the price formation process is centralized: a single price is announced to all linked traders at the same time. In recent work, Abreu and Manea (2012a, 2012b) study a model with decentralized matching: in every period a single pair of linked traders is picked to bargain. They show that decentralized trading has significant effects: bargaining may end in disagreement, a pair of traders may refuse to trade at one stage but agree to trade at a subsequent point. Moreover, decentralization creates the possibility of inefficient Markov perfect equilibrium.[8]

I have taken the network as given so far, but given the trading outcome on any network, we can now take a step back and ask what sort of networks would form if buyers and sellers can build links with each other. Consider the Corominas-Bosch (2004) model and suppose a link is two-sided and entails a cost $c > 0$ for each trader. As links are costly, the efficient network will entail a maximal set of disjoint pairs. Jackson (2008) shows that if $c < 1/2$ and the discount factor is close to 1, then pairwise stable networks coincide with efficient networks.

This simple model provides us a benchmark to assess the role of networks in shaping bargaining. The study of bargaining in networks remains an active field of research; for a recent survey, see Manea (2016a).

I now turn to the two alternative price formation protocols – posted prices and auctions.

Lever-Guzman (2011) considers the setting of a market with price setting firms. The firms and consumers are located in a bi-partite network (as in the Corominas-Bosch model). Consumers' reservation utility is 1 and is known to firms. Every firm sets a single price and the network is commonly known. This describes a game on a network, with prices set by sellers and consumer decisions on purchases. The goal is to understand how the network shapes pricing and the allocation of surplus.

It is easy to see that if all consumers have two or more links with firms then a firm knows that a consumer can always compare two prices and the competitive (Bertrand) price is the natural outcome. If, on the other hand, there is a consumer who has only one link then the firm who has this captive consumer can always make a profit of 1 by setting a price of 1. If this firm also has consumers with multiple links then there is a tension in the pricing strategy: a high price may lead to a loss of the other consumers. This suggests that in general networks, firms will use mixed strategies in prices. The same intuitions arise

---

[8] The models of bargaining I have discussed all assume that traders who agree leave and are not replaced. For a study of bargaining in networks where traders are replaced, see Manea (2011).

in search theory; a well known early paper on price dispersion is Burdett and Judd (1983).

I now turn to auctions on networks and discuss the work of Kranton and Minehart (2001). There are two stages. In stage 1, buyers unilaterally choose to form costly links with sellers. These links enable buyers to procure goods or inputs. Buyers trade-off expected gains from trade against costs of link formation.[9] In stage 2, the valuations of buyers are realized; they then engage in trade with sellers restricted by the network structure defined in the first stage. The trading in stage 2 takes place through a centralized auction where at each price efficient matches are determined. The paper establishes, somewhat surprisingly, that an efficient allocation mechanism (ex-post competitive environment) is sufficient to align the buyers' incentives to form ties with the social incentives. The following simple example illustrates the role of the link formation protocol – unilateral vs two-sided – in shaping the efficiency of networks.

Example 5 *Role of Linking Protocol*

There are two stages. In stage 1, players choose to form links. The links determine potential trade patterns. In stage 2, buyers simultaneously make bids to the seller. The winner is determined using a second price auction. Assume that the valuations of the buyers are uniformly distributed on the unit interval.

To fix ideas consider the simple case with 2 buyers and 1 seller. It is easy to see that in the single link network, the buyer will bid 0. In the two links network, buyers will submit valuations equal to their valuation, and so the expected price is the expected value of the second highest valuation. It maybe checked that the expected valuation of the winner is $2/3$ (which is also the total value of surplus generated), while the expected price is equal to $1/3$. Each buyer expects to earn $1/6$, together they expect to earn $1/3$, the seller expects to earn $1/3$.

What are the incentives of the traders to form a network? I first characterize the efficient networks: observe that expected social value of one buyer is $1/2$ while the expected social value of selling to two buyers is $2/3$. This immediately implies that empty network is efficient if $c > 1/2$, the single link network is efficient if $1/6 < c < 1/2$, and the two link network is efficient if $c < 1/6$.

Consider the case of unilateral links formed by buyers. Observe that the network is an equilibrium if no buyer has an incentive to form a link: simple computations reveal that if the cost of a link $c > 1/2$ then the empty network is an equilibrium. Next consider the single link network: if a buyer has formed a link then for him to retain it $c < 1/2$. On the other hand, for the second buyer not to form a link it must be the case that returns are less than cost of the link,

---

[9] For a related strand of the literature on buyer-seller networks with a different modeling approach – based on heuristic learning rules and random linking decisions – see Weisbuch, Kirman, and Herreiner (2000).

i.e., if $c > 1/6$. I have thus shown that a single link network is an equilibrium if $1/6 < c < 1/2$. Similarly, a comparison of expected payoffs from linking reveals that the two link network is an equilibrium if $c < 1/6$.

Jackson (2008) shows that the linking protocol matters: with two-sided linking, efficient networks are generally not pairwise stable except for very high and very low costs of linking.   □

This discussion brings out two general points. The first is that the network structure and price formation mechanism both shape the efficiency of trading and the allocation of surplus. The second is that the link formation protocol has a decisive impact on the architecture of networks and the efficiency of the trading system. For a systematic exploration on inefficiencies in bilateral trading networks, see Elliott (2015) and Elliott and Nava (2015). Finally, the existing work assumes that traders know the network. For a general treatment of games with incomplete network knowledge, see Galeotti, Goyal, Jackson, Vega-Redondo, and Yariv (2010).

7   INTERMEDIARIES

I have so far considered direct ties between sellers and final buyers. Supply, service and trading chains are a defining feature of the modern economy. They are prominent in agriculture, in transport and communication networks, in international trade, and in finance. The routing of economic activity, the allocation of surplus and the efficiency of the system depend on the prices set by these different intermediaries. This section discusses recent research on price formation in networks of intermediaries.[10]

I begin with a simple model of posted prices, taken from Choi, Galeotti, and Goyal (2016). By way of motivation, let us consider a tourist who wishes to travel by train from London to see the Louvre in Paris. The first leg of the journey is from home to St. Pancras Station. There are a number of different taxi companies, bus services and the Underground. Once at St. Pancras Station, the only service provider to Paris Nord Station is Eurostar. Upon arriving at Paris Nord, there are a number of alternatives (bus, Metro and taxi) to get to the Louvre. The network consists of alternative paths each constituted of local transport alternatives in London and in Paris and the Eurostar Company. Each of the service providers sets a price. The traveler picks the cheapest "path". Figure 6 represents this example.

This example suggests the following model: there is a source node, $\mathcal{S}$, and a destination node, $\mathcal{D}$. A path between the two is a sequence of interconnected nodes, each occupied by an intermediary. The source node and the destination

---

[10] In an early paper, Nava (2015) studies a model where traders choose how much *quantity* to buy and sell from neighbors. He finds that intermediation arises endogenously in equilibrium: traders buy in order to resell to others. Prices strictly increase along any intermediation chain. Efficiency is attained only in large economies and only when intermediation is negligible.

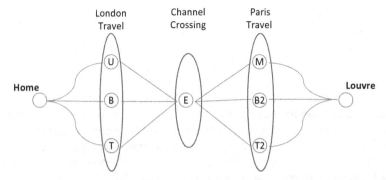

Figure 6 Transport Network: London to Paris.

node and all the paths between them together define a network. The passage of goods (or people) from source to destination generates surplus. Let us suppose that the value is known and for simplicity set it equal to 1. Intermediaries (who have zero cost) simultaneously *post a price*; the prices determine a total cost for every path between S and D. The tourist moves along a least cost path; so an intermediary earns payoffs only if she is located on it. This completes the description of a game on a network.

The aim is to understand how the network structure of intermediation shapes the prices and the allocation of surplus across traders.

To build some intuition let us consider two simple networks. The first network has two paths between S and D, each with a distinct node. The two intermediaries compete in price: this is a simple game of strategic complements. Standard arguments – à la Bertrand – tell us that the firms will set a price equal to 0. The second network contains a single line with two nodes between S and D. The two intermediaries are now engaged in bilateral Nash Bargaining and the strategies are strategic substitutes (assuming that the sum of demands must equal the value of surplus). As in the standard model, there are a number of possible outcomes. These examples illustrate how classical models of price formation and competition constitute special cases of our framework and also show how networks and the strategic structure are intimately related.

Moving on to general networks, a node is said to be *critical* if it lies on all paths between S and D. Choi, Galeotti, and Goyal (2016) develop a full characterization of equilibrium pricing. This result shows that critical traders are sufficient but not necessary for surplus extraction. The lack of necessity arises due to possible coordination failures along chains of traders that enhance the market power of non-critical traders. These coordination problems give rise to multiple equilibria. Standard refinements do not resolve the multiplicity problem, and so the authors take the model to the laboratory. The experiments establish that subjects avoid coordination problems. As a result, trade always takes place, and non-critical traders make very little profits. Summarizing the theory and the experiments yields:

Observation 3   *When value from exchange is common knowledge, the presence of critical traders in both necessary and sufficient for full surplus extraction by intermediaries. Subjects in the laboratory typically coordinate successfully and trading outcomes are efficient.*

In the benchmark setting with full information the number of critical intermediaries does not have an important impact on pricing and trading outcomes. However, in markets with multiple vertically related firms, double marginalization is a major concern for policy and regulation; see, e.g., Lerner (1934), Tirole (1994) and Spulber (1999). This motivates an extension of the benchmark model to a setting where value is uncertain. Suppose we fix ideas that value is uniformly distributed on the unit interval. This defines a new game on a network: the strategies remain as before but the payoffs are altered due to the incomplete information on valuations.

Consider the same two network examples as above. In the two path case, nothing essential changes: prices are still set at 0. But in the line network with two nodes, there is an outcome where both intermediaries set a price equal to $1/3$, so there is no trade with probability $2/3$. It is easy to see that with three intermediaries the price will be $1/4$ and so the probability of no trade is $3/4$. Thus individual prices are falling, aggregate price is rising and the probability of trade is falling in the number of critical traders. Using a combination of theory and experiments, Choi, Galeotti, and Goyal (2016) generalize this insight to cover networks in general.

The result on critical nodes is sharp but criticality may be seen as too demanding: a node that lies on most (but not all) paths has the same status as compared to a node that lies on only one path. Moreover, all critical paths have equal status in the model. It may be argued that location in the path – upstream or downstream – should matter. Related work with alternative pricing protocols develops these points. For auctions, see Kotowski and Leister (2014) and Gottardi and Goyal (2012); for bargaining, see Condorelli, Galeotti, and Renou (2016), Gofman (2011), and Manea (2016b); for bid-and-ask prices, see Acemoglu and Ozdaglar (2007), Blume et al. (2007) and Gale and Kariv (2009).[11]

I begin with bargaining. Following Manea (2016b), consider the following intermediation game. A seller is endowed with a single unit of an indivisible good, which can be resold through linked intermediaries until it reaches one of several buyers. At every stage in the game, the current owner of the good selects a bargaining partner among his downstream neighbors in the network. The two traders negotiate the price of the good via a random proposer protocol. With probability p, the current owner makes an offer and the partner either accepts or turns down the offer. With probability $1 - p$ the downstream trader makes an offer. Irrespective of the offer originator, once an offer is rejected bargaining ends. The current owner has an opportunity to select a new trader in

---

[11] For a comparison of outcomes under different pricing protocols, see Choi, Galeotti, and Goyal (2016).

the next stage. If an offer is accepted, then the two traders exchange the good at the agreed price. If the new owner is an intermediary, he has an opportunity to resell the good to downstream neighbors following the same protocol. The final buyer consumes the good upon purchase. Traders have a common discount factor $\delta \in (0, 1)$. The paper focuses on (Markov perfect) equilibria of this intermediation game.

To draw out the role of the network architecture, I focus on the simple setting where all traders have zero costs and all buyers have a common value $v > 0$. The following construction plays a key role in the analysis. Observe that any intermediary linked to two (or more) buyers will extract the full surplus of v, as traders become patient. This motivates the construction of the following layered graph. Start with the buyers, and add all intermediaries who are linked to at least two buyers, then add all intermediaries linked to at least two traders already present, and so on, until no more traders have two or more links to already present traders. This constitutes layer 0. Now consider traders left over: start with any trader who has one link with traders in layer 0, then add all intermediaries who have at least two links with intermediaries currently in layer 1 and proceed until there is no one with two or more links with traders in the emerging layer 1. Proceed recursively until all agents have been assigned to layers.

Manea (2016b) shows that, as $\delta \to 1$, the (Markov Perfect) equilibrium in any (acyclical) network can be characterized in terms of the resale values of different traders. These resale values are in turn defined by the different layers of the constructed multi-layered network.

To get a good sense of market power and behavior in the model it is useful to focus on a special class of networks, inspired by the example of travel from London to Paris (see Figure 6 above). A complete multipartite network has a single original seller and a single final buyer and there are L intermediating levels. Every node in a level is linked to every node in the adjacent levels above and below it. In this network, a node is critical if it is the unique member of a layer. Given the layer x, let k_x be the number of downstream layers that have critical traders. Let k be the number of "critical" layers in the entire network. In the context of complete multipartite networks, the analysis in Manea (2016b) yields us:

Observation 4 *Fix a complete multipartite network and let $\delta \to 1$. In equilibrium, the reservation value of intermediary i in level x converges to $p^{k_x+1}v$. The payoff of the initial seller converges to $p^{k+1}v$ and payoff of the buyer converges to $(1 - p)v$. The payoff of non-critical intermediaries converges to 0, while the payoff of critical trader at level x converges to $(1 - p)p^{k_x+1}v$.*

Thus the market power of any trader depends on the number of layers in the induced graph and number of traders in each layer of the downstream graph.[12]

---

[12] This application to complete multipartite networks is taken from Condorelli and Galeotti (2016).

So far, I have assumed that all players know the value of the good. I now turn to settings with incomplete information on valuations/surplus. Condorelli, Galeotti, and Renou (2016) study a setting where the good either has Low or High value to a trader. This valuation is independent of other's valuations and is private information. Trading proceeds as follows: the current owner makes a take-it-or-leave-it offer to a "neighbor." If the neighbor accepts then trade takes place, if not then he makes an offer to other neighbors. The process of bargaining gradually reveals information on the private valuations of traders. In equilibrium, High valuation traders always consume the product, while Low valuation traders seek out potential trading partners: the novelty here, relative to the earlier bilateral bargaining literature, is that search for a high valuation trader will involve possibly many other traders (in the network). A trader that lies on all paths between a trader i and the original seller – a suitably defined critical node – earns higher payoffs. For a general discount factor $\delta \in (0, 1)$, the analysis is intricate and trading exhibits complicated behavior: prices may be non-monotonic and trading inefficient. However, as $\delta \rightarrow 1$, trading is efficient: the traders manage to locate the High valuation trader (if one exists).

I turn next to auctions. Gottardi and Goyal (2012) and Kotowski and Leister (2014) study auctions in a network of intermediaries. I briefly describe the model and the main results from Kotowski and Leister (2014). There is a single source and possibly multiple eventual buyers (each of whom value the good at value $v > 0$). There are tiers of intermediaries between the original owner and buyers. In each tier, traders compete to provide intermediation services. The current owner conducts a second price auction among downstream traders to sell his good. The new owner does likewise until the good arrives at a buyer. The network is common knowledge but intermediaries have private information on their own costs. If the cost of trading is High then the intermediary drops out of the network.

Kotowski and Leister (2014) provide an elegant characterization of prices and profits. They show that behavior is defined by two network characteristics – number of layers and number of intermediaries in each layer – and the probability of High cost intermediaries. In the benchmark setting with two or more Low cost intermediaries in each layer the original owner will extract full surplus. Therefore, an intermediary earns rents only if it is the sole Low cost player in its layer, i.e., it is critical. With a greater probability of High cost, intermediate layers can in principle earn rents, in the event that their competitors in the same layer have turned out to be High cost. However, this possibility has correspondingly negative effects on the resale value for upstream traders. The authors show that the resale value is increasing in the probability of being Low cost and in the number of traders in each layer.

This discussion illustrates the ways in which standard price formation protocols – posted prices, bargaining and auctions – may be used to study intermediation in networks. In all cases, critical traders appear to be central to shaping market power. The models also clarify how the pricing protocol and the timing (sequential versus simultaneous) of decision making interacts with networks and with private information. In the posted price model, all prices are set at the same time. If prices were set in sequence then upstream traders will extract more of the surplus, just as in the bargaining and in the auction models. The extent of this extraction will be mitigated by private information downstream.

Network formation: The discussion above shows that location within a network and the structure of the network have powerful effects on earnings. So it is only natural that traders will seek to shape their network. The model of posted prices discussed above brings out the role of critical nodes. Given the potentially large rewards of being critical, firms and individuals will make investments in connections to make themselves critical. However, these efforts will face counter-efforts from other nodes who would like to keep intermediation rents down. What is the outcome of these pressures? I address this question with the help of a network formation model taken from Goyal and Vega-Redondo (2007).

Consider a link announcement game. Every player $i \in N$ announces a set of (intended) links with others $s_i = (s_{i1}, \ldots, s_{in})$. A link between i and j is formed, $g_{ij} = 1$, if $s_{ij} = s_{ji} = 1$. Upon formation of a link, both players incur a cost $c > 0$. As before, $\mathcal{N}_i(g)$ is the set of players whom player i accesses in network g. For any $k \in \mathcal{N}_i(g)$, define $\mathcal{C}(j, k; g)$ as the set of players who are critical to connect j and k in network g and let $c(j, k; g) = |\mathcal{C}(j, k; g)|$. Then, for every strategy profile of intended links, $s = (s_1, s_2, \ldots, s_n)$, the (net) payoffs to player i are given by:

$$\Pi_i(s_i, s_{-i}) = \sum_{j \in \mathcal{N}_i(g)} \frac{1}{e(i, j; g) + 2} + \sum_{j,k \in N} \frac{I_{\{i \in \mathcal{C}(j,k)\}}}{e(j, k; g) + 2} - \eta_i^d(g)c, \quad (9)$$

where $I_{\{i \in \mathcal{C}(j,k)\}} \in \{0, 1\}$ stands for the indicator function specifying whether i is essential for j and k, and $\eta_i^d(g) \equiv |\{j \in N : j \neq i, g_{ij} = 1\}|$ refers to the number of players with whom player i has a link.

Goyal and Vega-Redondo (2007) show that equilibrium networks are either connected or empty. The attempt of traders to extract rents from intermediation pushes towards a star structure in which there is a single central node. However, the desire of traders to avoid paying rents pushes toward a competitive network like a ring – with no critical traders – in which no one earns any intermediation rents. Their analysis reveals that with coordinated bilateral linking, the second pressure dominates and the star emerges as the unique (nonempty) stable network. I state this as:

Observation 5 *For a wide range of linking costs the star network is the unique (nonempty) stable network. The ratio of payoffs of the hub trader and a periphery trader is unbounded, as the number of traders grows.*

The idea of location advantages in networks has a long and distinguished history in sociology; see, e.g., Burt (1992). From an economic perspective, this work naturally motivates the question: can location advantages and large pay-off differences be sustained among otherwise identical individuals? The above model shows that the strategic struggle for these advantages leads to a star architecture – where a single player becomes essential to connect every other pair of players – and that such a network is robust with respect to individual and bilateral attempts to alter the structure.

While this is a very sharp prediction, there are three features of the result that are potentially unsatisfactory. The first is that it requires many links from a single player: capacity constraints may render the star infeasible in applications. The second is that it exhibits an extreme form of market power and this will attract entry and probably a larger and more coordinated rewiring of links. The third is that nodes are homogenous and that paths are perfectly competitive.

7.1   Financial Intermediaries

In recent years, following the financial crises of 2008, there has been renewed interest in the role of interconnections among financial institutions as a source for the transmission and possible amplification of shocks. The financial sector embodies intermediation in a pure form – that between the sources and the eventual users of savings. Traditional models of the banking sector generally pay little attention to the rich patterns of intermediation within the sector. A number of papers have documented the structure of the inter-bank lending network; see, e.g., Bech and Atalay (2010), Afonso and Lagos (2012), and Van Lelyveld and t' Veld (2012). The broad consensus is that this network has a core–periphery structure: there is a core of large banks that are densely interconnected, and a large number of smaller banks at the periphery who are connected to a few of the core banks. There is a net inflow of funds from the peripheral banks to the core banks. These empirical findings motivate the study of economic mechanisms underlying the formation of core–periphery financial networks. I briefly discus this work.

Van der Leij, Veld, and Hommes (2016) extend the Goyal and Vega-Redondo (2007) model presented above by allowing for smoother competition between paths. Their first result is that a core–periphery network is not stable when agents are homogeneous. On the other hand, such a network arises naturally if there is heterogeneity – with respect to valuations – among individuals. The higher value banks constitute the core. In particular, their model can reproduce the observed core–periphery structure in the Dutch interbank market for reasonable parameter values.

Farboodi (2014) also explores the role of heterogeneity across nodes. There are banks that have links with depositors and banks that have links with potential investors. A link between two banks is a durable relationship. Links are unilateral: a link from X to Y constitutes a commitment from X to honor any loan demand from Y. A bank has an incentive to form multiple links and be the intermediary between a source bank and a destination bank as it can then earn "rents". Farboodi (2014) shows that a core–periphery network emerges as an equilibrium outcome. An important result is that the network is inefficient as banks who lend to investors "over-connect", exposing themselves to excessive counter-party risk, while (depositor linked) banks who provide funding end up with too few connections. This creates excessive risk in the system at large.

In a recent paper, Wang (2015) explores the externalities in financial linking and the implications of contagion risk. In her model, firms form links by trading assets. Liquidation is costly. A link with a distressed firm percolates through the network: in a setting where contracts are not contingent on distant links, there is a externality generated by links. Her main insight is that when firms are highly dispersed in financial distress, the network features too many links with distressed firms and too few risk-sharing links among non-distressed firms. In an early paper, and using a more stylized model, Blume et al. (2011) obtain a related result on over-connected networks in a setting where shocks spread through a system, but contracts are not contingent on third party links.[13]

The discussion in this section brings out the importance of critical traders in shaping market power and the role of intermediation rents in the creation of trading and financial networks. The research also shows that profit motivated linking can lead to networks that sustain inefficiencies and exhibit systemic risk. The study of intermediation in networks remains a very active field of work; for recent work on related themes, see Galeotti and Goyal (2014) and Candogan, Bimpikis, and Ehsani (2015).

8 WORK, CONSUMPTION AND FINANCE

This section studies the role of social networks in labor, product, and financial markets.

8.1   Workers, unemployment and inequality

A significant fraction of all jobs are filled through the use of social networks (Granovetter, 1974; Rees, 1966; Cappellari and Tatsiramos, 2010; Cingano and Rosolia, 2012). There are two primary types of information for which contacts are used. First there is information on jobs: workers do not know which firms have vacancies while firms do not know the workers who are looking for a job.

---

[13] There is a large literature on financial contagion and systemic risk in networks; see, e.g., Acemoglu, Ozdaglar, and Tahbaz-Salehi (2015), Babus (2016), Cabrales, Gottardi, and Vega-Redondo (2016), Elliott and Nava (2016), Elliott, Golub, and Jackson (2014), Galeotti, Ghiglino, and Goyal (2015). For a survey, see Acemoglu, Ozdaglar, and Tahbaz-Salehi (2016).

The problem of network resilience also arises in communication, criminal and transport networks; for recent research on these topics, see Dziubinski and Goyal (2016), Baccara and Bar-Isaac (2008) and Goyal and Vigier (2014). For a survey of this line of work, see Dziubinski, Goyal, and Vigier (2016).

A second type of information concerns the ability of workers: a worker knows more about his own ability as compared to a potential employer. So firms seek information on quality and ability via personal contacts of their employees. This section examines the ways in which social networks affect the flow of information and thereby shape wages, unemployment and inequality.

Montgomery (1991) studies the adverse selection problem in labor markets. There are two periods. In each period a firm hires one worker. The output of a firm is equal to the ability of the worker in the firm. The ability of workers is private information. In period 1, firms pay wages equal to the (ex-ante) average ability of workers. During period 1, a firm learns the ability of its worker. At the start of period 2, it has a choice between asking the period 1 worker for the name of a contact and offering a referral wage *or* simply posting a wage in the market. The key assumption is that there is a assortativity in social ties: so a High ability worker is more likely to have ties with other High ability workers. Competition between firms means that wages equal expected ability of workers and, moreover, profits of firms are equal to zero (over the two periods).

Montgomery's (1991) analysis yields two insights. The *first* insight is that workers with more connections will earn a higher wage. The reason for this relation between connections and wages is simple: more connections implies a higher number of referral wage offers from firms and this translates in a higher accepted wage. The *second* insight is that an increase in the density of social connections raises the inequality in wages. This is a reflection of the lemons effect: an increase in social ties means that more high ability workers are hired via referrals, and this lowers the quality of workers who go into the open market. These considerations may be summarized as:

Observation 6 *Consider the model of referrals. A firm uses a referral offer when its current employee is a high-ability worker but not otherwise. Referral wage offers are dispersed over an interval. As firms entice higher quality workers through the referral wages, the average quality in the market falls: so wages in the market are lower than ex-ante average quality. An increase in the density of social connections or in the assortativity of social ties leads to a rise in the (maximal) referred wage and a fall in the market wage.*

The Montgomery (1991) paper studies the role of social networks in resolving adverse selection problems in labor markets. I now turn to the role of social networks in facilitating the flow of information on jobs.

Calvo-Armengol and Jackson (2004) study a model of information transmission on job vacancies. Information about new jobs arrives to individuals. If they are unemployed they take up the job; if employed they pass on information to their unemployed friends and acquaintances. With positive probability an employed worker may lose his job. The process of job loss, the arrival of new job information, and the transmission of this information via the network defines a dynamic process. The outcome is the employment status of individuals. The interest is in understanding how the properties of the social network affect the employment prospects of different individuals.

Calvo-Armengol and Jackson (2004) develop three main insights. The *first* insight is that the employment status of two individuals in a connected network is positively correlated. If Mr. A. is employed then it is more likely that he will pass on information about jobs to his neighbors who in turn will pass on information if they are employed. Thus if Mr. A. is employed then it is more likely that his neighbors are employed as well. The *second* insight is that the probability of an individual finding a job is declining with the duration of his unemployment. If Mr. A. has been unemployed for a long time then he must not have received information on jobs from others, and this is more likely if the neighbors are themselves unemployed. But this suggests that it is less likely that they will pass on new information concerning vacancies. Empirical research provides broad support for the positive correlation in employment rates of communities and neighborhoods and also shows that unemployment exhibits duration dependence. The *third* insight pertains to a multiplier effect on sustaining networks: a community with higher unemployment has lower incentives to keep connected. The loss in connections will, however, lower the employment rate, as information on jobs is not passed on. Thus small initial differences in unemployment rates can lead to a sequence of drop outs, which in turn can have large long-run effects on the employment prospects of the group.

Observation 7   *The employment status of workers in a connected network is positively correlated. There is positive duration dependence of unemployment. There is a network multiplier in unemployment: communities with high unemployment have lower incentives to maintain links, the lack of connections raises unemployment rates.*

In Calvo-Armengol and Jackson (2004), prices and competition do not play a role, while in Montgomery (1991) there is no modeling of network topology. There is also no explicit model of network formation in these papers. In a recent paper, Galeotti and Merlino (2014) examine the relation between labor market conditions and the role of social networks in matching vacancies with job seekers. They allow for workers to invest in connections with a view to accessing information that other workers may have. The arguments in Calvo-Armengol and Jackson (2004) suggest that if the firing rate is very high then social connections are less attractive as people will not pass on job information. On the other hand, if the firing rates are very low then there is little value in information on new jobs. So linking is attractive only when there is a moderate "separation" rate in the labor market. The authors build on this observation to show that the inverted-U relation between job separation rate and network investments determines an inverted-U relation between job separation rate and the probability that a worker finds a job through his social contacts. This prediction is consistent with data from the UK labor market.

There is a large literature on search and matching; in this literature search is random and workers are acting in isolation of each other (Rogerson, Shimer, and Wright, 2005). As the networks approach to the study of labor markets matures it would be important to develop models that combine random and network based search. This would be a first step to understanding the relative empirical significance of networks and random search in shaping wages and unemployment.[14]

8.2   Advertising and Pricing

In the standard product market model a firm chooses prices, advertising strategy and quality taking as given heterogenous consumer preferences (Tirole, 1994). The background assumption is that individuals are anonymous and act in isolation of each other. Empirical work, however, suggests that friends, neighbors, and colleagues play an important role in shaping consumer choice. This social influence arises out of information sharing and also due to compatibility pressures. In the past, the practical use of such social influences for advertising or pricing was limited due to the absence of good data on networks. The availability of large amounts of data on online social networking along with the other advances in information technology have led to an exciting new research programme on ways that firms and governments can harness the power of social networks to promote their goals. Practical interest has centered on questions such as: what are the relevant aspects of networks for marketing and competition? How much should a firm be willing to pay to acquire information about social networks?

Galeotti and Goyal (2009) study a simple model of large (directed) networks to study these questions. Their work distinguishes between the *level* and the *content* of social interaction. The level of interaction pertains to the number of people someone talks to (or the number of friends she has). Empirical work over the past decade has generated data on degree distributions across product categories as well as their relation to demographic characteristics of individuals which are traditionally used in design of influence strategies (Leskovec, Adamic, and Huberman, 2007, and Keller, Fay, and Berry, 2007).

The content of social interaction reflects the way in which actions of others' affect individual incentives. In the case of word of mouth communication about product quality and prices, the presence of a single informed neighbor leads to product awareness and possibly purchase. In the case of choice of language a sufficient proportion of neighbors need to choose an action before an individual will switch to this action.

---

[14] See Galenianos (2014) for a model of search and social networks. The role of social networks in addressing information problems is also relevant for an understanding of migration patterns; see, e.g., Munshi (2014) and Beaman (2016).

A first remark concerns the uses of network information: the use of such information reduces waste in advertising resources and generates greater sales. The effectiveness of social influence campaigns can be further increased by using more detailed information – such as the connections of different individuals in the social network. This leads naturally to a study of what is the right target in a network? Galeotti and Goyal (2009) find that that in the word of mouth context it is optimal to target individuals who are poorly connected. By contrast, in the proportional adoption externalities application, it is optimal to seed the most connected individuals (as they are unlikely to adopt via social influence)!

They also show that the effects of networks on profits turn on the content of the interaction. In the word of mouth context, an increase in connectivity enables greater spread of information: this increases sales and profits. On the other hand, if the product exhibits adoption externalities, an increase in connectivity makes it harder to satisfy the requirement that (say) all of them buy a product. Thus, an increase in social interaction in the presence of adoption externalities lowers profits. These considerations are summarized in:

Observation 8 *The nature of optimal targets in networks depends on the content of social interaction: if interaction takes the form of word of mouth communication then poorly connected nodes constitute optimal targets, while in the adoption externality context highly connected nodes are the optimal targets. Greater connectivity raises profits in the case of word of mouth communication, but lowers profits in the case of adoption externalities.*

Galeotti and Goyal (2009) focus on the case with one firm, with one step spread of advertisement, and the firm only chooses advertising. Current research expands the scope of the analysis significantly to include multiple firms, dynamics of spreading information, see, e.g., Fainmesser and Galeotti (2016), Goyal and Kearns (2012), and Campbell (2013). The use of social networks for the optimal diffusion of information remains an active field of research in economics.

In a related line of work, researchers have explored the use of optimal pricing in social networks. In the industrial organization literature, consumer value and hence, pricing, is conditional on the number of consumers who adopt different products (Farrell and Saloner, 1986; Katz and Shapiro 1985). Network externality often arises through the use of common products or services in personal interaction. So it is reasonable to suppose that the value of adopting a product to a consumer should depend on how many of her neighbors adopt the same product. This observation motivates the new strand of research on optimal pricing in networks.

Bloch and Querou (2013) and Candogan, Bimpikis, and Ozdaglar (2012) study the problem of optimal monopoly pricing in social networks where agents care about consumption of their neighbors. Given a profile of prices $\mathbf{p} = (p_1, \ldots, p_n)$, and consumption profile $\mathbf{q} = (q_1, \ldots, q_n)$, an agent i's utility is given by

$$U_i(q_1, ..., q_n) = a_i q_i - \frac{1}{2} b_i q_i^2 + q_i \sum_j g_{ij} q_j - p_i q_i \qquad (10)$$

where g_{ij} measures the influence of i on j and $a_i > 0$ and $b_i > 0$. Observe that an increase in neighbor's consumption raises marginal utility of consumption.[15]

Given prices **p**, under standard conditions there exists a unique consumption equilibrium. The analysis in Candogan, Bimpikis, and Ozdaglar (2012) and Bloch and Querou (2013) yields:

Observation 9 *Denote by G the adjacency matrix reflecting the social relations. The monopolist's optimal price vector satisfies*

$$p = a - \left[\Delta - \frac{G + G^T}{2}\right]^{-1} \frac{a - c\mathbf{1}}{2},$$

where Δ is a diagonal matrix with terms $2b_i$ on the diagonal, **a** the vector of a_is, c is the marginal cost of production and **1** is the vector of 1s.

Observe that if all influences are symmetric, $G = G^T$, and the monopoly sets a uniform price across the network. There are two forces at work: on the one hand, greater connectivity means greater utility and this pushes toward higher prices. On the other hand, greater connectivity also means greater externalities and this pushes towards lower prices to boost direct demand and hence the demand of neighbors. In the linear model under study, these two effects cancel out exactly. Observe that equilibrium consumptions do vary across nodes, and the authors show that they are proportional to the Katz–Bonacich centrality. Pricing in networks remains an active field of research; see Aoyagi (2015) for a model with competition among several firms.

The literature on social networks in product markets is motivated by practical concerns. The models incorporate asymmetric/incomplete information and network externalities. The analysis brings out the advantages of using networks to define optimal targets for advertising and also in shaping optimal pricing: degree distributions and network centrality are the relevant network features. The analysis also highlights the ways in which networks can amplify small differences in resources between competing firms. While much progress has been made, it is clear that we have only a partial understanding of how consumer search and word of mouth communication interacts with firms' advertising.[16]

---

[15] The specification here focuses on local externalities; it is possible to generalize this model to assign weights that decay in path length/distance. The case with no decay would then say that payoffs depend on membership of the same component: this would correspond to the traditional formulation in the industrial organization literature, where payoffs depend only on group size (as in Katz and Shapiro (1985)).

[16] See Galeotti (2010) for a model of social networks with search and pricing in product markets.

8.3   Financial Markets

Financial markets are one context where the paradigm of competitive markets, and common prices that reveal information of all traders, remains dominant. In recent years, empirical research has shown that social networks play a prominent role in shaping trading activity. I present a brief overview of this work.

Cohen, Frazzini, and Malloy (2008) show that portfolio managers place larger bets on firms where they have social connected senior managers or board members. Interestingly, these investments also yield higher returns. Similarly, Hong, Kubik, and Stein (2005) present evidence that US fund managers located in the same city commit to correlated investment decisions. Such correlated choices may be due to peer-to-peer communication or because fund managers in a given area base their decisions upon common sources of information. This empirical research motivates a formal analysis of the relation between information social networks and trader behavior and aggregate outcomes on volume and prices.

Ozsoylev and Walden (2011) and Colla and Melle (2010) study asset pricing in markets where traders are located in information networks. They study trader behavior and derive relations between trader behavior, prices and trading volume, and the network topology. For a general overview of networks in finance, see Allen and Babus (2009).

9   TRANSPORT NETWORKS

Firms (and governments) create infrastructure and price access on these networks. Traditionally, interest has focused on pricing issues; for a survey, see Altman and Wynter (2002) and Laffont and Tirole (2001). Moreover, as transport networks compete for passengers and for revenue, it is natural to view network formation as a competitive process. This section discusses the elegant work of Hendricks, Piccione, and Tan (1995, 1999) on airline networks.

Historically, airlines have been either publicly owned or heavily regulated. This has meant that both the routing as well as the pricing of services has been controlled in a variety of ways. In recent years, the airline market has been liberalized greatly in the US and Europe and also in other parts of the world. This has been accompanied by new entry and a significant fall in prices. Market concentration has gone up in direct flights but has come down in indirect flights. Airline networks increasingly exhibit a *hub–spoke* structure (with most flights being routed through a single city).

Following Hendricks, Piccione, and Tan (1995), consider a single airline serving set of cities $N = 1, 2, \ldots, n$, $n \geq 3$. Travel is one-way (from city i to city j). People living in a city wish to travel to other cities. Let i, j index cities. A direct connection is a nonstop flight from i to j. Operating the flight entails a variety of costs, such as check-in counters and ticketing. So suppose that one direct connection serves both routes i to j and j to i. For simplicity, suppose that there is a fixed cost of operating a direct link between any pair of cities, given by $F > 0$. The network of direct flights between the n cities is an (undirected) graph g. The profits of the airline is revenue minus fixed costs. The revenue (net of variable costs) is additively separable across city-market pairs. For each city pair, the revenue depends solely on the length of the path a traveler has to cross. Let $\pi(z)$ denote the revenue for a carrier when z is the length of path. It is reasonable to suppose that revenue is falling in path length. The analysis of Hendricks, Piccione, and Tan (1995) is summarized in:

Observation 10 *Suppose that revenue is falling in path length. Then there exist link cost levels F^* and F^{**}, such that for $F < F^*$ the complete network is optimal, for $F^* < F < F^{**}$ the hub–spoke network is optimal, and for $F^{**} < F$ the empty network is optimal.*

The proof builds on the trade-off between number of links versus path length: increasing direct flights is costly but raises revenue. The hub–spoke network balances the objectives perfectly: it contains the minimum number of links for any connected network and at the same time is also has short paths lengths (the maximum path length is 2). So if direct paths are attractive between two peripheral airports then, from separability, this must be true for all pairs of airports: the complete network with direct point-to-point flights between every pair of cities must be optimal.

In a subsequent paper, Hendricks, Piccione, and Tan (1999) study competition between two airlines who choose flight networks. They develop a two-stage game in which two carriers simultaneously choose their networks and then compete for travelers. The carrier offering the shorter path between any city pair has a competitive advantage because length is costly for the traveler. They restrict attention to costs where a point to point network is unattractive, even for a monopolist. The paper studies the relationship between the severity of competition and the architecture of routing networks. In the setting of aggressive competition (e.g., Bertrand-like behavior), monopoly is an equilibrium outcome: a single carrier operates a hub–spoke network. Both airlines operating hub–spoke networks cannot be sustained in equilibrium. By contrast, in the setting of nonaggressive competition, there exists an equilibrium with competing hub–spoke networks (when the number of cities is not too small). Figure 7 represents the outcomes.

We have discussed competition between networks within the specific setting of demand for transport. But the problem is of more general interest. The next section takes up networks in the context of the theory of the firm.

10   THE NATURE OF THE FIRM

Following the early work of Coase (1937), and more recently that of Williamson (1975), it is customary to partition economic exchange as taking place in the "market" (anonymous, arms-length) or within a firm (in a

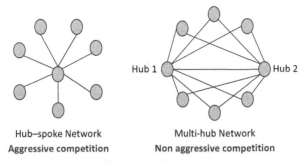

Hub-spoke Network   Multi-hub Network
Aggressive competition   **Non aggressive competition**

Figure 7 Airline Routing Networks.

hierarchy). Empirical work, however, suggests that firms maintain a variety of durable relationships; research alliances and capacity sharing agreements are two prominent examples. Moreover, individuals in a firm maintain social relations with individuals in other firms and these social relations shape the behavior of the different firms. These empirical observations have motivated the expression, "network forms of organization" (Powell, 1990). I start by discussing research alliances and capacity sharing agreements in a static setting and then turn to the dynamics of inter-firm relations.

In some industries, firms procure standardized inputs from arm's length markets, in others firms vertically integrate and produce their own specialized inputs, and there are prominent examples in which firms maintain ties with a stable set of suppliers (Uzzi, 1996). What determines these patterns? The discussion elaborates on the circumstances in which networks of buyers and sellers perform better than vertically integrated markets or spot exchange markets.

Following Kranton and Minehart (2000), suppose that there is a set of buyers $B = \{b_1, b_2, \ldots, b_m\}$ and a set of sellers $S = \{s_1, s_2, \ldots, s_n\}$. Every buyer demands a single unit of an input. This input can come in two types: it can be a (normalized) zero-value *standard* input or a positive-value *specialized* input. The buyer can buy the *standard* input from a competitive fringe of input suppliers at a price normalized to zero. Alternatively, a buyer can vertically integrate and produce a *specialized* input itself, by investing in a *dedicated* asset, at a cost $\alpha_d > 0$. Finally, a buyer can create links with sellers of *specialized* inputs ("specialists"). Each link costs $c > 0$ to a buyer.

A buyer i has a random valuation v_i for a specialized input, with $v_i = z + \varepsilon_i$, where z and ε_i are random variables. Assume that z is a common shock to all buyers, with mean $\bar{z} > 0$. The variable ε_i is a buyer-specific shock which has mean 0. There are S specialists who can produce just one specialized input. A buyer who acquires the input from a seller needs to have a link with that seller. As mentioned above, building the link costs $c > 0$ to the buyer. A seller needs to invest $\alpha_f > 0$ in a *flexible* asset to be able to produce a specialized input. Assume $\alpha_f = \alpha_d = \alpha$ for simplicity. Once the investment is made, the seller can satisfy the needs of different buyers, i.e., the seller is a *flexible* specialist.

An *industrial structure*, g, is formed by the investments of the buyers and the sellers. Networks involve buyers' specific investments and sellers' quasi-specific investments.

I start by looking at welfare maximizing industrial structures. Fix an industrial structure (or network) g and a vector $v = (v_1, v_2, \ldots, v_m)$ of (realized) buyers' valuations. Let $A(v, g)$ be an *allocation* of goods given buyers' valuations v and the industrial structure g. The economic surplus derived from an allocation of goods in an industrial structure g is $w(v, A(v, g))$. The allocation $A^*(v, g)$ is *efficient* if $w(v, A^*(v, g)) \geq w(v, A(v, g))$, for all feasible $A(v, g)$. For an industrial structure g, the expected surplus is $E_v[w(v, A^*(v, g))]$ and expected welfare is then

$$W(g) = E_v[w(v, A^*(v, g))] - \alpha \sum_{i=1}^{B} \delta_i(g) - c \sum_{i=1}^{B} l_i(g) - \alpha \sum_{j=1}^{S} \kappa_j(g), \quad (11)$$

where $\delta_i(g) = 1$ when buyer i is vertically integrated and equals zero otherwise, $l_i(g)$ is the number of links buyer i maintains, and $\kappa_j(g) = 1$ when seller j has invested in productive capacity and equals zero otherwise. We shall say that an industrial structure g is *efficient* if $W(g) \geq W(g')$ for all networks $g' \neq g$. Kranton and Minehart (2000) establish:

Observation 11 *If buyers valuations are widely dispersed, productive capacity is expensive, and costs of linking are modest, then a network structure is efficient.*

I now turn to the question of whether buyers and sellers have the right incentives to form efficient network structures. Consider the following simple two-stage game. In the first stage, buyers choose unilaterally whether to invest in a dedicated asset (which costs them α), or to create links (which costs them c), or not to invest at all. Likewise, sellers choose whether to invest in a flexible asset (which costs them α) or not to invest at all. In the second stage, buyers' valuations are realized and production and exchange takes place. I look at the case where the exchange is competitive (modeled as in Kranton and Minehart, 2001), i.e., as having sellers holding simultaneously ascending-bid auctions and buyers bidding truthfully).

In a network, sellers simultaneously hold ascending-bid auctions. It is optimal for a buyer to remain in the auction of all his linked sellers until the price reaches his valuation. Anticipating *competitive* revenues, what are buyers' incentives to create links? Kranton and Minehart (2000) show that, given sellers' investments, a link contributes to the buyer the same amount as it contributes to social welfare. The conclusion here is that with this price formation protocol, buyers and sellers will form network industrial structure when it is efficient. (This is reminiscent of the results in the Kranton and Minehart, 2001 model of buyer and seller networks.)

I next turn to research alliances among firms. Firms increasingly choose to collaborate in research with other firms. This research collaboration takes a variety of forms and is aimed both at lowering costs of production as well as improving product quality and introducing entirely new products. Indeed, Hagedoorn (2002) argues that there has been a significant increase in the level of collaborative research among firms. Two features of this collaboration activity have been highlighted. The first feature is that firms enter into a number of relationships with non-overlapping sets of firms: in other words, the relations are nonexclusive. The second feature is that firms often collaborate with other firms within the same market, giving rise to a complex relation which combines cooperation and competition. Example 2 (presented in Section 2), illustrated the effects of collaboration networks on firms' research activity and profits. I now discuss the formation of research networks.

Following Goyal and Joshi (2003), suppose there are $N = (1, 2, 3, \ldots, n)$, with $n \geq 2$ firms. Consider a link announcement game along the lines of Myerson (1991). A link costs $F > 0$ to each firm and lowers their marginal costs of production by $c > 0$. The links constitute an alliance network that defines a vector of firm costs. The rewards from a link depend on market competition. Strong competition refers to the case where only the unique lowest cost firm makes profits (Bertrand competition with homogenous goods is an example). Moderate competition refers to the case where lower costs imply higher profits (examples include Cournot competition with homogenous goods and price competition with differentiated goods).

Goyal and Joshi (2003) show that markets and linking activity interact in interesting ways with potentially large welfare effects. They show that with strong competition, the empty network (with no links), is the unique pairwise equilibrium. With moderate competition, the complete network (with all links present) is the unique pairwise equilibrium. The intuition is as follows: In the case of strong competition, no two firms can hope to make money in a non-empty network. Anticipating this outcome, firms form no links. On the other hand, under moderate competition, if two firms form a link, both lower costs, and therefore increase their profits, at the expense of other firms. Thus any incomplete network is vulnerable to a profitable deviation. Figure 8 represent these outcomes. This is a simple result but it has an important message: There is a two way flow of influence between markets and networks. Markets shape

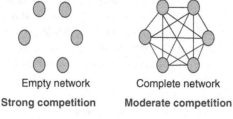

Empty network   Complete network

Strong competition   Moderate competition

Figure 8 Stable Collaboration Networks.

incentives to create links, but these networks in turn define costs and therefore shape the nature of competition.

These differences in the network can have potentially large welfare effects. Define social surplus as the sum of firm profits and consumers surplus. Goyal and Joshi (2003) show that under strong competition the efficient network entails a core–periphery network (with two fully linked firms in the core), whereas with moderate competition the efficient network is complete. These observations are summarized in:

Observation 12   *Suppose the cost of a link, F, is small.*

1. *With strong competition, the empty network, (with no links), is the outcome. With moderate competition, the complete network is the outcome.*
2. *Under strong competition the efficient network is a core–periphery network (with two fully linked firms); under moderate competition the efficient network is complete.*

Thus efficient networks are formed under moderate competition, but there is a divergence between individual incentives and efficiency under strong competition. This suggests that moderate competition may attain greater efficiency, due to the endogeneity of networks.

So far, the focus has been on the setting with small costs of linking. I now briefly discuss large costs of linking. To make progress, consider the linear demand homogenous good Cournot model. It turns out that, in this model, the marginal returns may be written in a compact form as a function of own links and of the sum of all links amongst the other firms. In particular, marginal returns are increasing in own links and they are declining in the sum of links of others. This property of payoffs immediately implies that if two firms have links then they must be linked. Thus, any (equilibrium) network must consist of a set of firms in a complete component and a set of isolated firms. The empty network and the complete network are limit cases of this class of networks.

This result also reveals that highly connected firms have an incentive to subsidize links with isolated firms (who may not find it profitable to form a link). Goyal and Joshi (2003) show that when firms can make transfers, the star network and multiple-hub networks are stable. Figure 9 represents these networks. The reason for these increasing marginal returns from own links and falling marginal returns in links of others: The central firm in a star has high marginal returns from an additional link, while peripheral firms with a single link have low marginal returns. Simple computations reveal that in these networks, the central highly connected firm earn higher profits compared to the peripheral firms. The analysis of efficient networks for large costs of linking is presented in Westbrock (2010).

More generally, given the increasing returns to own links, it follows that if a firm is linked to a firm with k links then it must also be linked to every firm

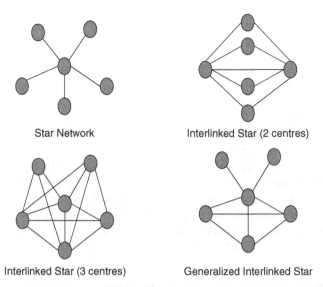

Star Network   Interlinked Star (2 centres)

Interlinked Star (3 centres)   Generalized Interlinked Star

Figure 9 Stable Collaboration Networks with Transfers.

with k or more links. This observation is central to the construction of nested graphs, that have been developed in the more recent work of Koenig, Tessone, and Zenou (2014).

I have discussed models of networks and firms where information is symmetric. In actual practice, a firm is more likely to know about the knowledge and skills of other firms with whom it has had past collaborations. Similarly, individual firms are likely to have significant private knowledge about own efforts and skills. In the context of research and development, formal contracts will typically not be able to address these problems fully. So firms may prefer repeated collaboration with existing collaboration partners or with firms about whom they can get reliable information via existing and past common partners. In other words, the network structure of past collaborations may well play an important role in shaping the performance of existing collaborations as well as the pattern of new collaborations. These considerations constitute key elements in the argument on the social embeddedness of economic activity (Granovetter, 1985; Raub and Weesie, 1990).[17]

Two questions have received attention: what types of firms enter into collaborative agreements and with whom? In a dynamic setting, there is the issue of how the existing pattern of collaboration links relates to the governance structure of a new collaboration partnership – do firms write a formal contract or are loose research sharing agreements sufficient? There

---

[17] Scientific collaboration shares some features in common with research alliances among firms; for an empirical investigation of the role of networks in fostering co-authorship in economics, see Fafchamps, Goyal, and van der Leij (2010) and Ductor, Fafchamps, Goyal, and van der Leij (2014).

is a large empirical literature on this question; see, e.g., Kogut, Sham, and Walker (1994), Gulati (2007), Powell, Koput, and Smith-Doerr (1996). The formal study of evolving relations in a network with asymmetric information, appears to be an open problem. For an early study of repeated games on fixed networks with exchange of information among players, see Haag and Lagunoff (2006). For a survey of the theory of repeated games on networks, see Nava (2016).

The second issue concerns the governance of network forms of organization. Empirical work has examined the nature of contracts and governance structures which define collaboration links between firms. This work suggests that collaboration agreements become less formal if partners are embedded in social networks of previous collaboration links (Gulati, 2007). This is suggestive of the growth of trust via participation of firms in a social network of collaborative links. We lack a formal model where the issue of contract form or complexity can be examined in relation to networks of trust.

11   THE GREAT TRANSFORMATION: SHIFTING BOUNDARIES

The Great Transformation refers to the large scale changes in political, legal and social structure during the process of industrialization. The traditional view, following Polanyi (1944) is that economic activity was more embedded in social ties in pre-industrial than it is in modern societies. In recent years, this view has been contested by a distinguished group of scholars; for an influential statement, see Granovetter (1985).[18]

While these arguments are timely, it is worth noting that arguments on the relation between social ties and markets have older, and very distinguished, antecedents. There is, on the one hand, the classical *doux-commerce* stance, going back to the eighteenth century (Montesquieu, 1748; Paine, 1792; Condorcet, 1795). It argues that markets create new opportunities for exchange, and these opportunities require that individuals cooperate with each other. Therefore, markets broaden the scope and hence reinforce social ties. Other scholars have argued that the expansion of markets are accompanied by wide ranging changes in attitudes and institutions, and these changes crowd out social ties (Polanyi, 1944; Thompson, 1971; Scott, 1977; Sandel, 2012). For eloquent accounts of this debate, see Hirschman (1977, 1982), and for a recent review of the debate, see Besley (2012). This argument takes the view that community-based economies, or *moral economies*, rest on norms of reciprocity and markets represent an outside option that undermine such norms. This section presents formal models and empirical evidence to assess the scope and validity of these arguments.

---

[18] The large literature on the role of social capital in economic and political performance must be mentioned here: Coleman (1988), Putnam (1993) and Dasgupta and Serageldin (1999).

I start with the discussion of an early paper by Kranton (1996) that develops an elegant model to explore the scope of the second line of reasoning.[19] She takes the view that community-based exchange involves reciprocity: I do you a favor today and you reciprocate in kind at a later date. Individuals who do not fulfill their obligations are punished by a termination of the favor exchange relationship; the seriousness of this punishment depends on the presence of alternatives. Thus the availability and size of a spot market where agents can anonymously exchange will affect the enforceability of reciprocal exchange. The size of the market is important because it shapes the costs of obtaining goods/services: thin markets raise the costs of search, while thick markets reduce them. The more individuals engage in reciprocal exchange, the less they need to rely on markets to obtain goods and services and vice versa. Thus there is a negative externality from markets to reciprocal exchange. These arguments are summarized in:

Observation 13 *Reciprocal-exchange and markets are substitutes and both constitute a self-sustaining system.*

What about welfare? The key issue here is substitutability of goods: in reciprocal relations individuals are obliged to accept whatever their partner provides. This restricts the range of goods. So if commodities are substitutable, reciprocal exchange is efficient while if goods are poor substitutes then markets are efficient. Putting together these points with the last observation above suggests the following reinforcement dynamics: starting from an initial situation in which most people are engaged in reciprocal exchange the system may well persist as no one wishes to enter the market due to the high search costs. On the other hand, if a large fraction of the population is in the market (or if a national government opens up its economy to global markets) then reciprocal relations may gradually shrink and disappear.

The defining feature of the above model is that markets and community are mutually exclusive: one can grow only as the expense of the other. But the empirical evidence on this subject is mixed. I present two examples to illustrate this point.

Example 6 *Caste Networks and Globalization*

Munshi and Rosenzweig (2006) explore the impact of economic liberalization of the Indian economy in the 1990s. This led to a shift toward the corporate and finance sectors, which increased the returns to white-collar jobs, for which knowledge of English was necessary. The authors estimate that in the city of Mumbai, the premium to English education (compared to education in the local

---

[19] For a recent study on the practice of bilateral favor exchange and its implications for the functioning of markets, see Bramoulle and Goyal (2016).

language, Marathi) went up by roughly 25 percent, over the 1990s. Crucially, the authors note that caste connections are (i) central for jobs search in the blue collar sector, but not in the white collar sector, and (ii) the networks are accessible to males but not the females.

Their main finding is about the effects of market liberalization on schooling. Boys adopted English language much less than their female counterparts: thus those with less access to the traditional network joined the market more. The gap in English education between girls of high and low castes shrank, but the gap for boys remained (roughly) intact. Moreover, participation in markets led to an erosion in the traditional networks.   □

Example 7 *The Digital Provide: Mobile Telephones and Social Connections*

The expansion of mobile telephony in developing countries and its potential for large development impact has been extensively commented upon (see, e.g., Aker and Mbiti, 2010). Jensen (2007) studies the impact of mobile telephones on fishermen in Kerala, India in the 1990s. Prior to the introduction of cellphones, fishermen fished and sold their catch almost exclusively within their local catchment zone. The adoption of cellphones had a large and differential impact. Fishermen could now exchange information with buyers, friends and relatives, and auctioneers while at sea, therefore obtaining precious information about the demand in different fish markets. By 2001, more than 65 percent of all fishing boats in Kerala owned a cellphone. Adoption was significantly higher for fishermen with larger boats.

Fishermen raised their participation in the market along with more intensive use of social connections (in communication). Moreover, it was the larger boats with a more extensive set of connections that took greater advantage of the new opportunities. This had significant implications for welfare and inequality.   □

These two empirical studies motivate a theoretical framework that includes both substitutes and complements relations between markets and networks and that that allows for heterogeneity in social connections.[20]

Following Gagnon and Goyal (2016), I consider a model where individuals located in a social structure choose a *network* action (x) and a *market* action (y). Payoffs to action x are increasing in the number of neighbors in the social structure who adopt the same action: this captures the local externalities in network activity. In contrast, market exchange is monetized, anonymous and short term, and agents are price-takers: payoffs to action y are independent of the decisions of others. The actions x and y may be *complements* or *substitutes*.

The authors start with the observation that behavior in this setting is described in terms of a simple network property: the q-core. To develop some

---

[20] Informal insurance remains important in developing countries (see Townsend, 1994; Ambrus, Mobius, and Szeidl, 2014; and Ambrus, Elliott, and Chandrasekhar, 2015). The relationship between social networks and markets is central to an understanding of the take-up of formal insurance schemes (see Gagnon and Goyal, 2016 and Mobarak and Rosenzweig, 2012).

intuition for this notion note that the payoffs to x depend on the number of one's neighbors who adopt x; adoption decisions of neighbors are in turn a function of how many of their neighbors adopt x, and so forth. This leads naturally to the notion of a set of individuals who each have a threshold number of neighbors, whose neighbors in turn each have this threshold neighbors, and so forth. The *q-core* of a graph is the maximal set of individuals having strictly more than q links with other individuals belonging to this set. Figure 10 illustrates the derivation of the 4-core in a network, through the progressive elimination of nodes that have 4 or fewer links.

The characterization of behavior in terms of the q-core allows a study of a number of questions.

First, consider the issue of who participates in markets and what sorts of social structure facilitate market participation. Gagnon and Goyal (2016) show that in the substitutes case, it is the individuals outside the q-core who take part in market exchange; by contrast, in the case of complements, it is the individuals within the (appropriate) q-core who do so. Denser networks will have a larger q-core and so will witness lower market participation in case of substitutes and higher adoption with complements.

Next consider welfare (defined as the sum of payoffs of all individuals). The authors show that markets may lower aggregate welfare when the actions are substitutes but that they always raise it in the case of complements. The intuition is that when someone joins the market (chooses y) and "leaves the network" (drops x) she imposes a network externality on her neighbors who stay with x. This negative effect may outweigh the personal rewards of joining the market. In the complements case, market exchange raises marginal payoffs of network action and thus "raises all boats".

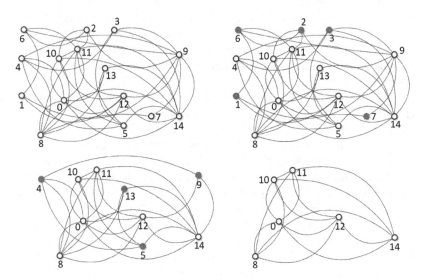

Figure 10 The 4-core.

The analysis also yields a crisp prediction on inequality: markets typically raise inequality in case of complements but always lower inequality in the case of substitutes. The reason is that with complements the marginal returns are highest for the "well-connected" members of the social network. In the substitutes case, the market action offers an outside option to individuals who benefit the least from the network, and therefore has the potential to reduce inequality. These points are summarized in:

Observation 14   *1. In the case of substitutes, members of the relevant q-core participate in the network activity and those outside it move to the market. The converse is true in case of complements.*

2. Market participation is higher in a denser network in case of complements but lower in the case of substitutes.

3. Welfare is always raised by the emergence of a market in case of complements, but may fall in case of substitutes.

4. Markets typically increase inequality in the case of complements but lowers inequality in the case of substitutes.

To close the circle, I now briefly return to the two empirical case studies discussed above and map them onto the model presented in Gagnon and Goyal (2016).

In the Caste Networks and Globalization setting, the action x refers to Marathi language while action y refers to English language schooling. The payoffs to x are correlated with participation in caste working class networks. The social connections mainly cover jobs for young men: so young men are well connected in large sub-castes; girls are poorly connected. The authors tell us that market liberalization raises returns to English. The model predicts that in response adoption of English should be higher for girls than for boys and that gender inequality should decrease. These predictions are consistent with the empirical patterns identified in Munshi and Rosenzweig (2006).

Turning to impact of mobile telephony, note that payoffs of fishermen are given by sales. The sales depend on information about prices in local fish markets. Let action x refer to "obtaining information," y refer to "owning a cell phone." Information sharing with social contacts becomes more profitable when combined with the purchase of a mobile phone. The model predicts that fishermen (with bigger boats and) with more contacts are more likely to adopt mobile telephony and that this will raise inequality. This is consistent with the empirical patterns identified in Jensen (2007).

More generally, these discussions suggest that the dynamics between markets and social networks exhibit interesting nonlinearities. One technology can lead to the relative decline in one function of social networks, while a subsequent technology can lead to a revival of the same function (or the development of a new role for social networks).[21] I illustrate this point with a topical example.

Through much of human history, news was passed on through private communication. Indeed, the Royal Society was set up in London in 1660 in an attempt to formalize such private communication through weekly meetings. The growth of newspapers, television and radio through the nineteenth and twentieth centuries gradually led to a decline in the role of social interaction in communication. It is possible that we are witnessing witnessing a reversal of this movement. The explosive growth of online social networks is a defining feature of the last decade. The Reuters Institute for the Study of Journalism (RISJ) reports that more than half the population of many countries (e.g., Brazil, Spain, Italy, and Finland) use Facebook for news purposes (RISJ, 2014). This rise of online news has proceeded in tandem with a sharp decline in traditional newspaper markets (Newman, 2009; Currah, 2009). For an entertaining account of the fall and rise of social networks as vehicles for communication of news, see Standage (2013).

12 CONCLUDING REMARKS

The origins of a systematic study of networks in economics can be traced to the 1990s. At the start, both the research on social learning and the research on network formation emerged in relative autonomy from applications and empirical work. As the theoretical findings came in contact with substantive issues in economics, research gathered momentum: networks now combine with the classical ideas of competition, prices and information to offer an encompassing framework for economic analysis.

References

Abreu, D., and M. Manea (2012a), "Markov Equilibria in a Model of Bargaining in Networks," *Games and Economic Behavior*, 75, 1–16.

Abreu, D., and M. Manea (2012b), "Bargaining and Efficiency in Networks," *Journal of Economic Theory*, 147, 43–70.

Acemoglu, D., V. Carvalho, A. Ozdaglar and A.Tahbaz-Salehi (2012), "The Network Origins of Aggregate Fluctuations," *Econometrica*, 80, 5, 1977–2016.

Acemoglu, D., M.A. Dahleh, I. Lobel, A. and Ozdaglar (2011), "Bayesian Learning in Social Networks," *Review of Economic Studies*, 78, 1201–46.

Acemoglu, D., and A. Ozdaglar (2007), "Competition and Efficiency in Congested Markets," *Mathematics of Operations Research*, 32, 1, 1–31.

Acemoglu, D., A. Ozdaglar and A. Tahbaz-Salehi (2015), "Systemic Risk and Stability in Financial Networks," *American Economic Review*, 105, 2, 564–608.

---

[21] For an overview of the impact of modern communication technologies on the relation between anonymous markets and social network based exchange, see Sundararajan (2016).

Acemoglu, D., A. Ozdaglar and A. Tahbaz-Salehi (2016), "Networks. Shocks and Systemic Risk," in *Oxford Handbook on Economics of Networks*, edited by Y. Bramoulle, A. Galeotti and B. Rogers. Oxford University Press.

Afonso, G., and R. Lagos (2012), "Trade dynamics in the market for federal funds." *Federal Reserve of New York Staff Report.*

Aker, J., and I. Mbiti (2010), "Mobile Telephones and Economic Development in Africa." *Journal of Economic Perspectives*, 24, 3, 207–32.

Allen, F., and A. Babus (2009), "Networks in Finance," in *Network-Based Strategies and Competencies*, edited by P. Kleindorfer and J. Wind, 367–82.

Altman, E., and L. Wynter (2002), "Equilibrium, Games, and Pricing in Transportation and Telecommunication Networks," *INRA Research Report* RR-4632.

Ambrus, A., Chandrasekhar, A. G. and M. Elliott (2015), "Social Investments, Informal Risk Sharing, and Inequality." *Economic Research Initiatives Duke (ERID) Working Paper*, no. 179.

Ambrus, A., M. Mobius and A. Szeidl (2014), "Consumption Risk-Sharing in Social Networks," *American Economic Review*, 104, 1, 149–82,

Antras, P. (2015), *Global Production: Firms, Contracts, and Trade Structure*. Princeton University Press.

Aoyagi, M. (2015), "Bertrand Competition Under Network Externalities," *The Institute of Social and Economic Research Discussion Paper 884*, Osaka University.

Aumann, R., and R. Myerson (1988), "Endogenous Formation of Links Between Players and Coalitions: An Application to the Shapley Value," in *The Shapley Value*, edited by A. Roth, 175–91, Cambridge: Cambridge University Press.

Babus, A. (2016), "The Formation of Financial Networks." *Rand Journal of Economics*, 47, 2, 239–72.

Baccara, M., and H. Bar-Isaac (2008), "How to Organize Crime," *Review of Economic Studies*, 75, 4, 1039–67.

Bala, V., and S. Goyal (1998), "Learning from Neighbours," *Review of Economic Studies* 65, 595–621.

Bala, V., and S. Goyal (2000), "A Non-Cooperative Model of Network Formation," *Econometrica*, 68, 5, 1181–31.

Bala, V., and S. Goyal (2001), "Conformism and Diversity Under Social Learning," *Economic Theory*, 17, 101–20.

Ballester, C., A. Calvo-Armengol and Y. Zenou (2006), "Who's Who in Networks. Wanted: The Key Player." *Econometrica*, 74, 1403–17.

Banerjee, A., A. Chandrasekhar, E. Duflo and M.O. Jackson (2013), "The Diffusion of Microfinance," *Science Magazine*, 341, 6144.

Beaman, L. (2016), "Social Networks and the Labor Market," in *Oxford Handbook on Economics of Networks*, edited by Y. Bramoulle, A. Galeotti and B. Rogers. Oxford University Press.

Bech, M. L., and E. Atalay (2010), "The Topology of the Federal Funds Market." *Physica A: Statistical Mechanics and its Applications*, 389, 22, 5223–46.

Besley, T. (2012), "What's the Good of the Market? An Essay on Michael Sandel's *What Money Can't Buy*." *Journal of Economic Literature*, 51(2), 478–95.

Bloch, F., and B. Dutta (2012), "Formation of Networks and Coalitions," in *Social Economics*, edited by A. Bisin, J. Benhabib and M. Jackson. Amsterdam: North Holland.

Bloch, F., and N. Querou (2013), "Pricing in Social Networks," *Games and Economic Behavior*, 80, 263–81.

Blochl, F., J. F. Theis, F. Vega-Redondo and E. O'N. Fisher (2011), "Vertex Centralities in Input-Output Networks Reveal the Structure of Modern Economies," *Physical Review E*, 83, 046127.

Blume, L., D. Easley, J. Kleinberg and E. Tardos (2007), "Trading Networks with Price-Setting Agents," in *Proceedings of the 8th ACM Conference on Electronic Commerce EC 2007* New York, NY, USA.

Blume, L., D. Easley, J. Kleinberg, R. Kleinberg and E. Tardos (2011), "Network Formation in the Presence of Contagious Risk," *Proceedings of the 12th ACM Conference on Electronic Commerce EC 2011EC.*

Bollobás, B. (1998), *Modern Graph Theory*, Berlin: Springer Verlag.

Boorman, S. (1975), "A Combinatorial Optimization Model for Transmission of Job Information Through Contact Networks," *Bell Journal of Economics*, 6, 1, 216–49.

Bramoulle, Y., A. Galeotti and B. Rogers (2016), *The Oxford Handbook of the Economics of Networks*. Oxford University Press.

Bramoulle. Y., and S. Goyal (2016), "Favoritism," *Journal of Development Economics*, forthcoming.

Bramoulle, Y., and R. Kranton (2007), "Public Goods in Networks," *Journal of Economic Theory*, 135, 478–94.

Bramoulle, Y., and R. Kranton (2016), "Games Played on Networks," in *Oxford Handbook on Economics of Networks*, edited by Y. Bramoulle, A. Galeotti and B. Rogers. Oxford University Press.

Burdett, K., and K. Judd (1983), "Equilibrium Price Dispersion," *Econometrica*, 51, 4, 955–69.

Burt, R. (1992), *Structural Holes: The Social Structure of Competition.* Harvard University Press.

Cabrales, A., P. Gottardi and F. Vega-Redondo (2016), "Risk-Sharing and Contagion in Networks." *Working paper*. Florence: EUI.

Calvo-Armengol, A., and M. O. Jackson (2004), "The Effects of Social Networks on Employment and Inequality," *American Economic Review*, 94, 3, 426–54.

Campbell, A. (2013), "Word-of-Mouth Communication and Percolation in Social Networks." *American Economic Review*, 103, 6, 2466–98.

Candogan, O., K. Bimpikis and S. Ehsani (2015), "Supply Disruptions and Optimal Network Structures," *mimeo*, Chicago and Stanford.

Candogan, O., K. Bimpikis, A. Ozdaglar (2012), "Optimal Pricing in Networks with Externalities," *Operations Research*, 60, 4, 883–905

Cappellari L. and K. Tatsiramos (2010), "Friends' Networks and Job Finding Rates," *IZA Discussion Paper No. 524, Institute for the Study of Labor (IZA).*

Carvalho, V. (2014), "From Micro to Macro via Production Networks." *Journal of Economic Perspectives*, 28, 4, 23–48.

Charness, G., M. Corominas-Bosch and G. Frechete (2007), "Bargaining and Network Structure: An Experiment," *Journal of Economic Theory*, 136, 1, 28–65.

Chandrasekhar, A. (2016), "The Econometrics of Network Formation," in *The Oxford Handbook of the Economics of Networks*, edited by Y. Bramoulle, A. Galeotti and B. Rogers. Oxford University Press.

Choi, S., A. Galeotti and S. Goyal (2016), "Trading in Networks: Theory and Experiments," *Journal of European Economic Association*, forthcoming.

Choi, S., E. Gallo, and S. Kariv (2016), "Networks in the Laboratory," in *The Oxford Handbook of the Economics of Networks*, edited by Y. Bramoulle, A. Galeotti and B. Rogers. Oxford University Press.

Cingano, F., and A. Rosolia (2012), "People I Know: Job Search and Social Networks," *Journal of Labor Economics*, 30, 291–332.

Coase, R. (1937), "The Nature of the Firm," *Economica* 4, 16, 386–405.

Cohen, L., A. Frazzini, and C. Malloy (2008), "The Small World of Investing: Board Connections and Mutual Fund Returns." *Journal of Political Economy*, 116, 951–79.

Coleman, J. (1966), *Medical Innovation: A Diffusion Study*. New York: Bobbs-Merrill.

Coleman, J. (1988), "Social Capital in the Creation of Human Capital," *American Journal of Sociology*, 94, S95–S120.

Colla, P., and A. Melle (2010), "Information Linkages and Correlated Trading," *Review of Financial Studies*, 23, 203–46.

Condorcet, M.J.A.C. (1998) [1795]. *Esquisse d'un Tableau Historique du Progres de l'Esprit Humain*. Paris: Flammarion.

Condorelli, D., and A. Galeotti (2016), "Strategic Models of Intermediation Networks," in *The Oxford Handbook of the Economics of Networks*, edited by Y. Bramoulle, A. Galeotti and B. Rogers. Oxford University Press.

Condorelli, D., A. Galeotti and L. Renou (2016), "Bilateral Trading in Networks," *Review of Economic Studies*, 01, 1–40.

Corominas-Bosch, M. (2004), "Bargaining in a Network of Buyers and Sellers," *Journal of Economic Theory*, 115, 1, 35–77.

Currah, A. (2009), *What's Happening to Our News: An Investigation into the Likely Impact of the Digital Revolution on the Economics of News Publishing in the UK*. Oxford: Reuters Institute for the Study of Journalism.

Costinot, A., J. Vogel and S. Wang (2012), "An Elementary Theory of Global Supply Chains," *Review of Economic Studies*, 80, 109–44.

Dasgupta, P., and I. Serageldin (1999), *Social Capital: A Multifaceted Perspective*. Washington, DC: World Bank Publications.

Ductor, L., M. Fafchamps, S. Goyal, and M. van der Leij (2014), "Social Networks and Research Output," *Review of Economics and Statistics*, 96, 5, 936–48.

Durlauf, S. (1993), "Nonergodic Economic Growth," *The Review of Economic Studies*, 60, 2, 349–66.

Dziubinski, M., and S. Goyal (2016), "How Do You Defend a Network?" *Theoretical Economics*, forthcoming.

Dziubinski, M., S. Goyal and A. Vigier (2016), "Conflict and Networks," in *The Oxford Handbook of the Economics of Networks*, edited by Y. Bramoulle, A. Galeotti and B. Rogers. Oxford University Press.

Easley, D., and J. Kleinberg (2010), *Crowds, Networks and Markets: Reasoning About a Highly Connected World*. Cambridge University Press.

Elliott, M. (2015), "Inefficiencies in Networked Markets," *American Economic Journal: Microeconomics*, 7, 4, 43–82

Elliott, M., B. Golub and M.O. Jackson (2014), "Financial Networks and Contagion." *American Economic Review*, 104, 10, 3115–53.

Elliott, M., and J. Hazel (2015), "Endogenous Financial Networks: Efficient Modularity and Why Shareholders Prevent it," *mimeo*, Cambridge.

Elliott, M. and F. Nava (2015), "Decentralized Bargaining: Efficiency and the Core," *mimeo*, Cambridge and LSE.

Fafchamps, M., S. Goyal, and M. van der Leij (2010), "Matching and Network Effects," *Journal of European Economic Association*, 8, 1, 203–31.

Fainmesser, I., and A. Galeotti (2016), "Pricing Network Effects," *Review of Economic Studies*, 83, 1, 165–98.

Farboodi, M. (2014), "Intermediation and Voluntary Exposure to Counter-Party Risk," *Working Paper*, University of Chicago.

Farrell, F. and G. Saloner (1986), "Installed Base and Compatibility: Innovation, Product Preannouncements, and Predation," *American Economic Review*, 76, 940–55.

Frank, R. (1993), *Choosing the Right Pond: Human Behavior and the Quest for Status*. Oxford University Press.

Gagnon, J. and S. Goyal (2016), "Networks, Markets and Inequality." *American Economic Review*, forthcoming.

Gale, D. and S. Kariv (2009), "Trading in Networks: A Normal Form Game Experiment." *American Economic Journal: Microeconomics*, 1, 2, 114–32.

Galenianos, M. (2014), "Hiring Through Referrals," *Journal of Economic Theory*, 152, 304–23.

Galeotti, A. (2010), "Talking, Searching and Pricing," *International Economic Review*, 51, 4, 1159–74.

Galeotti, A., C. Ghiglino and S. Goyal (2015), "Financial Linkages, Portfolio Choice and Systemic Risk," *mimeo*, Essex and Cambridge.

Galeotti, A., and S. Goyal (2009), "Influencing the Influencers: A Theory of Strategic Diffusion," *Rand Journal of Economics*, 40, 3, 509–32.

Galeotti A., and S. Goyal (2014), "Competing Chains," *mimeo*, Essex and Cambridge.

Galeotti, A., S. Goyal, M.O. Jackson, F. Vega-Redondo and L. Yariv (2010), Network Games, *The Review of Economic Studies*, 77, 1, 218–244.

Galeotti, A., D. Goyal, M. Jackson, F. Vega-Redondo, and L. Yariv (2010), "Network Games," *Review of Economic Studies*, 77, 1, 218–44.

Galeotti, A. and L. P Merlino (2014), "Endogenous Job Contact Networks," *International Economic Review*, 55, 1201–26.

Gallo, E. (2014), "Social Learning by Chit-Chat," *Journal of Economic Theory*, 153, 313–43.

Ghiglino, C., and S. Goyal (2010), "Keeping Up With the Neighbors: Social Interaction in a Market Economy," *Journal of the European Economic Association*, 8, 1, 90–119.

Gofman, M. (2011), "A Network-Based Analysis of Over-the-Counter Markets," *mimeo*, Wisconsin-Madison.

Golub, B., and M. O. Jackson (2010), "Naive Learning and the Wisdom of Crowds," *American Economic Journal: Microeconomics* 2, 1, 112–49.

Gottardi, P., and S. Goyal (2012), "Intermediation in Networks," *mimeo*, EUI and Cambridge.

Goyal, S. (1993), "Sustainable Communication Networks," *Tinbergen Institute Discussion Paper, TI 93–250*.

Goyal, S. (2007), *Connections: An Introduction to the Economics of Networks*. Princeton, NJ: Princeton University Press.

Goyal, S. (2012), "Learning in Networks," in *Handbook of Social Economics*, edited by. J. BenHabib, A. Bisin, M.O. Jackson. North Holland.

Goyal, S. (2016), "Networks in Economics: A Perspective on the Literature," in *The Oxford Handbook of the Economics of Networks*, edited by Y. Bramoulle, A. Galeotti and B. Rogers. Oxford University Press.

Goyal, S., and S. Joshi (2003), "Networks of Collaboration in Oligopoly," *Games and Economic Behavior*, 43, 1, 57–85.

Goyal, S., and M. Kearns (2012), "Competitive Contagion in Networks." *Symposium in Theory of Computing*, (STOC).

Goyal, S., and J. L. Moraga-Gonzalez (2001), "R&D Networks," *Rand Journal of Economics*, 32, 4, 686–707.

Goyal, S., and F. Vega-Redondo (2007), "Structural Holes in Social Networks," *Journal of Economic Theory*, 137, 460–92.

Goyal, S., and A. Vigier (2014), "Attack, Defence and Contagion in Networks," *Review of Economics Studies*, 81, 4, 1518–42.

Granovetter, M. (1974), *Getting a Job: A Study of Contacts and Careers*, Cambridge, MA: Harvard University Press.

Granovetter, M. (1985), "Economic Action and Social Structure: The Problem of Embeddedness," *American Journal of Sociology*, 3, 481–510.

Griliches, Z., (1957), "Hybrid Corn: An Exploration in the Economics of Technological Change," *Econometrica*, 2, 4, 501–22.

Gulati, R. (2007), *Managing Network Resources*. Oxford: Oxford University Press.

Haag, M., and R. Lagunoff (2006), "Social Norms, Local Interaction, and Neighborhood Planning," *International Economic Review*, 47, 1, 265–96.

Hagedoorn, J. (2002), "Inter-Firm R&D Partnerships: An Overview of Major Trends and Patterns Since 1960," *Research Policy*, 31, 477–92.

Hall, P. (1935), "On Representatives of Subsets," *Journal of London Mathematical Society*, 10, 1, 26–30.

Hendricks, K., M. Piccione and G. Tan (1995), "The Economics of Hubs: The Case of Monopoly," *The Review of Economic Studies*, 62, 1, 83–99.

Hendricks, K., M. Piccione and G. Tan (1999), "Equilibrium in Networks," *Econometrica*, 67, 6, 1407–34.

Hirschman, A. O. (1977), *The Passions and the Interests: Arguments for Capitalism Before its Triumph*. Princeton, NJ: Princeton University Press.

Hirschman, A. O. (1982), "Rival Interpretations of Market Society: Civilizing, Destructive or Feeble?," *Journal of Economic Literature*, 20, 1463–84.

Hong, H., J. D. Kubik, and J. C. Stein (2005). "Thy Neighbor's Portfolio: Word-of-Mouth Effects in the Holdings and Trades of Money Managers." *Journal of Finance*, 60, 2801–24.

Immorlica, N., R. Kranton, M. Manea and G. Stoddard (2016), "Social Status in Networks." *AEJ: Microeconomics*, forthcoming.

Jackson, M. O. (2006), "The Economics of Social Networks," in *Volume 1 in Advances in Economics and Econometrics: Theory and Applications* Ninth World Congress of the Econometric Society, edited by R. Blundell, W. Newey, and T. Persson, Cambridge University Press.

Jackson, M. O. (2008), *Social and Economic Networks*. Princeton, NJ: Princeton University Press.

Jackson, M. O., and A. Wolinsky (1996), "A Strategic Model of Economic and Social Networks," *Journal of Economic Theory*, 71, 1, 44–74.

Jackson, M. O., and Y. Zenou (2014), "Games on Networks," *Handbook of Game Theory, Vol. 4*, edited by P. Young and S. Zamir.

Jensen, R. (2007). "The Digital Provide: Information (Technology), Market Performance, and Welfare in the South Indian Fisheries Sector." *Quarterly Journal of Economics*, 122(3), 879–924.

Katz, E., and P. F. Lazarsfeld (1955), *Personal Influence: The Part Played by People in the Flow of Mass Communications*. New York: The Free Press.

Katz, M. and C. Shapiro, (1985), "Network Externalities, Competition and Compatibility," *American Economic Review*, 75, 3, 424–40.

Keller, E., B. Fay, and J. Berry (2007), "Leading the Conversation: Influencers' Impact on Word of Mouth and the Brand Conversation." *The Keller Fay Group, Word of Mouth Marketing Research Symposium.*

Kirman, A., and A. Vignes (1991), "Price Dispersion: Theoretical Considerations and Empirical Evidence from the Marseilles Fish Market," in *Issues in Contemporary Economics: Proceedings of the Ninth World Congress of the International Economic Association, Volume 1: Markets and Welfare,* edited by K. J. Arrow. New York: New York University Press.

Koenig, M., C. J. Tessone, and Y. Zenou (2014), "Nestedness in Networks: A Theoretical Model and Some Applications," *Theoretical Economics,* 9, 695–752.

Kogut, B., W. Sham and G. Walker (1994), "Interfirm Cooperation and Startup Innovation in the Biotechnology Industry," *Strategic Management Journal,* 15, 387–94.

Kotowski, M., and M. Leister (2014), "Trading Networks and Equilibrium Intermediation," *mimeo,* University of California, Berkeley.

Kranton, R. (1996), "Reciprocal Exchange as a Self-Sustaining System," *American Economic Review,* 86, 4, 130–51.

Kranton, R., and D. Minehart (2000), "Networks versus Vertical Integration," *Rand Journal of Economics,* 31, 3, 570–601.

Kranton, R., and D. Minehart (2001), "A Theory of Buyer-Seller Networks," *American Economic Review,* 91, 3, 485–508. Laffont, J.J., and J. Tirole (2001), *Competition in Telecommunications.* Cambridge, MA: MIT Press.

Lerner, A. P. (1934), "The Concept of Monopoly and the Measurement of Monopoly Power," *Review of Economic Studies.* 1, 3: 157–75.

Leskovec, J., Adamic, L.A., and Huberman, B.A. (2007), "The Dynamics of Viral Marketing." *ACM TWeb,* 1.

Lever-Guzman, C. (2011), "Price Competition on a Network," *Banco de Mexico Working Paper: 2011–04.*

Long, J. B., and C. I. Plosser (1983), "Real Business Cycles," *Journal of Political Economy,* 91, 39–69.

Laffont, J.J., and J. Tirole (2001), *Competition in Telecommunications.* MIT Press.

van der Leij, M., D. in 't Veld, C. Hommes (2016), "The Formation of a Core-Periphery Structure in Heterogeneous Financial Networks," *mimeo,* University of Amsterdam.

Manea, M. (2011), "Bargaining in Stationary Networks," *American Economic Review,* 101, 2042–80.

Manea, M. (2016a), "Models of Bilateral Trade in Networks," in *The Oxford Handbook of the Economics of Networks,* edited by Y. Bramoulle, A. Galeotti and B. Rogers. Oxford University Press.

Manea, M. (2016b), "Intermediation and Resale in Networks," *mimeo,* MIT.

Mobarak, A.M., and M. Rosenzweig, (2012). "Selling Formal Insurance to the Informally Insured." Yale Department of Economics Working Paper 97.

Montesquieu (1961) [1748]. *De l'esprit des lois.* Paris: Garnier.

Montgomery, J., (1991), "Social Networks and Labor-Market Outcomes: Toward an Economic Analysis," *The American Economic Review,* 81, 5, 1408–18.

Munshi, K. (2014), "Community Networks and the Process of Development," *Journal of Economic Perspectives,* 28, 4, 49–76.

Munshi, K., and M. Rosenzweig (2006), "Traditional Institutions Meet the Modern World: Caste, Gender, and Schooling Choice in a Globalizing Economy." *American Economic Review,* 96, 4, 1225–52.

Myerson, R. (1977), "Graphs and Cooperation in Games," *Mathematics of Operations Research*, 2, 3, 225–29.

Myerson, R. (1991), *Game Theory: Analysis of conflict*. Cambridge, MA: Harvard University Press.

Nava, F. (2015), "Efficiency in Decentralized Oligopolistic Markets," *Journal of Economic Theory*, forthcoming.

Nava , F. (2016), "Repeated Games on Networks," in *Oxford Handbook on Economics of Networks*, edited by Y. Bramoulle, A. Galeotti and B. Rogers (2015). Oxford University Press.

Newman, N. (2009), *The Rise of Social Media and its Impact on Mainstream Journalism: A Study of How Newspapers and Broadcasters in the UK and US Are Responding to a Wave of Participatory Social Media, and a Historic Shift in Control Towards Individual Consumers*. Oxford: Reuters Institute for the Study of Journalism.

Ozsoylev, H., and J. Walden (2011), "Asset Pricing in Large Information Networks," *Journal of Economic Theory*, 146, 6, 2252–80.

Paine, T., (1951) [1792]. *The Rights of Man*. New York: E.P. Dutton.

de Paula, A. (2016), "The Econometrics of Network Models," *mimeo*, UCL.

Polanski, A. (2007), "Bilateral Bargaining in Networks," *Journal of Economic Theory*, 134, 557–65.

Polanyi, K. (1944), *The Great Transformation: The Political and Economic Origins of Our Time*. New York: Rinehart.

Powell, W. (1990), "Neither market nor Hierarchy: Network Forms of Organization," *Research in Organizational Behavior*, 12, 295–336.

Powell, W.W., K. W. Koput, L. Smith-Doerr (1996), "Inter-Organizational Collaboration and the Locus of Innovation: Networks of Learning in Biotechnology," *Administrative Science Quarterly*, 116–45.

Putnam, R. (1993), *Making Democracy Work: Civic Traditions in Modern Italy*. Princeton, NJ: Princeton University Press.

Raub, W., and J. Weesie (1990), "Reputation and Efficiency in Social Interactions: An Example of Network Effects," *American Journal of Sociology*, 626–54.

Rees, A. (1966), "Information Networks in Labor Markets," *American Economic Review*, 56, 1, 559–66.

Reuters Institute for the Study of Journalism, (2014). *Reuters Institute Digital News Report 2014*, edited by N. Newman and D.A.L. Levy. Oxford.

Rogers, E.M. (1983), *Diffusion of Innovations*, 3rd Edition. New York: Free Press.

Rogerson, W., (1985), "Repeated Moral Hazard," *Econometrica*, 53, 1, 69–76.

Rogerson, R., R. Shimer and R. Wright (2005), "Search-Theoretic Models of the Labour Market: A Survey," *Journal of Economic Literature*, 43, 4, 959–88.

Ryan, B., and N. Gross (1943), "The Diffusion of Hybrid Seed Corn in Two Iowa Communities," *Rural Sociology*, 8, 15–24.

Sandel, M. (2012) *The Moral Limits of Markets*. Harvard University Press.

Scott, J., (1977). *The Moral Economy of the Peasant: Rebellion and Subsistence in Southeast Asia*. New Haven: Yale University Press.

Smelser, N. J. and R. Swedberg (2005), *The Handbook of Economic Sociology*, 2nd Edition. Russell Sage Foundation.

Spulber, D. (1999), *Market Microstructure: Intermediaries and the Theory of the Firm*. Cambridge University Press.

Standage, T. (2013), *The Writing on the Wall: The First 2000 Years.* London: Bloomsbury.

Sundararajan, A. (2016), *The Sharing Economy.* MIT Press.

Thompson, E. P., 1971. "The Moral Economy of the English Crowd in the 18th Century." *Past & Present*, 50, 76–136.

Tirole, J. (1994), *The Theory of Industrial Organization.* Cambridge, MA: MIT Press.

Townsend, R. (1994), "Risk and Insurance in Village India," *Econometrica*, 62, 539–91.

Uzzi, B. (1996), "The Sources and Consequences of Embeddedness: The Network Effect," *American Sociological Review*, 61, 4, 674–98.

Van Lelyveld I., and D. in t' Veld (2012), "Finding the Core: Network Structure in Interbank Markets." *DNB Working Paper No. 348.*

Vega-Redondo, F. (2007), *Complex Social Networks.* Cambridge: Cambridge University Press.

Wang, J. J. (2015), "Distress Dispersion and Systemic Risk in Networks," *mimeo*, Arizona State University.

Weisbuch, G., A. Kirman, and D. Herreiner (2000), "Market Organisation and Trading Relationships," *Economic Journal*, 110, 411–36.

Westbrock, B. (2010), *Inter-Firm Networks: Economic and Sociological Perspectives.* Ph.D Dissertation, Utrecht University.

Williamson, O. (1975), *Markets and Hierarchies: Analysis and Antitrust Implications.* Free Press.

Zenou, Y. (2016), "Key Players," in *The Oxford Handbook of the Economics of Networks*, edited by Y. Bramoulle, A. Galeotti and B. Rogers. Oxford University Press.

CHAPTER 8

Econometrics of Network Models

Áureo de Paula

In this article I provide a (selective) review of the recent econometric literature on networks. I start with a discussion of developments in the econometrics of group interactions. I subsequently provide a description of statistical and econometric models for network formation and approaches for the joint determination of networks and interactions mediated through those networks. Finally, I give a very brief discussion of measurement issues in both outcomes and networks. My focus is on identification and computational issues, but estimation aspects are also discussed.

1 INTRODUCTION

Networks are "vulgar." By that I mean: they are commonplace, ordinary. Although markets are the usual forum where economic phenomena take place, many social and economic behaviors are not mediated by prices. A great many studies have investigated the existence and quantification of spillover effects in education (e.g., Sacerdote, 2010), in the labor market (e.g., Topa, 2001) and, more recently, on non-cognitive outcomes (e.g., Neidell and Waldfogel, 2010 and Lavy and Sand, 2015). Many other behaviors are mediated through prices, but in such a way that it matters how agents are in contact with each other. Production and financial networks are natural examples (e.g., Atalay, Hortacsu, Roberts, and Syverson, 2011 for the first and Denbee, Julliard, Li, and Yuan, 2014 or Bonaldi, Hortacsu, and Kastl, 2014 for the second). The main conduit in these examples is the intervening role of "connections": who is

This article was prepared for the 2015 Econometric Society World Congress in Montréal, Canada. I am grateful to Anton Badev, Yann Bramoullé, Arun Chandrasekhar, Andreas Dzemski, Bo Honoré, Chris Julliard, Chuck Manski, Angelo Mele, Bryony Reich, Seth Richards-Shubik, Adam Rosen and Elie Tamer for comments on an earlier draft of the paper. The author gratefully acknowledges financial support from the European Research Council through Starting Grant 338187 and the Economic and Social Research Council through the ESRC Centre for Microdata Methods and Practice grant RES-589-28-0001.

in direct or indirect contact with whom. This structure defines (and is possibly defined by) how information, prices and quantities reverberate in a particular social or economic system. This recognition has sparked a growing literature on various aspects of networks and their role in explaining various social and economic phenomena among economic theorists, empirical researchers and, more recently, econometricians.

This article aims at providing a (selective) overview of some recent advances and outstanding challenges in the applied econometric literature on this topic. I focus on both the role of networks in aiding the measurement of outcomes determined on an underlying network structure and on the formation of such structures. I also provide a brief discussion on measurement issues related to both tasks. Given constraints in space and expertise, this article is not exhaustive. In fact, the identification and measurement of network-related phenomena has drawn increasing attention in fields as diverse as macroeconomics, industrial organisation, finance, and trade, which I do not discuss in this review. There are also subclasses of network-related phenomena of empirical and econometric interest that I do not cover, such as bargaining and matching in bipartite graphs. Some of the ideas below may prove useful to developments in those areas nonetheless.

The article proceeds as follows. The following section provides a palette of basic definitions and terminology used recurrently throughout this paper. Because those are well covered elsewhere, I am deliberately succint. Section 3 covers topics related to models where particular outcomes of interest are mediated by predetermined networks. The subsequent section focuses on econometric models for the determination of the networks themselves and also discusses the joint determination of outcomes and networks. Section 5 provides a brief discussion of measurement issues related to networks and outcomes. The last section concludes.

2 SOME BASIC TERMINOLOGY AND CONCEPTS

Networks are typically represented by graphs. A graph g is a pair of sets $(\mathcal{N}_g, \mathcal{E}_g)$ of *nodes* (or *vertices*) $\mathcal{N}_g$ and *edges* (or *links* or *ties*) $\mathcal{E}_g$. I will denote the cardinality of these sets by $|\mathcal{N}_g|$ and $|\mathcal{E}_g|$, respectively. For our purposes, vertices are economic agents: individuals, households, firms or other entities of interest. The set of nodes is usually conceived as a finite set of elements, though in principle the node set can also be infinite (e.g., Berge, 1962). An edge represents a link or connection between two nodes in $\mathcal{N}_g$. A graph is undirected when $\mathcal{E}_g$ is the set of unordered pairs with elements in $\mathcal{N}_g$, say $\{i, j\}$ with $i, j \in \mathcal{N}_g$. (The multiset $\{i, i\}$ with $i \in \mathcal{N}_g$ is a possibility, but I abstract away from self-links here.) This type of graph is appropriate in representing reciprocal relationships between two vertices. An example is (reciprocal) informal risk-sharing networks based on kinship or friendship (e.g., Fafchamps and Lund, 2003). To accomodate directional relationships, edges are best modeled as ordered pairs, say $(i, j) \in \mathcal{N}_g \times \mathcal{N}_g$. These graphs, known as directed graphs (or digraphs), are more adequate for handling relatioships that do not require reciprocity or for which direction carries a particular meaning, as in a supplier–client relationship in a production network (e.g., Atalay, Hortacsu, Roberts, and Syverson, 2011). Further generalizations allow for weighted links, perhaps representing distances between two individuals or the intensity of a particular relationship. Such weights can be represented as a mapping from the space of pairs (unordered or ordered) into the real line. Diebold and Yilmaz (2015), for example, consider a (directed, weighted) graph obtained from the forecast-error variance decomposition for a given class of economic variables of interest. The nodes in this case would be seen as different entities, like stocks or firms, for example, and the weight of a directed link from node i to node j gives the proportion of the forecast error variance in variable of interest for node i (e.g., return or volatility if nodes represent stocks) explained by shocks to node j.[1]

A common representation of a graph is through its $|\mathcal{N}_g| \times |\mathcal{N}_g|$ adjacency or incidence matrix W, where each line represents a different node. The components of W mark whether an edge between nodes i and j (or from i to j in a digraph) is present or not and possibly its weight (in weighted graphs). The adjacency matrix allows one to translate combinatorial operations into linear algebraic ones and can be quite useful in several settings. For an adjacency matrix W to a simple graph (i.e., no self-links and at most one link between any pair of nodes), the ij element of matrix $W^k, k \in \{1, \ldots, N-1\}$, for instance, produces the number paths of length k between i and j. Two graphs are said to be isomorphic if their adjacency matrices can be obtained from each other, through multiplication by a permutation matrix, for example. This translates into a relabeling of the vertices in the corresponding graphs.

2.1   Vertex Features

Various measures can then be defined to characterize a particular vertex in the graph, to relate two or more vertices on a graph, or to represent a global feature of the graph at hand. (Although some of the notions mentioned below apply to more general networks, in what follows I focus on simple, unweighted graphs for ease of exposition.) An important characteristic for a particular vertex i, for example, is the set of neighbors incident with that vertex in a graph g, denoted by $N_i(g)$. In an undirected graph g, this set is given by $\{j : \{i, j\} \in \mathcal{E}_g\}$, and a similar definition can be given for directed graphs. The cardinality of this set is known as the "degree" of that node, and one can then talk about the relative frequency of degrees in a given graph as a whole. (In directed graphs, one can further distinguish "in-degrees" and "out-degrees" relating to inward and outward edges from and to a given node.) A "dense" graph, for instance, is then

---

[1] They define a few measures based on this network representation to keep track of "connectedness" of a particular economic system through time. Their total connectedness measure, for example, is given by the total sum of the weights across edges divided by the number of nodes.

one in which nodes display a lot of connections, and a common measure of density is the average degree divided by $|\mathcal{N}_g| - 1$, which is the maximum number of possible links available to any given node. Given two nodes i and j in an undirected graph, a sequence of nodes $(i \equiv i_1, \ldots, i_{K-1}, i_K \equiv j)$ defines a "walk" if every edge $\{i_k, i_{k+1}\} \in \mathcal{E}_g$. A "cycle" is a walk where $i_1 = i_K$, and a tree is a graph without cycles. A "path" is a walk where no vertex is visited more than once. (One can similarly define paths and walks on directed graphs.) It is common to define the (geodesic) distance between these two as the shortest path between those two nodes. A graph is then said to be connected if the distance between any two vertices is finite (i.e., there is at least one path between those nodes). A component of a graph is a maximal connected subgraph, where a subgraph is defined by a subset of nodes from $\mathcal{N}_g$ together with a subset of edges from $\mathcal{E}_g$ between elements in the subset of nodes under consideration. (A maximal connected subgraph is not strictly contained in any other connected subgraph of g.) A quantity encoding the connectedness of a network is given by the second smallest eigenvalue of the Laplacian matrix, defined as $L = \text{diag}(W\mathbf{1}) - W$, where $\text{diag}(W\mathbf{1})$ is a diagonal matrix with the row-sums of W along the diagonal. This value, known as the algebraic connectivity or the Fiedler value of the graph, provides a measure of how easy it is to break the graph into disconnected components by selectively eliminating a small number of edges (see Kolaczyk, 2009).

One can also define various measures to characterize the typical network structure in the vicinity of a given vertex. For brevity, I only mention a basic taxonomy of such measures as specific definitions are available in most introductory texts on the subject (see, for example, the excellent overview in Jackson, 2009). An important network aspect of particular interest in social settings is the degree of "clustering" in the system, intuitively summarized by the propensity for two neighbors to a given node to also themselves be directly linked. Different clustering metrics are available to quantify this feature in a network. Studying volunteer work in the civil rights movement in the United States, for example, McAdam, 1986 suggests that "[a]lthough weak ties may be more effective as diffusion channels (Granovetter, 1973), strong ties embody greater potential for influencing behavior. Having a close friend engage in some behavior is likely to have more of an effect on someone than if a friend of a friend engages in that same behavior. Apparently, the above was true of the Freedom Summer project" (p. 80).[2] Theoretically, it may be easier for clustered individuals to coordinate on certain collective actions since clustering may facilitate common knowledge (Chwe, 2000).

Another feature of potential interest in economic and social networks is the degree of "centrality" of a given vertex, and various measures of centrality are also available. Those aim at characterizing how important a given node

---

[2] To properly parse the effect of clustering, one would of course like to account for homophily among those who would already be prone to activism. If those individuals tend to associate with other like-minded individuals, this effect of "strong ties" will be confounded.

is in comparison to the remaining nodes in g. Aside from how connected a given vertex is (degree centrality) or how far on average a vertex is from any other vertex in the network (closeness centrality), one can also compute the betweenness centrality, illustrating how crucial a given node is in connecting individuals. Another family of popular centrality measures includes those based on features of the adjacency matrix aimed at summarizing a node's centrality in reference to its neighbors centrality (more on this later). The simplest of these measures is the eigenvector centrality (a.k.a. Gould's index of accessibility), corresponding to the dominant eigenvector of the adjacency matrix (Gould, 1967; Bonacich, 1972).[3] Among the most popular metrics in this family were those proposed by Katz (1953) and Bonacich (1987). The Katz centrality of a node i can be motivated by ascribing a value of $\tilde{\beta}^k > 0$ to each connection reached by a walk of length k. Since the (i, j) entry in W^k counts the number of walks between i and j, if one adds up the weights for each individual, one has a centrality measure for each individual given by the components of the vector $\tilde{\beta} W \mathbf{1} + \tilde{\beta}^2 W^2 \mathbf{1} + \tilde{\beta}^3 W^3 \mathbf{1} + \ldots$ If $\tilde{\beta}$ is below the reciprocal of W's largest eigenvalue, we can write the above as $\tilde{\beta}(\mathbf{I} - \tilde{\beta} W)^{-1} W \mathbf{1}$, where $\tilde{\beta}$ is a small enough positive number. The Bonacich centrality generalizes this formula to a two-parameter index defined by the vector $\alpha(\mathbf{I} - \tilde{\beta} W)^{-1} W \mathbf{1}$. Recently, Banerjee, Chandrasekhar, Duflo, and Jackson, 2014 introduced another centrality measure, which they named *diffusion centrality* and which subsumes the degree, eigenvector, and Katz–Bonacich centralities as special cases. Such measures turn out to play an important role in the analysis of games and dissemination on networks (e.g., Ballester, Calvó-Armengol, and Zenou, 2006 and the survey by Zenou, 2015).

2.2   Random Graphs

Having characterized the objects of interest here, one is then well-positioned to discuss data-generating processes giving rise to potentially observable social and economic networks and their sampling. Letting $\mathcal{G}$ be a particular set of graphs, one can define a probability space $(\mathcal{G}, \sigma(\mathcal{G}), \mathbb{P})$, where $\sigma(\mathcal{G})$ is a σ-algebra of events in the sample space $\mathcal{G}$ and $\mathbb{P}$ is a probability measure on the measurable space $(\mathcal{G}, \sigma(\mathcal{G}))$. These models can and usually are indexed by features common to the graphs in $\mathcal{G}$, like the number of vertices and/or other features. One of the early models, for example, imposes a uniform probability on the class of graphs with a given number of nodes, $n = |\mathcal{N}_g|$, and a particular number of edges, $e = |\mathcal{E}_g|$, for $g \in \mathcal{G}$ (see Erdös and Rényi, 1959, 1960). Another basic, canonical random graph model is one in which the edges between any two nodes follow an independent Bernoulli distribution with equal probability, say p. For a large enough number of nodes and sufficiently small probability of link formation p, the degree distribution

---

[3] The most profitable of these measures is perhaps Google's PageRank index (Brin and Page, 1998).

approaches a Poisson distribution, and the model is consequently known as the Poisson random-graph model. This class of models appears in Gilbert (1959) and Erdös and Rényi (1960) and has since been studied extensively. Nevertheless, they fail to reproduce important dependencies observed in social and economic networks. One category of models that aims at a better representation of the regularities usually encountered in social systems involves models where nodes are incorporated into the graph sequentially and form ties more or less randomly. These models are able to reproduce features that the simple framework above is incapable of. For example, whereas the models above deliver degree distributions with exponential tails, many datasets appear to feature polynomial, Pareto tails. Models like the "preferential attachment" model (Barabási and Albert, 1999), whereby the establishment of new links is more likely for higher-degree existing nodes, produce Pareto tails (as well as other regularities usually observed; see the presentation in Jackson, 2009, or Kolaczyk, 2009 for a more thorough exposition).[4]

Another alternative is to rely on more general (static) random graph models that explicitly acknowledge the probabilistic dependencies in link formation. Such dependencies can be approached using probabilistic graphical models as in Frank and Strauss (1986). Probabilistic graphical models provide a (non-random) graphical representation of the probabilistic dependencies among a set of random vectors (e.g., Koller and Friedman, 2009). In the context of random (undirected) graphs with $|\mathcal{N}_g| = n$ vertices, those random variables are the $n(n-1)/2$ (random) edges potentially formed between the n nodes. To represent a given stochastic dependence structure in the formation of edges, Frank and Strauss rely on a (non-random) dependency graph having as vertices all the potential edges between the elements of an original set of nodes of interest. In this dependency graph, links between two nodes (i.e., (random) edges in the random graph of interest) are present if these two random variables are conditionally dependent given the remaining random variables (i.e., the remaining (random) edges in the original random graph of interest). For example, since edges form independently in the Poisson graph model, its dependency graph is an empty one, with no links among its nodes (which are the random edges in the original Poisson network of interest). On the other hand, if the probability that an edge between i and j depends on the existence of a link between i and k given the remaining edges in the graph, the dependency graph will feature a link between nodes that represent $\{i, j\}$ and $\{i, k\}$. Applying results previously employed in the spatial statistics literature (i.e., the Hammersley–Clifford Theorem; see Besag, 1974), one has

---

[4] It should be noted that, while polynomial tails characterize the degree distribution for many networks, the evidence in favor of Pareto tails is less consensual than it might appear from a casual reading of the literature. This is highlighted, for example, in Pennock, Flake, Lawrence, Glove, and Giles (2002), Jackson and Rogers (2007) and Clauset, Shalizi, and Newman (2009), who find that many networks appear to be better characterized by non-polynomial tails.

$$\mathbb{P}(G = g) \propto \exp\left(\sum_{C \subset g} \alpha_C\right),$$

where $\alpha_C \in \mathbb{R}$ and C indexes all completely connected subgraphs (i.e., "cliques") of the (nonrandom) dependency graph representing the random graph model of interest.[5]

In general, the task of enumerating the set of cliques can be computationally complex. This expression can nevertheless be simplified for many interesting specific dependency structures. Frank and Strauss (1986), for example, focus on (pairwise Markov) random graphs where two (random) edges that do not share a vertex are conditionally independent given the other remaining (random) edges (and hence are not linked in the dependency graph). It reflects the intuition that ties are not independent of each other, but their dependency arises only through those who are directly involved in the connections in question. This, and a homogeneity assumption (i.e., that all graphs that are the same up to a permutation of vertices have the same probability), delivers that

$$\mathbb{P}(G = g) \propto \exp\left(\alpha_0 t + \sum_{k=1} \alpha_k s_k\right),$$

where t is the number of triangles (completely connected triples of vertices) and s_k is the number of k-stars (tuples of $k+1$ vertices where one of the vertices has degree k and the remaining ones have degree one). (Notice that the Poisson model is a specific case of the above model, where $\alpha_0 = \alpha_2 = \cdots = \alpha_k = 0$.) This structure suggests a class of probabilistic models that reproduce the exponential functional form above even in cases where the Markov property used by Frank and Strauss does not hold. Those models are such that $\mathbb{P}(G = g) \propto \exp\left(\sum_{k=1}^{p} \alpha_k S_k(g)\right)$, where $S_k(g), k = 1, \ldots, p$ enumerate certain features of the graph g. These would be characteristics like the number of edges, the number of triangles and possibly many others. These models are known as exponential random graph models (or p^* models in the social sciences literature; see Robins, Pattison, Kalish, and Lusher, 2007) and can be extended beyond undirected random graphs. The models above constitute an exponential family of distributions over (random) graphs and exponential distributions (e.g., Bernoulli, Poisson) have well-known probabilistic and statistical properties. For example, the vector $(S_1(g), \ldots, S_p(g))$ constitutes a p-dimensional sufficient statistic for the parameters $(\alpha_1, \ldots, \alpha_p)$. All the models above (and many others) are presented in detail elsewhere (e.g., Bollobás, 2001; Jackson, 2009; Kolaczyk, 2009) and I will selectively discuss features and difficulties as they articulate with the literature reviewed here.

---

[5] This representation is sometimes expressed in terms of *maximal* cliques. Any representation based on non-maximal cliques can be converted into one based on maximal cliques by redefining α_C for a maximal clique as the sum of the αs on the subsets of that clique (Jordan and Wainwright, 2008).

3 OUTCOMES ON NETWORKS

As pointed out in the introduction, many social and economic outcomes are mediated by interactions among the entities involved (individuals, households, firms). In fact, the interaction structure can be instrumental in shaping the outcomes in various social and economic settings. Although the very determination of the social links on which those outcomes are resolved is plausibly informed by those outcomes or expectations about those outcomes in many cases, we start by assuming here that the peer structure, i.e., the ties among the various individuals involved, is determined independently.

3.1   Linear Models

The canonical representation for the joint determination of outcomes mediated by social interactions builds on the linear specification presented in Manski (1993). This representation postulates that the individual outcome variable for individual $i \in \{1, \ldots, N\}$, y_i, is determined according to

$$y_i = \alpha + \beta \sum_{j=1}^{N} W_{ij} y_j + \eta x_i + \gamma \sum_{j=1}^{N} W_{ij} x_j + \epsilon_i, \qquad \mathbb{E}(\epsilon_i | \mathbf{x}, W) = 0 \quad (1)$$

where $j \in \{1, \ldots, N\}$, x_i represents a covariate observed by the researcher (with $\mathbf{x} = [x_1 \ldots x_N]^\top$), ϵ_i represents a latent variable unobserved by the researcher, and W_{ij} are entries in the adjacency matrix that register the social network structure. For example, if y_i is affected by the average of all other individuals' outcomes and covariates, $W_{ij} = (N-1)^{-1}$ and $W_{ii} = 0$. (This model is a spatial auto-regressive model in spatial statistics.) I assume here that x is scalar though the arguments hold more generally. Stacking the individual equations above, one then obtains

$$\mathbf{y}_{N \times 1} = \alpha \mathbf{1}_{N \times 1} + \beta W_{N \times N} \mathbf{y}_{N \times 1} + \eta \mathbf{x}_{N \times 1} + \gamma W_{N \times N} \mathbf{x}_{N \times 1}$$
$$+ \epsilon_{N \times 1}, \qquad \mathbb{E}(\epsilon | \mathbf{x}, W) = 0 \qquad (2)$$

with $\mathbf{1}$ as a vector of 1s. Whereas I take this as the point of departure for my presentation of (linear) social interaction models, I note that the specification above can be obtained from more primitive foundations (e.g., Blume, Brock, Durlauf, and Jayaraman (2015)). Supposing that $1/\beta$ is not an eigenvalue of W, the equations above produce the following reduced form system:

$$\mathbf{y} = \alpha(\mathbf{I} - \beta W)^{-1} \mathbf{1} + (\mathbf{I} - \beta W)^{-1}(\eta \mathbf{I} + \gamma W)\mathbf{x} + (\mathbf{I} - \beta W)^{-1} \epsilon, \quad (3)$$

where $\mathbf{I}$ is an identity matrix of order N.

In his celebrated article, Manski examined the identification of the various parameters above (although using a different representation, see below). In doing so, he distinguished social influences between endogenous and exogenous (or contextual) effects. The latter represents any influence encoded by peer (observable) characteristics. The former translates into the influence of peers' outcomes on one's own outcomes. Although related, those two have different repercussions: endogenous effects act as conduits for the reverberation of shocks, leading to a multiplier effect, which is absent if contextual effects are the main driving mechanism for social influences. The separation of these two parameters is made more difficult by the possibility of correlation in unobservables, which Manski terms correlated effects. In the model above, this is reflected in the potential for $\mathbb{E}(\epsilon_i \epsilon_j | \mathbf{x}, W) \neq 0$ for $i \neq j$. (Notice that the covariance structure for the error vector is left unrestricted above.) As illustrated in that paper, if y represents school achievement, endogenous effects arise if one's achievement tends to vary with the average achievement in that person's reference group. If achievement is affected by the reference group's socio-economic background, there is an exogenous or contextual effect. Correlated effects may arise because pupils are exposed to the same teacher or have similar features that are relevant for achievement but are not observed by the researcher. Because all of these may explain similarities in outcomes, it gives rise to what Manski calls the "reflection problem."

The reduced form in (3) arises rather naturally in interaction models for maximizing agents endowed with quadratic payoffs. Blume, Brock, Durlauf, and Jayaraman (2015), for instance, suggest that observed outcomes can be construed as Bayes–Nash equilibria of a game with incomplete information. For a model of strategic complementarities in production, payoffs are given by

$$
U_i(\mathbf{y}; W) = \left(\alpha + \eta x_i + \gamma \sum_{j \neq i} W_{ij} x_j + z_i \right) y_i + \beta \sum_{j \neq i} W_{ij} y_i y_j - \frac{1}{2} y_i^2,
$$

$$(4)$$

where z_i is private information to individual i. The first two terms reflect a production function mapping effort into an outcome of interest where the second term reflects complementarity among individuals. The reduced form in (3) then corresponds to the equilibrium profile of the game where the unobservable error is a function of the private information z_i.[6]

Calvó-Armengol, Patacchini, and Zenou (2009) study a slightly different model of educational achievement. There, a pupil's educational achievement y_i is the sum of two effort choices, an idiosyncratic effort level e_i that is unaffected by peers' choices, and a "peer effect" effort level ϵ_i, which is potentially complemented by other individuals' efforts. The payoff function for a student is given by

$$
U_i(e_i, \epsilon; W) = \left(\eta x_i + \gamma \sum_{j \neq i} W_{ij} x_j \right) e_i - \frac{1}{2} e_i^2 + (\alpha W_i \mathbf{1} + v_i) \epsilon_i
$$

$$
- \frac{1}{2} \epsilon_i^2 + \tilde{\beta} \sum_{j=1}^{N} W_{ij} \epsilon_i \epsilon_j,
$$

---

[6] Blume, Brock, Durlauf, and Jayaraman (2015) focus their analysis on a different payoff structure corresponding to a narrative where individuals have preference for conformity. As they point out, the models are observationally equivalent.

where W_i is the ith row of W so that its multiplication by $\mathbf{1}$ produces the degree for individual i and ν_i is an idiosyncratic taste shock. The Nash equilibrium of this model leads to a reduced form econometric model given by[7]

$$
\begin{aligned}
y_i &= \eta x_i + \gamma \sum_{j=1}^{N} W_{ij} x_j + \epsilon_i \\
\epsilon_i &= \alpha W_i \mathbf{1} + \tilde{\beta} \sum_{j=1}^{N} W_{ij} \epsilon_j + \nu_i
\end{aligned}
\quad \Rightarrow \mathbf{y} = \frac{\alpha}{\tilde{\beta}} (\mathbf{I} - \tilde{\beta} W)^{-1} \tilde{\beta} W \mathbf{1}
$$

$$
+ (\eta \mathbf{I} + \gamma W)\mathbf{x} + (\mathbf{I} - \tilde{\beta} W)^{-1} \nu.
\tag{5}
$$

Notice that, since both e_i and ϵ_i are choice variables, endogenous effects are now encoded into $\tilde{\beta}$. It is also noteworthy that the simultaneity is in the determination of the unobservable error ϵ instead of the observable outcome variable $\mathbf{y}$. Finally, I should also point out that this special structure delivers a direct dependence of the outcome variable $\mathbf{y}$ on the Katz–Bonacich centrality index for each individual at $\tilde{\beta}$, listed in the vector $(\mathbf{I} - \tilde{\beta} W)^{-1} \tilde{\beta} W \mathbf{1}$ if the "peer effect" effort depends on the degree of the individual (i.e., $\alpha \neq 0$).[8] In their study of bank liquidity holdings in the United Kingdom, Denbee, Julliard, Li, and Yuan (2014) use a variation of this model and its connection with the Katz–Bonacich centrality to define a network impulse-response function of total outcome. In their analysis, W_{ij} is the (predetermined) borrowing by bank i from bank j. The variable e_i is interpreted as a bank's liquidity holdings when it is isolated, and the variable ϵ_i gives the liquidity holdings in a banking network.

In spite of the apparent differences between the preceding model and the model represented by (2)–(3), much of the identification and estimation analysis of this model follows along the same lines, and I will focus on the model given by (2)–(3) (unless explicitly stated).[9]

Earlier analyses of the model (2) focused on a peer structure given by a complete network where $\sum_{j=1}^{N} W_{ij} = 1$, $W_{ij} = W_{ik}$ for $j \neq k$ and it is customary to assume that $W_{ii} = 0$ (e.g., Moffitt, 2001).[10] It is also commonplace

---

[7] To guarantee uniqueness and interiority of the equilibrium, the authors impose the restriction that $\tilde{\beta}$ is less than the reciprocal of the largest eigenvalue of W. Whereas the estimates for the vast majority of the networks analyzed in the study satisfy this condition, 9 percent (=18/199) of the networks do not. It would be interesting to extend the analysis to incorporate the possibility of multiplicity and/or corner equilibria.

[8] If the rows of W add up to one, the intercept in the reduced form (3) is also given by a multiple of the Katz–Bonacich centrality index. Cohen-Cole, Kirilenko, and Patacchini (2014) estimate the model (2) on trading networks in financial futures markets and analyze the centrality indices for the traders in their sample.

[9] Calvó-Armengol, Patacchini, and Zenou (2009) use a variation of Proposition 4 below. If there are no correlated effects (i.e., correlation in ν_i), it might be possible to establish identification, as in Proposition 2 below.

[10] This weighting scheme amounts to collecting the endogenous and contextual covariates as the mean of one's peer group (sometimes termed the "exclusive mean"). As pointed out in Guryan, Kory, and Notowidigdo (2009), this mechanically generates a correlation between x_i and $\sum_{j \neq i} x_j / (N - 1)$ within the group even when x_i and x_j are independent for all pairs, and

to suppose that $|\beta| < 1$, which together with row-sum normalization, guarantees that $\mathbf{I} - \beta W$ is invertible and a well-defined reduced form exists. Under this specification and no further restrictions, it can be formally demonstrated that the structure represented by $(\alpha, \beta, \eta, \gamma)$ is not point-identified:

Proposition 1 *If* $|\beta| < 1$, $\eta\beta + \gamma \neq 0$, $W_{ij} = (N - 1)^{-1}$ *if* $i \neq j$ *and* $W_{ii} = 0$, $(\alpha, \beta, \eta, \gamma)$ *is not point-identified.*

This result is originally indicated in Manski (1993) and demonstrated, for instance, as a corollary to Proposition 1 in Bramoullé, Djebbari, and Fortin (2009). This negative result is also examined, for example, by Kelejian, Prucha, and Yuzefovich (2006) in an estimation context. The outlook on identification improves if one imposes further restrictions on the model and/or the available data. To illustrate this, I focus on the related representation originally considered in Manski (1993). Instead of specification (1), Manski studies a model akin to

$$y_i = \alpha + \beta\mathbb{E}(y_j|w) + \eta x_i + \gamma\mathbb{E}(x_j|w) + \epsilon_i, \quad \mathbb{E}(\epsilon_i|\mathbf{x}, w) = \delta w,$$

where w stands for a (scalar) identifier of the group, and expected values are taken so that the model is equilibrated and corresponds to a "social equilibrium."[11] The coefficients above retain the same interpretation as before, and $\delta \neq 0$ when there are correlated effects. Using this model, for example, a corollary to Proposition 2 in Manski is that, when $\delta = \gamma = 0$, the remaining parameters $(\alpha, \beta$ and $\eta)$ are point identified if 1, $\mathbb{E}(x_j|w)$ and x_i are "linearly independent in the population." Allowing for $\gamma \neq 0$, but (although not explicitly stated) otherwise under the same conditions (i.e., $\delta = 0$ and the variation previously implied by the linear independence condition), Angrist (2014; see also Acemoglu and Angrist, 2001, and Boozer and Cacciola, 2001) demonstrates an analogous result that β is point identified, drawing an interesting connection of this parameter to the population counterparts of the regression coefficient of y_i on x_i and a regression of group averages of y_i on group averages of x_i, which can be interpreted as the 2SLS estimator using group

a regression of the first on the second will lead to a biased estimator. This can be seen by noting that the usual requirement for OLS unbiasedness (strict exogeneity) is not satisfied, even though the covariance $\mathbb{C}(x_i, \sum_{j\neq i} x_j/(N - 1)) = 0$ and the Best Linear Projection slope coefficient is zero. This happens since x_i shows up either as regressand or as regressor (as part of the "exclusive mean") in all observations within the group. Whereas the regression will produce a biased estimator, the OLS estimators are still consistent (since contemporaneous exogeneity is preserved) and the problem is attenuated for larger groups as pointed out by those authors.

[11] In the literature, this structure is sometimes emulated by assuming that $\sum_{j=1}^{N} W_{ij} y_j$ is an "inclusive mean," where $W_{ii} \neq 0$ and $W_{ij} = N^{-1}$ for any i and j. This "expectational" equation can also be explained from more foundational models of behavior, as illustrated, for instance, in Blume, Brock, Durlauf, and Jayaraman (2015). As indicated there, whereas the appearance of $\mathbb{E}(y_j|w)$ or $\sum_{j=1}^{N} W_{ij} y_j$ may reflect different informational assumptions on the microeconomic model under consideration, they are in fact econometrically isomorphic.

dummies as instruments for x_i. As pointed out by Manski (1993) and using my notation, "the ability to infer the presence of social effects depends critically on the manner in which x varies with w" (p. 535). The non-identification result in Proposition 1 does not use this variation, whereas these positive identification results explore the between-group variation of the regressor x, without which the linear independence condition stated above fails and the variance $\mathbb{V}(\mathbb{E}(x_j|w)) = 0$, jeopardizing the results.

Alternative restrictions on the model (2) also allow us to achieve identification using higher moments. If there are no correlated effects, for example, and the conditional variance $\mathbb{V}(\epsilon|\mathbf{x}) = \sigma^2\mathbf{I}$, we have

$$\mathbb{V}(\mathbf{y}|\mathbf{x}) = \sigma^2(\mathbf{I} - \beta W)^{-2}.$$

This is enough to identify β and, consequently, the remaining parameters, even when $W_{ij} = (N-1)^{-1}$ if $i \neq j$ and $W_{ii} = 0$. In the peer effects literature, this result is indicated in Moffitt (2001) but is actually reminiscent of earlier results on covariance restrictions and identification of simultaneous equation models (see Fisher, 1966; Bekker and Pollock, 1986; Hausman, Newey, and Taylor, 1987). Below, I state it for the general case of N individuals, and a direct demonstration is available in the appendix.[12]

Proposition 2 *If* $|\beta| < 1$, $W_{ij} = (N-1)^{-1}$ *if* $i \neq j$, $W_{ii} = 0$, *and* $\mathbb{V}(\epsilon|\mathbf{x}) = \sigma^2\mathbf{I}$ *then* $(\alpha, \beta, \eta, \gamma)$ *is point-identified.*

Interestingly, the covariance restrictions above also imply a lower bound on the correlation among observable outcomes, which is strictly greater than the lower bound for the pairwise correlation of a collection of equi-correlated random variables when $N \geq 3$. The reasoning for this is as follows: If a person i's outcome is increased and β is negative, this has a downward direct influence on a given peer j. If a third individual k is also in the group, that person's outcome will also be negatively affected by the increase in i's outcome. This negative influence in k will, on the other hand, put upward pressure on j's outcome and the effect of the original increase in i's outcome will tend to be attenuated. (Of course, this indirect effect is not present if $N = 2$ and, accordingly, the lower bound there is exactly -1. The bound is nontrivial when $N > 2$.[13]) Although the restrictions contemplated here are strong (no correlated effects and equal variance across individuals), Proposition 2 suggests that covariance restrictions may not only be useful in identifying the parameters of interest, but also in providing testable implications. This result is summarised below.

---

[12] Covariance restrictions alone are not enough to identify the model without additional coefficient restrictions. The coefficient restrictions in the present model are different from those dealt with in the earlier works, which appear to focus on exclusion restrictions across equations.

[13] When $N = 3$, for example, the correlation implied by Proposition 3 is $-0.\overline{45}$. For three equi-correlated random variables, positive definiteness of the variance–covariance matrix implies a smaller lower bound of -0.50.

Proposition 3 *If* $|\beta| < 1$, $W_{ij} = (N-1)^{-1}$ *if* $i \neq j$, $W_{ii} = 0$, *and* $\mathbb{V}(\epsilon|\mathbf{x}) = \sigma^2\mathbf{I}$ *then*

$$\frac{\mathbb{C}(y_i, y_j|\mathbf{x})}{\mathbb{V}(y_i|\mathbf{x})} > \frac{4-3N}{4N^2 - 11N + 8}.$$

Since the presence of an additive common shock will tend to increase the correlation between two observable variables, I conjecture that a similar lower bound on correlations as in Proposition 3 is possible in that case. When correlated effects manifest themselves through an additive group effect (i.e., for a group $l = 1, \ldots, L$, the intercept is a random, possibly covariate dependent α_l), Davezies, d'Haultfoeuille, and Fougére (2009) show that the covariance restriction $\mathbb{V}(\epsilon|\mathbf{x}) = \sigma^2\mathbf{I}$ still provides identification if there are *at least* two groups of different sizes (see their Proposition 3.2). Recently, Rose (2015) examines identifiability using second moments under the (weaker) assumption that $\mathbb{V}(\epsilon|\mathbf{x}) = \sigma^2\mathbf{I} + \sigma_{\epsilon\epsilon}(W + W^\top)$. There, identification is established under conditions on W that are reminiscent of (though stronger than) the linear independence assumptions in Bramoullé, Djebbari, and Fortin (2009) (see below).

In fact, the use of restrictions on unobservables and higher moments for identification has been explored elsewhere in the literature for the identification and estimation of variations of the peer effects model presented in (2) (see Glaeser, Sacerdote, and Scheinkman, 1996 for an early example). Graham (2008), for instance, studies identification when outcomes within a group $l = 1, \ldots, L$ are defined by

$$\mathbf{y}_{l \ N_l \times 1} = \tilde{\gamma} W_{l \ N_l \times N_l} \epsilon_{l \ N_l \times 1} + \alpha_l \mathbf{1}_{N_l \times 1} + \epsilon_{l \ N_l \times 1},$$

where N_l is the number of individuals in group l, $W_{ij,l} = (N_l - 1)^{-1}$ if $i \neq j$ and $W_{ii,l} = 0$, and the group-specific intercept α_l is allowed to vary across groups.[14] (A similar model is also contemplated in Glaeser, Sacerdote, and Scheinkman, 2003.) The unobservables are separated into three components: an individual idiosyncratic component $\epsilon_{i,l}$, the average of that variable among a person's peers $\sum_{j \neq i} \epsilon_{j,l}/(N_l - 1)$, and a group-specific shock α_l. The main identification target is $\tilde{\gamma}$, which is interpreted as a contextual effect parameter on (unobservable) group characteristics.[15] Since the contextual effects here are unobserved, the difficulty lies is separating this unobservable component from the group-wide error α_l, which stand for the usual correlated effects.

Graham (2008) shows that $\tilde{\gamma}$ is identified if (i) two groups are available ($L \geq 2$), (ii) there is random assignment ($\Rightarrow \mathbb{E}(\epsilon_{i,l}\epsilon_{j,l}) = \mathbb{E}(\alpha_l\epsilon_{j,l}) = 0$ for any i, j, l; i.e., there is no sorting or matching in group formation); (iii) the variance of α_l does not differ across groups; and (iv) there is difference in within-group variance of outcomes. Recently, Blume, Brock, Durlauf, and

---

[14] Exogenous covariates $\mathbf{x}_l$ and (observed) contextual effects on those can be accomodated (see Blume, Brock, Durlauf, and Jayaraman, 2015), but are ommitted as in Graham (2008).

[15] Alternatively, it can be seen as an amalgam of contextual and endogenous effect parameters.

Jayaraman (2015) demonstrate how this result can be generalized to allow for identification of the model in (2) through higher moments (when there are no correlated effects; see their Theorem 5).

An interesting avenue for identification appears when the (observed) social network graph is not complete in a way that introduces enough exclusion restrictions into the equation system (2) to restablish the (necessary and sufficient) rank condition for point-identification. This insight is formalized in Bramoullé, Djebbari, and Fortin (2009):

Proposition 4 (Bramoullé, Djebbari, and Fortin, 2009) *If $\eta\beta + \gamma \neq 0$ and $\mathbf{I}, W, W^2$ are linearly independent, $(\alpha, \beta, \eta, \gamma)$ is point-identified.*

If $W_{ij} = (N-1)^{-1}$ if $i \neq j$ and $W_{ii} = 0$, $W^2 = (N-1)^{-1}\mathbf{I} + (N-2)/(N-1)W$ and the linear independence condition fails. One way in which that condition is satisfied is if W is block-diagonal with at least two blocks of different order. Suppose, for example, that the social network is composed of two complete subgraphs of size N_1 and N_2 such that $N_1 + N_2 = N$. In this case, $W^2 = \lambda_0\mathbf{I} + \lambda_1 W$. Whereas direct computation shows that W^2 has N_1 diagonal elements equal to $(N_1 - 1)^{-1}$ and N_2 diagonal elements equal to $(N_2 - 1)^{-1}$, the diagonal elements of $\lambda_0\mathbf{I} + \lambda_1 W$ all equal λ_0. This produces $\lambda_0 = (N_1 - 1)^{-1} = (N_2 - 1)^{-1}$ if we focus on diagonal elements of W^2. Another way to see how identification comes about in this case is to notice that the reduced form equation for individual i in group $l = 1, 2$ becomes

$$y_i = \frac{\alpha}{1-\beta} + \left[\eta + \frac{\beta(\eta\beta + \gamma)}{(1-\beta)(N_l - 1 + \beta)}\right] x_i + \frac{\eta\beta + \gamma}{(1-\beta)(1 + \frac{\beta}{N_l - 1})}\bar{x}_i + v_i,$$

where $\bar{x}_i$ is the average covariate in group l, and v_i is the corresponding reduced-form error. The variation of the reduced-form coefficients across groups of different sizes then allows one to identify the parameters of interest. Hence, if $N_1 \neq N_2$, the linear independence condition is satisfied and the model is identified. The use of groups with different sizes to obtain identification is also employed in Lee (2007) and Davezies, d'Haultfoeuille, and Fougére (2009).[16]

Identification is also made possible if there are vertices whose peers are linked to nodes that are not themselves directly connected to the original nodes. This allows one to use indirect peers to generate instrumental variables for the endogenous outcomes in the right-hand side of equation (2). These are naturally encoded in the requirement that $\mathbf{I}, W$, and W^2 be linearly independent. Suppose, for instance, that nodes $1, \ldots, N$ are placed on a circle, and links are directed from i to $i + 1$ (and N to 1) as represented in Figure 1.

In this case, $W_{i,i+1} = W_{N,1} = 1, i = 1, \ldots, N - 1$, and all other entries are zero. Each node i is affected directly by $i - 1$ and indirectly by every other

---

[16] Boucher, Bramoullé, Djebbari, and Fortin (2014) apply the estimator proposed in Lee (2007) to a study of peer effects in educational achievement.

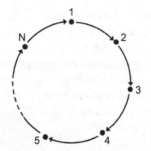

Figure 1 Directed Circle Network.

vertex. The matrix W^2 is such that $(W^2)_{N-1,1} = (W^2)_{N,2} = (W^2)_{i,i+2} = 1$ and records nodes that can be reached through a direct link. Since none of those is directly connected to the original vertices, they provide leverage for the model to identify the structure. This insight is used empirically in De Giorgi, Pellizari, and Redaelli (2010) and Bramoullé, Djebbari, and Fortin (2009). The model above is essentially a spatial autoregressive model and estimation can be pursued using spatial statistics methods (e.g., Kelejian and Prucha, 2010; Lin and Lee, 2010; Lee and Yu, 2010; or Lee, Liu, and Lin, 2010).[17]

A maintained assumption in the above identification result is that covariates are econometrically exogenous, which may be problematic as well. Bramoullé, Djebbari, and Fortin (2009) also extend the theoretical analysis above to the possibility of network-specific "fixed effects," α_l, potentially correlated with the covariates.[18] Of course, if excluded instruments are available, one may also employ them to identify the relevant parameters. It should be noted that the econometric exogeneity of the network structure itself is usually a maintained hypothesis. (Qu and Lee, 2015, provide an intrumental variable estimator that allows for endogeneity of W under certain conditions.)

Recently, Blume, Brock, Durlauf, and Jayaraman (2015) pointed out that, in fact, the identifying assumption on $\mathbf{I}$, W, and W^2 is the norm, rather than the exception! Indeed, when W is such that $\sum_{j=1}^{N} W_{ij} = 1$ and $W_{ii} = 0$ for any $i \in \{1, \dots, N\}$, the condition essentially only fails for the case when the social network is made up of equally-sized components with equal nonzero entries.[19] This is indicated in Theorem A2 in that paper:

---

[17] The command `spreg` in Stata, for example, implements maximum likelihood and GS2SLS estimators (see Drukker, Egger, and Prucha, 2013).

[18] An uncorrelated "random effect" α_l would still allow for identification under the conditions above. Bramoullé, Djebbari, and Fortin (2009) difference away the "fixed effect," which requires the linear independence condition to be strengthened to the linear independence of $\mathbf{I}$, W, W^2, and W^3.

[19] The row-sum normalization corresponds to what Liu, Patacchini, and Zenou (2014) call *local average* interactions, as opposed to, say, *local aggregate* interactions, where entries in W would correspond to 0 or 1.

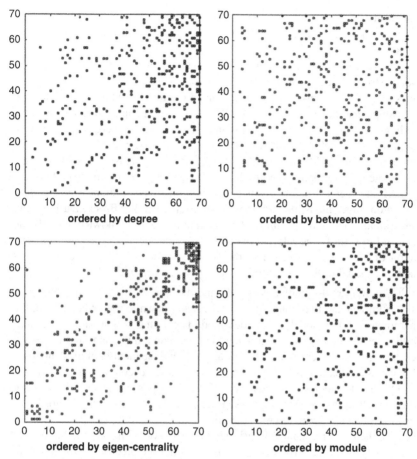

Figure 2 Adjacency Matrix: High School Friendships.
Note: In 1957 and 1958, boys in a small high school in Illinois were asked the following: "What fellows here in school do you go around with most often?" The data aggregates information from both years and appears in Coleman (1964). The panels display nodes ordered by degree centrality, betweenness centrality, eigenvector centrality, and modularity. The latter is a measure used to detect community structure in a graph.

Proposition 5 (Blume, Brock, Durlauf, and Jayaraman, 2015) *If W is such that $\sum_{j=1}^{N} W_{ij} = 1$ and $W_{ii} = 0$ for any $i \in \{1, \ldots, N\}$ and $\mathbf{I}$, W, and W^2 are linearly dependent, then W is block diagonal with blocks of the same size, say $N_l \ (\leq N)$, and any nonzero entry is given by $(N_l - 1)^{-1}$.*

In fact, many social graphs appear to display a connection structure that greatly departs from the block diagonal and complete within each block. Figure 2, a pictorial representation for the adjacency matrix of a network of friendships among teenagers, displays such an instance, with patterns that are much distinct from those obtained from a partition of individuals into completely connected subnetworks leading block diagonality in the subplots from Figure 2.

The setup described up to this point presumes that researchers observe the social structure represented by W. Whereas connections are sometimes elicited in survey instruments (e.g., the National Longitudinal Study of Adolescent to Adult Health, known as AddHealth), "[i]f researchers do not know how individuals form reference groups and perceive reference-group outcomes, then it is reasonable to ask whether observed behavior can be used to infer these unknowns" (Manski, 1993, p. 536). Although this is not possible with a complete social graph, because observed outcomes are informative about the underlying social structure acting as conduit, one may still hope to retain identification under plausible additional restrictions. Blume, Brock, Durlauf, and Jayaraman (2015), for example, demonstrate that partial knowledge of W can be used to identify the relevant parameters. In particular, they focus on a variation of the setup above, where the social structures mediating endogenous and contextual effects may differ (i.e., $y_i = \alpha + \beta \sum_{j=1}^{N} W_{ij,y} y_j + \eta x_i + \gamma \sum_{j=1}^{N} W_{ij,x} x_j + \epsilon_i$ with possibly distinct W_x and W_y). They show that when W^x is known and two (known) nodes are also known to not be connected, the parameters of the model can be identified (Theorem 6 in that paper). An analogous result demonstrates that when there are enough unconnected nodes for each of the graphs represented by W_x and W_y, and the identity of those nodes is known, identification is also (generically) possible (Theorem 7 in that paper).

Observed outcomes can possibly offer further possibilities when W is not directly observed. As Manski (1993) suggests, "[i]f researchers do not know how individuals form reference groups and perceive reference-group outcomes, then it is reasonable to ask whether observed behavior can be used to infer these unknowns" (p. 536). Such possibilities are investigated in de Paula, Rasul, and Souza (2015).[20] Letting Π denote the matrix of reduced-form coefficients in the system (3), one has

$$\Pi = (\mathbf{I} - \beta W)^{-1}(\eta \mathbf{I} + \gamma W).$$

Under the assumption that $|\beta| < 1$, one obtains that W and Π in fact share eigenvectors and Π's eigenvalues are functions of W's eigenvalues and the parameters of interest. Among other things, this indicates that the eigenvector centrality of W – corresponding to the dominant eigenvector – can also be directly obtained from Π. Additional restrictions often employed in the literature, such as $\eta\beta + \gamma \neq 0$, linear independence of $\mathbf{I}$, W and W^2 and row-sum normalization (which implies that the largest eigenvalue for W and W^2 is one) allow one to provide a tight characterisation for the set of observationally

---

[20] Blume, Brock, Durlauf, and Ioannides (2011) show local identification when there is a partial order on individuals and W displays weights decaying exponentially in distance. Souza (2014) suggests a probabilistic model for W and an integrated likelihood method for the estimation of the (identified set of) parameters in model (2).

equivalent parameters. This and other similar results are demonstrated in detail by de Paula, Rasul, and Souza (2015).

If Π can be estimated, an estimator for (at least one element in the set of identified) parameters of interest can be obtained (say, via indirect least squares). Since the number of parameters (reduced or structural) is $O(N^2)$ though, to estimate those one would in practice need obtain at least as many observations of $(\mathbf{y}, \mathbf{x})$ for a given social system (i.e., $TN > N^2$). Whereas this is empirically conceivable when N is small, it is less plausible for even moderately sized networks.[21] Estimation can nonetheless be possible with further, empirically credible restrictions on the system. Many social and economic networks (though not all) tend to be sparse, for instance. The density of the production networks examined in Atalay, Hortacsu, Roberts, and Syverson (2011) for the United States, for example, amounts to less than 1 percent of possible links.[22] Also relying on United States data, Carvalho (2014) finds an edge density of about 3 percent.[23] If one defines an undirected network from reciprocal friendship nominations in the AddHealth dataset, which elicits teenage friendships, the density is about 2 percent.

This, potentially coupled with additional restrictions, opens the possibility of application of penalization methods well suited to handle sparse models, like the Least Absolute Shrinkage and Selection Operator (LASSO) (Tibshirani, 1996; see Belloni, Chernozhukov, and Hansen, 2013, for a recent review focused on econometric applications), the Smoothly Clipped Absolute Deviation (SCAD) penalty (Fan and Li, 2001), the Elastic Net (Zou and Hastie, 2005), or the Minimax Concave Penalty (MCP) (Zhang, 2010). If T is the number of observed instances of $(\mathbf{y}, \mathbf{x})$, applying those methods directly to the reduced form would entail an estimator defined as

$$\hat{\pi}_i = \mathrm{argmin}_{\pi_i} \frac{1}{T} \sum_t (y_{it} - \pi_i^\top \mathbf{x}_t)^2 + \lambda \sum_j p_T(\pi_{ij}),$$

for each $i \in \{1, \ldots, N\}$, where π_i is a column-vector corresponding to the ith row from Π, and $p_T(\cdot)$ is a sample-size-related penalty function that depends on the particular penalization method used. (The adequate notion of sparsity here is that T be sufficiently large compared to nonzero entries in the adjacency

---

[21] There are, nevertheless, data environments, like financial systems, where information on outcomes is collected frequently and reduced-form parameters can potentially be estimated without additional restrictions.

[22] Atalay, Hortacsu, Roberts, and Syverson (2011) used data from Compustat from 1979 to 2007 to study supply networks. The average number of suppliers (indegrees) reported in the study was 3.67 over the sample period. The number of firms in the sample varied between 631 (in 1979) and 1848 (in 2002). The total number of possible links in the directed graph is $N(N-1)$, and the density of links, defined as the ratio of observed links to potential links, is then given by the average (in)degree divided by $N-1$. Assuming that the average indegree is constant across years, the density is then between 0.2 percent (for $N = 1848$) and 0.6 percent (for $N = 631$).

[23] Carvalho (2014) uses input–output tables from the Bureau of Economic Analysis in 2002, defining 417 sectors as nodes in the network.

matrix.) This reduced form estimator (using the Elastic Net penalty function) is applied by Bonaldi, Hortacsu, and Kastl (2014), for example, to study the evolution and interconnection of banks' cost-of-funding inferred from bank bids in the main refinancing operation (MRO) auctions by the European Central Bank. There, y_{it} gives bank i's cost of funding, and covariates $\mathbf{x_t}$ are *lagged* cost-of-funding measures for all banks in the system. The authors use the estimated parameters to construct centrality indices for the banks in their sample. This estimator is also pursued by Manresa (2013) in a version of the model in (2) without endogenous effects ($\beta = 0$), in which case $\Pi = \eta \mathbf{I} + \gamma W$ (using my notation), allowing on the other hand for time- and individual-fixed effects.[24]

The estimation strategy above relies on sparsity of the reduced-form coefficients. Since $\Pi = \eta \mathbf{I} + \gamma W$ when $\beta = 0$ (as in Manresa, 2013), row-sum normalization of W (as required previously) is unnecessary for identification (one can normalize $\gamma = 1$, and the entries in each row can be heterogeneous). In this case, given that Π is a linear function of η and W, sparsity of W is clearly transferred to sparsity in Π. Nevertheless, because

$$\Pi = (\mathbf{I} - \beta W)^{-1} (\eta \mathbf{I} + \gamma W) \Leftrightarrow W = (\Pi - \eta \mathbf{I}) (\beta \Pi + \gamma \mathbf{I})^{-1},$$

it is not immediate that sparsity of W translates into sparsity of the reduced-form coefficient matrix Π. This will be the case when β is small (in which case $\Pi \approx \eta \mathbf{I} + \gamma W$ and sparsity in $\mathbf{I}$ and W carries over). Take, for example, the directed circle analyzed earlier, where $W_{i,i+1} = W_{N,1} = 1, i = 1, \ldots, N-1$, and all other entries are zero. Since there are N links out of possibly $N(N-1)$ directed connections, the density of edges is given by $1/(N-1)$. A directed circle with 100 nodes hence has an edge density of (approximately) 1 percent. Assume then that $\gamma = \eta = 1$ for simplicity. Figure 3 plots the proportion of zeros in Π as a function of β for a directed circle with $N = 100$.

Alternatively, note that (for $|\beta| < 1$) we can expand the inverse using a Neumann series and obtain

$$\Pi = \eta \mathbf{I} + (\beta \eta + \gamma) \sum_{k=1}^{\infty} \beta^{k-1} W^k.$$

Since $\beta \eta + \gamma \neq 0$, $\pi_{ij} = 0$ if, and only if, there are no paths between i and j in W. The (i, j) entry in W^k is nonzero whenever there is a path of length k between i and j. If a pair is not connected at any length, that entry is zero for every k. Therefore, Π is sparse if there is a large number of (i, j) unconnected pairs in W. When that is the case, de Paula, Rasul, and Souza (2015) say that W is "sparsely connected." (Note that the circular graph used above is sparse, but not sparsely connected.) A sparsely connected network, where many pairs

---

[24] Manresa suggests a computational procedure that alternates between the individual LASSO estimator for individual specific parameters (individual fixed effects and individual row in W), penalizing the L^1 norm of W_i, given the remaining parameters and a pooled ordinary least squares estimator for the remaining parameters given individual specific parameters until convergence.

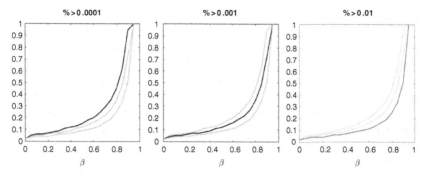

Figure 3 Sparsity of Π for Directed Circle. *Note:* The dark lines in the first, second, and third panels show the proportion of entries in $(\mathbf{I} - \beta W)^{-1}(\mathbf{I} + W)$ that are larger than 0.0001, 0.001 and 0.01, respectively, as a function of β. The matrix W is a 100×100 matrix ($N = 100$), such that $W_{ii+1} = W_{100,1} = 1$ for $i = 1, \ldots, 100$ and zero, otherwise. The density (proportion of nonzero entries) of W is 1 percent, and the density of $\mathbf{I} + W$, corresponding to $\beta = 0$, is 2 percent.

are not linked, will exhibit many components. A notion of *approximate* sparse connectedness can then be envisioned where the (i, j) entry of W^k is nonzero, but small. Because the number of components in a network equals the multiplicity of the zero eigenvalue of the Laplacian matrix (i.e., diag($W\mathbf{1}$) $- W$) (see Kolaczyk, 2009), the spectrum of this matrix can be used as a measure of sparse connectedness; the more eigenvalues there are in the vicinity of zero, the closer the matrix is to a sparsely connected matrix. The directed circle above is not approximately sparsely connected either.

I should note that there is a built-in tension between sparse connectedness and the linear independence assumption used for the identification of the model. For a (row-)stochastic matrix, for example, the nth smallest eigenvalue for the Laplacian matrix diag($W\mathbf{1}$) $- W$ corresponds to one minus the nth largest eigenvalue of W.[25] Then, if the spectrum of the Laplacian matrix is close to zero, the spectrum of the matrix W is close to a constant vector (of ones) and $\mathbf{I}$, W, and W^2 are linearly dependent. An alternative is to introduce the penalization directly on W, which may be more naturally expected to be sparse. In this case, it should be pointed out that the identification condition that W be nonnegative, row-sum normalized to one implies that the L_1-norm of W equals N. Hence, within this class of models, penalty schemes used in the LASSO or the Elastic Net might find difficulties discriminant among adjacency matrices. Other penalization strategies using non-convex penalty functions that also allow for sparse estimates, like the Smoothly Clipped Absolute Deviation (SCAD) penalty (Fan and Li, 2001) or the Minimax Concave Penalty (Zhang, 2010), will not be constant within the class of unit row-normalized, nonnegative matrices and might be employed. On the other hand, I should note that sparsity of W itself can potentially provide identification power *per se*,

---

[25] This is because (diag($W\mathbf{1}$) $- W$)$\mathbf{v} = (\mathbf{I} - W)\mathbf{v} = \lambda\mathbf{v}$ implies that $W\mathbf{v} = (1 - \lambda)\mathbf{v}$.

as it provokes a relatively large number of entries in W to be zero. In this sense, unrestricted estimation is a possibility using the LASSO or Elastic Net. (The relaxation of positivity and row-sum normalization could be regarded as allowing for individual heterogeneity in the magnitude and sign of β.)

The penalization of W is pursued, for example, by Lam and Souza (2013), after dispensing with the positivity and normalization assumption on W. They estimate the parameters of the model by minimizing an objective function written directly in terms of the structural system. In terms of our specific model and notation,

$$\min_{(W,\beta,\delta,\gamma)} \frac{1}{T} \sum_t \|\mathbf{y}_t - \alpha - \beta W \mathbf{y}_t - \eta \mathbf{x}_t - \gamma W \mathbf{x}_t \|_2^2 + \lambda \sum_{i \neq j} p_T(W_{ij}),$$

(6)

where $\| \cdot \|_2$ is the Euclidean norm and the penalty term depends on the L_1 norm of W. Since y is endogenous, it is expected that additional assumptions need to be imposed, and Lam and Souza (2013) suppose that the variance of the structural errors ϵ_{it} vanishes asymptotically (see their Assumption A2). (The asymptotics are in N and T.) Intuitively, this assumption can be seen as a version of the Proximity Theorem: "[I]f the variance–covariance matrix of the regressors is bounded away from singularity, the least-squares estimator approaches consistency either as the variance of the disturbance approaches zero or as the probability limits of the correlations between the disturbance and regressors approach zero" (see Theorem 3.9.1 in Fisher, 1966). The estimator, then, may be best suited for circumstances when error variances are relatively small, but less suited when the variance of the structural errors is comparatively large (see, e.g., Table 5 in Lam and Souza, 2013, for Monte Carlo results when error variances are comparatively large).[26]

In lieu of the above strategy, we can instead opt to minimize the following objective function:

$$\min_{(W,\beta,\delta,\gamma)} \frac{1}{T} \sum_t \|\mathbf{y}_t - \Pi \mathbf{x}_t\|_2^2 + \lambda \sum_{i \neq j} p_T(W_{ij})$$
$$\text{s.t. } (\mathbf{I} - \beta W)\Pi - (\eta \mathbf{I} + \gamma W) = 0.$$

Absent the penalization term, this can be seen to correspond to an indirect least squares estimator. This estimator nevertheless penalizes the adjacency matrix W directly (as opposed to the previous estimator focusing on the reduced form). A potential complication is that the objective function will no longer be convex since $\Pi = (\mathbf{I} - \beta W)^{-1}(\eta \mathbf{I} + \gamma W)$.[27] Of course, if the row-sum normalization condition is imposed also, one would also likely have to resort

---

[26] If the errors are normally distributed with a diagonal variance–covariance matrix, a full-information maximum likelihood estimator based on the model 2 would involve a term on the $(\log)$-L^2 norm of W (corresponding to the logarithm of the Jacobian term), and a penalized (quasi-)maximum likelihood estimator could be employed.

[27] Another possibility which may attenuate the computational issues is to minimize the above objective function with respect to both Π and W. (I thank Lars Nesheim for this suggestion.)

to a non-convex penalization scheme (like SCAD or MCP). The analysis and performance of this estimator are subjects of ongoing research.[28]

Aside from its role in estimation, sparsity of W can also be useful in identification as it essentially imposes exclusion restrictions on the different structural equations. Supposing enough sparsity, for example, Rose (2015) obtains identification results under additional conditions on the reduced-form coefficient matrix Π. These conditions are rank restrictions on sub-matrices of Π (whose verification is nevertheless computationally demanding). Intuitively, given two observationally equivalent systems, sparsity guarantees the existence of pairs that are not connected in either. Since observationally equivalent systems are linked via the reduced-form coefficient matrix, this pair allows one to identify certain parameters in the model and, having identified those, one can then proceed to identify other aspects of the structure. (This is related to the ideas in Theorem 6 of Blume, Brock, Durlauf, and Jayaraman, 2015; see discussion above.)

3.2   Nonlinearities and Multiple Equilibria

One can enumerate various empirical circumstances where a linear model may not be ideal (see, e.g., Kline and Tamer, 2011). Nonlinearities can occur through two possible, *non-mutually exclusive*, avenues: by nonlinearities in the "link" function through which the (possibly weighted) average of peer outcomes determine an individual's outcome (i.e., $y_i = f\left(\sum_{j=1}^{N} W_{ij} y_j, x_i, \sum_{j=1}^{N} W_{ij} x_j, \epsilon_i\right)$) or through nonlinear aggregation of peer outcomes (e.g., $\min_{j:W_{ij}\neq0} y_j$ instead of $\sum_{j=1}^{N} W_{ij} y_j$).

As noted by Manski (1993), even under nonlinearities, nonparametric versions of the social interactions system with global interactions analyzed earlier (i.e., $W_{ij} = 1/(N-1), i \neq j$ and $W_{ii} = 0, i, j = 1, \ldots, N$) are not identified. Brock and Durlauf (2001) show that this is not the case in a (parametric) binary choice model with social interactions (without correlated effects), and Brock and Durlauf (2007) extend the analysis to nonparametric binary choice models showing various point- and partial-identification results.[29] Blume, Brock, Durlauf, and Ioannides (2011) provide a comprehensive survey of social interactions in nonlinear models covering, for example, multiple discrete choice (Brock and Durlauf, 2006), duration models (Sirakaya, 2006; de Paula, 2009; Honoré and de Paula, 2010). Recently, Bramoullé, Kranton, and D'Amours (2014), investigated a class of game theoretic models on general networks and suggested a Tobit-type social interactions econometric model (on this, see Xu and Lee, forthcoming).

---

[28] If instrumental variables are available for each of the endogenous variables, (penalized) IV estimators could also provide an estimation avenue (see Gautier and Tsybakov, 2014; Lam and Souza, 2014).

[29] Bisin, Moro, and Topa (2011) and Menzel (2015) investigate alternatives for estimation of these models (and others) for interaction systems with a large number of players.

Manski (1993) also points out that "social effects might be transmitted by distributional features other than the mean" (p. 534). Tao and Lee (2014) consider, for example, peer effects defined by the minimum outcome among one's peers. Also looking at a model where individuals are affected by nonlinear functionals of their peers' outcome distribution, Tincani (2015) obtains testable implications and finds evidence of nonlinearities in education peer effects in Chile using a recent earthquake and its differential impact on students at different distances from its rupture. Whereas these models use a global interactions network structure, more general network structures could prove useful in many respects.

One interesting aspect in such nonlinear models is the possibility for multiple equilibria. In their study of social effects on fertility choices, for example, Manski and Mayshar (2003) explore a utility-maximizing model where nonlinear child allowance schemes may lead to multiple social equilibria. Whereas multiplicity can, at times, pose issues for identification, this is not necessarily always the case. Once again, Manski (1993), for instance, suggested that "[t]he prospects for identification may improve if [the model] is nonlinear in a manner that generates multiple social equilibria" (p. 539). Indeed, identification is facilitated in certain cases, as suggested by the analysis of a binary choice model (without correlated effects) in de Paula and Tang (2012) (see de Paula, 2013, for a general survey on econometric analysis of interaction models with multiplicity).

Recently, Manski (2013) contemplated the analysis of potential outcomes in a social interactions context. Letting $x_i = \{0, 1\}$ denote a particular (binary) treatment for individual i and $\mathbf{x}$ be a vector collecting treatments for the group as a whole, the potential outcome for individual i when the group is faced with the treatment profile $\mathbf{x}$ is denoted by $y_i(\mathbf{x})$. Manski enumerates a few circumstances where individual treatments may spill over to other network members. The epidemiology of infectious diseases provides a salient example, where vaccination of an individual presumably affects that person's likelihood of infection, which is additionally influenced by the infection status of others in the community (there is a well-established epidemiology literature on network diffusion of infectious diseases). Using the conditional cash transfer program Progresa in Mexico and using consumption as an outcome, Angelucci and De Giorgi (2009) found evidence of spillovers operating mostly through insurance and credit relationships. Dieye, Djebbari, and Barrera-Osorio (2014) investigate the effects of a scholarship program in Colombia with possible spillovers. Using our notation, we can represent the setup envisioned by Manski as

$$y_i(\mathbf{x}) = f\left(W_i, \mathbf{y}_{-i}(\mathbf{x}), \mathbf{x}, \epsilon_i\right),$$

where $y_i(\mathbf{x})$ is the potential outcome for individual i when the network receives treatment $\mathbf{x}$.[30] Manski provides characterizations on the set of identified

---

[30] Manski also mentions the possibility that the treatment vector may affect the reference group for each individual, in which case $W_i = W_i(\mathbf{x})$). In fact, Comola and Prina (2014), studying

distributions for the potential outcomes $\mathbf{y}(\mathbf{x}), \mathbf{x} \in \{0, 1\}^N$ when the above system has a single solution. As he points out, a nonlinear system may lead to multiple solutions (or maybe no solution at all), complicating the characterization of the identified set of potential outcome distributions. These ideas are further investigated (theoretically and empirically) by Lazzati (2015), who further imposes monotonicity restrictions on the treatment effects.

3.3   Other Considerations

Spillovers mediated through network structures are, of course, present in a myriad of economic and social circumstances. Demand externalities arise naturally in goods and services whose values depend on the topology and volume of the network of consumers and producers involved. There is a enough literature in theoretical and applied industrial organization on the topic to fill a completely separate survey article.

More traditional industries are nevertheless also interconnected via input–output-directed relationships (see Kranton and Minehart, 2001, for a theoretical analysis of buyer-seller networks). Carvalho, Nirei, and Saito (2014), for instance, examined supply chain disruptions following the 2011 earthquake in Japan. Also using Japanese data, Bernard, Moxnes, and Saito (2014) studied buyer–seller networks and firm performance using infrastructure developments (high-speed trains) for variation in travelling costs, leading to the creation of new buyer-seller linkages. In fact, supplier–client networks present many of the same features described earlier (e.g., clustering, sparsity, intransitivities) (e.g., Atalay, Hortacsu, Roberts, and Syverson, 2011; and Carvalho, 2014). It is *conceivable* that some of the ideas highlighted in previous subsections (e.g., the use of indirect peers' outcomes or the output of suppliers of one's suppliers for identification) could be used in the identification of these relationships and primitives of interest, like production or value-added functions (e.g., Gandhi, Navarro, and Rivers, 2013 for a recent article with a good overview on the econometric literature about production and value-added functions). Production networks and their composition have obvious connections to the macroeconomy (e.g., Acemoglu, Carvalho, Ozdaglar, and Tahbaz-Salehi, 2012) and trade (e.g., Antras and Chor, 2013), and I refer the reader to Carvalho, 2014, and Acemoglu, Ozdaglar, and Tahbaz-Salehi, forthcoming) for recent reviews on the propagation of microeconomic shocks in production and financial systems.

Buyer-seller networks have repercussions in other dimensions as well. One interesting dimension is in taxation chains. The collection of value-added taxes is usually done via a credit mechanism, for example, whereby firms remit taxes on their revenues and claim tax credits on their inputs. Theoretically, this binds compliance through the network and is another channel through

the introduction of a savings product in Nepal, found that insurance-motivated connections are likely to be rewired after the intervention.

which individual firm decisions may reverberate through the network (e.g., de Paula and Scheinkman, 2010, and Pomeranz, forthcoming).[31] Again, the insights described previously could prove useful here.

4   NETWORK FORMATION

As seen above, the connection structure among networked agents can assist with the identification and estimation of models describing the resolution of economic and social outcomes of interest. It is nevertheless apparent that, whereas in some cases the peer structure can be taken as (econometrically) exogenous or predetermined, many times the very formation of a connection arises in response to incentives that may or may not articulate with the outcomes to be determined using the networks as a conduit. Models of network formation are, then, of interest on their own as well as in conjunction with the simultaneous equation models covered in the previous section.

4.1   Statistical Models

We can posit a data-generating process summarized by the statistical model $(\mathcal{G}, \sigma(\mathcal{G}), \mathcal{P})$, where $\sigma(\mathcal{G})$ is a σ-algebra of events in the sample space of graphs $\mathcal{G}$, and $\mathcal{P}$ is a class of probability distributions on the measurable space $(\mathcal{G}, \sigma(\mathcal{G}))$. In the Ërdos–Rényi model defined on N vertices, for example, $\mathcal{P}$ would be the parametric class of models indexed by the probability $p \in (0, 1)$ that an undirected link is independently formed between any two vertices under consideration, defining a probability distribution over the set of $2^{N(N-1)/2}$ possible graphs on the set of N nodes. (I will focus here on undirected networks, though versions of many of the estimators below exist for more general graphical structures.) A great many statistical models for network formation can be seen as enrichments of this simple model (just as a probit or logit and mixture versions of those can be seen as generalizations of a Bernoulli statistical model). For the statistical models listed in this subsection, the analyst is assumed to have data on at least one network (*but not necessarily more than one*). (The estimation of a classical Ërdos–Rényi model with only one network of N individuals, for instance, would essentially amount to the estimation of Bernoulli parameter on $N(N-1)/2$ observations.)

Zheng, Salganik, and Gelman (2006), for example, used a heterogeneous version of this simple random graph model to obtain estimates for the total size of hard-to-count populations. In the Ërdos–Rényi model above, the expected degree for a given individual when there are N nodes equals Np, and the proportion of total links involving individuals in group k (e.g., incarcerated individuals) is given by N_k/N. The answer to the question of how many individuals of group k an individual i knows is then well-approximated by

---

[31] Network spillovers can also be present at the individual compliance level (e.g., Fortin, Lacroix, and Villeval, 2007, Galbiati and Zanella, 2012, and Kopczuk, Alstadsaeter, and Telle, 2014).

a Poisson distribution with parameter pN_k (similar to the approximation of the degree distribution by a Poisson distribution, as mentioned earlier). The authors show that a better model for the data analyzed is one where not only individual "gregariousness" (i.e., the expected degree of the individual) but also the individual propensity to know individuals in a given group k are heterogeneous. The distribution of answer counts is then given by a mixture of Poisson distributions (mixing over the heterogeneity in the relevant parameters), overdispersed relative to a (homogeneous parameter) Poisson distribution. Using this statistical model and Bayesian statistical methods, they were able to estimate the distribution of links (to any other individual) in the wider population of interest. This model is adapted by Hong and Xu (2014) to study local networks among fund managers using their portfolio allocation to local investments, where they find similar evidence of heterogeneity. Many other estimation strategies seek to characterize the degree distribution as a means to infer a well-suited probabilistic data-generating model for the network (e.g., Ërdos–Rényi, preferential attachment, etc.).

A well-known generalization of the Ërdos–Rényi model is the class of exponential random graph models introduced earlier in this article. For those models,

$$\mathbb{P}(G = g) = \exp \left(\sum_{k=1}^{p} \alpha_k S_k(g) - A(\alpha_1, \ldots, \alpha_k) \right), \tag{7}$$

where $A(\alpha_1, \ldots, \alpha_k)$ is a normalization constant ensuring that probabilities integrate to one and $S_k(g), k = 1, \ldots, p$ enumerate certain features of the graph g. These would be characteristics like the number of edges, the number of triangles, and possibly many others. (If only the number of edges is considered, we obtain the Ërdos–Rényi model.) Since the probability mass function is in the exponential class, the model shares some well-understood properties. For example, the vector $(S_k(g))_{k=1}^{p}$ is a sufficient statistic for $(\alpha_k)_{k=1}^{p}$, which is called the natural parameter for the exponential family, and $A(\alpha_1, \ldots, \alpha_k) = \ln \left[\sum_{g \in \mathcal{G}} \exp \left(\sum_{k=1}^{p} \alpha_k S_k(g) \right) \right]$ is its cumulant generating function or log partition function (i.e., the logarithm of its moment-generating function). (The distribution (7) is sometimes referred to as the Gibbs measure in the literature, given its connection to similar models in physics.) This model allows one to define probabilities using prevalent features of observed networks such as triads, clusters, and other topological characteristics.

In principle, it is also amenable to likelihood-based inference just like any other exponential class distribution. The ensuing computational difficulties are nevertheless sizeable. This relates to the fact that the normalization constant (i.e., $\exp(-A(\alpha_1, \ldots, \alpha_k))$) requires summing over all $2^{N(N-1)/2}$ graphs. If $N = 24$, the number of graphs (approximately 1.21×10^{83}) amounts to more than the estimated number of atoms in the observable universe. To circumvent this issue, considerable effort has been devoted to providing computational tools and approximation results that allow one to estimate this constant and carry out inference. Two main avenues are the use of variational principles and Markov chain Monte Carlo (MCMC) methods, both rooted in statistical mechanics.

Exploring properties of the cumulant function (e.g., convexity), one can use variational methods to represent the constant as a solution to an optimization problem. Consider, for instance, an Ërdos–Rényi graph on two nodes i and j. The (random) edge between these two vertices can be written as a Bernoulli random variable W_{ij}, and its probability mass function can be parameterized as $\mathbb{P}(W_{ij} = w_{ij}) = \exp(\alpha w_{ij})/(1+\exp(\alpha)) = \exp(\alpha w_{ij} - A(\alpha))$, $w_{ij} = 0, 1$. In this case, $A(\alpha) = \ln(1 + \exp(\alpha))$, and notice that $A''(\alpha) = \exp(\alpha)/(1 + \exp(\alpha))^2 > 0$, so $A(\alpha)$ is convex. Using results from convex analysis, one can express $A(\alpha)$ as

$$A(\alpha) = \sup_{\mu \in [0,1]} \{\alpha\mu - A^*(\mu)\}, \tag{8}$$

where $A^*(\mu) = \sup_{\alpha \in \mathbb{R}}\{\mu\alpha - A(\alpha)\} = \mu \ln \mu + (1 - \mu)\ln(1 - \mu)$ (i.e., the *convex conjugate* or Legendre–Fenchel transformation of $A(\alpha)$). Note also that $A^*(\mu)$ equals the negative of the solution to the problem: $\max_p H(p)$ subject to $\mathbb{E}_p(g_{ij}) = \mu$, where $H(p) \equiv -p \ln p - (1 - p)\ln(1 - p)$ is known as the Shannon entropy (for the Bernoulli distribution). The conjugate dual $A^*(\mu)$ can be obtained using the entropy measure more generally. Having obtained $A^*(\mu)$, if one then explicitly maximizes $\alpha\mu - A^*(\mu) = \alpha\mu - \mu \ln \mu - (1 - \mu)\ln(1 - \mu)$ over $\mu \in [0, 1]$, it can be seen that the maximum is attained at $A(\alpha)$ defined above. The key here is to use the fact that the necessary conjugate function is related to the entropy measure H and represents the sum over possible networks $A(\alpha)$ as the solution to an optimization problem. In practice, the computation of the dual function will involve calculation of the entropy measure H, and the optimization (8) is performed over a space that is not always easily characterized (in this case, it is $\{\mu : 0 \le \mu \le 1\}$). In high-dimensional problems, various approximations to the constraint set and the dual $A^*(\mu)$ are then pursued to provide a computationally tractable estimate of the cumulant function $A(\alpha)$ (see Section 3.3 in Jordan, 2004 or Jordan and Wainwright, 2008 and Braun and McAuliffe, 2010 for an application to high-dimensional discrete choice models). Using variational methods, for example, Chatterjee and Diaconis, 2013 provide an approximation of the cumulant function for dense graphs when the number of nodes goes to infinity,[32] and Chatterjee and Dembo, 2014 provide error bounds for this approximation when there is a small degree of sparsity.

Perhaps a more familiar class of techniques involves MCMC methods. Such procedures have also been developed to produce maximum likelihood estimators and Bayesian posterior distributions for $(\alpha_1, \ldots, \alpha_k)$ in exponential network models. Different approaches are summarized in Kolaczyk (2009).[33]

---

[32] Their arguments are based on approximations to large, dense graphs.

[33] The software suite `statnet` offers a package for the analysis of ERGMs in R.

It should be noted that various issues may arise in simulating ERGMs. The procedure can be very slow to converge to an invariant distribution. This is highlighted, for instance, in the discussion by Chandrasekhar and Jackson (2014) and Mele (2015) and formally demonstrated in Bhamidi, Bresler, and Sly (2011). In particular, for certain regions of the parameter space (defined as "low temperature" regions, in analogy to spin systems in physics), where the distribution (7) is multimodal, the mixing time for the MCMC procedure, i.e., the time it takes for the MCMC procedure to be within e^{-1} in total variation distance from the desired distribution, is exponential on the number of nodes (Theorem 6 in that paper). In other regions ("high temperature" ones), where the distribution (7) is unimodal, the mixing time is $O(n^2 \ln n)$ (Theorem 5 in that article).

One recurrent related issue in the application of ERGMs is what the literature terms *degeneracy* or *near degeneracy*, whereby "depending on the parameter values, the exponential random graph distribution can have a bimodal shape in the sense that most of the probability mass is distributed over two clearly separated subsets of the set of all digraphs, one subset containing only low-density and the other subset containing only high-density digraphs. The separation between these two subsets can be so extreme that [...] stochastic updating steps which change only a small number of arc variables [...] have a negligible probability of taking the Markov process from one to the other subset" (Snijders, 2002, p. 13). This again will lead at times to very slow convergence of a Markov chain Monte Carlo procedure to an invariant distribution. It is not uncommon either to observe abrupt changes on the class of probable graphs as parameters change, and all of these "oddities" are characterized as *degeneracy* or *near degeneracy* of the ERGM. In fact, this behavior is not at all unusual and is related to the general properties of discrete exponential distribution families as investigated in Rinaldo, Fienberg, and Zhou (2009) and Geyer (2009) (see Handcock, 2003 for an earlier analysis). In such models, when the observed sufficient statistics are at (or, for all practical purposes, near) the boundary of their support, the MLE will not exist, and, even when it does, Markov chain-ML estimators will tend to not behave well. For instance, the sample average is the sufficient statistic for the natural parameter α of a Bernoulli random variable (as in the two-node Erdos–Rényi random graph above). When that sample average is one or zero, the ML estimator for the natural parameter does not exist! As indicated by Rinaldo, Fienberg, and Zhou (2009), "ERG modeling based on simple, low dimensional network statistics [...] can be rather coarse. In fact, those ERG models are invariant with respect to the relabeling of the nodes and even to changes in the graph topologies, depending on the network statistics themselves. As a result, they do not specify distributions over graphs per se, but rather distributions over large classes of graphs having the same network statistics" (pp. 459–60). Hence, when the model is not sufficiently rich and/or observed networks are moderately sparse, the sufficient statistics will act as a coarse classifier of networks, and one may well find herself facing the issues highlighted above. The stark "discontinuities" in the distribution of graphs generated by the model as parameters are varied are also investigated in Chatterjee and Diaconis (2013) for dense, large networks. They also discuss the (troublesome) issue that for certain regions of the parameter space – the "high temperature" ones, where the distribution (7) is unimodal, graph draws from the model are very close to those of an Ërdos–Rényi model with independent link formation (see their Theorem 4.2). A similar point is made in Bhamidi, Bresler, and Sly (2011) (see their Theorem 7).[34]

An early alternative estimation strategy, adapted to ERGMs by Strauss and Ikeda (1990) (but originally suggested by Besag, 1975), is to rely on the (log) pseudo-likelihood

$$\sum_{\{i,j\}} \ln \mathbb{P}(W_{ij} = 1 | W_{-ij} = w_{-ij}; \alpha),$$

where $\mathbb{P}(W_{ij} = 1 | W_{-ij} = w_{-ij}; \alpha)$ denotes the probability that the link W_{ij} is formed conditional on the remainder of the network, which I denote by W_{-ij}. Upon inspection, it can be seen that this does not correspond to the likelihood function for the model unless links form independently. In fact, if the dependence is not sufficiently weak, this estimator is bound to produce unreliable estimates (e.g., Robins, Snijders, Wang, Handcock, and Pattison, 2007).

If links are independently formed, the objective function is such that $\mathbb{P}(W_{ij} = 1 | W_{-ij} = w_{-ij}; \alpha) = \mathbb{P}(W_{ij} = 1; \alpha)$. In this case, one can easily focus on dyads (i.e., pairs of vertices and the existing links between them) and incorporate covariates. This dyadic model has often been used in the social sciences to study network links (see Wasserman and Faust, 1994). One well-known dyadic model is that of Holland and Leinhardt (1981), where the authors focus on directed links. Their model, which they call the p_1 model, postulates that:

$$\mathbb{P}(W_{ij} = W_{ji} = 1) \propto \exp(\alpha^{\text{rec}} + 2\alpha + \alpha_i^{\text{out}} + \alpha_i^{\text{in}} + \alpha_j^{\text{out}} + \alpha_j^{\text{in}})$$

and

$$\mathbb{P}(W_{ij} = 1, W_{ji} = 0) \propto \exp(\alpha + \alpha_i^{\text{out}} + \alpha_j^{\text{in}}).$$

Here, the parameter α_i^{out} encodes the tendency of node i to send out links irrespective of the target (its "gregariousness"), and α_j^{in} captures node j's tendency to receive links regardless of the sender's identity (its "attractiveness"). The parameter α^{rec} registers the tendency for directed links to be reciprocated: large, positive values of α^{rec} will increase the likelihood of symmetric adjacency matrices. (Note that when $\alpha_i^{\text{out}} = \alpha_i^{\text{in}} = \alpha^{\text{rec}} = 0$ for all i, links

---

[34] These difficulties in distinguishing the model from an Ërdos–Rényi one also lead to identification issues as pointed out in Mele (2015), which analyses an ERGM obtained from a network formation model (see dicussion below). As he indicates, these identification challenges are less troublesome when multiple networks are observed (as in Nakajima, 2007), but are germane when identification relies on a single network.

form independently with probability given by $\exp(\alpha)/(1 + \exp(\alpha))$, and the model would correspond to a logit.) It is straightforward to add dyad-specific covariates to the specification above.

Generalizations and special cases for this model have been suggested and extensively analyzed. Hoff (2005), for example, considers an augmented model where *multiplicative* interactions between individual unobserved factors are added to the probability specification above (i.e., $\mathbf{z}_i \times \mathbf{z}_j$, where $\mathbf{z}_i$ is a vector of i-specific factors), and those plus the additive "gregariousness" and "attractiveness" features defined previously (i.e., α_i^{out} and α_i^{in}) are modeled as random effects. Building on tools from the (large-N, T) panel data literature (Fernandez-Val and Weidner, 2014) and focusing on the additive structure above with possibly additional observed covariates, Dzemski (2014) on the other hand treats α_i^{out} and α_i^{in} as fixed effects, hence allowing for an arbitrary correlation between those and with any observed characteristic in the model.[35] He provides a test of the model based on the prevalence of transitive triads (i.e., vertex triples where links are transitive) and an application to the microfinance-related networks collected and analyzed in Banerjee, Chandrasekhar, Duflo, and Jackson (2014) (among other papers).[36] Graham (2014) investigates a similar model (with observed covariates), but for undirected networks (see also Charbonneau, 2014). There, the undirected links are formed with a probability that is proportional to $\exp(\alpha + \alpha_i + \alpha_j)$. This is related to the Rasch model (Rasch, 1960) and can be seen as a pairwise stable arrangement when direct transfers are possible (see Bloch and Jackson, 2007). In the absence of covariates, its MLE large sample properties (for dense networks) are analyzed by Chatterjee, Diaconis, and Sly (2011) and Yan and Xu (2013), who call it the β-model. In this case, the distinction between "sender productivity" and "receiver attractiveness" for a given node disappears, but the parameters α_i can be interpreted as the proclivity by node i to establish connections. Those parameters are also treated as fixed effects. Aside from providing large sample characterizations for the ML estimator, Graham (2014) also analyzes the conditional ML estimator constructed using sufficient statistics for α_i, allowing him to "condition those parameters out" and circumvent the incidental parameters problem when estimating the observable covariate coefficients.

Instead of zooming in on individual pairs and the links established between them, Chandrasekhar and Jackson (2014) proposed a framework focusing on additional classes of subgraphs, which they call subgraph generation model (SUGM). The model specifies a set of K subgraphs, $(G_l)_{l=1}^{K}$, possibly involving a different number of nodes each and probabilities for each one of those. For example, one could specify $K = 2$ and G_1 to be the class of (undirected) edges between two nodes, taking probabiliy p_1, and G_2 to be the class of (undirected) triangles, to form with probability p_2. (I focus on undirected

---

[35] Hoff (2005) parameterized the correlation between α_i^{out} and α_i^{in}, whereas Dzemski (2014) can allow for more general dependencies.

[36] Interestingly, the estimated distribution of "gregariousness" and "attractiveness" appear to cluster in a few groups, suggesting group-level heterogeneity.

graphs, but their analysis can also be extended to directed ones.) A possible narrative for this specification could be that the establishment of certain connections only requires dyads (e.g., a tennis match), whereas others elicit participation from triples (e.g., a proper rock'n'roll band). One version of their model has subgraphs form at random and produce a graph realization defined by the union of edges formed by the initial subgraph draws. Note that some edges drawn in the initial protocol will be redundant. The edge $\{i, j\}$ from the first class of subgraphs may form independently as well as part of a triangle, say $\{i, j, k\}$, with probability $p_1 \times p_t$: two bandmates in a trio may also be tennis partners. (Chandrasekhar and Jackson, 2014, also consider a protocol where subgraphs are formed sequentially, avoiding redundancies.) Furthermore, realized isolated edges, triangles, and more generally modeled subgraphs can possibly get "meshed" in the final observed network. For instance, a triangle involving nodes i, j and k could be the outcome of independently formed edges $\{i, j\}$, $\{j, k\}$, and $\{k, i\}$ (which occurs with probability p_1^3), a genuine triangle $\{i, j, k\}$ (happening with probability p_t), or a combination of independent edges and triangles involving those nodes (and possibly others). Disentangling the count of subgraphs in the model that are genuinely formed or just happenstance from the composition of other subgraphs can be done by noting that the count of each subgraph $(G_l)_{l=1}^K$ is a mixture of both genuinely and incidentally formed subgraphs. This provides a system of equations that can be solved for the parameters of interest. This system of equations also produces a simple method of moments estimator for the desired quantities, and Chandrasekhar and Jackson (2014) provide large sample characterizations for the estimator. The probabilities for each subgraph can also be made to depend on covariates. Finally, the authors also relate SUGM to mutual consent and search intensity network formation models. They provide an application to microfinance-related network data collected by the authors in several Indian villages (e.g., Banerjee, Chandrasekhar, Duflo, and Jackson, 2014).

4.2   Strategic Network Formation

Most of the literature above relates to statistical models not (or at least not directly) related to economic models of network formation. Here I consider econometric models where agents purposefully form networks according to an explicit equilibrium notion and a payoff structure whereby node i's utility function $U_i(g)$ depends on the network g and vertex and/or pairwise-specific variables, observable and unobservable to the econometrician. (I omit observable covariates below for simplicity.) Though more general specifications are possible, one common specification (for undirected networks) involves variations of

$$U_i(g) \equiv \sum_{j \neq i} W_{ij} \times \left(u + \epsilon_{ij}\right) + \left|\cup_{j: W_{ij}=1} N_j(g) - N_i(g) - \{i\}\right| v$$

$$+ \sum_j \sum_{k > j} W_{ij} W_{ik} W_{jk} \omega, \tag{9}$$

where $N_i(g)$ denotes the set of nodes directly connected to node i and $|\cdot|$ is the cardinality of a given set. The vector $\epsilon_i \equiv (\epsilon_{ij})_{j \neq i}$ enumerates link-specific payoff shifters. I also retain the notation of using $W_{ij} \in \{0, 1\}$ to denote the establishment of a link from i to j. The first term in this payoff function enumerates the utility of direct connections and is indexed by the parameter u. The second term represents the payoff from indirect connections (one link away), and v is the payoff per such an indirect link. The last term expresses any utility from mutual connections between vertices directly linked to node i. Whereas specific implementations may differ, they typically involve terms relating to each of these three aspects (direct connections, indirect connections, and mutual connections). Similar specifications exist for directed networks. Finally, the analysis may also differ depending on whether utility is transferable or not (see Jackson, 2009 for a definition). Here I focus on non-transferable utility models, although transferable utility models have also been examined (see Lee and Fong, 2011).

One class of models focuses on an iterative network formation protocol and includes the papers by Christakis, Fowler, Imbens, and Kalianaraman (2010), Mele (2015) and Badev (2013). At each iteration of the meeting protocol, a pair of individuals and the relevant unobservable errors are drawn and (myopically) determine the formation or dissolution of an edge according to the payoff structure. This relates, for example, to earlier analyses on stochastic best response dynamics by Blume (1993) (for non-cooperative games) and, in the context of network formation models, to Watts (2001) and Jackson and Watts (2002). A meeting protocol is also employed in the precursor article by Currarini, Jackson, and Pin (2009) (which focuses on direct links). (I mention in passing that, given the nature of the myopic sequential optimization process, a structural interpretation of the unobserved taste shocks and meeting protocol as a component of the data-generating process will be more or less adequate, depending on the empirical context.) The first paper above considers an undirected network. While Christakis, Fowler, Imbens, and Kalianaraman (2010) do not explicitly consider an equilibrium notion, if unobservable preference shocks are absent (or fixed) throughout the meeting protocol, the (undirected) network would converge to *a* pairwise stable configuration if one exists (see below for definition) or cycle if one does not exist (see Watts, 2001). In the models above, new unobservables are drawn at each meeting, and one can view these "perturbations" as producing a version of the stochastic stability analysis in Jackson and Watts (2002).

Mele (2015) and Badev (2013), on the other hand, study directed networks (Badev, 2013 extends Mele, 2015 to model link formation and behavioral choices – smoking – simultaneously). Under some conditions, Mele (2015) demonstrates the existence of a potential function to characterize the Nash equilibria of the model absent the unobservable error. (Badev, 2013, who also relies on a potential function, on the other hand, introduces and focuses his analysis of the unobservable-error-free model on the concept of k-Nash stability, building on previous work by Bala and Goyal, 2000.) Mele (2015) then shows that the meeting protocol and myopic best response dynamic form an ergodic Markov chain on the space of networks and converges to a unique invariant distribution (with modes at the maximands of the potential function alluded to above). In fact, when the unobservables are assumed to be i.i.d. extreme value distributed, the limiting distribution corresponds to that of an ERGM.[37] Given the practical difficulties in the estimation of ERGMs pointed out previously, I should mention that Mele (2015) also proposes a modified MCMC procedure and analyzes the procedure for this particular model along the lines of Bhamidi, Bresler, and Sly (2011), demonstrating that the slow convergence regions in the parameter space are relatively small for parsimonious parameterizations of the utility function where only direct links matter (see Mele, 2015 for further details). Intuitively, the most parsimonious parameterization of an ERGM would correspond to an Ërdos–Rényi model, for which the parameter space would be in the "high temperature" regime.

All three models above are fit to a network of friendships obtained from the AddHealth data and use MCMC methods to produce Bayesian estimates of the parameters of interest. Whereas Christakis, Fowler, Imbens, and Kalianaraman (2010) use data from one school network, Mele (2015) estimates his model on three school networks, and Badev (2013) uses data from 14 school networks. (The AddHealth data has a total of 16 schools for which all information was collected.) The goodness of fit analysis provided by Christakis, Fowler, Imbens, and Kalianaraman (2010) demonstrates that a model with utility functions extending to indirect connections matches patterns of the observed networks well.

A different class of models focuses instead on a static framework. For undirected networks, a common solution concept adopted in those papers is that of pairwise stability (see Jackson and Wolinsky, 1996). A pairwise stable network is one for which:

$$\{i, j\} \in g \Rightarrow U_i(g) \geq U_i(g - \{i, j\}) \tag{10}$$

and

$$\{i, j\} \notin g \Rightarrow U_i(g \cup \{i, j\}) < U_i(g) \text{ or } U_j(g \cup \{i, j\}) < U_j(g). \tag{11}$$

The notation $g - \{i, j\}$ stands for the graph obtained by the deletion of the link $\{i, j\}$ from g, and $g \cup \{i, j\}$ denotes the graph obtained by adding the edge $\{i, j\}$ to g. This solution concept incorporates the idea that any link can be severed unilaterally, but the formation of a link requires mutal consent. Other solution concepts exist for undirected networks and related solution concepts can be employed for directed networks (Nash stability, for example) and when transfers are possible (see Jackson, 2009). As pointed out above, pairwise stable networks would be rest points for link formation sequences produced via a meeting protocol if the payoff structure does not change at each new meeting.

---

[37] The connection between potential games and ERGMs was independently noticed by Butts (2009).

In that case, the realized sequence of meetings could be seen as a selection among the possible stable networks which the approaches described below try to be agnostic about. The articles described above circumvent this issue by introducing noise in the meeting process (as unobservables are drawn anew at each meeting opportunity). A (latent) meeting protocol would still need to be specified.[38] Furthermore, the multiplicity partly reappears as the MCMC procedures used in the estimation tend to have the most difficulty in regions of the parameter space where the distribution of networks is multimodal (i.e., the "low temperature" regions), which in turn correspond to there being multiple (Nash or Nash stable) equilibria in the underlying game (without econometric errors).

Aside from the proliferation of possible networks as the number of nodes grows, an added difficulty in the analysis of such models is the possible multiplicity of equilibria for given realizations of the payoff-relevant variables. To illustrate this, consider a simple three-node graph with payoffs given by

$$U_i(g) = \sum_{j \in 1,\ldots,n, j \neq i} \delta^{d(i,j;g)-1} \left(1 + \epsilon_{ij}\right) - |N_i(g)|,$$

where $\delta \in (0, 1)$ and $d(i, j; g)$ is the shortest distance between i and j in the graph g. This is an econometric version of the connections game in Jackson and Wolinsky (1996) where player i collects $1 + \epsilon_{ij}$ if directly connected to node j and $\delta^{d(i,j;g)-1} \left(1 + \epsilon_{ij}\right)$ if indirectly connected to j and any direct connection cost her one util. The set of possible links is $\{12, 13, 23\}$, and there are eight possible networks (2^3). (To economize on notation, I use ij instead of $\{i, j\}$ to denote the edge between nodes i and j.) To visualize the multiplicity of solutions, I map the possible pairwise stable networks for a realization of ϵs where $\epsilon_{ij} = \epsilon_{ji}$ for any i, j in the ($\epsilon_{12} \times \epsilon_{13}$)-space for $0 < \epsilon_{23} < \delta/(1 - \delta)$ (see appendix for a more detailed description).

To emulate the approach usually adopted in the empirical games literature (see de Paula, 2013), one could generate bounds on the parameters of interest (i.e., δ in this model) by noting that the model implies probability bounds for each (pairwise stable) network to be observed. For example, the probability of observing the network $\{12, 13\}$ is bounded below by the probability that it arises as a unique equilibrium (e.g., the probability of the NE corner of the figure) and bounded below by that quantity plus the probability that it is a pairwise stable network (but not the only one) (e.g., the positive quadrant). The first bound corresponds to the possibility that this network is never selected when other equilibrium networks are possible and the upper bound corresponds to the opposite scenario where this network is always selected. Such bounds would depend on the parameters of the model. *If one has access to a sample of networks*, one could estimate the identified set of parameters

---

[38] In the directed network case, Badev (2013) shows nevertheless that, under certain restrictions on the class of meeting protocols, the invariant network distribution does not depend on the specification of the meeting process.

302   Áureo de Paula

by collecting all those parameters for which the bounds contain the observed frequency of networks. It should be apparent that this task becomes computationally quite complex as the number of nodes increases: the dimensions of both the latent variable space and possible networks to be checked for stability increase relatively quickly. (Remember that with 24 nodes, the number of graphs is more than the estimated number of atoms in the observed universe.)

To ameliorate the computational difficulties highlighted above, Sheng (2014) focuses instead on subnetworks (i.e., subsets of vertices and the edges among them), checking whether those subgraphs are consistent with pairwise stability (with or without transferable utility) for undirected networks. A lower bound on the probability of observing a particular subgraph to a pairwise stable network is the probability that this subgraph be the only one to satisfy the pairwise stability conditions given any (potentially not pairwise stable) complementary network (i.e., the network after deletion of the subgraph's edges from the overall graph, including the edges incident with the subgraph nodes). An upper bound is the probability that this subgraph satisfies the pairwise stability condition given some (potentially not pairwise stable) complementary network. As explained by Sheng (2014), these bounds are not sharp (even when considering subnetworks only) since the upper bound is larger than the probability that the subgraph is part of a pairwise stable network, and the lower bound is lower than the probability that it is a subgraph to a unique pairwise stable network given the payoff structure. Consider, for instance, the game depicted in Figure 4, and take the subgraph $\{12\}$. Because this link satisfies the pairwise stability condition when $\epsilon_{12} > 0$, given no links between 1 and 3 and between 2 and 3, the upper bound will be larger than the region where $\{12\}$ is

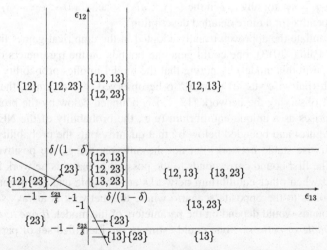

Figure 4 Multiplicity of Pairwise Stable Networks. *Note:* The figure shows the pairwise stable networks for different realization of ϵ_{12} and ϵ_{13}, assuming that $0 < \epsilon_{23} < \delta/(1 - \delta)$. A detailed description is given in Appendix B.

a subgraph to any pairwise stable network (which would exclude the triangle where {23} is the only pairwise stable network). Since the set of complementary networks may still be sizeable, the author imposes additional restrictions (payoffs of a link only depend on the remaining graph up to each player's immediate neighborhood and a cap on the number of links each node can form). Using these bounds, usual techniques in the estimation of partially identified models can then be implemented, and the dimensionality of the problem is reduced from the cardinality of the vertex set to the count of vertices in the subgraphs analyzed. One possible issue is that the restrictions imposed may sacrifice identification power when networks involve a large number of nodes and yield larger bounds.

The computational burden can also be alleviated by exploring particular features of the model. Miyauchi (2014) studies a model with non-transferable utility, where payoffs are supermodular, and pairwise stable networks consequently correspond to a fixed point of a monotone mapping. The supermodularity condition requires that $U_i(g) - U_i(g - \{ij\})$ if $\{ij\} \in g$ and $U_i(g \cup \{ij\}) - U_i(g)$ for $\{ij\} \notin g$ be increasing in the adjacency matrix for every pair of nodes i and j. (The connections game depicted in Figure 4 does not satisfy this condition.) Since the set of fixed points in this case possesses a minimal and maximal element by Tarski's fixed-point theorem, these can be used directly to formulate a computationally tractable estimator for the identified set. Miyauchi (2014) provides Monte Carlo experiments and an empirical illustration using the AddHealth data. Boucher and Mourifié (2013) analyze a very similar framework, assuming high-level conditions on pointwise identification through a pseudo-likelihood objective function and (weak) dependence across agents in observed pairwise stable networks. Weak dependence and other conditions (e.g., homophily and diversity) are further explored in Leung (2015a) to study large sample properties of estimators in a network formation model where a link is formed whenever those involved receive a positive "joint surplus" (which may depend on other edges in the network). The assumptions in his model (which can also accomodate non-transferable utilities) deliver a sparse network as the number of nodes grows, and he provides an application to a network of physician referrals.

Sheng (2014) and Miyauchi (2014) focus on a sample scheme where a number of networks of (at most) moderate size are observed. An alternative empirical scenario is one in which one has access to very few networks (perhaps only one) and many nodes. de Paula, Richards-Shubik, and Tamer (2015) developed an algorithm to compute the identified set for the preference parameters in the context of large (pairwise stable) networks (without transferable utility). They approximate this large community by a continuum of nodes, where agents can only form a finite number of links, and payoffs depend only on a finite number of direct and indirect connections.[39] A

---

[39] Formally, one needs to be careful in working with the continuum. Since unobservables are assumed to be independently drawn across individual nodes, measurability complications need

pairwise network will then be represented by a continuous graph with bounded degrees (since nodes have a finite number of incident edges), corresponding to a sparse network (see previous discussion about the empirical plausibility of such social and economic graphs). Such mathematical objects, called *graphings* in the applied mathematics literature, are sometimes used to approximate large networks as limits for large discrete graphs under a well-defined convergence metric (e.g., Lovasz, 2012 for a recent survey).[40] To further reduce the dimensionality of the problem, they also assume that unobservable taste shocks depend only on the covariates of putative connections and not on their identity. If covariates have a finite support, individual nodes can be classified into a finite (albeit possibly large) number of "network types," which provide a description of an individual node's local network. In the example introduced above, for instance, if 1, 2, and 3 stand for possible characteristics of a node (from a continuum of vertices) and individuals can only establish one connection, a given individual node would have three unobservable taste shocks: one for each one of the possible neighbour covariates. (The payoff to being isolated is normalized to zero.) In this example, a network type would describe the characteristic of a node (1, 2, or 3) and that of this neighbor (1, 2, 3 or whether the node has no neighbors).

The proportion of network types in an observed pairwise stable network is an equilibrium outcome, potentially estimable even from *incompletely observed* networks. Hence, whereas the number of vertices may be overly numerous, the cardinality of the set of network types is controlled. This allows them to verify whether observed networks correspond to pairwise stable networks for a given preference parameter vector using a computationally tractable quadratic program! To do so, they first define a partition of the space of unobservable variables. A set in this partition, called a "preference class," corresponds to the set of network types for which an individual agent with given realization for the unobservable preference shocks would not be inclined to drop a connection from. In the running example used here, those individuals for whom all the taste shocks are positive would prefer a link to any individual (regardless of whether her covariate is 1, 2 ,or 3) to being isolated. Her preference class would comprise network types connected to each of the three characterizing labels and the isolated type (since there are no links to drop in that case). Then, one can presumably allocate nodes to network types, and the proportion of nodes in a preference class allocated to a specific network type is called by them an "allocation parameter".

to be handled using results such as those presented in, e.g., Uhlig (1996) or Sun (2006). Another issue that appears in working in coalitional games on the continuum, when coalitions themselves can be a continuum, is avoided in this framework by restricting individuals to form a finite number of links where only the characteristics on the potential connection (and not her identity) matter.

[40] The corresponding approximation to dense graphs, known as *graphons*, is used, for example, by Chatterjee and Diaconis (2013) in their asymptotic study of ERGMs.

Given preference parameters, a pairwise stable network will correspond to allocation parameters satisfying certain restrictions. The requirement that a link in a pairwise stable network should be beneficial to both parties involved (i.e., (10)) is encoded in the definition of preference classes (since by definition connections characterizing network types in a preference class would not be dropped) and allocations from any preference class to network types not in that class are set to zero. de Paula, Richards-Shubik, and Tamer (2015) also show that the requirement that absent links be detrimental to at least one of the parties involved (i.e., (11)) implies that a quadratic form (on the vector of allocation parameters) be equal to zero. (This necessary condition is also sufficient in certain models and can thus yield sharp identified sets.) Using the restriction that the proportion of network types corresponds to observed ones, which guarantees that the supply and demand of links are balanced, and positivity constraints, the authors express the verification in terms of a quadratic program attaining a minimand equal to zero. Hence, instead of checking for pairwise stability among all possible networks involving a potentially large number of vertices and realizations of the unobservables for a given parameter value, the verification task is reduced to the solution of a quadratic program defined on the vector allocation parameters and whether the attained minimum is equal to zero and is computationally appealing. For example, de Paula, Richards-Shubik, and Tamer (2015) present a simulation study on a model based on (9), where individuals can form up to three connections on 500 nodes, and covariates take two values. The evaluation of the quadratic program takes on average less than 30 seconds.[41] It should also be pointed out that the computations above rely on the estimated proportion of network types. This can be regarded as an aggregate over observed pairwise stable networks with sampling variability stemming from differently selected equilibrium networks or as an estimate of network-type proportions from an incompletely observed network. As long as a distributional theory is provided for these statistics, the distributional features of the structural parameters can be obtained since the quadratic programming provides a mapping between the two.

The models above presume a complete information framework, where payoffs to all players involved are known to each one. An alternative strand of models focuses on directed networks and an incomplete information environment, whereby an individual node's preference shocks are unobservable, not only to the econometrician but also to other nodes. This is analyzed, for example, in Gilleskie and Zhang (2009) and Leung (2015b). Both articles employ a

---

[41] Miyauchi (2014) considers a simulation study on a similar payoff structure (setting $\nu = 0$) and covariates taking four values (gender × race). The simulation studies are not directly comparable since they employ different machines, and the model there is simpler in some dimensions (no preference for indirect connections, other than for mutual connections), but more complex in others (dimension of covariate support). For 200 nodes (as opposed to 500 nodes in de Paula, Richards-Shubik, and Tamer, 2015, the evaluation of the model for a single parameter takes about 2286 seconds ($\approx$ 38 minutes) for 100 sampled networks and using 100 simulations for the construction of his objective function.

multi-step estimation strategy where equilibrium beliefs are estimated at a first step from linking decisions and used in the estimation of payoffs in a second stage. The first step is made possible because private information is independent across agents, and beliefs about other agents' linking decision do not depend on one's private information. Analogous multi-stage conditional choice probability-based strategies have been employed in the dynamic programming discrete choice and empirical games literature under similar assumptions (e.g., de Paula, 2013), and Gilleskie and Zhang (2009) use a related framework, so only direct neighbors enter the utility function. Their main goal is to empirically study peer effects in smoking behavior (as in Badev, 2013) while allowing for links to be formed purposefully by the agents involved. As in previous studies, they employed the AddHealth data in their analysis. Leung (2015b) offers a related estimator focusing on the network formation. Here, though, the payoff structure involves the usual graph theoretic configurations as in (9), and the statistical analysis is performed for a small number of large networks instead of a large number of small games (as in Bisin, Moro, and Topa, 2011 and Menzel, 2015). An empirical illustration using microfinance-related data from Banerjee, Chandrasekhar, Duflo, and Jackson (2014) is also given. Both papers employ the assumption that a unique equilibrium is present in the data (even if the payoff structure is amenable to multiple solutions), which is not uncommon in the empirical games literature.

Finally, the models discussed previously are static or, at best, myopically dynamic models of network formation. Whereas farsighted models of network formation exist in the theoretical literature (e.g., Jackson, 2009), partly due to data (un)availability and/or the computational complexities even in static settings, they have not been very explored in the applied econometric literature. Alternative models for network formation, based on non-cooperative equilibrium concepts and exploring dynamics with forward-looking behavior, have nevertheless been proposed and could be used in data scenarios where network evolution is observable. Lee and Fong (2011), for instance, propose a dynamic network formation model for bipartite networks, where agents are split into two groups and across-group connections are established. There, payoffs are transferable, and a link is interpreted as a negotiation channel entailing a bargaining game over a contemporaneous surplus and quantifies the value of a particular edge. Connections are established via a link announcement game, where negotiations are open if two parties announce a putative link with each other. Because costs of establishing a negotiation link depend on the previous state of the bargaining connections, the model lends itself to dynamic incentives, and the authors focus on Markov perfect equilibria for the network formation process. This brings them closer to the empirical dynamic games literature and the estimation strategies suggested there (using methods developed after the paper by Hotz and Miller, 1993, for individual dynamic decisions and adapted to strategic interactions by various authors in the 2000s). Lee and Fong (2011) provide an illustration on insurer-provider contracting in health care through a series of simulations studies. Similar ideas appear in Johnson (2012).

I end this subsection by pointing to surveys in statistics and econometrics that encompass the class of network formation models in this and the previous subsections. Those surveys are distinct in focus and serve as an adequate complement to the discussion provided above. Those are Kolaczyk (2009), Goldenberg, Zheng, Fienberg, and Airoldi (2009), and Hunter, Krivitsky, and Schweinberger (2012) (in statistics) and Graham (2015) and Chandrasekhar (2015) (in econometrics).

4.3 Network Formation and Outcomes

Whereas network formation may be of interest in its own right, the models discussed above can be seen as a stepping stone for modeling outcomes discussed in the previous section, since the decision to establish links may be informed by any outcomes determined via the ensuing social structure. As mentioned earlier, for example, Gilleskie and Zhang (2009) and Badev (2013) studied econometric models for simultaneous link formation and discrete behavior (i.e., smoking behavior).

Goldsmith-Pinkham and Imbens (2013) model the joint determination of social networks and a continuous outcome (high school grade) using a dyadic edge formation framework for the former and a linear-in-means model for the latter using the AddHealth data. Because the network is observed on two different occasions, they postulate that the links are formed through pairwise stability based on a felicity function that depends solely on direct links (i.e., parameters v and ω are set to zero in (9)), and the previously observed network as a state variable.[42] Link formation and outcomes are connected by the presence of individual specific unobservables ξ_i and covariates (in this case, previous grade point average). Both ingredients affect an individual's outcome directly in the linear-in-means model, and links are formed based on an affinity between the covariates and the individual specific unobservables for the two parties involved in the putative link (which can be seen as a "latent position model" as in Hoff, Raftery, and Handcock, 2002). The presence of this individual effect introduces network endogeneity in the linear-in-means system as links are related to unobservables that determine those very outcomes. In their empirical application, estimated using Bayesian methods, the authors find that the individual specific unobservable driving both network formation and grades determination improves the fit for the network formation model but does not do so appreciably for the estimation of the linear-in-means model.

One natural approach to integrating network formation and outcome interactions takes the payoffs from network formation as indirect utilities, subsuming the potential payoffs from the economic system determining outcomes after the network is formed. One econometric model that can be cast along

---

[42] Since indirect edges are not payoff-relevant and there are no restrictions on the number of links formed, there is a single pairwise stable network given realizations for the unobservable preference shocks.

those lines is Hsieh and Lee (2013) (who also applied their model to the AddHealth, looking at smoking and grades as outcomes of interest). Link formation is formed based on a joint surplus function that depends on the network in a way similar to Mele (2015) and behaviors (as in Badev, 2013), producing an ERG model at the network formation stage (as in the papers cited above). Outcomes are determined through a linear-in-means model (for grades) and a Tobit version of the linear-in-means model (for smoking, measured as the frequency in the year preceding the survey). The model is estimated using Bayesian methods, as in those other articles. Hsieh and Lee (2013) found that behaviors appear significantly in link formation and that network interactions matter for both outcomes.[43]

One important aspect affecting the joint econometric analysis of network formation and interactions is the possibility of multiplicity in network formation and/or at the outcome determination system. As seen earlier, this is a possibility depending on the solution concept adopted and on other details of the framework at hand (e.g., whether utility is transferable or not). In this case, partial identification in either stage – formation or interactions – will likely be transmitted to other parameters of the model. For example, even if point identification at the network interactions model is achieved along the lines highlighted previously, if the network formation protocol is subject to partial identification, parameters in a linear-in-means model will possibly only be partially identified. An illustration of this is given, for example, in Ciliberto, Murry, and Tamer (2015) in the context of an empirical entry-exit game in industrial organization. Aside from joint modeling and estimation of both network formation and interactions, another possibility is to consider instruments for networks as suggested, for example, in Qu and Lee (2015). Of course, if network formation is prone to multiplicity, the model is incomplete without an equilibrium selection rule (see Tamer, 2003). New developments in the partial identification literature may nonetheless prove useful here (e.g., Chesher and Rosen, 2014).

5 MEASURING NETWORKS AND OUTCOMES

It should be noted that a few econometric models for network formation highlighted in the previous section presume the availability of data on the complete

---

[43] Hsieh and Lee (2013), Goldsmith-Pinkham and Imbens (2013), and Badev (2013) use different subsets of the AddHealth data. They also rely on different outcome measurements and covariates – Badev (2013) uses a binary variable related to smoking behavior in the month prior to the survey, whereas Hsieh and Lee (2013) use a multivalued measure for the past year; Badev (2013) incorporates the price of cigarettes, whereas Hsieh and Lee (2013) do not. Furthermore, they all employ different models – Badev's model for smoking does not correspond to a binary model of the linear-in-means model, for instance, and Goldsmith-Pinkham and Imbens (2013) use network data from two survey waves to construct their model. Hence the estimates across these three models are hard to compare. From a practitioner's viewpoint, it would be interesting to compare these competing frameworks.

network. Whereas some strategies do not require observation of the whole network (e.g., in independent dyadic models), others are more demanding. ERG models, for example, are typically not "projective," which implies that estimators based on subgraphs are not consistent (see Shalizi and Rinaldo, 2013). As indicated by those authors, if incomplete network information is available and "an ERGM is postulated for the whole network, then inference for its parameters must explicitly treat the unobserved portions of the network as missing data (perhaps through an expectation-maximization algorithm), though of course there may be considerable uncertainty about just how much data is missing" (p. 523). On this latter point, see, e.g., Handcock and Gile (2010) or Koskinen, Robins, and Pattison (2010). When repeated outcomes are observed for a given system, the methods suggested in Manresa (2013) and de Paula, Rasul, and Souza (2015) may also be useful for network information retrieval.

For some of the econometric models described above, though, complete observation of the network may not be necessary, and relevant features of the network can be estimated, provided that a suitable sampling scheme is given. Kolaczyk (2009), for example, provides estimators for various network features like the total number of edges or the total number of triangles. These could presumably be used for the estimation of the SUG model proposed by Chandrasekhar and Jackson (2014). The proportion of "network types" contemplated in de Paula, Richards-Shubik, and Tamer (2015) could potentially be estimated along similar lines. A review of available methods for the estimation of graph features from sampled subnetworks is given in Kolaczyk (2009).

In the context of outcome interactions, Moffitt (2001) and Angrist (2014) aptly point out that measurement issues may compromise any identification results assuming no mismeasurement (see also Ammermueller and Pischke, 2009). When using between-group variation in covariates to identify β through its connection to OLS and 2SLS coefficients, measurement errors in covariates will typically produce attenuation in the first, though not the second.[44] In the covariance restriction case studied by Moffitt (2001) (Proposition 2), if outcomes or covariates are measured with error, measurement error variances will be confounded in the variance of observed outcomes. These are indeed empirically relevant considerations that researchers should be aware of. In his study of randomly assigned roommates, for example, Sacerdote (2001) accounts for the possibility of mismeasured covariates by including classical measurement error, which precludes him from using covariance restrictions as suggested in Moffitt (2001). Ammermueller and Pischke (2009) carefully discuss the consequences of measurement error in covariates in their analysis for peer effects in education. Under classical measurement error in *outcomes*, a related strategy

---

[44] As pointed out by Angrist (2014), other considerations may also drive a wedge between those two, even when there are no peer effects.

can nevertheless be employed to obtain the endogenous effect. If classical measurement errors are independent across peers in a given group, their covariance washes out as we consider observed outcome covariances, and contrasts in those covariances across groups may still allow for point identification of the endogenous effect. Below I demonstrate this for groups of size two and three (double and triple rooms in Sacerdote's context). In the proposition below, $\tilde{y}_{i,g}$ denotes the observed outcome for individual i in group g, and $v_{i,g}$ denotes the measurement error.

Proposition 6 *Suppose there are two groups $g = 1, 2$ such that $N_1 = 2$ and $N_2 = 3$. If $|\beta| < 1$, $W_{ij,g} = (N_g - 1)^{-1}$ if $i \neq j$, $W_{ii,g} = 0$, $\mathbb{V}(\epsilon_g | \mathbf{x}_g) = \sigma^2 \mathbf{I}_g$ and $\tilde{y}_{i,g} = y_{i,g} + v_{i,g}$ where $v_{i,g} \perp\!\!\!\perp v_{j,h}$ and $v_{i,g} \perp\!\!\!\perp y_{j,h}$ for any i, j, g and h, then β is identified.*

Of course, that measurement errors be classical is in itself a strong assumption, and Proposition 6 above should be interpreted with that in mind. It also assumes that covariates are *not* measured with error, which was the focus of the above-mentioned concerns. The result nevertheless demonstrates that network interaction models may themselves provide additional structure to be explored in the estimation of measurement error-ridden models.

6 CONCLUSION

This article provided a (selective) review of recent works on networks and outcomes mediated through networks. This is an area of active research, but much remains to be learned.

Regarding models of network effects on outcomes, I should mention that heterogeneity is an important issue that I have not explicitly discussed in this work. As pointed out by Sacerdote (2010) in his review of peer effects studies in education, a "linear-in-means model masks considerable heterogeneity in the effects experienced by different types of students." Nonlinear and heterogeneous effects models could prove useful. Tincani (2015) provides an interesting empirical examination of nonlinearities in social interactions. Of course, should nonlinearities be relevant, multiple social equilibria are a possibility. Some of the ideas mentioned in this article allow for heterogeneous peer coefficients (e.g., de Paula, Rasul, and Souza, 2015, if adequate data is available) and Masten (2015) is a recent contribution in the development of random coefficient versions to the models considered here. Measurement issues present important practical difficulties. As indicated by Ammermueller and Pischke (2009), more attention to measurement issues could bring in important rewards. As far as network formation models are concerned, econometric methodologies that take into account sampling and measurement peculiarities are also important in practice. Computational and identification difficulties are also a primary concern, and integrated models of network formation and interactions will typically inherit those.

In both cases, most models examined are static. Dynamic, forward-looking models may be adequate for many applications (e.g., industrial organization and banking), especially as more detailed and abundant data on the evolution of networks and outcomes becomes available.

A PROOFS

A.1 Proof of Proposition 2

If $\mathbb{V}(\epsilon|\mathbf{x}) = \sigma^2\mathbf{I}$, then $\mathbb{V}(\mathbf{y}|\mathbf{x}) = \sigma^2(\mathbf{I} - \beta W)^{-2}$. Since $|\beta| < 1$ and W is (row-)stochastic, we obtain

$$(\mathbf{I} - \beta W)^{-1} = \mathbf{I} + \beta W + \beta^2 W^2 + \dots$$

It can be verified that $W^k, k = 1, 2, \dots$ is symmetric with diagonal elements $(W^k)_{ii} = a_{k-1}$ and off-diagonal entries $(W^k)_{ij} = a_k, i \neq j$, where

$$a_0 = 0, \qquad a_{-1} = 1 \quad \text{and} \quad a_k = (a_{k-2} + a_{k-1}(N-2))/(N-1).$$

Let $S = \sum_{k=1}^{\infty} \beta^k W^k$. Then,

$$
\begin{aligned}
S_{ii} &= \sum_{k=1}^{\infty} \beta^k a_{k-1} = \sum_{\tilde{k}=0}^{\infty} \beta^{\tilde{k}+1} a_{\tilde{k}} = \sum_{\tilde{k}=1}^{\infty} \beta^{\tilde{k}+1}(a_{\tilde{k}-2} + a_{\tilde{k}-1}(N-2))/(N-1) \\
&= \frac{\beta^2}{N-1}\left(1 + \sum_{\tilde{k}=2}^{\infty} \beta^{\tilde{k}-1} a_{\tilde{k}-2}\right) + \frac{N-2}{N-1}\beta \sum_{\tilde{k}=1}^{\infty} \beta^{\tilde{k}} a_{\tilde{k}-1} \\
&= \frac{\beta^2}{N-1}\left(1 + \sum_{\bar{k}=1}^{\infty} \beta^{\bar{k}} a_{\bar{k}-1}\right) + \frac{N-2}{N-1}\beta \sum_{\tilde{k}=1}^{\infty} \beta^{\tilde{k}} a_{\tilde{k}-1} \\
&= \frac{\beta^2}{N-1}(1 + S_{ii}) + \frac{N-2}{N-1}\beta S_{ii}
\end{aligned}
$$

where the second and fifth equalities set $\tilde{k} = k - 1$ and $\bar{k} = \tilde{k} - 1$ respectively, the third equality acknowledges that $a_0 = 0$ and uses the definition of a_k above, and the last equality uses the definition of S_{ii}. This implies that

$$S_{ii} = \frac{\beta^2}{(N-1) - (N-2)\beta - \beta^2}.$$

(The denominator is nonzero as long as $|\beta| < 1$.) On the other hand, $S_{ij} = \sum_{k=1}^{\infty} \beta^k a_k = \beta^{-1} S_{ii}$ (for $i \neq j$).

Since $(\mathbf{I} - \beta W)^{-1} = \mathbf{I} + \beta W + \beta^2 W^2 + \dots = \mathbf{I} + S$, its diagonal elements are then given by $1 + S_{ii} = [(N-1) - (N-2)\beta]/C$, and its off-diagonal entries are given by $\beta^{-1} S_{ii} = \beta/C$, where $C = (N-1) - (N-2)\beta - \beta^2$.

Using then the fact that $\mathbb{V}(\mathbf{y}|\mathbf{x}) = \sigma^2(\mathbf{I} + S)^2$, the ratio between covariance and variance among observable outcome variables is given by

$$\kappa(\beta, N) \equiv \frac{\mathbb{C}(y_i, y_j|\mathbf{x})}{\mathbb{V}(y_i|\mathbf{x})} = \frac{2\beta(N - 1) - (N - 2)\beta^2}{((N - 1) - (N - 2)\beta)^2 + (N - 1)\beta^2}. \tag{12}$$

Notice that $\beta = 0 \Rightarrow \mathbb{C}(y_i, y_j|\mathbf{x}) = 0$, and the Cauchy–Schwarz inequality implies that $|\kappa(\beta, N)| \leq 1$. Furthermore, the denominator above is always positive and $\text{sgn}(\kappa(\beta, N)) = \text{sgn}(2\beta(N - 1) - (N - 2)\beta^2)$. If $N = 2$, the right-hand side in (12) becomes $2\beta/(1 + \beta^2)$, which is increasing in β and the equation above has a unique solution. I will thus focus on $N > 2$. In this case, the numerator is a quadratic, concave polynomial with two roots: $\beta_1 = 0$ and $\beta_2 = 1 + N/(N - 2) > 1$. It is then negative for $\beta \in (-\infty, \beta_1) \cup (\beta_2, \infty)$ and positive for $\beta \in (\beta_1, \beta_2)$. Since $|\beta| < 1$, it is then straightforward to see that

$$\beta \geq 0 \Leftrightarrow \kappa(\beta, N) \geq 0.$$

Let $\overline{\kappa}$ be the observed covariance–variance ratio among outcome variables. The parameter β is then a solution to the quadratic equation $p(b; \overline{\kappa}, N) = 0$ obtained from (12), where $p(b; \overline{\kappa}, N)$ is given by

$$\left\{ \overline{\kappa} \left[(N - 2)^2 + (N - 1) \right] + (N - 2) \right\}$$
$$\times b^2 - 2(N - 1)[1 + \overline{\kappa}(N - 2)]b + \overline{\kappa}(N - 1)^2.$$

By the Fundamental Theorem of Algebra, there are at most two solutions to the equation above. As noted earlier, $\text{sgn}(\overline{\kappa}) = \text{sgn}(\beta)$. There are then three cases to consider:

i) If $\overline{\kappa} = 0$, then $\beta = 0$ and the model is identified since the remaining parameters can then be obtained from the reduced-form coefficients.

ii) If $\overline{\kappa} > 0$, then $\beta > 0$, and the coefficient on the quadratic term in the equation above is positive and the polynomial $p(b; \overline{\kappa}, N)$ is convex in b. Furthermore, $p(0; \overline{\kappa}, N) = \overline{\kappa}(N - 1)^2 > 0$ (since $\overline{\kappa} > 0$) and $p(1; \overline{\kappa}, N) = N(\overline{\kappa} - 1) \leq 0$ (since $\overline{\kappa} \leq 1$, see above). Together, these imply that both roots are greater than zero, that one of the roots is greater than one and the other is less than one. Hence, only one root is positive and below one, and the model is identified as the remaining parameters again can be obtained from the reduced-form coefficients.

iii) If $\overline{\kappa} < 0$, then $\beta < 0$. Notice that the linear coefficient in $p(b; \overline{\kappa}, N)$ is negative when $N = 2$. For $N > 2$, it is positive if, and only if,

$$\overline{\kappa} < \frac{1}{2 - N} < 0.$$

Since $\overline{\kappa}$ is bounded below by $\kappa(-1, N)$ (see Proposition 3) and

$$\kappa(-1, N) - \frac{1}{2 - N} = \frac{N(N - 1)}{\{[(N - 1) + (N - 2)]^2 + (N - 1)\}(N - 2)} > 0,$$

the linear coefficient in $p(b; \overline{\kappa}, N)$ is always negative.

On the other hand, the quadratic coefficient in $p(b; \overline{\kappa}, N)$ is positive if, and only if,

$$\overline{\kappa} > \frac{-(N-2)}{(N-2)^2 + (N-1)}.$$

For $N \geq 4$, it can be seen that

$$\kappa(-1, N) > \frac{-(N-2)}{(N-2)^2 + (N-1)}.$$

In this case, the quadratic polynomial is convex, and its minimizer is positive (since the linear coefficient is negative, and the quadratic coefficient is positive). This implies that only one of its roots can be negative and the model is then identified.

If $N = 3$, the roots to $p(b; \overline{\kappa}, 3)$ are given by $2 \pm 2/\sqrt{1 + \overline{\kappa}}$. (The lower bound on $\overline{\kappa}$ is $\kappa(-1, 3) = -5/11 > -1$, so the denominator will always be nonzero.) Since $-1 < \overline{\kappa} < 0, 2 - 2/\sqrt{1 + \overline{\kappa}} < 0 < 2 + 2/\sqrt{1 + \overline{\kappa}}$, and only one root is admissible. The model is identified as before. ∎

A.2   Proof of Proposition 3

The derivative of $\kappa(\beta, N)$ defined in (12) with respect to β is given by

$$\frac{\partial \kappa(\beta, N)}{\partial \beta} = \frac{(N-1)^2(N-1-\beta^2 - \beta(N-2))}{\{((N-1) - (N-2)\beta)^2 + (N-1)\beta^2\}^2}$$

$$> \frac{(N-1)^2(N-2)(1-\beta)}{\{((N-1) - (N-2)\beta)^2 + (N-1)\beta^2\}^2}$$

$$\geq 0,$$

where both inequalities use the assumption that $|\beta| < 1$. Hence, a lower bound for $\kappa(\beta, N) \equiv \mathbb{C}(y_i, y_j|\mathbf{x})/\mathbb{V}(y_i|\mathbf{x})$ is given by $\kappa(-1, N) = (4-3N)/(4N^2 - 11N + 8)$. ∎

A.3   Proof of Proposition 6

Because the measurement error is classical and independent across individuals,

$$\mathbb{C}(\tilde{y}_{i,g}, \tilde{y}_{j,g}|\mathbf{x}_g) = \mathbb{C}(y_{i,g}, y_{j,g}|\mathbf{x}_g).$$

From the proof of Proposition 2, we obtain

$$\mathbb{C}(y_{i,1}, y_{j,1}|\mathbf{x}_1) = 2\beta\sigma^2/(1 - \beta^2)^2$$

for the group with two individuals and

$$\mathbb{C}(y_{i,2}, y_{j,2}|\mathbf{x}_1) = \beta(4 - \beta)\sigma^2/[(1 - \beta) + (1 - \beta^2)]^2$$

for the group with three individuals. Then,

$$\psi(\beta) = \frac{\mathbb{C}(y_{i,1}, y_{j,1}|\mathbf{x}_1)}{\mathbb{C}(y_{i,2}, y_{j,2}|\mathbf{x}_1)} = \frac{8 + 8\beta + 2\beta^2}{4 + 7\beta + 2\beta^2 - \beta^3}.$$

It can be checked that $\psi'(\beta) < 0$ for $|\beta| < 1$ and consequently $\psi(\beta) > \psi(1) = 1.5$.

Let $\overline{\psi}$ be the observed covariance ratio among outcome variables. The parameter β is then a solution to a cubic equation $q(b; \overline{\psi}) = 0$ obtained from the expression above, where $q(b; \overline{\psi}) \equiv -\overline{\psi}\beta^3 + 2(\overline{\psi} - 1)\beta^2 + (7\overline{\psi} - 8)\beta + 4(\overline{\psi} - 2)$. To show that only one root to this equation is below 1 in absolute value, I make use of Rouché's theorem (see Rudin, 1987, pp. 225 and 229). The result is stated for general complex-valued functions. In our context, it establishes that, if the functions f and g are continuous on a compact set C and differentiable on its interior with $|g(x)| < |f(x)|$ on the boundary of C, then f and $f + g$ have the same number of zeros in the interior of C, where each zero is counted as many times as its multiplicity. Taking $f(x) = a_1 x$ (so that $f(x) = 0 \Rightarrow x = 0$) and $g(x) = a_0 + a_2 x^2 + \cdots + a_K x^K$ and $C = [-1, 1]$, one obtains the following corollary:

If $|a_1| > |a_0| + |a_2| + \cdots + |a_K|$, then there is exactly one root for the polynomial $a_0 + a_1 x + \cdots + a_K x^K$ with absolute value less than 1.

When $\overline{\psi} \geq 2$, $7\overline{\psi} - 8 > |-\overline{\psi}| + |2(\overline{\psi} - 1)| + |4(\overline{\psi} - 2)| = 7\overline{\psi} - 10$. When $\overline{\psi} < 2$, we have that $|-\overline{\psi}| + |2(\overline{\psi} - 1)| + |4(\overline{\psi} - 2)| = 6 - \overline{\psi}$. Then, $7\overline{\psi} - 8 > 6 - \overline{\psi} \Leftrightarrow \overline{\psi} > 14/8$, which is true since $\overline{\psi} > 1.5$. This implies that there is only one solution with absolute value below one (i.e., β) and completes the proof. ∎

B   CONNECTIONS GAME

Here I examine the three-player connections game where $u_i(g) = \sum_{j \in 1, \ldots, n, j \neq i} \delta^{d(i,j;g)-1} (1 + \epsilon_{ij}) - |N_i(g)|$. The set of possible links is $\{12, 13, 23\}$, and there are eight possible networks (2^3). However, there are only four distinct topologies, which can be characterized by the number of links (0 to 3). These networks and respective payoffs are characterized below:

(i) One network with 0 links ($g = \emptyset$): $u_i = 0$ for each player. For this network to be pairwise stable, one needs $\epsilon_{ij} < 0$ or $\epsilon_{ji} < 0$ for every pair ij.

(ii) Three networks with 1 link ($g = \{ij\}$): $u_i = \epsilon_{ij}$ and $u_j = \epsilon_{ji}$ for the two connected players, $u_k = 0$ for the isolated player (three possible networks with distinct isolated players). For this network to be pairwise stable, one needs $\epsilon_{ij} \geq 0$ and $\epsilon_{ji} \geq 0$ (for the ij link); $\epsilon_{ik} < 0$ or $\epsilon_{ki} < 0$ (for the absent ik link); and $\epsilon_{jk} < 0$ or $\epsilon_{kj} < 0$ (for the absent jk link).

(iii) Three networks with two links ($g = \{ij, jk\}$): $u_i = \epsilon_{ij} + \delta(1 + \epsilon_{ik})$, $u_k = \epsilon_{kj} + \delta(1 + \epsilon_{ki})$ and $u_j = \epsilon_{ji} + \epsilon_{jk}$ (three possible networks with different middle players). For this network to be pairwise stable, one needs $\epsilon_{ij} + \delta(1 + \epsilon_{ik}) \geq 0$ and $\epsilon_{ji} \geq 0$ (for the ij link); $\epsilon_{kj} + \delta(1 + \epsilon_{ki}) \geq 0$ and $\epsilon_{jk} \geq 0$ (for the kj link); and $\epsilon_{ik} < \delta(1 + \epsilon_{ik})$ or $\epsilon_{ki} < \delta(1 + \epsilon_{ki})$ (for the absent ik link).

(iv) One network with three links ($g = \{12, 13, 23\}$): $u_i = \epsilon_{ij} + \epsilon_{ik}$ and similar expressions for the other players. For this network to be pairwise stable, one needs $\epsilon_{ij} \geq \delta(1 + \epsilon_{ij})$ and $\epsilon_{ji} \geq \delta(1 + \epsilon_{ji})$ for every ij pair.

If $0 < \epsilon_{23} < \delta/(1 - \delta)$ and $\epsilon_{ij} = \epsilon_{ji}$ for every pair, we can establish the conditions on ϵ_{12} and ϵ_{13} for each of the 2^3 possible graphs to be pairwise stable:

$$\emptyset : \qquad \text{not pairwise stable}$$
$$\{12\} : \qquad \epsilon_{12} \geq 0; \epsilon_{13} \leq 0; \epsilon_{13} < \epsilon_{23}/\delta - 1$$
$$\{13\} : \qquad \epsilon_{13} \geq 0; \epsilon_{12} \leq 0; \epsilon_{12} < \epsilon_{23}/\delta - 1$$
$$\{23\} : \qquad \epsilon_{12} < 0, \epsilon_{13} < 0$$
$$\{12, 13\} : \epsilon_{12}, \epsilon_{13} \geq -\delta(1 + \epsilon_{23}); \epsilon_{13}, \epsilon_{12} > 0; \epsilon_{23} < \delta/(1 - \delta)$$
$$\{12, 23\} : \epsilon_{12}, \epsilon_{23} \geq -\delta(1 + \epsilon_{13}); \epsilon_{12}, \epsilon_{23} > 0; \epsilon_{13} < \delta/(1 - \delta)$$
$$\{13, 23\} : \epsilon_{13}, \epsilon_{23} \geq -\delta(1 + \epsilon_{12}); \epsilon_{13}, \epsilon_{23} > 0; \epsilon_{12} < \delta/(1 - \delta)$$
$$\{12, 13, 23\} : \qquad \text{not pairwise stable}$$

References

Acemoglu, D., and J. Angrist (2001): "How Large are Human-Capital Externalities? Evidence from Compulsory-Schooling Laws," in *NBER Macroeconomics Annual*, ed. by B. S. Bernanke, and K. Rogoff, vol. 15 of *9-74*. MIT Press.

Acemoglu, D., V. Carvalho, A. Ozdaglar, and A. Tahbaz-Salehi (2012): "The Network Origins of Aggregate Fluctuations," *Econometrica*, 80(5), 1977–2016.

Acemoglu, D., A. Ozdaglar, and A. Tahbaz-Salehi (forthcoming): "Networks, Shocks, and Systemic Risk," in *The Oxford Handbook on the Economics of Networks*, ed. by Y. Bramoullé, A. Galeotti, and B. Rogers. Oxford University Press.

Ammermueller, A., and J.-S. Pischke (2009): "Peer Effects in European Primary Schools: Evidence from the Progress in International Reading Literacy Study," *Journal of Labor Economics*, 27(3), 315–48.

Angelucci, M., and G. De Giorgi (2009): "Indirect Effects of an Aid Program: How Do Cash Transfers Affect Ineligibles' Consumption?" *American Economic Review*, 99(1), 486–508.

Angrist, J. (2014): "The Perils of Peer Effects," *Labour Economics*, 30, 98–108.

Antras, P., and D. Chor (2013): "Organizing the Global Value Chain," *Econometrica*, 81(6), 2127–204.

Atalay, E., A. Hortacsu, J. Roberts, and C. Syverson (2011): "Network Structure of Production," *Proceedings of the National Academy of Sciences*, 108(13), 5199–202.

Badev, A. (2013): "Discrete Games with Endogenous Networks: Theory and Policy," Working Paper, University of Pennsylvania.

Bala, V., and S. Goyal (2000): "A Noncooperative Model of Network Formation," *Econometrica*, 68(5), 1181–229.

Ballester, C., A. Calvó-Armengol, and Y. Zenou (2006): "Who's Who in Networks. Wanted: The Key Player," *Econometrica*, 74, 1403–17.

Banerjee, A., A. Chandrasekhar, E. Duflo, and M. Jackson (2014): "Gossip: Identifying Central Individuals in a Social Network," MIT Working Paper.

Barabási, A., and R. Albert (1999): "Emergence of Scaling in Random Networks," *Science*, 286, 509–12.

Bekker, P., and D. Pollock (1986): "Identification of Linear Stochastic Models with Covariance Restrictions," *Journal of Econometrics*, 31(2), pp. 179–208.

Belloni, A., V. Chernozhukov, and C. Hansen (2013): "Inference Methods for High-Dimensional Sparse Econometric Models," in *Advances in Economics and Econometrics, Theory and Applications: Tenth World Congress of the Econometric Society*, ed. by D. Acemoglu, and M. Arellano, vol. 3. Cambridge: Cambridge University Press.

Berge, C. (1962): *The Theory of Graphs and Its Applications*. Methuen Wiley.

Bernard, A. B., A. Moxnes, and Y. Saito (2014): "Geography and Firm Performance in the Japanese Production Network," RIETI Discussion Paper 14-E-034.

Besag, J. (1974): "Spatial Interactions and the Statistical Analysis of Lattice Systems (with Dicusssions)," *Journal of the Royal Statistical Society B*, 36, 196–236.

——— (1975): "Statistical Analysis of Non-Lattice Data," *The Statistician*, 24(3), 179–95.

Bhamidi, S., G. Bresler, and A. Sly (2011): "Mixing Time of Exponential Random Graphs," *The Annals of Applied Probability*, 21(6), 2146–70.

Bisin, A., A. Moro, and G. Topa (2011): "The Empirical Content of Models with Multiple Equilibria in Economies with Social Interactions," NBER Working Paper 17196.

Bloch, F., and M. Jackson (2007): "The Formation of Networks with Transfers among Players," *Journal of Economic Theory*, 113(1), 83–110.

Blume, L. (1993): "The Statistical Mechanics of Strategic Interaction," *Games and Economic Behavior*, 5, 387–424.

Blume, L., W. Brock, S. Durlauf, and Y. Ioannides (2011): "Identification of Social Interactions," in *Handbook of Social Economics*, ed. by J. Benhabib, A. Bisin, and M. Jackson, vol. 1B, pp. 853–964. North-Holland, Amsterdam.

Blume, L., W. Brock, S. Durlauf, and R. Jayaraman (2015): "Linear Social Interaction Models," *Journal of Political Economy*, 123(2), 444–96.

Bollobás, B. (2001): *Random Graphs*. Cambridge University Press, Cambridge.

Bonacich, P. (1972): "Factoring and Weighting Approaches to Status Scores and Clique Identification," *Journal of Mathematical Sociology*, 2, 113–20.

——— (1987): "Power and Centrality: A Family of Measures," *American Journal of Sociology*, 92, 1170–1182.

Bonaldi, P., A. Hortacsu, and J. Kastl (2014): "An Empirical Analysis of Systemic Risk in the EURO-zone," University of Chicago Working Paper.

Boozer, M. A., and S. E. Cacciola (2001): "Inside the 'Black Box' of Project STAR: Estimation of Peer Effects Using Experimental Data," Yale Economic Growth Center Discussion Paper No. 832.

Boucher, V., Y. Bramoullé, H. Djebbari, and B. Fortin (2014): "Do Peers Affect Student Achievement? Evidence From Canada Using Group Size Variation," *Journal of Applied Econometrics*, 29(1), 91–109.

Boucher, V., and I. Mourifié (2013): "My Friend Far Far Away: Asymptotic Properties of Pairwise Stable Networks," Université Laval and University of Toronto Working Paper.

Bramoullé, Y., H. Djebbari, and B. Fortin (2009): "Identification of Peer Effects Through Social Networks," *Journal of Econometrics*, 150, 41–55.

Bramoullé, Y., R. Kranton, and D'Amours (2014): "Strategic Interaction and Networks," *American Economic Review*, 104(3), 898–930.

Braun, M., and J. McAuliffe (2010): "Variational Inference for Large-Scale Models of Discrete Choice," *Journal of the American Statistical Association*, 105(489), 324–35.

Brin, S., and L. Page (1998): "The Anatomy of a Large Scale Hypertextual Web Search Engine," *Computer Networks*, 30, 107–17.

Brock, W., and S. Durlauf (2001): "Discrete Choice with Social Interactions," *Review of Economic Studies*, 68, 235–61.

——— (2006): "Multinomial Choice with Social Interactions," in *The Economy as an Evolving Complex System*, ed. by S. Durlauf, and L. Blume, vol. 3, pp. 175–206. New York: Oxford University Press.

——— (2007): "Identification of Binary Choice Models with Social Interactions," *Journal of Econometrics*, 140(1), 57–75.

Butts, C. (2009): "A Behavioral Micro-Foundation for Cross-Sectional Network Models," UC Irvine Working Paper.

Calvó-Armengol, A., E. Patacchini, and Y. Zenou (2009): "Peer Effects and Social Networks in Education," *Review of Economic Studies*, 76(4), 1239–67.

Carvalho, V. (2014): "From Micro to Macro via Production Networks," *Journal of Economic Perspectives*, 28(4), 23–48.

Carvalho, V., M. Nirei, and Y. Saito (2014): "Supply Chain Disruptions: Evidence from the Great East Japan Earthquake," Cambridge University Working Paper.

Chandrasekhar, A. (2015): "Econometrics of Network Formation," in *Oxford Handbook on the Economics of Networks*, ed. by Y. Bramoullé, A. Galeotti, and B. Rogers. Oxford University Press.

Chandrasekhar, A. G., and M. O. Jackson (2014): "Tractable and Consistent Random Graph Models," Working Paper 20276, NBER.

Charbonneau, K. B. (2014): "Multiple Fixed Effects in Binary Response Panel Data," Bank of Canada Working Paper 2014–17.

Chatterjee, S., and A. Dembo (2014): "Nonlinear Large Deviations," Stanford University Working Paper, arXiv:1401.3495v5.

Chatterjee, S., and P. Diaconis (2013): "Estimating and Understanding Exponential Random Graph Models," *Annals of Statistics*, 41(5), 2428–61.

Chatterjee, S., P. Diaconis, and A. Sly (2011): "Random Graphs with a Given Degree Sequence," *The Annals of Applied Probability*, 21(4), 1400–35.

Chesher, A., and A. Rosen (2014): "Generalized Instrumental Variable Models," CeMMAP Working Paper 04/14.

Christakis, N., J. Fowler, G. Imbens, and K. Kalianaraman (2010): "An Empirical Model of Strategic Network Formation," Harvard University Working Paper.

Chwe, M. (2000): "Communication and Coordination in Social Networks," *Review of Economic Studies*, 67, 1–16.

Ciliberto, F., C. Murry, and E. Tamer (2015): "Inference on Market Power in Markets with Multiple Equilibria," University of Virginia and Harvard University Working Paper.

Clauset, A., C. Shalizi, and M. Newman (2009): "Power-Law Distributions in Empirical Data," *SIAM Review*, pp. 661–703.

Cohen-Cole, E., A. Kirilenko, and E. Patacchini (2014): "Trading Network and Liquidity Provision," *Journal of Financial Economics*, 113, 235–51.

Coleman, J. S. (1964): *Introduction to Mathematical Sociology*. London Free Press Glencoe.

Comola, M., and S. Prina (2014): "Do Interventions Change the Network? A Dynamic Peer Effect Model Accounting for Network Changes," PSE Working Paper.

Currarini, S., M. Jackson, and P. Pin (2009): "An Economic Model of Friendship: Homophily, Minorities and Segregation," *Econometrica*, 77(4), 1003–45.

Davezies, L., d'Haultfoeuille, and D. Fougére (2009): "Identification of Peer Effects Using Group Size Variation," *Econometrics Journal*, 12(3), 397–413.

De Giorgi, G., M. Pellizari, and S. Redaelli (2010): "Identification of Social Interactions through Partially Overlapping Peer Groups," *American Economic Journal: Applied Economics*, 2(2), 241–75.

de Paula, A. (2009): "Inference in a Synchronization Game with Social Interactions," *Journal of Econometrics*, 148, 56–71.

―――― (2013): "Econometric Analysis of Games with Multiple Equilibria," *Annual Review of Economics*, 5, 107–31.

de Paula, A., I. Rasul, and P. C. Souza (2015): "Identifying and Estimating Social Connections from Outcome Data," UCL and PUC-Rio Working Paper.

de Paula, A., S. Richards-Shubik, and E. Tamer (2015): "Identification of Preferences in Network Formation Games," UCL Working Paper.

de Paula, A., and J. A. Scheinkman (2010): "Value Added Taxes, Chain Effects and Informality," *American Economic Journal: Macroeconomics*, 2, 195–221.

de Paula, A., and X. Tang (2012): "Inference of Signs of Interaction Effects in Simultaneous Games with Incomplete Information," *Econometrica*, 80(1), 143–172.

Denbee, E., C. Julliard, Y. Li, and K. Yuan (2014): "Network Risk and Key Players: A Structural Analysis of Interbank Liquidity," LSE Working Paper.

Diebold, F. X., and K. Yilmaz (2015): *Financial and Macroeconomic Connectedness: A Network Approach to Measurement and Monitoring*. Oxford University Press.

Dieye, R., H. Djebbari, and F. Barrera-Osorio (2014): "Accounting for Peer Effects in Treatment Response," IZA Discussion Paper 2014.

Drukker, D., P. Egger, and I. Prucha (2013): "On Two-Step Estimation of a Spatial Autoregressive Model with Autoregressive Disturbances and Endogenous Regressors," *Econometric Reviews*, 32(5-6), 686–733.

Dzemski, A. (2014): "An Empirical Model of Dyadic Link Formation in a Network with Unobserved Heterogeneity," University of Mannheim Working Paper.

Erdös, P., and A. Rényi (1959): "On Random Graphs," *Publicationes Mathematicae Debrecen*, 6, 290–97.

(1960): "On the Evolution of Random Graphs," *Publications of the Mathematical Institute of the Hungarian Academy of Sciences*, 5, 17–61.

Fafchamps, M., and S. Lund (2003): "Risk Sharing Networks in Rural Philippines," *Journal of Development Economics*, 71, 261–87.

Fan, J., and R. Li (2001): "Variable Selection via Nonconcave Penalized Likelihood and its Oracle Properties," *Journal of the American Statistical Association*, 96(456), 1348–60.

Fernandez-Val, I., and M. Weidner (2014): "Individual and Time Effects in Nonlinear Panel Models with Large N, T," Boston University Working Paper.

Fisher, F. (1966): *The Identification Problem in Econometrics*. New York: McGraw-Hill.

Fortin, B., G. Lacroix, and M.-C. Villeval (2007): "Tax Evasion and Social Interactions," *Journal of Public Economics*, 91(11-12), 2089–112.

Frank, O., and D. Strauss (1986): "Markov Graphs," *Journal of American Statistical Association*, 81, 832–42.

Galbiati, R., and G. Zanella (2012): "The Tax Evasion Social Multiplier: Evidence from Italy," *Journal of Public Economics*, 96, 485–94.

Gandhi, A., S. Navarro, and D. Rivers (2013): "On the Identification of Production Functions: How Heterogeneous is Productivity?" University of Wisconsin Working Paper.

Gautier, E., and A. Tsybakov (2014): "High-Dimensional Instrumental Variables Regression and Confidence Sets," Working Paper CREST.

Geyer, C. J. (2009): "Likelihood Inference in Exponential Families and Directions of Recession," *Electronic Journal of Statistics*, 3, 259–89.

Gilbert, E. (1959): "Random Graphs," *Annals of Mathematical Statistics*, 30(4), 1141–44.

Gilleskie, D., and Y. S. Zhang (2009): "Friendship Formation and Smoking Initiation Among Teens," University of North Carolina Working Paper.

Glaeser, E., B. Sacerdote, and J. A. Scheinkman (2003): "The Social Multiplier," *Journal of the European Economic Association*, 1(2-3), 345–53.

(1996): "Crime and Social Interactions," *Quarterly Journal of Economics*, 111(2), 507–48.

Goldenberg, A., A. Zheng, S. E. Fienberg, and E. M. Airoldi (2009): "A Survey of Statistical Network Models," *Foundations and Trends in Machine Learning*, 2(2), 129–333.

Goldsmith-Pinkham, P., and G. Imbens (2013): "Social Networks and the Identification of Peer Effects," *Journal of Business and Economic Statistics*, 31(3), 253–64.

Gould, P. (1967): "On the Geographical Interpretation of Eigenvalues," *Transactions of the Insititute of British Geographers*, 42, 53–86.

Graham, B. (2008): "Identifying Social Interactions through Conditional Variance Restrictions," *Econometrica*, 76(3), 643–60.

(2014): "An Empirical Model of Network Formation: Detecting Homophily when Agents are Heterogeneous," University of California at Berkeley Working Paper.

(2015): "Methods of Identification in Social Networks," *Annual Review of Economics*, 7, University of California at Berkeley Working Paper.

Granovetter, M. (1973): "The Strength of Weak Ties," *American Journal of Sociology*, 78, 1360–80.

Guryan, J., K. Kory, and M. J. Notowidigdo (2009): "Peer Effects in the Workplace: Evidence from Random Groupings in Professional Golf Tournaments," *American Economic Journal: Applied Economics*, 1(4), 34–68.

Handcock, M. (2003): "Assessing Degeneracy in Statistical Models for Social Networks," University of Washington Working Paper.

Handcock, M., and K. Gile (2010): "Modeling Social Networks from Sampled Data," *The Annals of Applied Statistics*, 4(1), 5–25.

Hausman, J., W. Newey, and W. Taylor (1987): "Efficient Estimation and Identification of Simultaneous Equation Models with Covariate Restrictions," *Econometrica*, 55(4), 849–74.

Hoff, P. (2005): "Bilinear Mixed-Effects Models for Dyadic Data," *Journal of the American Statistical Association*, 100, 286–95.

Hoff, P., A. Raftery, and M. Handcock (2002): "Latent Space Approaches to Social Network Analysis," *Journal of the American Statistical Association*, 97, 1090–98.

Holland, P. W., and S. Leinhardt (1981): "An Exponential Family of Probability Distributions for Directed Graphs," *Journal of the American Statistical Association*, 76, 33–65.

Hong, H., and J. Xu (2014): "Count Models of Social Networks in Finance," Princeton University Working Paper.

Honoré, B. E., and A. de Paula (2010): "Interdependent Durations," *Review of Economic Studies*, 77, 1138–63.

Hotz, V. J., and R. A. Miller (1993): "Conditional Choice Probabilities and the Estimation of Dynamic Models," *Review of Economic Studies*, 60(3), 497–529.

Hsieh, C.-S., and L.-F. Lee (2013): "Specification and Estimation of Network Formation and Network Interaction Models with the Exponential Probability Distribution," OSU Working Paper.

Hunter, D. R., P. N. Krivitsky, and M. Schweinberger (2012): "Computational Statistical Methods for Social Network Models," *Journal of Computational and Graphical Statistics*, 21(4), 856–82.

Jackson, M. (2009): *Social and Economic Networks*. Princeton University Press.

Jackson, M., and B. Rogers (2007): "Meeting Strangers and Friends of Friends: How Random Are Social Networks?" *American Economic Review*, 97(3), 890–915.

Jackson, M., and A. Watts (2002): "The Evolution of Social and Economic Networks," *Journal of Economic Theory*, 106, 265–95.

Jackson, M., and A. Wolinsky (1996): "A Strategic Model of Social and Economic Networks," *Journal of Economic Theory*, 71(1), 44–74.

Johnson, T. (2012): "Dynamic Network Formation: Theory and Estimation," University of Notre Dame Working Paper.

Jordan, M. I. (2004): "Graphical Models," *Statistical Science*, 19(1), 140–55.

Jordan, M. I., and M. J. Wainwright (2008): "Graphical Models, Exponential Families, and Variational Inference," *Foundations and Trends in Machine Learning*, 1(1-2), 1–305.

Katz, L. (1953): "A New Status Index Derived from Sociometric Analysis," *Psychometrica*, 18, 39–43.

Kelejian, H. H., and I. R. Prucha (2010): "Specification and Estimation of Spatial Autoregressive Models with Autoregressive and Heteroskedasticity Disturbances," *Journal of Econometrics*, 157, 53–67.

Kelejian, H. H., I. R. Prucha, and Y. Yuzefovich (2006): "Estimation Problems in Models with Spatial Weighting Matrices which Have Blocks of Equal Elements," *Journal of Regional Science*, 46(3), 507–15.

Kline, B., and E. Tamer (2011): "Some Interpretation of the Linear-in-Means Model of Social Interactions," Northwestern University Working Paper.

Kolaczyk, E. (2009): *Statistical Analysis of Network Data.* Springer-Verlag.

Koller, D., and N. Friedman (2009): *Probabilistic Graphical Models: Principles and Techniques.* MIT Press.

Kopczuk, W., A. Alstadsaeter, and K. Telle (2014): "Social Networks and Tax Avoidance: Evidence from a Well-Defined Norwegian Tax Shelter," Columbia University Working Paper.

Koskinen, J. H., G. Robins, and P. Pattison (2010): "Analysing Exponential Random Graph (p-star) Models with Missing Data using Bayesian Data Augmentation," *Statistical Methodology*, 7, 366–84.

Kranton, R., and D. Minehart (2001): "A Theory of Buyer-Seller Networks," *American Economic Review*, 91(3), 485–508.

Lam, C., and P. C. Souza (2013): "Regularization for High-Dimensional Spatial Models Using the Adaptive LASSO," LSE Working Paper.

——— (2014): "One-Step Regularized Spatial Weight Matrix and Fixed Effects Estimation with Instrumental Variables," LSE Working Paper.

Lavy, V., and E. Sand (2015): "The Effect of Social Networks on Students' Academic and Non-Cognitive Behavioral Outcomes: Evidence from Conditional Random Assignment of Friends in School," University of Warwick and Hebrew University Working Paper.

Lazzati, N. (2015): "Treatment Response with Social Interactions: Partial Identification via Monotone Comparative Statics," *Quantitative Economics*, 6, 49–83.

Lee, L.-F. (2007): "Identification and Estimation of Econometric Models with Group Interactions, Contextual Factors and Fixed Effects," *Journal of Econometrics*, 140(2), 333–74.

Lee, L.-F., X. Liu, and X. Lin (2010): "Specification and Estimation of Social Interaction Models with Network Structures," *Econometrics Journal*, 13, 145–76.

Lee, L.-F., and J. Yu (2010): "Estimation of Spatial Autoregressive Panel Data Models with Fixed Effects," *Journal of Econometrics*, 154, 165–85.

Lee, R. S., and K. Fong (2011): "Markov-Perfect Network Formation: An Applied Framework for Bilateral Oligopoly and Bargaining in Buyer-Seller Networks," NYU Working Paper.

Leung, M. (2015a): "A Random-Field Approach to Inference in Large Network Models," Stanford University Working Paper.

——— (2015b): "Two-Step Estimation of Network Formation Models with Incomplete Information," *Journal of Econometrics*, 188(1), 182–195.

Lin, X., and L.-F. Lee (2010): "GMM Estimation of Spatial Autoregressive Models with Unknown Heteroskedasticity," *Journal of Econometrics*, 157, 34–52.

Liu, X., E. Patacchini, and Y. Zenou (2014): "Endogenous Peer Effects: Local Aggregate or Local Average," *Journal of Economic Behavior and Organization*, 103, 39–59.

Lovasz, L. (2012): *Large Networks and Graph Limits.* American Mathematical Society.

Manresa, E. (2013): "Estimating the Structure of Social Interactions using Panel Data," CEMFI Working Paper.

Manski, C. F. (1993): "Identification of Endogenous Social Effects: The Reflection Problem," *The Review of Economic Studies*, 60(3), 531–42.

——— (2013): "Identification of Treatment Response with Social Interactions," *Econometrics Journal*, 16(1), S1–S23.

Manski, C. F., and J. Mayshar (2003): "Private Incentives and Social Interactions: Fertility Puzzles in Israel," *Journal of the European Economic Association*, 1(1), 181–211.

Masten, M. A. (2015): "Random Coefficients on Endogenous Variables in Simultaneous Equation Models," Duke University Working Paper.

McAdam, D. (1986): "Recruitment to High-Risk Activism: The Case of Freedom Summer," *American Journal of Sociology*, 92(1), 64–90.

Mele, A. (2015): "A Structural Model of Segregation in Social Networks," Johns Hopkins Working Paper.

Menzel, K. (2015): "Inference for Games with Many Players," NYU Working Paper.

Miyauchi, Y. (2014): "Structural Estimation of a Pairwise Stable Network with Nonnegative Externality," MIT Working Paper.

Moffitt, R. (2001): "Policy Interventions, Low-Level Equilibria and Social Interactions," in *Social Dynamics*, ed. by S. Durlauf, and P. Young. MIT Press.

Nakajima, R. (2007): "Measuring Peer Effects on Youth Smoking Behaviour," *Review of Economic Studies*, 74(3), 897–935.

Neidell, M., and J. Waldfogel (2010): "Cognitive and Noncognitive Peer Effects in Early Education," *Review of Economics and Statistics*, 92(3), 562–76.

Pennock, D., G. Flake, S. Lawrence, E. Glove, and C. Giles (2002): "Winners Don't Take All: Characterizing the Competition for Links on the Web," *Proceedings of the National Academy of Sciences*, 99(8), 5207–11.

Pomeranz, D. (forthcoming): "No Taxation without Information: Deterrence and Self-Enforcement in the Value Added Tax," *American Economic Review*.

Qu, X., and L.-F. Lee (2015): "Estimating a Spatial Autoregressive Model with an Endogenous Spatial Weight Matrix," *Journal of Econometrics*, 184(2), 209–32.

Rasch, G. (1960): *Probabilistic Models for Some Intelligence and Attainment Tests*. University of Chicago Press.

Rinaldo, A., S. E. Fienberg, and Y. Zhou (2009): "On the Geometry of Discrete Exponential Families with Application to Exponential Random Graph Models," *Electronic Journal of Statistics*, 3, 446–84.

Robins, G., P. Pattison, Y. Kalish, and D. Lusher (2007): "An Introduction to Exponential Random Graph (p^*) Models for Social Networks," *Social Networks*, 29(2), 173–191.

Robins, G., T. Snijders, P. Wang, M. Handcock, and P. Pattison (2007): "Recent Developments in Exponential Random Graph (p^*) Models for Social Networks," *Social Networks*, 29(2), 192–215.

Rose, C. (2015): "Essays in Applied Microeconometrics," PhD thesis, University of Bristol.

Rudin, W. (1987): *Real and Complex Analysis*. McGraw-Hill.

Sacerdote, B. (2001): "Peer Effects with Random Assignment: Results for Dartmouth Roomates," *Quarterly Journal of Economics*, 106(2), 681–704.

——— (2010): "Peer Effects in Education: How Might They Work, How Big Are They and How Much Do We Know Thus Far?," in *Handbook of the Economics of Education*, ed. by E. A. Hanushek, S. Machin, and L. Woessmann, vol. 3. North-Holland.

Shalizi, C., and A. Rinaldo (2013): "Consistency under Sampling of Exponential Random Graph Models," *Annals of Statistics*, 41(2), 508–35.

Sheng, S. (2014): "A Structural Econometric Analysis of Network Formation Games," UCLA Working Paper.

Sirakaya, S. (2006): "Recidivism and Social Interactions," *Journal of the American Statistical Association*, 101(475), 863–77.

Snijders, T. (2002): "Markov Chain Monte Carlo Estimation of Exponential Random Graph Models," *Journal of Social Structure*, 3(2), 1–40.

Souza, P. C. (2014): "Estimating Network Effects without Network Data," LSE Working Paper.

Strauss, D., and M. Ikeda (1990): "Pseudolikelihood Estimation for Social Networks," *Journal of the American Statistical Association*, 85(409), 204–12.

Sun, Y. (2006): "The Exact Law of Large Numbers via Fubini Extension and Characterization of Insurable Risks," *Journal of Economic Theory*, 126, 31–69.

Tamer, E. (2003): "Incomplete Simultaneous Discrete Response Model with Multiple Equilibria," *The Review of Economic Studies*, 70(1), 147–65.

Tao, J., and L.-F. Lee (2014): "A Reaction Function Model with the First Order Statistic," *Econometrics Journal*, 17(3), 197–240.

Tibshirani, R. (1996): "Regression Shrinkage and Selection via the Lasso," *Journal of the Royal Statistical Society B (Methodological)*, 58(1), 267–88.

Tincani, M. (2015): "Heterogeneous Peer Effects and Rank Concerns: Theory and Evidence," UCL Working Paper.

Topa, G. (2001): "Social Interactions, Local Spillovers and Unemployment," *Review of Economic Studies*, 68(2), 261–95.

Uhlig, H. (1996): "A Law of Large Numbers for Large Economies," *Economic Theory*, 8, 41–50.

Wasserman, S., and K. Faust (1994): *Social Network Analysis: Methods and Applications*. Cambridge University Press.

Watts, A. (2001): "A Dynamic Model of Network Formation," *Games and Economic Behavior*, 34, 331–41.

Xu, X., and L.-F. Lee (forthcoming): "Maximum Likelihood Estimation of a Spatial Autoregressive Tobit Model," *Journal of Econometrics*.

Yan, T., and J. Xu (2013): "A Central Limit theorem in the β-Model for Undirected Random Graphs with a Diverging Number of Vertices," *Biometrika*, 100(2), 519–24.

Zenou, Y. (2015): "Key Players," in *Hanbook on the Economics of Networks*, ed. by Y. Bramoullé, B. Rogers, and A. Galeotti. Oxford University Press.

Zhang, C.-H. (2010): "Nearly Unbiased Variable Selection Under Minimax Concave Penalty," *Annals of Statistics*, 38(2), 894–942.

Zheng, T., M. J. Salganik, and A. Gelman (2006): "How Many People Do You Know in Prison?: Using Overdispersion in Count Data to Estimate Social Structure in Networks," *Journal of the American Statistical Association*, 101(474), 409–23.

Zou, H., and T. Hastie (2005): "Regularization and Variable Selection via the Elastic Net," *Journal of the Royal Statistical Society B*, 67(2), 301–20.

CHAPTER 9

Networks in Economics: Remarks

Rachel E. Kranton

The past fifteen years have seen a burst in research on the economics of networks. Researchers have been studying a wide range of economic settings, and in each case, links between individuals arguably play critical roles in individual and aggregate outcomes. The following are some examples, with specified settings and links: peer effects with friendship links, innovation/research and development with links between researchers and colleagues, local public goods with geographic and social links, oligopoly and firms' interlinked markets, macroeconomic shocks and supply chain links, information transmission and people's social links, banking and links due to cross-holdings, and markets and links between buyers and sellers.

The mathematical structure of networks ties together all this research. In a network, agents have pairwise "links" that affect their dealings. These links collectively give the "adjacency matrix," also called the "graph," or the "network," that impacts outcomes for all agents. At the individual level, an agent's payoffs depend directly on the actions of her "neighbors," i.e., the agents to whom she is linked. Distant agents also shape payoffs and incentives to the extent that they are indirectly linked, by "paths" in the network.

These remarks give a bird's eye view of this research, providing a road map to bring together the detailed accounts of the empirical and theoretical research provided by the two papers in this session. Following the road map, these remarks give a whirlwind tour of research objectives and themes and present challenges for future studies.

Research papers in this area typically begin with documenting an economic outcome of interest and recognizing that a network underlies this outcome. Figure 1 gives a road map. Starting at the top, a theoretical study typically posits pairwise links between N agents that form a network G. An empirical study will also typically begin with data on the links that make up the network,

See the presented papers (de Paula, 2017 and Goyal, 2017) for extensive references; only a few illustrative articles are cited here. For further reading, the forthcoming *Oxford Handbook on the Economics of Networks* (Bramoullé, Galeotti, and Rogers, 2016), provides a compendium of detailed papers reviewing the literature.

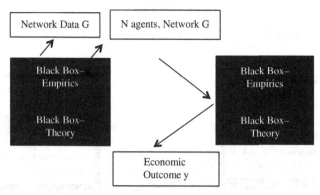

Figure 1 Road Map of Research in the Economics of Networks.

i.e., who is linked to whom in the relevant population. There are then two black boxes to be filled in. The first box concerns how networks shape outcomes, i.e., the theory and empirics of how individual actions, given a network, lead to the economic outcome. The second black box concerns network formation, i.e., how links come about in the first place.

Research efforts fill in (parts of) these black boxes, as outlined in Figure 2.

Networks Shape Outcomes: Starting with the black box on the right, the first track of research considers how, given links between agents and the overall network, structures shape individual and aggregate outcomes. Econometric research develops techniques to use network data to identify peer effects; consider the impact of agent 1 on agent 2. The actions of agent 3, who is linked to agent 2 but not to agent 1, can serve as an instrument for the impact of the original relationship. Theoretical research develops games played on networks. Agents strategically choose actions $(y_1, y_2, y_3, \dots)$ as individual payoffs depend on neighbors' actions. The equilibrium of the game gives the overall economic outcome y.

Network Formation: The second track of research begins to fill in the black box on the left to consider how links are formed. Since actions of neighbors affect payoffs, people would have the incentive to make and break links. To capture this possibility, theorists develop models of strategic link formation. Empirical researchers study the statistical patterns that would emerge from such processes. Research also considers "mechanical" network formation processes, where agents' links are generated by some random process.

To give a sense of the material covered in the two papers presented in the session: Goyal (2017) focuses on the two areas of theoretical research (in the lower halves of each black box) and de Paula (2017) focuses on the two areas of the empirical research (in the upper halves of each black box).

In all of these efforts, researchers often must develop new techniques and methods. Networks are discrete mathematically and the analysis of networks does not lend itself easily to traditional tools used in economics, such as

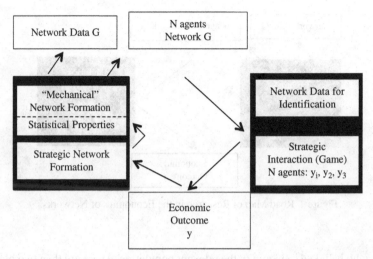

Figure 2 Filling in the Black Boxes.

calculus. The computational complexity of networks also requires new statistical methods. To have a sense of these efforts, again follow the outline of this research in Figure 2, starting from the right.

Networks Shape Outcomes: In the econometric research on exploiting network data to identify social interactions, sufficient conditions involve the linear independence of powers of a network graph (Bramoullé, Djebbari, and Fortin, 2009). For strategic interaction on given networks, researchers must specify actions, game structure, and payoffs that incorporate the network structure. Researchers posit new games of local public goods, bargaining, price-setting, and collaboration that take into account the combinatorics of links.

Network Formation: For strategic formation of networks, new equilibrium concepts take into account links and the complexity of the network setting. For example, since links are formed by pairs of agents, "pairwise stability" gives an alternative to Nash equilibrium. In a dynamic game, since completely forward-looking agents seem unrealistic, agents are posited to play myopic best replies, which lead (possibly) to a convergent set of networks. Ërdos–Rény random graphs and the generalization to exponential random graphs are prominent mechanical models of network formation, where each agent is linked to another probabilistically. Features of graphs are then analyzed by maximum likelihood and Markov Chain Monte Carlo (MCMC) methods.

The primary objective of all this research is to uncover network properties that determine individual and aggregate outcomes. To illustrate, there is perhaps now one setting that has been sufficiently well studied to take us around the full circle of the map (with results from each of the speakers in this session). Consider peer effects or local public goods and more generally the set of models that all share an underlying structure where agents' optimal action is linear in his neighbors' actions.

Networks Shape Actions: Starting on the right, first, network data can identify peer effects when the network is sufficiently "sparse" (de Paula, Rasul, and Souza, 2015). In a strategic game on a network, individual actions are proportional to their Bonacich centralities, which give the weighted sum of the paths in a network starting from that individual (Ballester, Calvó-Armengol, and Zenou, 2006). The lowest eigenvalue of the network determines the equilibrium set, giving the critical measure of the overall extent of strategic substitutabilities (Bramoullé, Kranton, and D'Amours, 2014).

Network Formation: For network formation, in a model of local public goods where agents choose directed links simultaneously with actions, stars are Nash equilibrium outcomes; one agent is providing the local public good (Galeotti and Goyal, 2010). In a peer effect setting, models where agents can choose directed links give stronger predictions that better match friendship data (Badev, 2013; Mele, 2013).

While collectively researchers have greatly advanced the economics of networks, several challenges remain. The first set of challenges is perhaps most obvious and related to similar issues in other fields. The second set is perhaps particular to the study of networks.

The first set of challenges concerns multiple equilibria and identification. First, multiple equilibria arise in many games played on networks and in network formation games. Both in theory and empirics, researchers are already addressing this challenge by developing equilibrium refinements and computational and statistical methods to estimate outcomes. Second, beyond the concerns from multiple equilibria, identifying a network effect per se remains an empirical challenge when data are particularly light on individual characteristics. Since networks are endogenous, an individual might occupy a particular position within a network because of characteristics (such cognitive and non-cognitive skills) that are also directly related to the economic outcome of interest (such as success in school).

The second set of challenges concerns more deeply the overall research agenda and what can be learned from the economic analysis of networks. First, when studying network settings, researchers must pay close attention to which of the many possible connections between individuals are relevant for the economic outcome at hand. For example, in the study of peer effects, the available data might enumerate school friendships. But school friendships might not be critical to a student's educational and health outcomes. Enemies (or bullies) might be critical, or students who set the tone for the entire school, such as star athletes. The relevant links might be "virtual," and in general researchers are challenged to uncover the relationships that actually matter, and which relationships matter is, of course, itself an empirical question. The specification of empirical and theoretical models should rely on detailed descriptions of the environment, perhaps in literatures other than economics.

The second of these deeper challenges lies in the economic interpretation of the network features which emerge from our analyses. The holy grail in much of this research is to uncover some general empirical or theoretical regularity that is applicable to any network or any network data set. Eigenvalues, centrality measures, network structures such as stars or nested split graphs, all appear in results. The questions then become: What insights do these mathematical features lend to our understanding of the social and economic world? How do these mathematical expressions relate to observed patterns of interaction? To answer these questions, economists could again learn from researchers in other fields such as physics, sociology, and computer science, who are engaged in such pursuits as defining network notions of communities and constructing algorithms to find communities given network data.

References

Badev, A. 2013. "Discrete Games with Endogenous Networks: Theory and Policy," Working Paper, University of Pennsylvania.

Ballester, C., A. Calvó-Armengol, and Y. Zenou. 2006. "Who's Who in Networks. Wanted: The Key Player," *Econometrica*, 74, 1403–17.

Bramoullé, Y., H. Djebbari, and B. Fortin. 2009. "Identification of Peer Effects Through Social Networks," *Journal of Econometrics*, 150, 4–55.

Bramoullé, Y., R. Kranton, and M. D'Amours. 2014. "Strategic Interaction and Networks," *American Economic Review*, 104(3), 898–930.

Bramoullé, Y., A. Galeotti and B. Rogers. 2016. *The Oxford Handbook of the Economics of Networks*. Oxford: Oxford University Press.

de Paula, À. 2017. "Econometrics of Networks Models," *Advances in Economics and Econometrics: Theory and Applications, Eleventh World Congress*.

de Paula, À., I. Rasul, and P. C. Souza. 2015. "Identifying and Estimating Social Connections from Outcome Data," UCL and PUC-Rio Working Paper.

Galeotti, A., and S. Goyal. 2010. "The Law of the Few." *American Economic Review*, 100(4), 1468–92.

Goyal, S. 2017. "Networks and Markets," *Advances in Economics and Econometrics: Theory and Applications, Eleventh World Congress*.

Mele, A. 2013. "A Structural Model of Segregation in Social Networks," Johns Hopkins Working Paper.

Index

Other titles in the series (continued from page iii)

Donald P. Jacobs, Ehud Kalai, and Morton I. Kamien, Editors, *Frontiers of research in economic theory: The Nancy L. Schwartz Memorial Lectures, 1983–1997*, 9780521632225, 9780521635387

A. Colin Cameron and Pravin K. Trivedi, *Regression analysis of count data*, 9780521632010, 9780521635677

Steinar Strom, Editor, *Econometrics and economic theory in the 20th century: The Ragnar Frisch Centennial Symposium*, 9780521633239, 9780521633659

Eric Ghysels, Norman R. Swanson, and Mark Watson, Editors, *Essays in econometrics: Collected papers of Clive W. J. Granger (Volume I)*, 9780521772976, 9780521774963

Eric Ghysels, Norman R. Swanson, and Mark Watson, Editors, *Essays in econometrics: Collected papers of Clive W. J. Granger (Volume II)*, 9780521792073, 9780521796491

Cheng Hsiao, *Analysis of panel data, second edition*, 9780521818551, 9780521522717

Mathias Dewatripont, Lars Peter Hansen, and Stephen J. Turnovsky, Editors, *Advances in economics and econometrics – Eighth World Congress (Volume I)*, 9780521818728, 9780521524117

Mathias Dewatripont, Lars Peter Hansen, and Stephen J. Turnovsky, Editors, *Advances in economics and econometrics – Eighth World Congress (Volume II)*, 9780521818735, 9780521524124

Mathias Dewatripont, Lars Peter Hansen, and Stephen J. Turnovsky, Editors, *Advances in economics and econometrics – Eighth World Congress (Volume III)*, 9780521818742, 9780521524131

Roger Koenker, *Quantile regression*, 9780521845731, 9780521608275

Charles Blackorby, Walter Bossert, and David Donaldson, *Population issues in social choice theory, welfare economics, and ethics*, 9780521825511, 9780521532587

John E. Roemer, *Democracy, education, and equality*, 9780521846653, 9780521609135

Richard Blundell, Whitney K. Newey, and Thorsten Persson, *Advances in economics and econometrics – Ninth World Congress (Volume I)*, 9780521871525, 9780521692083

Richard Blundell, Whitney K. Newey, and Thorsten Persson, *Advances in economics and econometrics – Ninth World Congress (Volume II)*, 9780521871532, 9780521692090

Richard Blundell, Whitney K. Newey, and Thorsten Persson, *Advances in economics and econometrics – Ninth World Congress (Volume III)*, 9780521871549, 9780521692106

Fernando Vega-Redondo, *Complex social networks*, 9780521857406, 9780521674096

Itzhak Gilboa, *Theory of decision under uncertainty*, 9780521517324, 9780521741231

Krislert Samphantharak and Robert M. Townsend, *Households as corporate firms: an analysis of household finance using integrated household surveys and corporate financial accounting*, 9780521195829, 9780521124164

Rakesh Vohra, *Mechanism design: A linear programming approach*, 9781107004368, 9780521179461

Daron Acemoglu, Manuel Arellano, Eddie Dekel, *Advances in economics and econometrics – Tenth World Congress (Volume I)*, 9781107016040, 9781107638105

Daron Acemoglu, Manuel Arellano, Eddie Dekel, *Advances in economics and econometrics – Tenth World Congress (Volume II)*, 9781107016057, 9781107674165

Daron Acemoglu, Manuel Arellano, Eddie Dekel, *Advances in economics and econometrics – Tenth World Congress (Volume III)*, 9781107016064, 9781107627314

Andrew Harvey, *Dynamic models for volatility and heavy tails: With applications to financial and economic time series*, 9781107034723/9781107630024

Cheng Hsiao, *An analysis of panel data, second edition*, 9781107038691/9781107657632

Jean-François Mertens, Sylvain Sorin, Shmuel Zamir, *Repeated games*, 9781107030206/9781107662636

Christopher P. Chambers and Federico Echenique, *Revealed Preference Theory*, 9781107087804

Stephen Maurer, *On the Shoulders of Giants: Colleagues Remember Suzanne Scotchmer's Contributions to Economics* 9781107131163, 9781107578968

Printed in the United States
by Baker & Taylor Publisher Services